CONTENTS

D0453064

TO THE STUDENT

The aim of this book is to help make your study of advanced biology interesting and successful. It includes examples of modern issues, developments and applications that reflect the continual evolution of scientific knowledge and understanding. We hope it will encourage you to study science further when you complete your course.

USING THIS BOOK

Biology is a fascinating, but complex subject – underpinned by some demanding ideas and concepts, and by a great deal of experimental data ('facts'). This mass of information can sometimes make its study daunting. So don't try to achieve too much in one reading session and always try to keep the bigger picture in sight.

There are a number of features in the book to help with this:

- Each chapter starts with a brief example of how the biology you will learn has been applied somewhere in the world, followed by a short outline of what you should have learned previously and what you will learn through the chapter.

- Important words and phrases are given in bold when used for the first time, with their meaning explained. There is also a glossary at the back of the book. If you are still uncertain, ask your teacher or tutor because it is important that you understand these words before proceeding.

- Throughout each chapter there are many questions, with the answers at the back of the book. These questions enable you to make a quick check on your progress through the chapter.

- Similarly, throughout each chapter there are checklists of key ideas that summarise the main points you need to learn from what you have just read.

- Where appropriate, worked examples are included to show how calculations are done.

- There are many assignments throughout the book. These are tasks relating to pieces of text and data that show how biological ideas have been developed or applied. They are not required knowledge for an A-level examination. Rather, they provide opportunities to apply the science you have learned to new contexts, practise your maths skills and practise answering questions about scientific methods and data analysis.

- Some chapters have information about the 'required practical' activities that you need to carry out during your course. These sections provide the necessary background information about the apparatus, equipment and techniques that you need to be prepared to carry out the required practical work. There are questions that give you practice in answering questions about equipment, techniques, attaining accuracy, and data analysis.

At the end of each chapter there are Practice Questions, which are exam-style questions including some past paper questions. There are a number of sections, questions, Assignments and Practice Questions that have been labelled 'Stretch and challenge', which you could try to tackle. In places these go beyond what is required for the specification but they will help you build upon the skills and knowledge you acquire and better prepare you for further study beyond advanced level.

Good luck and enjoy your studies. We hope this book will encourage you to study biology further when you complete your course.

PRACTICAL WORK IN BIOLOGY

Practical work is a vital part of biology. Biologists apply their practical skills in a wide variety of contexts – from conservation to food production; from tracking invasive species to controlling disease. In your A-level Biology course you need to learn, practise and demonstrate that you have acquired these skills.

WRITTEN EXAMINATIONS

Your practical skills will be assessed in the written examinations at the end of the course. Questions on practical skills will account for about 15% of your marks. The practical skills assessed in the written examinations are:

Independent thinking
- solve problems set in practical contexts
- apply scientific knowledge to practical contexts

Use and application of scientific methods and practices
- comment on experimental design and evaluate scientific methods
- present data in appropriate ways
- evaluate results and draw conclusions with reference to measurement uncertainties and errors
- identify variables including those that must be controlled

Numeracy and the application of mathematical concepts in a practical context
- plot and interpret graphs
- process and analyse data using appropriate mathematical skills
- consider margins of error, accuracy and precision of data

Instruments and equipment
- know and understand how to use a wide range of experimental and practical instruments, equipment and techniques appropriate to the knowledge and understanding included in the specification

Throughout this book there are questions and longer assignments that will give you the opportunity to develop and practise these skills. The contexts of some of the exam questions will be based on the 'required practical activities'.

Figure 1 *Biologists often use techniques and apparatus in the field as well as in the laboratory.*

Figure 2 *It is important to be able to interpret and analyse data – this doctor is analysing an electrocardiogram; understanding anomalies is crucial when making a diagnosis.*

Figure 3 *You will need to use a variety of equipment correctly and safely.*

ASSESSMENT OF PRACTICAL SKILLS

Some practical skills can only be practised when you are doing experiments. The following **practical competencies** will be assessed by your teacher:

- follow written procedures
- apply investigative approaches and methods when using instruments and equipment
- safely use a range of practical equipment and materials
- make and record observations
- research, reference and report findings

You must show your teacher that you consistently and routinely demonstrate the competencies listed above during your course. The assessment will not contribute to your A-level grade, but will appear as a 'pass' alongside your grade on the A level certificate.

These practical competencies must be demonstrated by using a specific range of **apparatus and techniques**:

- use appropriate apparatus to record a range of quantitative measurements (to include mass, time, volume, temperature, length and pH)
- use appropriate instrumentation to record quantitative measurements, such as a colorimeter or potometer
- use laboratory glassware apparatus for a variety of experimental techniques to include serial dilutions
- use a light microscope at high power and low power, including use of a graticule
- produce scientific drawing from observation with annotations
- use qualitative reagents to identify biological molecules
- separate biological compounds using thin layer/paper chromatography or electrophoresis
- safely and ethically use organisms to measure plant or animal responses, and physiological functions
- use microbiological aseptic techniques, including the use of agar plates and broth
- safely use instruments for dissection of an animal organ, or plant organ
- use sampling techniques in fieldwork
- use ICT such as computer modelling or data logger to collect data, or use software to process data.

REQUIRED PRACTICAL ACTIVITIES

During the A-level course you will need to carry out 12 **required practical** activities. These are the main sources of evidence that your teacher will use to award you a pass for your competency skills.

Figure 4 *Aseptic techniques must be used when handling agar plates and broth.*

Figure 5 *Dissection tools – such as this scalpel being used to cut a sheep kidney – must be handled with care; they are often surgically sharp, but not always surgically clean!*

1. Investigation into the effect of a named variable on the rate of an enzyme-controlled reaction

2. Preparation of stained squashes of cells from plant-root tips; set-up and use of an optical microscope to identify the stages of mitosis in these stained squashes and calculation of a mitotic index

3. Production of a dilution series of a solute to produce a calibration curve with which to identify the water potential of plant tissue

4. Investigation into the effect of a named variable on the permeability of cell-surface membranes

5. Dissection of animal or plant gas exchange or mass transport system or of organ within such a system

6. Use of aseptic techniques to investigate the effect of antimicrobial substances on microbial growth

7. Use of chromatography to investigate the pigments isolated from leaves of different plants, for example leaves from shade-tolerant and shade-intolerant plants, or leaves of different colours

8. Investigation into the effect of a named factor on the rate of dehydrogenase activity in extracts of chloroplasts

9. Investigation into the effect of a named variable on the rate of respiration of cultures of single-celled organisms

10. Investigation into the effect of an environmental variable on the movement of an animal using either a choice chamber or a maze

11. Production of a dilution series of a glucose solution and use of colorimetric techniques to produce a calibration curve with which to identify the concentration of glucose in an unknown 'urine' sample

12. Investigation into the effect of a named environmental factor on the distribution of a given species

Information about the apparatus, techniques and analysis of required practicals 1 to 6 are found in Student Book 1.

You will be asked some questions in your written examinations about skills developed as result of carrying out these required practicals.

Practical skills are really important. Take time and care to learn, practise and use them.

1 PHOTOSYNTHESIS

PRIOR KNOWLEDGE

You will probably remember the equation for photosynthesis, in which plants use light energy, absorbed by chlorophyll, to react water and carbon dioxide together to produce carbohydrates and oxygen. You may also remember that ATP is the molecule used as the energy currency in cells, and that it is made by combining ADP and inorganic phosphate.

LEARNING OBJECTIVES

In this chapter, we look at the process of photosynthesis, in which plants harness light energy to split water and combine hydrogen atoms from it with carbon dioxide, forming carbohydrates that contain some of the energy from the light.

(Specification 3.5.1)

Humans have an insatiable demand for energy. Today, much of our energy supply still comes from fossil fuels, despite the universal acknowledgement that these will eventually run out, and that burning fossil fuels is causing an increase in the carbon dioxide concentration in the atmosphere, which is leading to increased global temperatures.

Artificial photosynthesis represents one of several potential options for obtaining more of our energy supplies from renewable sources. Photosynthesis is a very efficient energy-transfer process, in which energy from light is transferred to energy in carbohydrates. We can already grow plants and algae (Figure 1) to produce biofuels that can be burnt. Now, researchers are looking into various approaches that would enable us to transfer energy from light to produce fuels such as methanol, using processes similar to photosynthesis, but without involving plants.

For example, in 2014, researchers at Monash University, in Melbourne, Australia, described the significant progress that they have made in developing a kind of artificial photosynthesis. The researchers are working on developing two new catalysts – one that can split water, and one that can absorb carbon dioxide and react it with the hydrogen from the water to form methanol. When supplied with carbon dioxide dissolved in water, and irradiated with sunlight, these new catalysts can produce methanol.

Figure 1 *These tanks contain the green unicellular alga, Chlorella, which is being grown to produce biofuels.*

As yet, this process needs much more development before it can be scaled up and used commercially. But the promise is there, and other research groups working on different systems are also reporting success. It is a tall order, however, to try to produce a system for transferring light energy to fuels that betters that of plants. After all, they have millions of years of evolution behind them, which have helped to make photosynthesis work with such efficiency.

1.1 ENERGY FOR LIVING ORGANISMS

All living cells need a constant supply of energy in order to remain alive. Cells use energy for a whole range of processes – for example, active transport to move substances into and out of the cell, moving substances around inside the cell, building protein molecules, replicating DNA – the list is almost endless. When we look at a whole organism (for example, yourself), we can identify many other uses of energy. At this moment, you are using energy to contract the muscles between your ribs, to draw air into your lungs. Your brain cells are using energy to transfer electrical signals, helping you to make sense of what you are reading. The immediate source of almost all of this energy is **ATP**.

You learned a little about ATP in your AS level course (see *Chapter 4 of Year 1 Student Book*). ATP is a phosphorylated nucleotide. ATP can be hydrolysed by the enzyme **ATP hydrolase**, separating one of the phosphate groups from the ATP molecule to produce ADP and inorganic phosphate (Figure 2).

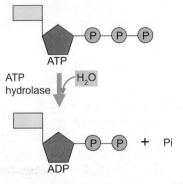

Figure 2 The hydrolysis of ATP

This reaction releases energy that the cell can then use for any process that requires energy. The energy is in a small enough 'packet' to make sure that not too much is wasted – exactly the right amount of ATP can be hydrolysed to provide just the required amount of energy. Moreover, it can be released from ATP exactly when and where it is required.

In this chapter and the next, we will look, in some detail, at how the cell produces ATP. Every cell makes its own ATP, synthesising it by recombining inorganic phosphate groups with ADP molecules. The quantity of ATP used each day is quite staggering. Your body contains approximately 250 g of ATP, but over the course of one day you probably turn over your own body weight of ATP. This means that the ATP molecules making up that 250 g are constantly being hydrolysed and reformed, over and over again.

ATP synthesis

Because energy cannot be created or destroyed, the production of an energy-containing substance such as ATP requires an input of energy. The reaction is catalysed by an enzyme called **ATP synthase** (often just called ATPase) (Figure 3).

There are two main ways in which cells produce ATP. In green plants, and also in many types of micro-organisms, ATP is made during **photosynthesis**. In this case, the energy used to synthesise the ATP comes from light. In this chapter, you will learn where and how this happens.

The ATP made in photosynthesis, however, is very short-lived. It is broken down almost straight away to release energy that is then used to produce other energy-containing compounds, in particular carbohydrates. These carbohydrates can be stored, or transported to other parts of the plant, where they can later be broken down to release their energy again. This energy is then used to make more ATP, in every cell of the plant. The reactions involved are called **respiration**. The reactions of respiration are described in Chapter 2.

Animals, such as ourselves, obtain energy-containing compounds by eating them. The ultimate source of the energy in our bodies is the carbohydrates and other organic compounds made by plants. Just as in the plant cells, these are broken down by respiration, inside our body cells, releasing energy to produce ATP (Figure 4).

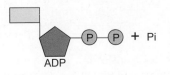 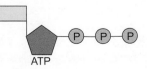

Figure 3 The formation of ATP

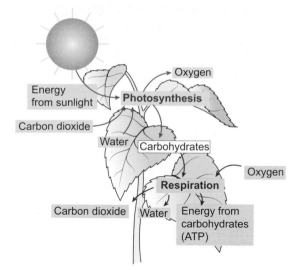

Figure 4 *Energy transfers in photosynthesis and respiration*

Oxidation and reduction reactions

Photosynthesis and respiration involve two types of chemical reaction:

1. Reduction reactions involve the addition of electrons or hydrogen atoms to a molecule, or removal of oxygen. Molecules that supply these electrons or hydrogen atoms are called reducing agents.

2. Oxidation reactions involve the removal of electrons or hydrogen atoms, or the addition of oxygen. Molecules that accept these electrons or hydrogen atoms are called oxidising agents.

You can probably see that reduction and oxidation reactions have to occur together. If one substance is giving away electrons to another, then the giver is being oxidised, and the acceptor is being reduced.

In this chapter and the next, you will meet many reactions in which electrons or hydrogen atoms are passed from one molecule to another. A very important oxidising agent in photosynthesis is a phosphorylated nucleotide called **NADP**, which has the essential role of accepting protons (hydrogen ions) and electrons from one substance, and then passing them on to others.

QUESTIONS

1. Give an example of:
   a. a part of the body that generates a lot of heat
   b. a part of the body where active transport is used to pump substances into or out of cells

   c. a reaction that is involved in synthesising large molecules, and which uses energy.

2. Cells use ATP rather than glucose as their direct energy supply. Explain the advantage of this.

KEY IDEAS

> Cells require energy for many life-maintaining processes. The immediate source of this energy is ATP.

> Every cell makes its own ATP.

> ATP is synthesised during photosynthesis and respiration, in a reaction catalysed by ATP synthase.

> NADP is an oxidising agent that is involved in photosynthesis, where it accepts and passes on protons and electrons.

1.2 AN OVERVIEW OF PHOTOSYNTHESIS

In the rest of this chapter we will look in detail at exactly what happens inside a chloroplast during photosynthesis. The fundamental event is the transfer of energy from light into chemical energy in glucose. This involves two main stages – the **light-dependent reaction** and the **light-independent reaction** – each of which is itself made up of many smaller steps. As you will see, ATP is involved in this process. ATP is made in the light-dependent reaction using energy from sunlight. It is then used in the light-independent reaction, releasing energy to be stored in a glucose molecule.

Figure 5 summarises what happens during these two stages. In the light-dependent reaction, energy from sunlight is used to split water into hydrogen and oxygen, and to cause electrons to be ejected from chlorophyll molecules. The oxygen is given off as a waste product. The hydrogen and electrons are used to make ATP and reduced NADP.

The reduced NADP and the ATP are then used in the light-independent reaction. In this stage, carbon dioxide is converted to carbohydrates (sugars), using the reducing power and energy of the reduced NADP and ATP.

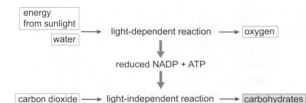

Figure 5 *The two stages of photosynthesis*

Both stages of photosynthesis take place inside **chloroplasts**. The light-dependent stage happens on the **thylakoids** – membranes in which **chlorophyll** and other pigments are embedded. The light-independent stage takes place in the **stroma**. Figure 6 shows the structure of a chloroplast.

Both sets of reactions are kept separate from other reactions in the cell by the outer chloroplast membranes. There are two of these, forming an **envelope**. Carbon dioxide readily diffuses through the outer membranes of the chloroplasts into the stroma. Sugars that are made in photosynthesis can be transported out though these membranes. However, not all the sugar is exported from the chloroplast; some is converted into starch and stored in starch grains inside the stroma. When needed, carbohydrate may be released from the starch grains and translocated to other parts of the plant, in the form of sucrose.

KEY IDEAS

❯ The light-dependent reactions of photosynthesis take place on the membranes of the thylakoids, inside a chloroplast.

❯ During the light-dependent reactions, energy from light is used to split water molecules; the oxygen from the water is given off as a waste product.

❯ Also during the light-dependent reactions, energy from light causes electrons to be ejected from chlorophyll molecules.

❯ The hydrogen from the water and the high-energy electrons from the chlorophyll are used to make ATP and reduced NADP.

❯ The light-independent reactions of photosynthesis take place in the stroma of a chloroplast.

❯ During the light-independent reactions, energy from ATP and reduced NADP are used to convert carbon dioxide to carbohydrates.

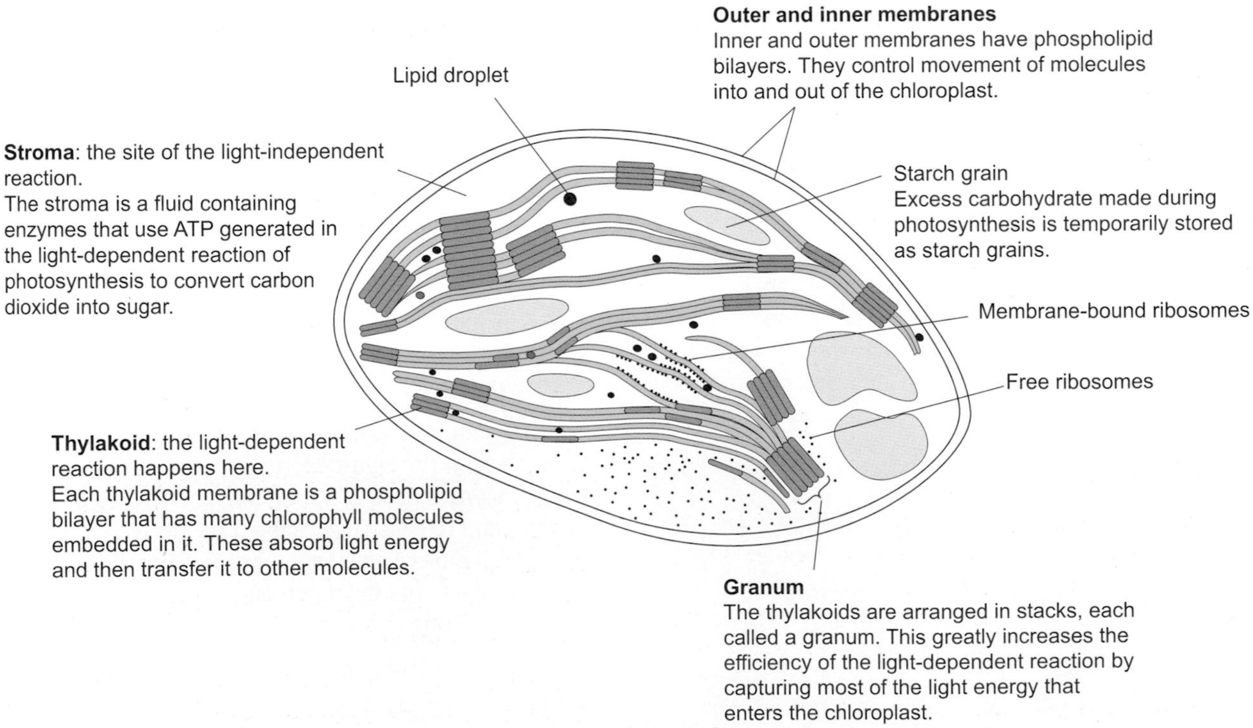

Outer and inner membranes
Inner and outer membranes have phospholipid bilayers. They control movement of molecules into and out of the chloroplast.

Lipid droplet

Starch grain
Excess carbohydrate made during photosynthesis is temporarily stored as starch grains.

Stroma: the site of the light-independent reaction.
The stroma is a fluid containing enzymes that use ATP generated in the light-dependent reaction of photosynthesis to convert carbon dioxide into sugar.

Membrane-bound ribosomes

Free ribosomes

Thylakoid: the light-dependent reaction happens here.
Each thylakoid membrane is a phospholipid bilayer that has many chlorophyll molecules embedded in it. These absorb light energy and then transfer it to other molecules.

Granum
The thylakoids are arranged in stacks, each called a granum. This greatly increases the efficiency of the light-dependent reaction by capturing most of the light energy that enters the chloroplast.

Figure 6 *Inside a chloroplast*

1.3 THE LIGHT-DEPENDENT REACTIONS

In this stage of photosynthesis, energy captured from sunlight by pigment molecules is used to split water, to synthesise ATP, and to produce reduced NADP (Figure 7).

Photoionisation

The thylakoid membranes have a similar basic structure to other cell membranes. They are phospholipid bilayers with various proteins within them. However, thylakoid membranes also contain many pigment molecules. These are arranged in little groups called **photosystems**. Each photosystem contains numerous chlorophyll molecules, of two types – chlorophyll *a* and chlorophyll *b* – and other pigments known as carotenoids.

When light falls on any of these pigments, the energy is passed through the photosystem and transferred to a chlorophyll *a* molecule. Chlorophyll *a* is one of a special group of compounds that can absorb light energy and use it to boost the energy level of electrons. Electrons can be thought of as orbiting around the nucleus of an atom. If the right amount of energy is absorbed, this can boost an electron into a higher orbit, or even remove it from the atom completely. The atom that has lost the electron has become a positively charged ion. When the energy that makes this happen comes from light, the process is known as **photoionisation**.

When a chlorophyll *a* molecule absorbs energy from sunlight, photoionisation takes place and an electron is ejected from the molecule. As we will see, these high-energy electrons have a key role to play.

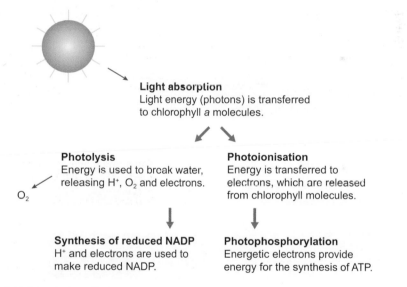

Figure 7 *Overview of the light-dependent reactions*

ASSIGNMENT 1: PIGMENTS

(PS 3.1)

White light is a mixture of light of different colours; these are easily seen in a rainbow, or when light is passed through a prism. Each colour of light has a different wavelength. Blue light has a wavelength of approximately 450 nm, red light has a wavelength of approximately 650 nm, and the other visible colours have wavelengths in between.

Objects appear to be different colours because of the wavelengths of light that they absorb and reflect. A white object reflects all wavelengths of light, while a black object absorbs all and reflects none. A yellow object reflects yellow light and absorbs other colours.

An absorption spectrum shows how much light specific objects or molecules absorb at each wavelength. Figure A1a shows the absorption spectra of the different pigments in a chloroplast.

Figure A1b shows a complete absorption spectrum for a leaf, involving all its different pigments.

This graph also shows an action spectrum for photosynthesis – that is, the rate of photosynthesis at different wavelengths of light.

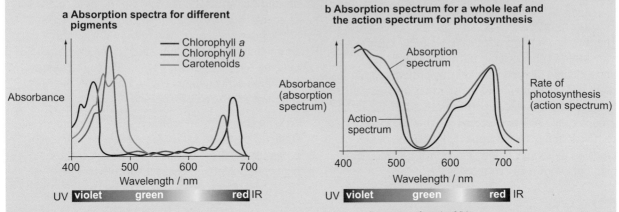

a Absorption spectra for different pigments

— Chlorophyll *a*
— Chlorophyll *b*
— Carotenoids

Absorbance

Wavelength / nm

UV violet green red IR

b Absorption spectrum for a whole leaf and the action spectrum for photosynthesis

Absorption spectrum

Absorbance (absorption spectrum)

Action spectrum

Rate of photosynthesis (action spectrum)

Wavelength / nm

UV violet green red IR

Figure A1 *Absorption spectra for some pigments in a leaf (a) and absorption and action spectra for a leaf (b)*

As can be seen in the absorption spectrum, chlorophyll is not one single compound but a mixture of several different pigments.

Questions

A1. What are the main colours of light absorbed by chlorophyll *b*?

A2. Explain why chlorophyll appears green.

A3. Copy the graph axes in Figure A1. On your copy, draw the action spectrum for a leaf if it contained only chlorophyll *a* and no other pigments.

A4. Suggest why it is an advantage to a plant to have several different pigments in its chloroplasts.

A5. Light does not penetrate very far into water. Short wavelengths penetrate to greater depths than long wavelengths. Different types of seaweeds contain different photosynthetic pigments. Low down on the shore, where they are covered by deep water when the tide is in, seaweeds tend to be red or orange. Higher up the shore, where they are covered only by shallow water for short periods of the day, they are usually green (Figure A2). Suggest how these different colours may be useful adaptations to their environments.

Figure A2 *Seaweeds come in many colours. Here you can see green, brownish-orange and dark red species.*

REQUIRED PRACTICAL ACTIVITY 7: APPARATUS AND TECHNIQUES

(MS 4.1, PS 2.3, PS 2.4, AT a, AT b, AT g)

Use of chromatography to investigate the pigments isolated from leaves of different plants, for example, leaves from shade-tolerant and shade-intolerant plants, or leaves of different colours.

This practical activity gives you the opportunity to show that you can:

> use appropriate instrumentation to record quantitative measurements

> use laboratory glassware apparatus

> separate biological compounds using thin layer/ paper chromatography.

We have seen that chloroplasts contain several different pigments, including chlorophyll *a*, chlorophyll *b* and carotenoids. We can separate these pigments using chromatography.

To do this, you first have to extract the pigments from the leaves. The pigments are not soluble in water, so instead you use an organic solvent, such as propanone. Care is needed, because propanone is very volatile (it forms a vapour), highly flammable and is an irritant. You therefore must not have any flames in the vicinity of your experiment and must always wear eye protection.

A good way of extracting the pigments is to grind some leaves in a pestle and mortar, adding a little sand to help to crush them and break open the cells, and some propanone to dissolve the pigments. Use only a small amount of propanone, and crush the leaves very thoroughly, to try to get a really concentrated solution of pigments.

Next, you need to prepare the chromatography paper and apparatus. This is shown in Figure P1.

Handle the chromatography paper with forceps rather than with your fingers, as lipids and other substances on your skin may interfere with the movement of the pigment up the paper, or show up as spots on the chromatogram. Use a pencil and ruler to draw a straight line a couple of centimetres up from the base of the strip of chromatography paper.

Pour some propanone into the base of a beaker, just deep enough so that you will be able to place the paper into it without the propanone reaching the pencil line.

Now you are ready to load the pigment extract onto the paper. Use a narrow-ended glass pipette, or the head of a large pin, for this. Dip it into the pigment extract, and very carefully make a small spot of the pigment exactly on the pencil line on the paper. Repeat many times, allowing each drop to dry before adding the next one. Try to make each spot as small as possible, containing as much pigment as possible.

Support the paper in the beaker as shown in Figure P1, and cover it.

As the propanone soaked into the chromatography paper is drawn upwards, it passes through the pigment spots that you made, and the pigments dissolve in the propanone. The pigments are carried upwards as the solvent moves upwards. Due to a combination of, for example, different particle size, solubility in propanone and adhesion/attraction to paper, the different pigments move different distances (Figure P2).

When the solvent has reached a level close to the top of the paper, carefully remove the paper, and draw a pencil line at the highest level reached by the solvent. This is known as the solvent front.

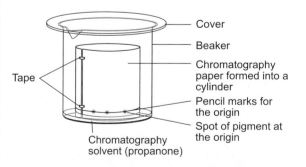

Figure P1 Apparatus for chloroplast pigment chromatography

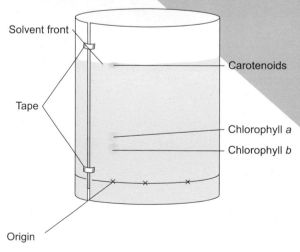

Figure P2 A chromatogram of chloroplast pigments

R_f values for each spot on the chromatogram are calculated by the equation:

$$R_f = \frac{\text{distance travelled by pigment spot}}{\text{distance travelled by solvent}}$$

Each type of pigment has its own characteristic R_f value, so even if you cannot see the colours clearly, you can still identify the pigment by calculating its R_f. Although R_f values vary for different solvents, in general carotenoids tend to have values very close to 1 (that is, they are so mobile that they are carried all the way up the paper with the solvent), chlorophyll *b* has a fairly small R_f value, and chlorophyll *a* is somewhere in between. With some kinds of leaves and some solvents, you may be able to see even more pigment spots. For example, you may see yellow spots as well as the chlorophyll ones, which are formed by pigments called xanthophylls.

QUESTIONS

P1. Suggest why:
   a. the pigment spot is loaded onto a pencil line on the chromatography paper
   b. the pigment spot is made as small and as concentrated as possible
   c. the pencil line must not be below the surface of the solvent
   d. a pencil line is drawn to show the solvent front immediately the paper is removed from the solvent.

P2. Outline how you could use chromatography to compare the pigments found in the leaves of two different plants.

P3. Figure P3 shows chromatograms obtained from seaweed and from spinach leaves. The same solvent was used in both cases.

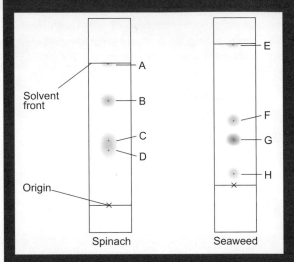

Figure P3 *Chromatograms for seaweed and spinach leaves*

   a. Calculate the R_f value for each pigment spot. Measure to the middle of the spot, as indicated by the pencil dot.
   b. The table shows the R_f values for each pigment, using the solvent that produced the chromatograms in the diagrams. Identify each pigment.

Pigment	R_f value
beta carotene	almost 1
chlorophyll *a*	0.45
chlorophyll *b*	0.38
chlorophyll *c*	0.01
fucoxanthin	0.32
xanthophyll	0.74

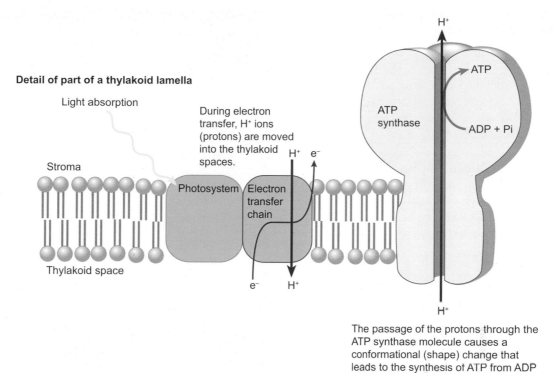

Detail of part of a thylakoid lamella

Light absorption

During electron transfer, H⁺ ions (protons) are moved into the thylakoid spaces.

Stroma

H^+ e^-

Photosystem / Electron transfer chain

Thylakoid space

e^- H^+

H^+

ATP synthase

ATP

ADP + Pi

H^+

The passage of the protons through the ATP synthase molecule causes a conformational (shape) change that leads to the synthesis of ATP from ADP and Pi.

Figure 8 Photophosphorylation

Photophosphorylation

The high-energy electrons that are ejected from chlorophyll molecules are used to make ATP.

As well as the photosystems described earlier, the thylakoid membranes inside the chloroplast contain a number of different **electron carriers**. These are arranged in a particular sequence, so that the electron is passed from one to the next (Figure 8). Each time the electron is passed on, it loses a little energy. The energy that is released is used to pump protons, H^+, across the membranes and into the spaces between them.

The result of this is a higher concentration of protons inside the spaces between the membranes than outside them, producing a diffusion gradient for protons. There is also an electrical gradient, because protons carry a positive charge. Thinking about the two gradients together, we say that there is an **electrochemical gradient**. Protons can diffuse down this gradient, from their high concentration to their lower concentration, and from a place with a high positive charge towards a less positively charged area, through the thylakoid membranes.

They can only do this through particular channels, which are formed by **ATP synthase** molecules. As

the hydrogen ions diffuse through, losing the energy that was given to them as they were pumped through the membrane, the ATP synthases use this energy to catalyse the synthesis of ATP from ADP and Pi.

The movement of the protons through the membrane, down their electrochemical gradient, is called **chemiosmosis**. This is rather a confusing name, because of course it has nothing at all to do with 'normal' osmosis, which involves the movement of water molecules.

The whole process, in which the high-energy electrons are used to make ATP, is called **photophosphorylation**.

Photolysis

As well as containing light-absorbing pigments, one of the types of photosystem found in chloroplasts contains an enzyme that can split water molecules in the presence of light. This produces protons (hydrogen ions, H^+), electrons (e^-) and oxygen.

water	$\rightarrow$	protons	+	electrons	+	oxygen
$2H_2O$	$\rightarrow$	$4H^+$	+	$4e^-$	+	O_2

This reaction is known as **photolysis** (photo = light, lysis = splitting). The oxygen is released into the atmosphere. This reaction is the source of almost all the oxygen that makes up 20 per cent of the air around us. Millions of tonnes of oxygen are present in the atmosphere, almost all produced by photolysis.

The electrons from the water are used to replace the electrons ejected from the chlorophyll molecules during photoionisation. The protons are picked up by NADP, as described below.

Production of reduced NADP

At the end of the electron transport chain, the electrons are picked up by NADP, along with the protons from the split water molecules. In the process, the NADP is reduced, becoming reduced NADP.

NADP + protons + electrons → reduced NADP

Remember that a hydrogen atom is made up of a proton and an electron, so effectively the NADP is combining with hydrogen, which originally came from water.

Products of the light-dependent reaction

So, at the end of the light-dependent reaction we have three products:

- oxygen, which is a waste product from the photolysis of water, and which diffuses out of the chloroplast and eventually into the atmosphere
- ATP, which was made by photophosphorylation, and contains energy that originated in the light energy absorbed by chlorophyll
- reduced NADP, which contains protons and electrons (hydrogen) derived from water molecules that were split by photolysis.

The ATP and reduced NADP are now used in the light-independent reaction.

QUESTIONS

3. Which of these terms matches each description below?

| photoionisation | photolysis | photophosphorylation |

a. The formation of ATP using energy that originally came from light.

b. The emission of an electron from a molecule, as a result of the absorption of light energy.

c. The splitting of water in the presence of light.

KEY IDEAS

- An enzyme present in the thylakoid membranes splits water molecules into protons, electrons and oxygen in the presence of light. This is called photolysis.

- Energy from light also causes electrons to be ejected from chlorophyll a, in a process called photoionisation.

- These high-energy electrons are used to make ATP, in a process called photophosphorylation.

- ATP is made when electrons are passed along the electron transfer chain, on the thylakoid membranes. The energy from these electrons is used to pump protons (hydrogen ions) across the membrane. As they diffuse back, the protons pass through an ATP synthase enzyme, which uses the energy of the gradient to combine ADP with inorganic phosphate.

- The products of the light-dependent reaction are oxygen, reduced NADP and ATP.

1.4 THE LIGHT–INDEPENDENT REACTION

As we have seen, the light-dependent reactions of photosynthesis require energy from sunlight. They can therefore occur during the day, but not at night.

However, the next stage of photosynthesis does not need an input of light energy. It can therefore take place even in the dark. In practice, however, it cannot go on all night, because it needs the ATP and reduced NADP that have been made in the light-dependent reactions. Once these have been used up, the light-independent reaction grinds to a halt.

In the light-independent stage of photosynthesis, the energy from ATP and the electrons from reduced NADP are used to reduce carbon dioxide from the atmosphere and build it into carbohydrate. This carbohydrate can provide a long-term store of energy. It can also be used as building blocks to produce all the other organic molecules – such as lipids, proteins and nucleic acids – that are needed for growth.

Figure 9 summarises the events that take place during the light-independent reaction. It is often known as the **Calvin cycle**, after the person who first worked out the series of reactions involved in the cycle.

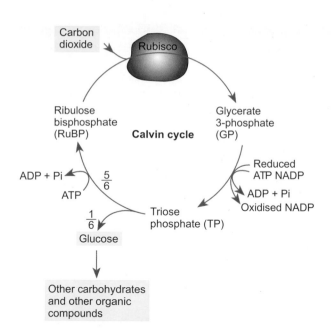

Figure 9 *The light-independent reaction*

As this is a cycle, we could start anywhere, but let's begin at the top left, where carbon dioxide first comes into the picture. The carbon dioxide combines with a substance called **ribulose bisphosphate**, generally known as **RuBP** for short. The reaction is catalysed by an enzyme called **rubisco**. Rubisco is the most abundant enzyme in the world.

An RuBP molecule contains five carbon atoms, and a carbon dioxide molecule contains one, so this reaction produces a 6-carbon molecule. This instantly splits into two, forming two 3-carbon molecules, called **glycerate 3-phosphate** (**GP**). The carbon dioxide is now said to be fixed, meaning that it has become part of a compound within the plant.

GP is not actually a carbohydrate. It is converted to carbohydrate using energy from ATP and hydrogen from reduced NADP, both of which are supplied from the light-dependent stage of photosynthesis. This is a reduction reaction. The GP is reduced to form **triose**

phosphate (**TP**). This *is* a carbohydrate – it is a 3-carbon sugar.

All of these reactions take place in the stroma of the chloroplast.

Various things can now happen to the TP. Most of it – about five-sixths – is used to regenerate RuBP. If this did not happen, the chloroplast would quickly run out of RuBP and the reaction would stop. The rest is used to make other kinds of useful organic molecules.

TP is a 3-carbon compound, so two molecules of it can be combined to form the 6-carbon hexose sugar, glucose. Other carbohydrates, such as sucrose, starch or cellulose, can be synthesised, dependent upon the cell's needs. TP can also be converted to fats (lipids) and – with the addition of nitrate or ammonium ions – to amino acids and proteins.

QUESTIONS

4. Students sometimes write: In photosynthesis, carbon dioxide is converted to oxygen. Explain why this is not correct.

5. Look at the diagram of the Calvin cycle in Figure 9. Give an example of a redox reaction. State which substance is being oxidised, and which is being reduced.

6. Figure 9 shows that ADP, Pi and oxidised NADP are formed. Suggest what happens to these substances.

7. In your own words, summarise how energy from light is transferred to energy in glucose, during photosynthesis.

8. Using Figure 9 and what you now know about the light-dependent and light-independent reactions of photosynthesis, explain how the structure of a chloroplast is adapted to its functions.

ASSIGNMENT 2: WORKING OUT THE CALVIN CYCLE

(PS 1.2, 2.1, 3.1, 4.1)

In the 1950s, researchers led by Melvin Calvin were the first to find out what happened during the light-independent stage of photosynthesis. The researchers used apparatus similar to that shown in Figure A1.

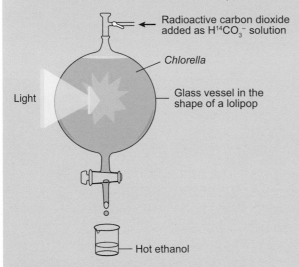

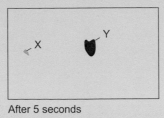
Radioactive carbon dioxide added as $H^{14}CO_3^-$ solution

Chlorella

Glass vessel in the shape of a lolipop

Light

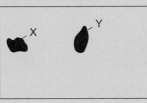

Hot ethanol

Figure A1 *The apparatus used by Melvin Calvin's team*

The glass-sided disc contained cells of a tiny one-celled photosynthetic organism called *Chlorella*. The apparatus was placed in a dark room and the *Chlorella* cells were supplied with carbon dioxide that contained radioactive carbon.

The contents of the apparatus were mixed thoroughly and then a light was switched on. At five-second intervals a member of Calvin's team extracted a few of the *Chlorella* cells from the apparatus and placed them into hot ethanol to kill them. The cells were then homogenised (mashed up to form a liquid).

The liquid was analysed to find out what it contained. This was done using two-way paper chromatography. This technique involves running the chromatogram with one solvent, then turning the paper through 90° and running it again with a different solvent.

Although the substances being separated were not coloured, Calvin could find where they were

on the paper because they contained radioactive carbon. Figure A2 shows two of the chromatograms he obtained. The dark spots contain radioactive carbon compounds.

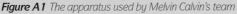

After 5 seconds

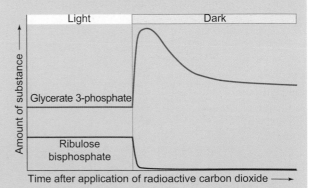

After 30 seconds

Figure A2 *Chromatograms obtained from the Chlorella experiments*

The researchers were able to collect samples of these compounds and find out exactly what they were. By using this technique, Calvin's team was able to investigate the sequence in which different organic compounds were produced.

In another series of experiments, Calvin's team used similar techniques to investigate the effect of light and dark periods on the compounds formed in the light-independent reaction. Figure A3 shows the results from one of these investigations.

Figure A3 *Changes in concentrations of GP and RuBP during light and darkness*

TASKS

A1. Suggest the advantages of using two-way chromatography, rather than just using one solvent that carries the compounds in one direction.

Stretch and challenge

A2. Using your knowledge of the light-independent stage of photosynthesis, suggest the identities of compound X and compound Y in Figure A2.

A3. Using the graphs in Figure A3, explain why:

   a. When the light is switched off, the curve for ribulose bisphosphate falls.

   b. When the light is switched off, the curve for glycerate 3-phosphate rises.

   c. Eventually, the curve for glycerate 3-phosphate levels off.

KEY IDEAS

> During the light-independent reaction, energy from ATP and electrons from reduced NADP are used to reduce carbon dioxide and produce carbohydrates.

> The enzyme rubisco, which is present in the stroma of chloroplasts, catalyses the combination of carbon dioxide with ribulose bisphosphate (RuBP), to produce a 6-carbon compound.

> The 6-carbon compound immediately splits into two molecules of glycerate 3-phosphate (GP).

> GP is reduced by reduced NADP, using energy from ATP. This produces the carbohydrate triose phosphate (TP).

> Five-sixths of the TP is used to regenerate RuBP. The remainder is used to synthesise other carbohydrates, lipids and amino acids.

Light and air

(MS 0.1, 0.2, 0.3)

Light is very important for humans and for many other living things. Plants use light to photosynthesise, and the resulting energy accumulates in the food chain (see *Chapter 3*). Light has inspired people, including artists and scientists, throughout history.

Light travels at approximately 186 000 miles per second.

The speed of sound is approximately 340 metres per second.

   a. Express the approximate speed of light in kilometres per hour, using standard form.

   b. At this speed, how far can light travel in four seconds? Express your answer in standard form.

   c. Express the speed of sound as a fraction and a decimal of the speed of light, using standard form.

Typically, most of the air around us is made up of oxygen and nitrogen. Oxygen is approximately $\frac{1}{5}$ of the air we breathe, and nitrogen makes up about $\frac{39}{50}$.

   d. Express the relative quantities of oxygen and nitrogen in the air, as percentages.

   e. Air also contains small quantities of other gases, such as carbon dioxide and argon. According to your answer for **d**, what fraction of the air must these gases occupy?

Part a

First, it is important to understand how a kilometre relates to a mile.

1 mile equates roughly to 1.61 kilometres:

$1 \div 1.61 = 0.62$

So, the value in miles $\div 0.62$
= the equivalent in kilometres

Similarly, the value in kilometres $\times 0.62$
= the value in miles

186 000 miles per second $\div 0.62$
= 300 000 kilometres per second

$186\,000 = 186 \times 1000 = 1.86 \times 100\,000$

This can be expressed as 1.86×10^5 in standard form.

$300\,000 = 3.0 \times 10^5$ kilometres per second, in standard form.

Part b

Speed is a measure of the distance travelled over the time it has taken, and is generally shown algebraically as:

$$S(m\ s^{-1}) = \frac{D(m)}{T(s)}$$

The equation needs to be re-arranged, taking care to use the correct units, to calculate the distance:

Distance = 3.0×10^5 km s^{-1} × 4 s
= 1 200 000 = 1.2×10^6 kilometres

Part c

First, it is important for the values to have the same units. This can be done by converting the speed of sound to miles per second:

340 meters per second ÷ 1000
= 0.34 kilometres per second

$0.34 \times 0.62 = 0.21$ miles per second
= 0.21 ÷ 186 000 = 0.0000011 = 1.1×10^{-6}

So, sound travels at approximately 1.1×10^{-6} of the speed of light.

Part d

Oxygen: 1 ÷ 5 = 0.2

0.2 × 100 (to convert to a percentage) = 20%

Nitrogen: 39 ÷ 50 = 0.78

0.78 × 100 (to convert to a percentage) = 78%

Part e

The total percentage of air occupied so far by oxygen and nitrogen is 98% (20% + 78%).

100% (total air) − 98%
= 2% remaining for the other gases

2% as a fraction = 2 ÷ 100 = 1 ÷ 50 = $\frac{1}{50}$

1.5 FACTORS AFFECTING THE RATE OF PHOTOSYNTHESIS

What determines how fast a plant can photosynthesise? Obviously, light intensity will have an effect, as this is the energy source that drives the whole process. Carbon dioxide and water are the two raw materials, so supplies of these will be critical. Temperature is also likely to have an effect, because high temperatures speed up particle movement and therefore increase the frequency of collisions between reacting molecules in the Calvin cycle. On the other hand, very high temperatures denature proteins in living organisms and therefore stop enzyme-catalysed reactions from taking place at all.

The rate of photosynthesis is important in food production because it determines the crop yield. All the factors mentioned above can affect the rate of photosynthesis of a crop. Good crop management involves the manipulation of these factors so as to maximise photosynthesis and achieve good yields.

A factor that is in short supply will limit the rate of photosynthesis, and is called a **limiting factor**.

Light

The effect of light on photosynthesis depends on:

> light quality – that is, the wavelengths that it contains; plants can use only certain wavelengths for photosynthesis

> light duration – that is, the day length

> light intensity – that is, how strong the light is.

At low light intensities, an increase in the rate of photosynthesis is directly proportional to increasing light intensity (Figure 10). But as light intensity increases, photosynthesis reaches a maximum rate and fails to increase further. This could be because:

> The photosynthetic reactions are proceeding as fast as is possible for the photosynthetic pathways in that particular plant.

> Some other environmental factor is now limiting the rate, such as carbon dioxide concentration or temperature.

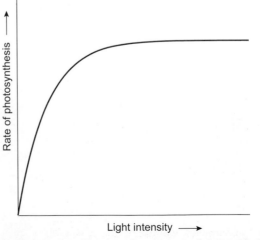

Figure 10 *Effect of light intensity on the rate of photosynthesis*

The maximum light that can be used in photosynthetic reactions is estimated to be about 10 000 lux (the SI unit of illuminance, equal to one lumen per square metre). On a clear summer day in Britain, solar illumination may reach 100 000 lux. At this time of year in a sunny field, therefore, light intensity is not the limiting factor. The plants have as much light as they can possibly use.

At very high light intensities there may be damage to the chlorophyll molecules, resulting in a drop in the rate of photosynthesis.

Temperature

When light intensity and carbon dioxide are not limiting factors, increasing temperature can increase the rate of photosynthesis. Between the range 10 °C to about 35 °C, a 10 °C rise in the temperature will double the rate of photosynthesis (Figure 11).

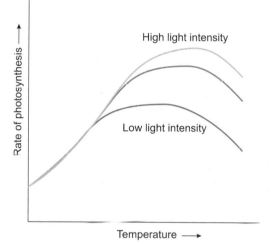

Figure 11 *Effect of temperature on the rate of photosynthesis*

It is interesting to note that temperature does not have a direct effect on the light-dependent reactions of photosynthesis. This is because, unusually for a metabolic reaction, the energy that drives the reaction is light energy. The kinetic energy of the particles involved is almost irrelevant. However, temperature does affect the rate of the light-independent stage, just as it does any other metabolic reaction.

Carbon dioxide

In tropical areas, temperature and light intensity are not usually the limiting factors for photosynthesis, but carbon dioxide may be limiting. Carbon dioxide is the source of carbon atoms used to make all the organic products of photosynthesis. Carbon dioxide is needed in the light-independent reactions of photosynthesis, where it is reduced to carbohydrate and other organic compounds. Atmospheric carbon dioxide usually makes up only about 0.04% of the volume of the air. This is a tiny proportion. For most plants, this is lower than the optimum value for photosynthesis (Figure 12).

Crop management in glasshouses

Imagine that a grower in the UK produces tomatoes to sell in bulk to supermarkets (Figure 13). In the UK climate, tomatoes can only be grown outdoors for a few months of the year, as they are killed by frost and the fruits grow poorly in low temperatures. So the grower produces the crop in glasshouses.

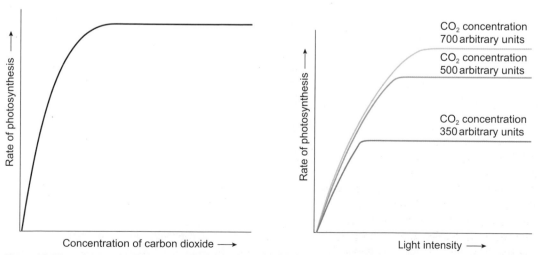

Figure 12 *Effect of carbon dioxide concentration on the rate of photosynthesis*

Figure 13 *Growing crops in glasshouses can produce very high rates of photosynthesis, and therefore high yields.*

Glasshouse cultivation allows:

> better yields to be achieved

> some crops to be grown out of season and so provide a better economic return

> some plants to be grown in regions where they would not normally grow.

In order to achieve maximum yields, possible limiting factors inside the glasshouse need to be controlled.

The faster the plants can photosynthesise, the more carbohydrates they can make. This provides them with both the materials and the energy required to make new cells for growth, and for fruit formation. Rapid photosynthesis means rapid production of a large crop of tomatoes.

Over short periods, 0.5% carbon dioxide has been found to be the optimum concentration for photosynthesis. Over longer periods, however, this concentration may cause the stomata to close, resulting in a drop in photosynthesis. For glasshouse crops such as tomatoes, 0.1% carbon dioxide is the optimum over long periods.

Tomato plants die when the temperature falls below about 2 °C. At the other extreme, temperatures above 30 °C can damage tomato plants. The grower aims to keep the temperature somewhere between 15 °C and 25 °C. This allows the plants to photosynthesise rapidly, without there being any danger of cells being damaged.

It is just as important to stop temperatures from rising too high in the summer as it is to keep them from dropping too low in the cooler spring and autumn months. At the ideal temperatures for tomato growth, water loss by transpiration is likely to be high, so the plants will need to be kept well watered. Excessive water loss can lead to closure of the stomata,

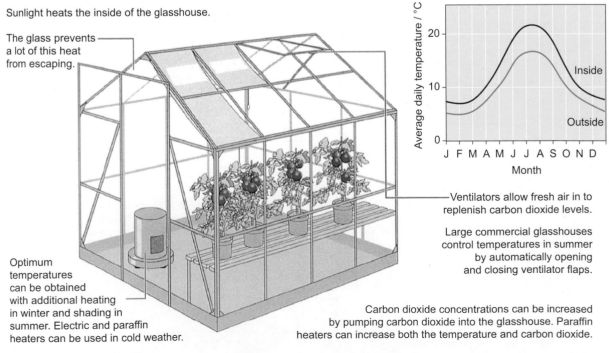

Figure 14 *Glasshouse cultivation*

meaning that carbon dioxide will not be able to enter the leaves and photosynthesis will come to a halt. Many glasshouses have automatic watering systems with sprinklers and humidifiers. However, it is also important to regulate humidity in order to limit fungal diseases, which can increase when the humidity is too high.

Artificial lighting can be used in glasshouses when the natural light intensity falls too low. The light sources that are used provide a mix of the wavelengths that can be absorbed by the plant pigments – a spectrum similar to the absorption spectrum shown in Figure A1 in Assignment 1. This way, the grower is not spending money on electricity to produce light of wavelengths that will be wasted.

All of these factors can be controlled by computers. Sensors are used to monitor the level of each factor and the feedback is processed by the computer.

Keeping carbon dioxide concentration, temperature and light intensity at their optima is expensive. Carbon dioxide can be added from generators or from cylinders, which have to be bought in. Sometimes, it is generated by burning fuels such as paraffin, which has the added bonus that this also increases temperature. Lights run from electricity. The grower has to calculate the expense of controlling all of these factors, and balance it against the price that he or she expects to get from the crop. The increase in yield has to be worth more than the costs of environmental control, if it is to be worth the investment.

Crop management in open fields

It is much less easy to control potential limiting factors when crops are growing in fields. However, there are still measures that can be taken to keep rates of photosynthesis, and therefore growth rates, as high as possible.

Weeds are plants that grow among the crop, but are not wanted. They compete with the crop plants for light, water and carbon dioxide, as well as for mineral ions from the soil, some of which will be needed to produce the enzymes, chlorophyll and cell structures that are needed for photosynthesis. Killing weeds and applying fertilisers therefore helps to increase photosynthesis in the crop plants.

In dry conditions, the stomata on the leaves of the crop plants may close, so that the plant can conserve water. This decreases rates of photosynthesis, because carbon dioxide cannot diffuse into the leaves. Irrigation to keep an adequate water supply can prevent this from happening.

Crops that are sensitive to temperature, such as strawberries, can be covered with fleece or polythene to help to increase the temperature around them and allow them to grow earlier in the year than might otherwise be possible.

Figure 15 *Spraying herbicides to kill weeds in a field of young wheat plants*

REQUIRED PRACTICAL ACTIVITY 8: APPARATUS AND TECHNIQUES

Investigation into the effect of a named factor on the rate of dehydrogenase activity in extracts of chloroplasts

(PS 2.4, PS 3.1, PS 4.1, MS 3.2, AT a, AT b, AT c)

This practical activity gives you the opportunity to show that you can:

> use appropriate apparatus to record a range of quantitative measurements

> use laboratory glassware apparatus for a variety of experimental techniques.

During the light-dependent reaction, NADP acts as an electron acceptor, becoming reduced in the process. The reaction is catalysed by a dehydrogenase enzyme. We can investigate this reaction using a different electron acceptor – one that changes colour when it accepts electrons.

A good substance to use is a blue dye that you may have used before to test for the presence of vitamin C. This dye is called DCPIP. It is blue when oxidised, but becomes colourless when it accepts electrons and is reduced.

The first step is to extract some chloroplasts (Figure P1). Chop up some leaves, add them to a small amount of an ice-cold solution containing sucrose, potassium chloride and a buffer (called an isolation medium), and grind them vigorously in an ice-cold pestle and mortar. The sucrose and potassium chloride ensure that the solution has a similar water potential to the cells in the leaves. The buffer keeps the pH at 7. The resulting mixture is then filtered through muslin to get rid of any big bits of leaves. The green filtrate contains the chloroplasts.

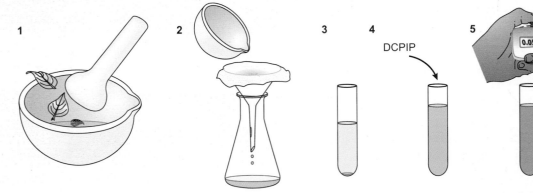

Figure P1 *Procedure for investigating dehydrogenase activity in chloroplasts*

The filtrate can now be centrifuged. This produces a little green pellet at the base of each centrifuge tube. The pellet contains most of the chloroplasts. Pour off the liquid (called the supernatant) and replace with a little of the ice-cold isolation medium. Mix the chloroplasts into it, using a glass rod or a pipette. (You might like to look at this mixture under a microscope, where you should be able to see the chloroplasts.) Stand each tube containing these resuspended chloroplasts in an ice-cold water bath.

You now have a suspension of chloroplasts in each tube. If you place some of this suspension into a clean test tube, add a measured quantity of DCPIP, and

shine light onto it, you will see that the blue DCPIP quickly loses its colour. This happens because the chloroplasts are absorbing light and emitting electrons, which are being picked up by the DCPIP and reducing it. If you do the same in a tube wrapped in black paper, the DCPIP will remain blue.

You can now investigate how different factors affect the rate at which this happens. For example, you could shine light of different colours (wavelengths) onto the tubes, and time how long it takes for the DCPIP to decolourise. Keep all other factors constant. You could also investigate the effect of light intensity, or temperature.

QUESTIONS

P1. Suggest why the isolation medium:
  a. is kept ice cold
  b. contains a buffer to keep the pH at 7
  c. has a water potential similar to that of the leaf cells.

P2. If you have access to a colorimeter, you can measure the depth of colour every minute, rather than just timing how long it takes for the DCPIP to change from blue to colourless. The reading on the colorimeter is called the absorbance. The greater the absorbance, the darker the blue colour of the DCPIP.

Table P1 shows the results obtained when DCPIP was added to a tube containing resuspended chloroplasts, and another containing the supernatant. Both tubes were kept in light of the same intensity.

Time / minutes	Absorbance / arbitrary units	
	Resuspended chloroplasts	Supernatant
0	10.0	10.0
2	8.4	9.3
4	6.7	8.4
6	5.2	7.1
8	4.9	6.3
10	2.4	4.5
12	1.0	3.2
14	0.3	2.6

Table P1

a. Plot line graphs for these results, drawing lines of best fit. Draw both lines on the same pair of axes.

b. Explain the results for the resuspended chloroplasts.

c. Suggest reasons for the differences between the two sets of data.

ASSIGNMENT 3: MAXIMISING THE YIELD

(PS 1.2, 2.1, 2.4, 3.1)

Tomatoes are an important crop in many parts of the world. They may be used locally for food, but more often they are an important export crop, bringing in significant income for farmers. Growers have to decide whether it is best to use a low-tech approach and simply growing the tomatoes in open fields, or whether it may be worth making a substantial investment to build glasshouses where they can control the conditions in which the plants are growing.

An investigation was carried out into the effect of temperature on the growth of tomatoes. Tomato plants of the same variety – one that grows well at higher temperatures – were grown in an open field and also in three different glasshouses. The experiment was carried out in a subtropical country, where the outside temperature never dropped below 29.5 °C.

Even when not heated, the temperature inside a glasshouse is generally higher than outside. This is because of the greenhouse effect – short wavelength rays from the Sun pass through the glass into the glasshouse, and are reflected from the surfaces inside the glasshouse as longer wavelengths, which cannot escape. These longer wavelengths warm the air inside the glasshouse.

The glasshouses in the experiment had different coverings.

Figure A1 shows the variations in temperature in the four growing environments throughout the 10 months of the investigation.

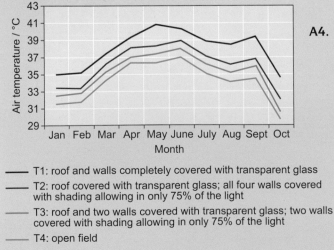

— T1: roof and walls completely covered with transparent glass

— T2: roof covered with transparent glass; all four walls covered with shading allowing in only 75% of the light

— T3: roof and two walls covered with transparent glass; two walls covered with shading allowing in only 75% of the light

— T4: open field

Figure A1 Temperature variation in four growing environments

Equal numbers of one-month-old plants of the same tomato variety were planted into each of the growing environments in February. Table A1 shows the growth yields of fruit from the plants in each of the four growing environments.

Growing environment	Mean plant height / cm	Mean fruit yield per plant / g
T1	97.50	1348.5
T2	105.83	2145.2
T3	104.83	2055.0
T4	75.40	981.0

Table A1

Questions

A1. a. Compare the temperatures in growing environments T1 and T2.

   b. Explain the reasons for the differences that you have described.

A2. What appears to be the temperature range at which this variety of tomato plants produces the highest yield? Use the information in the graphs and in the table to support your answer.

A3. Suggest one factor, other than temperature, which may have been partly responsible for the differences in yield between T1 and T4. How significant might this factor have been? Do you think that it brings the reliability of the results into question?

A4. Discuss the extent to which the results of this investigation could be used by growers in a temperate country such as the UK to help them to determine the best environment in which to grow tomatoes.

KEY IDEAS

> Low light intensity, low concentrations of carbon dioxide and temperatures that are above or below the optimum can limit the rate of photosynthesis.

> Agricultural practices can help to reduce the effects of these limiting factors. In glasshouses, temperature, lighting and carbon dioxide concentration can be controlled. In open fields, the rates of photosynthesis, and therefore yields of crop plants, can be increased by removing weeds that compete for light, carbon dioxide and minerals, and by providing irrigation and adding fertilisers.

PRACTICE QUESTIONS

1. An experiment was carried out to investigate the effect of two different carbon dioxide concentrations, and three different day and night temperatures, on the rate of growth of cereal plants. The results are shown in Table Q1.

CO_2 concentration / mmol mol^{-1}	Day and night temperatures / °C	Mean grain yield per plant / g	Mean above-ground biomass per plant / g	Harvest index
330	26/19	9.0	17.1	0.53
	31/24	10.1	19.8	
	36/29	10.1	22.2	
660	26/19	13.1	26.6	
	31/24	12.5	27.6	
	36/29	11.6	70.1	

Table Q1

a. The harvest index is calculated by dividing the mean grain yield per plant by the mean above-ground biomass per plant. One value for harvest index is included in the table. Calculate the other five values for the harvest index.

b. With reference to the data in the table, describe the effect of carbon dioxide concentration on:

  i. the mean grain yield per plant

  ii. the harvest index.

c. With reference to the data in the table, describe the effect of temperature on:

  i. the mean grain yield per plant

  ii. the harvest index.

d. Suggest reasons for the patterns that you have described in your answers to **b** and **c**.

e. Suggest why farmers may be more interested in achieving a high harvest index rather than a high mean grain yield per plant.

2. Scientists investigated the effect of iron deficiency on the production of triose phosphate in sugar beet plants. They grew plants under the same conditions with their roots in a liquid growth medium that contained all the necessary nutrients. Ten days before the experiments, they transferred half the plants to a liquid growth medium that contained no iron. The scientists measured the concentration of triose phosphate

(continued)

produced in these plants and in the control plants:

❯ at the end of six hours in the dark

❯ then for 16 hours in the light.

Their results are shown in Figure Q1.

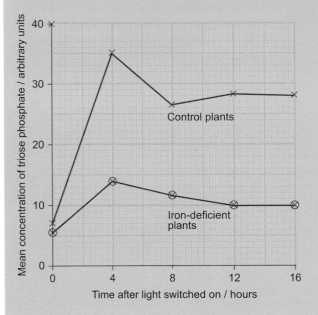

Figure Q1

a. i. The experiments were carried out at a high carbon dioxide concentration. Explain why.

ii. Explain why it was important to grow the plants under the same conditions up to ten days before the experiment.

iii. The plants were left in the dark for six hours before the experiment. Explain why.

b. Iron deficiency reduces electron transport. Use this information and your knowledge of photosynthesis to explain the decrease in production of triose phosphate in the iron-deficient plants.

c. Iron deficiency results in a decrease in the uptake of carbon dioxide. Explain why.

AQA June 2013 Paper 4 Question 5

3. During photosynthesis, carbon dioxide reacts with ribulose bisphosphate (RuBP) to form two molecules of glycerate 3-phosphate (GP). This reaction is catalysed by the enzyme rubisco. Rubisco can also catalyse a reaction between RuBP and oxygen to form one molecule of GP and one molecule of phosphoglycolate. Both the reactions catalysed by rubisco are shown in Figure Q2.

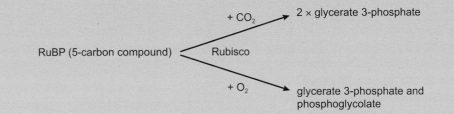

Figure Q2

a. i. Where exactly in a cell is the enzyme rubisco found?

ii. Use the information provided to give the number of carbon atoms in one molecule of phosphoglycolate.

b. Scientists investigated the effect of different concentrations of oxygen on the rate of absorption of carbon dioxide by leaves of soya bean plants. Their results are shown in Figure Q3.

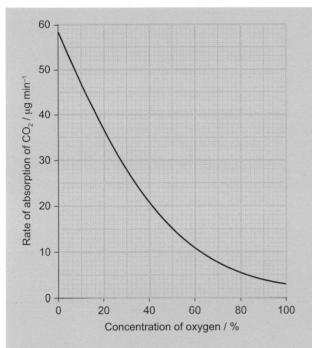

Figure Q3

Tube	Contents of tube	Uptake of radioactively labelled CO_2 / counts per minute
A	Stroma and grana	96 000
B	Stroma, ATP and reduced NADP	97 000
C	Stroma	4000

a. Name the substance that combines with carbon dioxide in a chloroplast.

b. Explain why the results in tube B are similar to those in tube A.

c. Use the information in the table to predict the uptake of radioactively labelled carbon dioxide if tube A was placed in the dark. Explain your answer.

d. Use your knowledge of the light-independent reaction to explain why the uptake of carbon dioxide in tube C was less than the uptake in tube B.

e. DCMU is used as a weed killer. It inhibits electron transfer during photosynthesis. The addition of DCMU to tube A decreased the uptake of carbon dioxide. Explain why.

AQA June 2012 Unit 4 Question 4

Use Figure Q2 to explain the results obtained in Figure Q3.

c. Use the information provided and your knowledge of the light-independent reaction to explain why the yield from soya bean plants is decreased at higher concentrations of oxygen. Phosphoglycolate is not used in the light-independent reaction.

AQA January 2013 Unit 4 Question 5

4. A scientist investigated the uptake of radioactively labelled carbon dioxide in chloroplasts. She used three tubes, each containing different components of chloroplasts. She measured the uptake of carbon dioxide in each of these tubes. Her results are shown in the table.

5. Researchers have investigated the effect of introducing a form of rubisco from cyanobacteria into tobacco leaves, using gene technology. They measured the amount of CO_2 fixed in leaves of normal tobacco plants, and in leaves of tobacco plants containing the cyanobacterial rubisco, exposed to different concentrations of CO_2. The rate was measured as the amount of CO_2 fixed per mole of rubisco per second.

(continued)

The results are shown in Figure Q4.

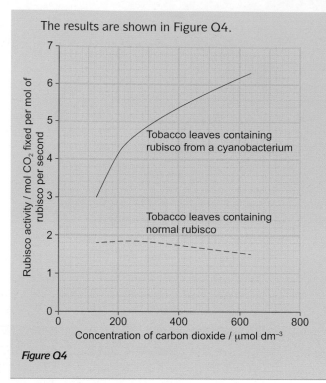

Figure Q4

a. Describe the role of rubisco in the light-independent reaction of photosynthesis.

b. In which part of the chloroplast does the reaction catalysed by rubisco take place?

c. Compare the effects of increasing carbon dioxide concentration on tobacco leaves containing normal and those containing cyanobacterial rubisco.

d. Suggest how growing genetically engineered plants containing cyanobacterial rubisco might increase yields.

2 RESPIRATION

PRIOR KNOWLEDGE

Respiration is one of the seven signs of life – it is a biochemical process that releases the energy in organic molecules. You will probably remember that the process can be summarised as:

glucose + oxygen → carbon dioxide + water + energy

The energy released in this process is used to make ATP, a compound that, in one simple step, delivers instant energy for various processes.

Respiration is largely an enzyme-controlled process and so you will need to recall your knowledge of enzyme action and activation energy.

LEARNING OBJECTIVES

In this chapter we look at the two types of respiration. Aerobic respiration provides a lot of ATP but needs oxygen. Anaerobic respiration provides less energy as ATP for a given amount of respiratory substrate.

In order to understand respiration you need to appreciate where each of the stages takes place, what goes in, what comes out and how the products of one stage are the starting point for the next. There are four main stages to full aerobic respiration.

(Specification 3.5.2)

Forensic scientists can estimate the time of death by several different means, one of which is the onset of rigor mortis – the 'stiffness of the dead'.

Several different factors combine to determine the time that rigor mortis sets in, but it is usually between two and six hours after death. Smaller muscles are affected first, such as those of the hands and face. When the larger muscles lock in place, it is very difficult to reposition the body. It can be a challenge to get an awkwardly shaped and rigid corpse into a coffin.

So why do corpses go stiff? It's all about ATP.

ATP is constantly being used and needs to be re-synthesised – that is why we respire. After death, respiration stops, and so does the production of ATP. Being a relatively unstable molecule, ATP has a half-life. It breaks down rather quickly, and when that happens, the cross-bridges that join the muscle fibres lock in place, fixing the muscles. The corpse will remain stiff until enzyme activity begins to break down the muscle fibres, at which point the muscles become moveable again.

Rigor mortis is very important in the meat industry. If meat is chilled after slaughter, a process called cold shortening takes place. The release of calcium ions causes the ATP to react with the muscle fibres, and the muscles shorten, resulting in tough, dense meat. To prevent this, newly-slaughtered meat is often zapped with electricity, which causes rapid contraction and relaxation of the fibres – a bit like shivering – and this uses up all the ATP. After this, the muscle cannot develop rigor mortis. Result: more tender meat.

2.1 THE STAGES OF RESPIRATION

All cells in all organisms respire all the time, unless they are dormant. Respiration is a series of oxidation reactions. The first stage of respiration occurs in the fluid part of the cytoplasm. Afterwards, the products of this first stage pass into the **mitochondria** for the rest of the process.

A good way to understand respiration is to focus on the electrons. Basically, the reactions of respiration remove electrons from the glucose – or what's left of it. These high-energy electrons are picked up by molecules called **coenzymes**. Whenever you see the expression 'reduced coenzyme', think 'an electron being carried'. These reduced enzymes are a bit like casino chips, or credit notes. The energy in the electrons can be cashed in for ATP at the end of the process, the **electron transfer chain**.

$$NAD^+ + e^- \rightarrow \text{reduced NAD (NADH)}$$

$$FADH^+ + e^- \rightarrow \text{reduced FAD (FADH}_2)$$

Both these equations are simply showing that a coenzyme picks up an electron to become a reduced coenzyme. The plus on the NAD is a proton, and combines with an electron to make a hydrogen atom, hence the H. NADH and FADH$_2$ are **reduced coenzymes** carrying electrons whose energy can be used to produce ATP.

The four stages of full aerobic respiration are:

1 **Glycolysis** – literally 'sugar splitting'. 6-carbon glucose molecules are split into two 3-carbon molecules of **pyruvate**. The process starts with an input of ATP to make the glucose more reactive, but the end product is a small net gain in ATP, as well as some reduced coenzyme. This stage requires no oxygen – it is **anaerobic** – and happens in the cytoplasm of the cell. Anaerobic respiration is basically glycolysis that can't go any further.

2 **The link reaction** – the pyruvate made in glycolysis passes into the mitochondria where it is oxidised to produce **acetate**, which is picked by **coenzyme A** to form **acetyl coenzyme A**. This stage makes reduced coenzyme NADH but no ATP.

3 **The Krebs cycle** – the acetate has electrons and carbon dioxide removed from it. The Krebs cycle is the main source of reduced coenzymes, and produces a small amount of ATP.

4 **The electron transfer chain** – the electrons harvested in the first three processes are used, indirectly, to power the production of ATP. This happens on the membranes of the cristae inside the mitochondrion, and is known as **oxidative phosphorylation**.

Figure 1 shows the structure of a mitochondrion, and summarises the stages of respiration that take place in the different parts.

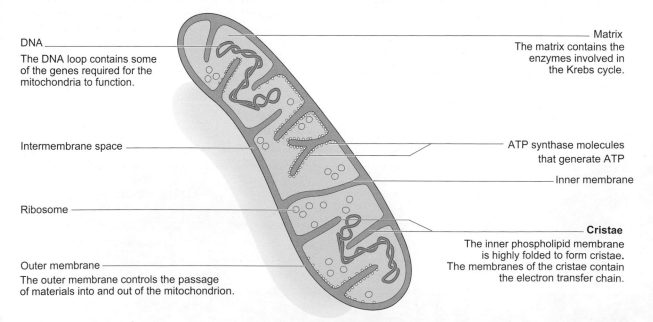

DNA
The DNA loop contains some of the genes required for the mitochondria to function.

Intermembrane space

Ribosome

Outer membrane
The outer membrane controls the passage of materials into and out of the mitochondrion.

Matrix
The matrix contains the enzymes involved in the Krebs cycle.

ATP synthase molecules that generate ATP

Inner membrane

Cristae
The inner phospholipid membrane is highly folded to form cristae. The membranes of the cristae contain the electron transfer chain.

Figure 1 *A mitochondrion. The mitochondria of cells with a high energy demand have more cristae, increasing the surface area for ATP production.*

QUESTION

1. What similarities are there between the structure of a mitochondrion and a chloroplast?

KEY IDEAS

> Respiration is the oxidation of glucose, or other organic molecules, such as lipids or amino acids. During the process energy is released from glucose molecules, and much of this energy is used to synthesise ATP.

> Aerobic respiration involves four stages. Glycolysis takes place in the cytoplasm. The link reaction and the Krebs cycle take place in the matrix (inner fluid) of a mitochondrion. The electron transfer chain takes place in the inner membrane (on the cristae) of a mitochondrion.

2.2 GLYCOLYSIS

The overall process of glycolysis is illustrated in Figure 2. It is a ten-step process, with each step being controlled by a different enzyme. These enzymes are found in the cytoplasm of virtually all cells, making glycolysis a property of living tissue. There is no organelle as such for glycolysis.

Glucose is not very reactive, so to start the process two molecules of ATP are used to add two phosphate groups. This produces a more reactive phosphorylated 6-carbon sugar. The phosphorylated sugar is then broken down into two molecules of the 3-carbon sugar **triose phosphate** and then into two molecules of pyruvate. This is an oxidation process: electrons are removed from the triose phosphate and transferred to a coenzyme, producing **reduced NAD (NADH)**.

The conversion of two triose phosphates to pyruvate also releases enough energy to produce four molecules of ATP. Two ATP in and four out gives a net gain of two. At the end of glycolysis we have, per glucose:

> two molecules of ATP

> two molecules of reduced NAD

> two molecules of pyruvate.

KEY IDEAS

> In glycolysis, glucose is converted to pyruvate in a series of small steps. Each glucose molecule is phosphorylated, and then split to form two triose phosphate molecules. This uses two molecules of ATP for each molecule of glucose. NAD takes electrons from each triose phosphate molecule, becoming reduced NAD.

> As the triose phosphate is converted to pyruvate, enough energy is released to make two molecules of ATP for every triose phosphate – so there is a net gain of two molecules of ATP for every glucose molecule.

2.3 THE LINK REACTION

The link reaction is named as such because it links the anaerobic reactions of glycolysis with the aerobic reactions in the mitochondria. Figure 3 gives an overview of the link reaction.

At the start of the link reaction the pyruvate that is made in glycolysis moves from the cytoplasm into the mitochondrial matrix – the fluid in the centre of the mitochondrion. In this matrix, NAD removes electrons from the pyruvate, oxidising it to a 2-carbon acetate molecule and carbon dioxide. The acetate is picked up by a carrier molecule – coenzyme A – to form acetyl coenzyme A.

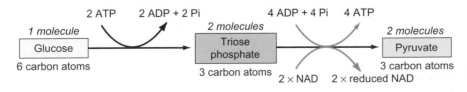

Figure 2 Glycolysis

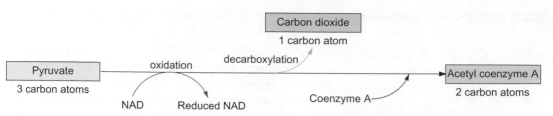

Figure 3 The link reaction

For each glucose molecule, the link reaction produces:

> two molecules of acetyl coenzyme A

> two molecules of reduced NAD

but no ATP.

2.4 THE KREBS CYCLE

Acetyl coenzyme A enters a series of reactions called the Krebs cycle, named after Hans Krebs, who discovered the sequence while working at Sheffield University in the 1950s. The reactions of the Krebs cycle, summarised in Figure 4, also occur in solution in the matrix of the mitochondria. Overall, the reactions of the Krebs cycle remove electrons that originate from the 2-carbon acetate group. These oxidation reactions produce carbon dioxide and reduced NAD and FAD.

Krebs cycle, step-by-step:

1 The 2-carbon acetate from acetyl coenzyme A combines with a 4-carbon organic acid to form a 6-carbon molecule.

2 A molecule of carbon dioxide is removed, forming a 5-carbon compound. This step produces one molecule of NADH.

3 Another molecule of carbon dioxide is removed, making a 4-carbon compound. This step produces one molecule of NADH, one of $FADH_2$ and one of ATP.

4 In the final step, the 4-carbon compound is converted back into the substance that starts the cycle. This step produces a third molecule of NADH and one of $FADH_2$.

The Krebs cycle itself produces only a small amount of ATP directly. Like the two ATPs made by glycolysis, this is ATP production by **substrate-level phosphorylation**.

Remember that each glucose produces two pyruvate molecules and so, per glucose, the Krebs cycle turns twice. So, overall, per glucose, the Krebs cycle makes:

> two molecules of ATP

> six molecules of NADH

> two molecules of $FADH_2$

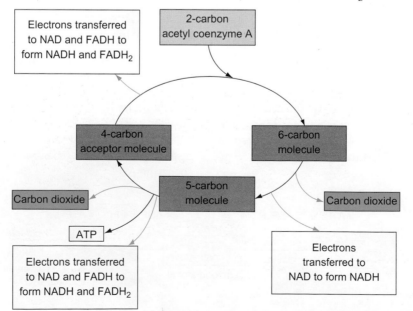

Figure 4 The Krebs cycle. Note: the carbon dioxide comes directly from these reactions, without the need for oxygen

> four molecules of carbon dioxide (the 'remains' of the acetate).

If we add these to the products of glycolysis and the link reaction, we have:

> four molecules of ATP

> ten molecules of NADH

> two molecules of $FADH_2$.

So, that's four molecules of ATP that are ready to be used, and 12 electrons that can be used to make more ATP by cashing them in at the electron transfer chain.

We have included the numbers of the different molecules here to help you understand the Krebs cycle and to give you a sense of the difference between aerobic and anaerobic respiration. However, you won't be expected to remember them in an examination.

You may have noticed that so far there has been no mention of oxygen. This is because there is no need for oxygen throughout the first three stages of respiration (glycolysis, the link reaction and the Krebs cycle); carbon dioxide is **not** made using oxygen breathed in. However, oxygen is vital for the next and final stage, which is the production of ATP in the electron transfer chain.

2.5 THE ELECTRON TRANSFER CHAIN

The purpose of the electron transfer chain is to use the energy associated with the electrons to make ATP. The reduced coenzymes – NADH and $FADH_2$ – deliver their electrons to the inner mitochondrial membrane.

A summary of the reactions that occur in the electron transfer chain is shown in Figure 5.

The inner mitochondrial membrane is folded to increase its surface area. Each fold is known as a **crista**, the plural being **cristae**. Embedded in this membrane are the proteins of the electron transfer chain, and stalked granules, which are **ATP synthase** enzymes. These impressive molecular machines turn, like turbines in a windmill, to make ATP.

How ATP is made:

1   The reduced coenzymes deliver their electrons to the first protein in the electron transfer chain. This protein, by definition, becomes reduced.

2   The electron passes to the next protein in the carrier. In this way, the first protein is oxidised and the second one becomes reduced. This happens all the way along the electron transfer chain. The electron is transferred from one

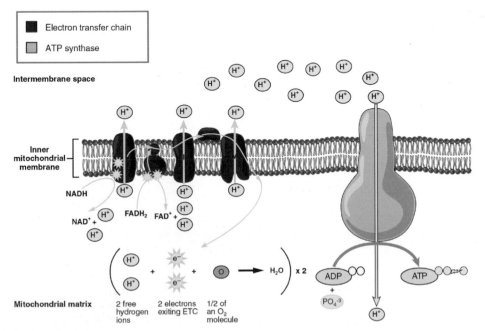

Figure 5 *The electron transfer chain*

protein to the next, and each step represents a redox reaction that releases energy.

3 This energy is used to pump hydrogen ions (H^+ ions, protons) into the intermembrane space.

4 This maintains a higher concentration in the intermembrane space, forming a diffusion gradient. Due to the charge on the protons, there is also an electrochemical gradient: a difference in charge across the inner mitochondrial membrane.

5 The H^+ ions diffuse back into the centre of the mitochondria through the only route available to them – the ATP synthase enzyme. The flow of H^+ ions causes the ATP synthase enzyme to turn, making ATP from ADP and Pi as it does so. This process is called **chemiosmosis**.

So how much ATP is produced? Each electron provided by NADH produces three ATP molecules, while each $FADH_2$ produced two ATPs.

So the final balance sheet is:

> $10 \times 3 = 30$ ATP molecules from NADH

> $2 \times 2 = 4$ ATP molecules from $FADH_2$.

That's 34 ATPs from the electron transfer chain. Making ATP in this way is known as **oxidative phosphorylation**. In contrast, making the four molecules of ATP from glycolysis and the Krebs cycle is known as **substrate-level phosphorylation**.

(Again, we have added the numbers to help with understanding, but you won't need to remember them in an examination.)

So, now we can see how respiration generates large amounts of ATP. But still no oxygen has been involved. It is not until the end of the process that its role becomes clear.

The end products of the electron transfer chain are electrons and protons. Each oxygen atom picks up two protons and two electrons to produce a molecule of water, which is released back into the cell. If you like balanced equations:

$$O_2 + 4e^- + 4H^+ \rightarrow 2H_2O$$

So, that's why you are breathing at the moment. Without oxygen, there is nowhere for the electrons to go once they arrive at the end of the electron transfer chain. So the electrons remain in the chain. This means that the reduced NAD and reduced FADH

molecules cannot offload their electrons, so the whole system backs up and none of the previous stages can occur due to a lack of coenzymes to accept the electrons.

QUESTIONS

2. Three out of the four stages of aerobic respiration produce ATP. Name them.

3. Three out of the four stages of aerobic respiration produce reduced coenzyme. Name them.

Other respiratory substrates

So far we have just looked at glucose as a respiratory substrate. However, in practice organisms can use a variety of other organic molecules. Lipids and amino acids can both be broken down into two carbon fragments, like acetate, and fed into the Krebs cycle. Many organisms get much of their energy in this way. Carnivores, for example, respire a lot of amino acids from their high protein diet. When humans are starving, or dieting, the lack of glucose leads to increased lipid metabolism. This leads to a reduction in stored triglyceride. In plain English, it is fat burning.

KEY IDEAS

> In the link reaction, the pyruvate produced in glycolysis moves into the mitochondria, where CO_2 is removed (decarboxylation) from pyruvate, leaving a 2-carbon (acetyl) fragment that reacts with coenzyme A to form acetyl coenzyme A.

> The Krebs cycle occurs in the matrix of the mitochondrion, where the 2-carbon fragment from acetyl, acetyl coenzyme A – the acetate – is combined with a 4-carbon compound to make a 6-carbon compound. This is converted back to the 4-carbon compound in a series of enzyme-controlled steps. In several of these steps, carbon dioxide and/or electrons

are removed. The electrons are picked up by coenzymes. In one step, ATP is synthesised from ADP and Pi.

> The reduced coenzymes pass their electrons to the first compound in a series of electron carriers that are situated in the inner membrane of the mitochondrion, and which are collectively called the electron transfer chain. The electrons are passed along the chain, and are finally accepted by oxygen, forming water.

> The energy released from the electrons as they pass along the electron transfer chain is used to pump hydrogen ions (protons) from the matrix, across the inner membrane and into the space between the two membranes. As the hydrogen ions move back down their concentration gradient, they pass through ATP synthase and energy from them is used to synthesise ATP.

> The movement of hydrogen ions down their concentration gradient through ATP synthase to produce ATP is known as chemiosmosis.

2.6 ANAEROBIC RESPIRATION

In humans and other organisms that depend mainly on aerobic respiration, if oxygen is not available, the electron transfer chain, the Krebs cycle and the link reaction grind to a halt. However, if the cell can re-synthesise some NAD, it will be able to carry on with glycolysis and make some vital ATP. Two out of 38 possible ATP molecules may not seem impressive, but it can be enough to keep cells going, especially as the process is a lot quicker than full aerobic respiration. Anaerobic respiration provides a lot of ATP, very quickly. The problem is that it is not very efficient in terms of energy from the respiratory substrate, and not sustainable for very long.

So how do cells re-synthesise NAD? It is done by converting pyruvate into another substance, usually **lactate** (a 3-carbon compound) or **ethanol** and **carbon dioxide**. Generally, animal and bacterial cells convert pyruvate to lactate (Figure 6). However, plants and fungi, including yeast, convert pyruvate to ethanol and carbon dioxide (Figure 7). The fact that yeast, under anaerobic conditions, will produce ethanol and carbon dioxide has long been used by humans in baking, brewing and wine-making.

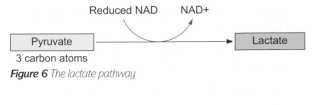

Figure 6 *The lactate pathway*

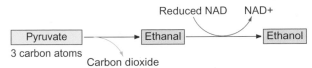

Figure 7 *The ethanol pathway*

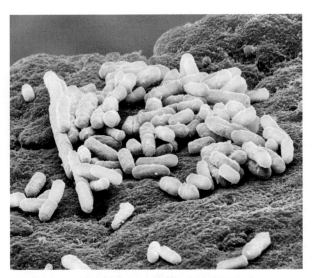

Figure 8 *Scanning electron micrograph of Lactobacillus bacteria. The tangy taste of yoghurt is largely due to lactobacilli respiring anaerobically to produce lactate.*

To a sprinter, anaerobic respiration is absolutely vital and is the source of much of the ATP for events such as the 400 m. However, the lactic acid produced is toxic and we cannot continue to produce it indefinitely. It has to be removed from the respiring cells and broken down.

The lactic acid produced in our anaerobically respiring muscle cells diffuses into the blood plasma, and is carried away in solution to be broken down by the cells of the liver. To do this, the liver cells need oxygen. So, carrying out anaerobic respiration does not mean that we manage to do without oxygen – we just delay the moment when it is needed. Even after completing strenuous exercise, we continue to breathe heavily, taking in extra oxygen that the liver cells need to break down the lactic acid.

REQUIRED PRACTICAL ACTIVITY 9: APPARATUS AND TECHNIQUES

(ATa, ATb, ATc)

Investigation into the effect of a named variable on the rate of respiration of cultures of single-celled organisms.

This practical activity gives you the opportunity to show that you can:

> ⟩ use appropriate apparatus and instrumentation to record a range of quantitative measurements

> ⟩ use laboratory glassware apparatus

> ⟩ use microbiological aseptic techniques.

Apparatus and techniques

There are many single-celled organisms – such as bacteria – that could be used for this required practical activity. Yeast is one of the easiest to use. Yeasts are single-celled fungi that can respire aerobically or anaerobically. To make them respire anaerobically, you simply deny them access to air.

> ⟩ You can use a **respirometer** to measure the rate of aerobic or anaerobic respiration (Figure P1). Gas exchange changes the volume of air in a sealed chamber. This change can be seen, and measured, by the movement of fluid or a bubble in a tube.

> ⟩ You can measure the volume of carbon dioxide gas given off to monitor anaerobic respiration. Yeast cells are grown in an airtight container, and the gas given off can be collected in a measuring cylinder.

> ⟩ You can use methylene blue to measure the rate of aerobic respiration. It starts off blue and goes colourless as the yeast cells respire. The faster it goes colourless, the faster the rate of aerobic respiration.

Measuring rate of respiration using a respirometer

When yeast respires aerobically, it takes in oxygen and releases carbon dioxide. The sodium hydroxide absorbs the carbon dioxide as fast as it is made, so it's just as if CO_2 isn't being made at all. The volume of the sodium hydroxide solution does not change significantly as it absorbs the CO_2.

So, as the yeast respires and absorbs oxygen, the volume of gas in the apparatus decreases and the coloured water moves along the tube. The faster the yeast respires, the more oxygen it uses and the faster the coloured water moves to the left. It is easier if the tube with the coloured water is calibrated with units of volume, such as a syringe or measuring cylinder. Otherwise, you have to work out the volume of oxygen used by calculating the volume of a cylinder from the formula $\pi r^2 h$ where r is the radius of the tube and h is the distance moved by the fluid.

Measuring yeast respiration by carbon dioxide production

In this variation the yeast cells are made to respire anaerobically by giving them sugar but preventing access to oxygen. This is achieved by putting them in a sealed flask, or by placing a layer of oil on the top of the solution.

Yeast will respire anaerobically according to the equation:

glucose → ethanol and carbon dioxide

The faster the yeast respires, the faster it will make carbon dioxide.

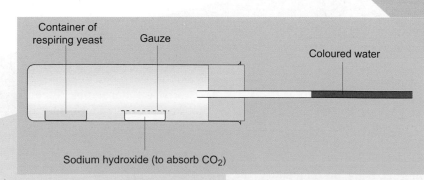

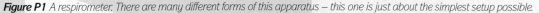

Figure P1 *A respirometer. There are many different forms of this apparatus – this one is just about the simplest setup possible.*

Measuring rate of respiration using methylene blue

Methylene blue is an indicator. It acts as an alternative to NAD as a coenzyme. In its blue form it is oxidised. When it gains electrons, it becomes colourless. If the blue form is added to respiring yeast, it will go colourless as it accepts electrons that have been removed from the glucose. The faster the yeast respires, the faster the solution turns colourless.

There are several variables that can be studied, including:

- type of substrate (such as glucose, fructose or lactose)
- concentration of substrate
- temperature.

For example, if investigating temperature:

Step 1: Set up a water bath at 20 °C.

Step 2: Take a clean test tube and add yeast and methylene blue. Label this 'Tube 1' and add your initials.

Step 3: Take another tube and add yeast, methylene blue and glucose. Label it 'Tube 2' and add your initials.

Step 4: Take a third test tube and add *boiled* yeast, methylene blue and glucose. Label it 'Tube 3' and add your initials.

Step 5: Place all three tubes into the water bath and time how long it takes for the blue colour to disappear.

Step 6: Repeat steps 2–5 at temperatures of 30 °C, 40 °C and 50 °C.

As a rough guide, in the tubes labelled '2', the methylene blue should go clear within about five minutes when the experiment is conducted at 35 °C.

QUESTIONS

P1. Using the apparatus shown in Figure P1, a student recorded the rate of respiration as 3.5 mm^3 g^{-1} min^{-1}.

    a. What measurement would need to be taken in order to work out the rate of respiration using these units?

    b. Suggest how you could modify the apparatus to allow the liquid to be moved back to the start without assembling the apparatus from scratch.

    c. Suggest how you could modify the apparatus to measure the rate of respiration in a culture of algae.

P2. For the methylene blue investigation, list:

    a. the independent variable

    b. the dependent variable

    c. three variables that were controlled.

P3. 'End point determination' can be a problem with this investigation. Suggest what is meant by this term.

P4. What is the purpose of repeating the investigation with boiled yeast?

P5. What is the purpose of the glucose?

P6. The blue colour disappeared in tube 1, even when no glucose was added. Suggest an explanation for this.

P7. If the tubes are shaken, the blue colour returns. Suggest an explanation for this.

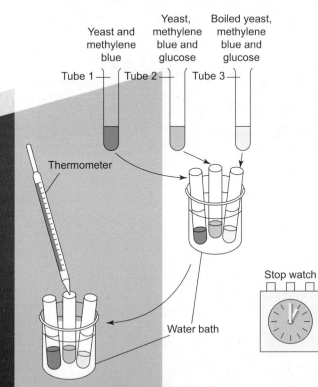

Yeast and methylene blue — Tube 1

Yeast, methylene blue and glucose — Tube 2

Boiled yeast, methylene blue and glucose — Tube 3

Thermometer

Water bath

Stop watch

Figure P2 *The apparatus for this investigation*

2.7 ENERGY TRANSFER IN PHOTOSYNTHESIS AND RESPIRATION

A comparison of some of the fundamental features of photosynthesis and respiration is shown in Figure 9.

Both processes are energy transfer systems. In photosynthesis, sunlight energy is transferred to chemical energy. In respiration, one form of chemical energy is transferred to another, but of a type that is instantly available to the cell.

In photosynthesis, reduced NADP acts as an electron donor to carbon (in carbon dioxide). In respiration, a similar compound, NAD, accepts high-energy electrons from carbon (in glucose) and becomes reduced NAD (NADH) in the process. An easy way to remember which of these is involved in photosynthesis and which in respiration is if you remember that the one with the P (NADP) is used in photosynthesis and the other (NAD) is used in respiration.

During respiration, carbon is oxidised. Four electrons are removed from each atom of carbon, which is exactly the opposite of photosynthesis. Whereas energy is required to add electrons to organic molecules in photosynthesis, removing electrons in respiration releases energy.

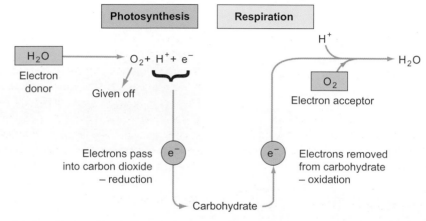

Figure 9 *Comparison of photosynthesis and respiration*

ASSIGNMENT 1: THE RESPIRATORY QUOTIENT

(MS 2.2, 2.3, 2.4)

"We can tell what you've had for breakfast just by analysing your breath". Well, not exactly, but that's the idea behind the respiratory quotient (RQ). An analysis of an organism's gas exchange gives us some idea as to which food types are being respired. Different respiratory substrates result in a different ratio of carbon given out to oxygen taken in.

Look at the basic equation for the respiration of glucose:

$$C_6H_{12}O_6 + 6O_2 \rightarrow 6CO_2 + 6H_2O$$

The formula for working out a respiratory quotient is:

$$\text{respiratory quotient (RQ)} = \frac{\text{volume of } CO_2 \text{ produced}}{\text{volume of } O_2 \text{ used}}$$

So, for glucose:

$$RQ = \frac{6}{6} = 1$$

Organisms don't just respire glucose – they can also respire lipid, amino acids and a variety of other organic molecules. In carnivores, such as cats, a lot of energy comes from the respiration of amino acids – a result of their high protein diet.

There is no general formula for a triglyceride because this group of organic molecules varies.

The general rule is that lipids have a higher ratio of hydrogen to oxygen than carbohydrates.

Questions

A1. This equation summarises the respiration of palmitic acid, a fatty acid:

$$C_{16}H_{32}O_2 + 23O_2 \rightarrow 16CO_2 + 16H_2O$$

Work out the RQ, to two decimal places, from the information given.

A2. Explain how you could use a respirometer (such as the one shown in Figure P1) to work out the respiratory quotient.

A3. An organism had an RQ of 0.9. Suggest a reason for this.

A4. Is it possible to work out a respiratory quotient for anaerobic respiration? Explain your answer.

A5. The RQ for a protein is generally around 0.8. Suggest why there is no definitive value for a protein, in the way that there is for glucose.

A6. A scientist wanted to lose weight, and so went on a 'calorie-controlled diet'. Explain how a measurement of their RQ could tell them whether their diet was working or not.

ASSIGNMENT 2: AEROBIC TRAINING

(MS 0.3, 3.1; PS 3.1)

Athletic events and sports can generally be divided into two categories – those that require strength/power, such as sprints, and those that require endurance, or stamina.

Endurance athletes need to keep their muscles working at a high level without accumulating lactate, which means that the muscles have to be provided with enough fuel and oxygen.

Training for endurance events – known as **aerobic training** – produces changes in the structure and

physiology of the fibres that make up the muscles. These fibres contain a dark-red pigment called myoglobin. This is similar in structure to one of the four polypeptides that make up haemoglobin; both of these pigments are able to combine with oxygen and then release it again. Myoglobin, however, only releases oxygen when the oxygen concentration has become very, very low. It therefore acts as an oxygen store in muscle tissues, providing oxygen when the rate of supply by the blood is not enough. Aerobic training increases the quantity of myoglobin stored in muscles by up to 75%.

Figure A1 *British long-distance runner Mo Farah is the current Olympic, World and European champion in the 5000 metres and 10 000 metres; from the start of each race, he sets a punishing pace.*

Another change brought about by aerobic training is an increase in the number and size of mitochondria in the muscles, and also the ability of mitochondria to use oxygen rapidly and make large quantities of ATP at great speed. This latter improvement is due to increased production of the enzymes involved in the various stages of respiration. Figure A2 shows how the activity of one of the enzymes of the Krebs cycle, called succinate dehydrogenase, changed in an athlete undergoing aerobic training for a period of seven months.

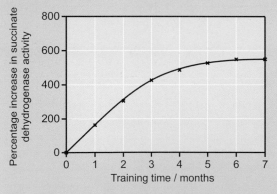

Figure A2 *Changes in the activity of succinate dehydrogenase*

It can also be useful to measure the rate at which a sample of muscle from an athlete is able to use oxygen. A scientist obtained a small specimen of muscle using a needle biopsy. He ground the sample

into a solution. This released the mitochondria, which started to use oxygen and generate ATP. Figure A3 shows the maximum rate at which muscle extracts taken from three people were able to use oxygen.

Figure A3 *Maximum rates at which muscles use oxygen*

Questions

A1. Suggest which of these activities could be part of an aerobic training regime: swimming, weight lifting, running. Explain your answer.

A2. Think back to your AS work. Sketch a dissociation curve for haemoglobin. On the same axes, sketch the dissociation curve for myoglobin.

A3. Explain how an increased quantity of myoglobin in a muscle, such as is produced by aerobic training, could give a 5000 m runner an edge over a rival with less myoglobin.

A4. Explain how the changes in succinate dehydrogenase activity shown in Figure A2 could help to improve an athlete's performance.

A5. Calculate the maximum rate of oxygen use by the muscles of the marathon runner as a percentage of the maximum rate of oxygen use by the muscles of the untrained runner.

A6. Discuss the changes in muscle structure and physiology that could account for the improved rate of oxygen use (shown in Figure A3) by a muscle sample taken from a marathon runner compared with a sample of muscle taken from an untrained person. (Some are mentioned here, but you may be able to think of others as well.

Remember, though, that we are looking at the performance of a sample of muscle in a test tube, not in the person's body.)

A7. The following are all changes that can occur as a response to exercise. Some of them are short term and some are longer term – what we generally refer to as 'getting fitter'. Make a table with two columns, 'Short term' and 'Long term', and organise the following responses.

   ❭ Increase in haematocrit (the volume of red blood cells in the blood)

   ❭ Increase in stroke volume

   ❭ Increase in the mitochondrial density in muscle fibres

   ❭ Increase in cardiac output

   ❭ Increase in oxygen usage

   ❭ Increase in capillarisation (more blood vessels in the muscles)

   ❭ Increase in ventilation rate

   ❭ Increase in vital capacity

   ❭ Increase in succinate dehydrogenase concentration in the muscles

PRACTICE QUESTIONS

1. The boxes in Figure Q1 represent substances in glycolysis, the link reaction and the Krebs cycle.

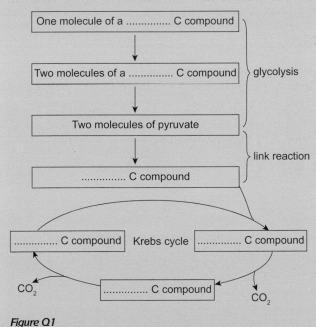

Figure Q1

   a. Complete Figure Q1 to show the number of carbon atoms present in one molecule of each compound.

   b. Other substances are produced in the Krebs cycle in addition to the carbon compounds shown in Figure Q1. Name three of these other products.

   AQA January 2005 Unit 4 Question 2

2. **a.** Mitochondria in muscle cells have more cristae than mitochondria in skin cells. Explain the advantage of mitochondria in muscle cells having more cristae.

   b. Substance X enters the mitochondrion from the cytoplasm. Each molecule of substance X has three carbon atoms.

      i. Name substance X.

      ii. In the link reaction substance X is converted into a substance in which the molecules effectively contain only two carbon atoms. Describe what happens in this process.

   c. The Krebs cycle, which takes place in the matrix, releases hydrogen ions. These hydrogen ions provide a source of energy for the synthesis of ATP, using coenzymes and carrier proteins in the inner membrane of the mitochondrion.

   Describe the roles of the coenzymes and carrier proteins in the synthesis of ATP.

   AQA June 2004 Unit 4 Question 7

(continued)

3. a. Table Q1 contains some statements relating to biochemical processes in a plant cell. Complete the table with a tick if the statement is true or a cross if it is not true for each biochemical process.

Statement	Glycolysis	Krebs cycle	Light-dependent reaction of photosynthesis
NAD is reduced			
NADP is reduced			
ATP is produced			
ATP is required			

Table Q1

b. An investigation was carried out into the production of ATP by mitochondria.

ADP, phosphate, excess substrate and oxygen were added to a suspension of isolated mitochondria.

i. Suggest the substrate used for this investigation.

ii. Explain why the concentration of oxygen and amount of ADP fell during the investigation.

iii. Further investigation was carried out into the effect of three inhibitors, A, B and C, on the electron transfer chain in these mitochondria. In each of three experiments, a different inhibitor was added. Table Q2 shows the state of the electron carriers, W–Z, after the addition of inhibitor.

Give the order of the electron carriers in this electron transfer chain. Explain your answer.

AQA June 2006 Unit 4 Question 7

4. Figure Q2 shows glycolysis and the Krebs cycle.

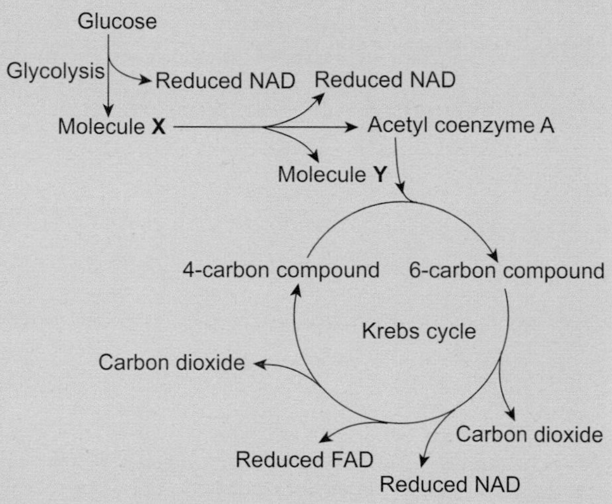

Figure Q2

a. Name:

i. molecule X

ii. molecule Y.

b. Where, in a cell, does glycolysis occur?

	Electron carrier			
Inhibitor added	W	X	Y	Z
A	oxidised	reduced	reduced	oxidised
B	oxidised	oxidised	reduced	oxidised
C	reduced	reduced	reduced	oxidised

Table Q2

c. High concentrations of ATP inhibit an enzyme involved in glycolysis.

   i. Describe how inhibition of glycolysis will affect the production of ATP by the electron transfer chain.

   ii. Explain this effect.

   AQA June 2007 Unit 4 Question 1

5. In an investigation of aerobic respiration, isolated mitochondria were added to a prepared medium containing succinate and inorganic phosphate. Succinate is a 4-carbon compound, which occurs in the Krebs cycle, and can be used as a respiratory substrate. The medium was saturated with oxygen. Equal amounts of ADP were added at one-minute intervals, and measurements were taken of the oxygen concentration in the medium. Figure Q3 shows the results.

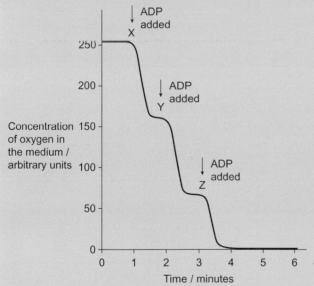

Figure Q3

a. Why was inorganic phosphate added to the medium?

b. Explain why the oxygen concentration in the medium decreased after adding ADP at X.

c. Explain why the fall in oxygen concentration was the same following the addition of ADP at X and at Y.

d. Explain why the fall in oxygen concentration, following the addition of ADP, was less at Z than at Y.

e. Fresh mitochondria were isolated from cells and a similar experiment was carried out. This time the medium contained glucose instead of succinate. Again, the medium was saturated with oxygen, and excess ADP was added. However, there was almost no fall in oxygen concentration, even after 10 minutes.

   i. Suggest and explain a reason for this observation.

   ii. Explain, in outline only, how you could test your suggestion.

   AQA January 2002 Unit 4 Question 10

6. a. Describe the part played by the inner membrane of a mitochondrion in producing ATP.

   b. A scientist investigated ATP production in a preparation of isolated mitochondria. He suspended the mitochondria in an isotonic solution and added a suitable respiratory substrate, together with ADP and phosphate. He bubbled oxygen through the preparation.

   i. Why was the solution in which the mitochondria were suspended isotonic?

   ii. Explain why the scientist did **not** use glucose as the respiratory substrate.

   iii. Explain why the oxygen concentration would change during this investigation.

   AQA June 2010 Unit 4 Question 6

7. a. A student measured the rate of aerobic respiration of a woodlouse using the apparatus shown in Figure Q4.

   i. The student closed the tap. After thirty minutes the drop of coloured liquid had moved to the left. Explain why the drop of coloured liquid moved to the left.

   ii. What measurements should the student have taken to calculate the rate of aerobic respiration in mm^3 of oxygen g^{-1} h^{-1}?

(continued)

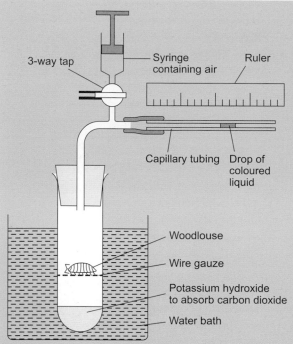

Figure Q4

b. DNP inhibits respiration by preventing a proton gradient being maintained across membranes. When DNP was added to isolated mitochondria the following changes were observed.

> less ATP was produced

> more heat was produced

> the uptake of oxygen remained constant.

Explain how DNP caused these changes.

AQA January 2011 Unit 4 Question 6

8. Yeast is a single-celled organism. A student investigated respiration in a population of yeast growing in a sealed container. His results are shown in Figure Q5.

a. Calculate the rate of oxygen uptake in arbitrary units per hour between 2 and 4 hours.

b. i. Use the information provided to explain the changes in oxygen uptake during this investigation.

ii. Use the information provided to explain the changes in production of ethanol during this investigation.

c. Sodium azide is a substance that inhibits the electron transfer chain in respiration. The student repeated the investigation but added sodium azide after 4 hours. Suggest and explain how the addition of sodium azide would affect oxygen uptake and the production of ethanol.

AQA January 2013 Unit 4 Question 6

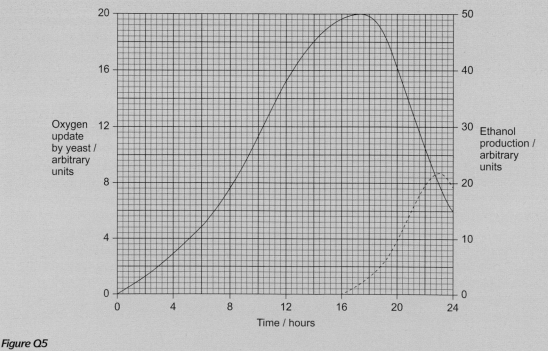

Figure Q5

3 ENERGY AND ECOSYSTEMS

PRIOR KNOWLEDGE

In Chapter 1 we saw how plants use photosynthesis to transfer energy from sunlight into organic molecules such as glucose, starch and cellulose. In Chapter 2 we saw how all organisms use respiration to transfer energy from glucose into ATP. The ATP is then used as the energy currency of the cell – the immediate source of energy for the myriad of energy-consuming metabolic reactions that maintain life.

LEARNING OBJECTIVES

In this chapter we take a wider look at the idea of energy in biological systems. We look at what happens to the energy as it passes through the producers and is passed on – in organic molecules – to the organisms higher up the food chain. You need to understand where and why energy is lost. You also need to appreciate how an understanding of energy loss can lead to more efficient food production.

(Specification 3.5.3)

One of the most important steps in the history of mankind was the development of agriculture. Early humans were hunter-gatherers. We know something about their lifestyle because there are still some small groups of people who live in a similar way today, for example, the Hadza tribe in Tanzania. In many ways hunter-gatherers have a laid-back lifestyle; generally, the men hunt animals for meat and skins, while the women collect food plants.

About 10 000 years ago, people in Britain began to take control over the sources of their food. They became agriculturalists. They had already domesticated dogs, which must have helped with hunting. Now they also began to domesticate grazing animals, including cattle, sheep, goats and pigs. Crops were planted, tended and harvested, to provide food and other resources such as clothing and building materials. As soon as you don't have to worry about where your next meal is coming from, you are free to do other things.

Agriculture has allowed our population to grow much larger than hunting and gathering could ever do. We are able to use a greater proportion of the Sun's energy to produce large quantities of food in a relatively small area. Selective breeding, fertilisers, pesticides and machinery have allowed us to do this using relatively few person-hours, so that most of us now have nothing to do with food production and can spend our time doing other things. In the distant past, before farming began, finding food would have been the main activity of almost everyone in society. Without agriculture, human culture could never have developed to produce the complex society that exists today.

3.1 PLANTS SYNTHESISE ORGANIC COMPOUNDS

Within any ecosystem there must be organisms that are capable of harvesting energy. The community contains organisms that produce energy-containing organic molecules, using an external energy source. These organisms are called **producers**. Most producers photosynthesise but this doesn't mean that all producers are plants: algae and some bacteria can also photosynthesise. Globally speaking, the algae in the oceans produce more organic molecules and oxygen than all of the land plants put together.

There are a few ecosystems where other sources of energy are used, for example, in the communities found around deep-sea volcanic vents, where bacteria use energy from minerals to synthesise organic molecules.

Most of the sugars made by the producers are used in respiration. The remainder is converted into larger carbohydrates such as starch and cellulose, and other vital molecules such as proteins and lipids. These compounds make up the **biomass** of the organisms. The rest of the community relies on the producers. All the other organisms are known as **consumers**, because their energy source comes from the organic nutrients that they consume – which originally came from the producers.

Knowledge of how energy is passed from one organism to another is of great value in helping us to understand the interrelationships between the different species in a community. It is also vital for helping us to maximise producing our own food. How can we harness more of the Sun's energy to make more food to feed everyone in the world? And can we do this without destroying the habitats and livelihoods of other species? As the human population continues to grow, these are questions that we urgently need to address.

Food chains
Let us recap some basic information about food chains that you may remember from Year 1 and possibly GCSE: Organisms that feed directly on producers are called **primary consumers**, and they are usually **herbivores** (because producers are usually plants or algae). Animals that eat primary consumers are **secondary consumers**. Above them are the **tertiary consumers** and so on. Secondary and tertiary consumers are **carnivores** or **omnivores**. This sequence forms a **food chain**. A food chain shows feeding relationships and the related energy transfers – how energy is transferred from one organism to another, in the form of chemical energy in organic molecules. Figure 1 shows two food chains; one based on land (terrestrial) and one in water (aquatic).

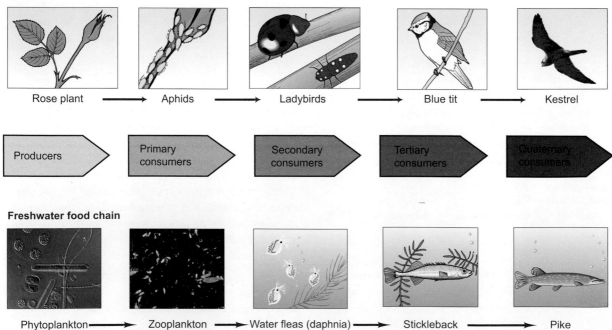

Figure 1 *Two examples of food chains. The arrows show the direction of energy flow from one trophic level to the next.*

Each step in a food chain is a **trophic level**. 'Trophic' means 'feeding'. In both food chains in Figure 1, there are five trophic levels.

One group of organisms that is often overlooked when constructing food chains is the **decomposers**. All fungi and most bacteria are decomposers. These organisms feed on the dead organic material, such as the dead bodies, leaves and waste materials of organisms, from all the trophic levels. Some animals, such as earthworms and woodlice, also feed on rotting organic material. Overall, these organisms play a vital role in recycling, as we shall see in Chapter 4.

QUESTIONS

1. If decomposers were added to the food chains in Figure 1, at what point(s) would they appear?
2. Use the information in Figure 2 to draw complete food chains containing:
   a. four organisms
   b. five organisms
   c. six organisms.
3. List all the secondary consumers in the British woodland food web.

British woodland ecosystem

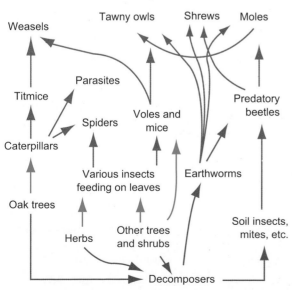

Figure 2 *Interrelationships in a British wood*

Food webs

Food chains are an over-simplification of the actual feeding relationships in an ecosystem. Many animals feed on both plants and other animals, so they may feed at two or more trophic levels. It would be almost impossible to work out all the feeding relationships that exist within a community.

Food web diagrams show how different food chains within an ecosystem interact with one another. Figure 2 shows *some* of the possible interrelationships in a British wood. In reality, there are thousands of species in this ecosystem (including hundreds of different kinds of insects, and thousands of species of bacteria), so even this diagram is far too simple an example of the true situation. Notice, too, that the diagram should really have arrows going from every single organism to the decomposers – and that there are hundreds of different species of decomposers, each of which really deserves its own individual listing in the food web.

Biomass

If you are a farmer with a field of wheat you will be interested in how much grain you are going to be able to sell, and how long it will be before you can sell it. In short, you are interested in biomass.

Biomass is defined as biological material from living or recently living organisms. It can refer to just one organism, a whole population, a whole crop or a whole trophic level. In practice, biomass usually refers to the mass of the producers. Generally, the biomass on land (terrestrial biomass) decreases as you go up the trophic levels – so, grasses, trees and shrubs, for example, have much higher biomass than the animals that eat them. Take trees, for example: there is an awful lot of carbon locked up in wood, mainly as the polymers cellulose and lignin.

Biomass can be measured in terms of mass of carbon or, more practically, the dry mass of tissue produced per given area per given time. In practice, the measurement of biomass involves destroying the organisms in question. For example, to estimate the biomass of a field of wheat, you would collect all the wheat plants in one square metre, dry them at 80 °C, weigh them, and then repeat the process until there is no further change in weight, showing that all the water has been removed. To calculate the biomass of the field, multiply the answer by the number of square metres in the field.

To go one step further and estimate the potential energy in the wheat, you would burn the dry mass from several sample areas, find the mean and multiply up by the total area (see **calorimetry** later in this chapter).

Units are important to allow comparisons

It is important to appreciate the importance of units here. Scientists are usually interested in how much biomass is being produced in a certain time, rather than how much is already there – it is a measure of the **productivity** of the ecosystem. Biomass is measured as the dry mass of material produced **per unit area per unit time** – for example $kg\ m^{-2}\ y^{-1}$. Without these 'pers', you can't compare different situations.

Energy loss at each trophic level

If you consider the energy flow through each trophic level, diagrams can be drawn, such as the one in Figure 3. They enable us to compare the amount of energy that enters the producers in an ecosystem, as well as the amount that flows through to each trophic level. They are always pyramid-shaped – wider at the base – because the energy reduces significantly at each trophic level. The units used to construct pyramids of energy must include a consideration of area and time, for example $kJ\ m^{-2}\ y^{-1}$.

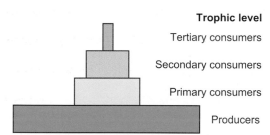

Trophic level

Tertiary consumers

Secondary consumers

Primary consumers

Producers

Figure 3 *A pyramid of energy*

Where does all the energy go?

Basic thermodynamics tells us two things:

1. Energy cannot be created or destroyed, just transferred.

2. No energy transfer is 100% efficient; some is always transferred to the surroundings as heat.

Biological systems are no exception. Only a very small proportion of the solar energy that reaches the Earth's surface is actually captured in photosynthesis and conserved inside organic molecules, but that is all that is available to the higher trophic levels.

Of the sunlight energy that reaches the Earth, some heats up the atmosphere while a lot is absorbed by rocks or water.

Of the solar energy that does fall on plant leaves:

- Some is reflected.

- Some passes straight through the leaves, missing the chloroplasts.

- Some is the wrong wavelength; only visible light in the wavelength range of 380 nm to 720 nm (red to blue light) excites electrons in the chlorophyll and starts the light-dependent reaction.

- Some is converted to heat during the reactions of photosynthesis.

At best, something approaching 10% of the solar energy is incorporated into carbon compounds by photosynthesis, but a significant proportion of this is available to the plants for their own metabolic needs. Respiration of the plants themselves further reduces the energy available for growth. It is rare for more than 3% or 4% of the solar energy that falls on a plant to be incorporated into its growth. It is often much less.

Energy transfer from producers to consumers

In plants, most of the available energy is locked inside carbohydrates such as cellulose and starch. How efficient is a herbivore – a cow, for example – at transferring the energy available in the grass that they eat, into its own tissues; its meat or milk? The simple answer is, not very.

Firstly, the cattle will not eat all the grass. The roots usually remain in the ground.

Secondly, the animals will not be able to digest all of the grass that they do eat. After water, grass is mostly composed of cellulose – the most abundant polysaccharide on Earth. Strangely, animals do not make cellulase enzymes, and so any cellulose breakdown that does happen is due to microorganisms in the gut. The energy in any undigested food passes straight through their digestive systems and out of the body as faeces, never having been part of the cow's body. This energy becomes available to the decomposers, but is not much use to us.

Think about the next organisms in the food chain – us – and the efficiency of energy transfer is even worse. Imagine that the cows are killed to produce beef. Most of the (potential) chemical energy that the cows managed to digest and absorb will have been used as substrate for respiration. Cows are mammals that move about to keep warm. So only a small proportion of the total energy that they absorbed from their gut will be incorporated into their tissues, but that is what is theoretically available to us. Yet, once again, we only obtain a small amount of this energy. We don't eat every part of a cow. Some parts, such as the hide, hair, hooves, teeth and bones, are not eaten and we are unable to digest every molecule of the tissue that we do actually consume.

The net production of consumers can be calculated by considering these values:

> **N** is the **net** production – the energy available in the tissues of the animal (meat and/or milk)

> **I** is the potential energy in the **ingested** food (in our example, the energy in the grass)

> **F** is the energy lost in **faeces** and urine

> **R** is the energy lost via **respiration**, lost to the environment as heat.

This gives us the equation $N = I - (F + R)$.

This can be represented diagrammatically.

You are expected to know this equation and may be asked to recall and use it in an examination.

Why are there so few links in the chain?

At each step the efficiency of energy transfer is only about 10%. As similar losses happen at each successive trophic level, there can be only a limited number of trophic levels in a food chain before the energy 'runs out' (Figure 4).

Most communities are so complex that it is difficult to obtain accurate data about the efficiency of energy transfer. Figure 5 shows a simplified pyramid of energy

for an aquatic ecosystem in Florida. Figure 6 shows the energy data that the researchers found.

Flow diagrams can also be constructed for individual animals. Figure 7 shows energy flow through four types of animals: an invertebrate herbivore, an invertebrate carnivore, a mammalian herbivore and a mammalian carnivore. The diagrams are drawn to scale, so that the widths of the arrows enable comparisons to be made.

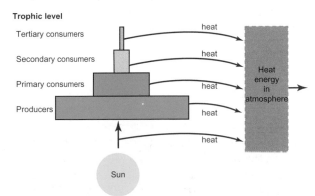

Figure 4 Heat losses from each trophic level

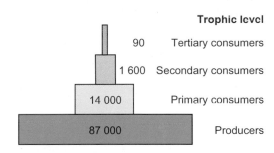

Figure 5 Pyramid of energy for an aquatic ecosystem in Florida (arbitrary units)

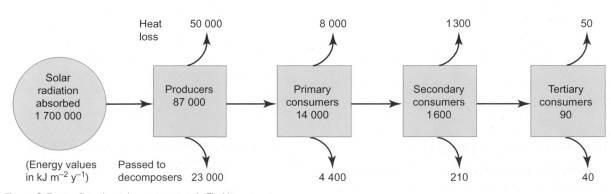

Figure 6 Energy flow through an ecosystem in Florida

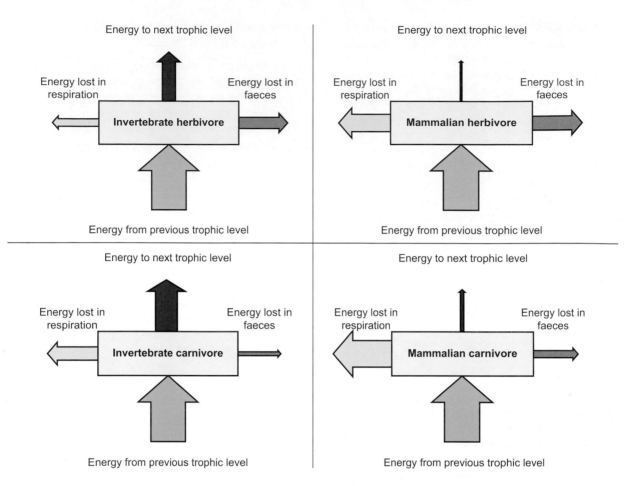

Figure 7 *Energy flow diagrams; the size of each arrow represents the amount of energy.*

QUESTIONS

4. Look at Figure 7.

   a. Suggest why the proportion of energy lost in respiration is greater in the mammals than it is in the invertebrates. (Clue – think about homeostasis.)

   b. Suggest explanations for the differences in the proportions of energy that are lost in the faeces of herbivores and carnivores. (Clue – think about digesting plant cells compared with animal cells.)

   c. Using all the information in Figure 7, describe and explain the differences between these four organisms in the efficiency of energy transfer to the next trophic level.

KEY IDEAS

❯ Energy enters most ecosystems as light, which is transferred by photosynthesis into chemical energy in organic compounds.

❯ Food chains and food webs show the direction of energy flow from producers and through each level of consumers.

❯ Energy is lost as heat, at and between each trophic level. The proportion of the energy that is passed on from one trophic level to the next is known as the efficiency of energy transfer. It is rarely more than 10%.

❯ Net production can be worked out from the equation N = I – (F + R).

3.2 PRODUCTION

Gross and net production

First, two vital definitions:

Gross primary production (GPP) is the chemical energy store in plant biomass, in a given area or volume, in a given time. Think of it as all the energy that was captured by photosynthesis.

Net primary production (NPP) is the chemical energy store in plant biomass after respiratory losses to the environment have been taken into account. It is basically what's left after the plant has taken what it requires.

It is the NPP that represents the potential food available to primary consumers.

As an equation: NPP = GPP − R

When crop plants are grown for food, we are essentially using the plants to transfer energy in sunlight into chemical energy in carbohydrates and other nutrients. The rate at which plants do this is known as **primary production**.

Primary production is often measured in terms of the amount of energy that is transferred from light energy into chemical energy, over an area of one square metre, during one year. Its units are therefore $kJ\ m^{-2}\ year^{-1}$. It is important to remember that production is a **rate**, and therefore its units must include time.

Another way of measuring primary production is the mass of new plant matter that is produced over an area of one square metre per day. In this case, its units are $g\ m^{-2}\ day^{-1}$. Table 1 shows productivity per day in $g\ m^{-2}$ for six important food crops. (Only five of these are grown in the UK – rice cannot grow in our temperate climate.)

You can see that the mean production for each crop is much lower than the highest value that can be obtained. If we could somehow move the world mean average closer towards the maximum, we could produce much, much more food each year – which perhaps could be one way of helping to feed the millions of people who do not get enough to eat.

Crop	Production per day of growing season / $g\ m^{-2}$	
	World mean	Highest production in ideal conditions
Wheat	2.3	8.3
Oats	2.4	6.2
Maize	2.3	4.4
Rice	2.7	4.4
Potatoes	2.6	5.6
Sugar beet	4.3	8.2

Table 1 *Crop productivity*

Table 2 gives some values for NPP in a range of different ecosystems. You can see that intensive agriculture (where the land is farmed to get as high a yield as possible, by using inputs such as pesticides and inorganic fertilisers) comes very high on the list, second only to tropical rainforests.

Ecosystem	NPP/ $kJ\ m^{-2}\ year^{-1}$
Extreme desert	260
Desert scrub	2 600
Subsistence agriculture	3 000
Open ocean	4 700
Shallow seas over continental shelf	13 500
Temperate grasslands	15 000
Temperate deciduous forest	26 000
Intensive agriculture	30 000
Tropical rainforest	40 000

Table 2 *Net primary production (NPP) in different ecosystems*

Factors affecting primary production

Primary production is affected by a wide range of abiotic and biotic factors. Production is related directly to the rate of photosynthesis. The rate at which plants can photosynthesise is determined by:

> the intrinsic capabilities of the particular species and variety of plants

> the intensity of sunlight that falls onto them

> the duration of light each day

> the amount of water that is available

> the temperature

> the concentration of carbon dioxide in the atmosphere

> the availability of inorganic ions such as nitrate in the soil

> competition for light and other resources

> damage to the plants by fungi, insects and other pests.

5. a. Which of the factors listed in *Factors affecting primary production* are abiotic factors, and which are biotic factors?

   b. Suggest which factors are likely to contribute to the high productivity in the two most productive ecosystems in Table 2.

   c. Suggest which factors are likely to be reducing productivity in the two least productive ecosystems in Table 2.

ASSIGNMENT 1: PHOTOSYNTHETIC EFFICIENCY

(MS 0.3; PS 3.2)

Globally, the mean energy value of solar radiation during the daytime is approximately 1 kJ m^{-2} s^{-1}. Figure A1 shows what happens to each 1000 units of solar radiation that falls on the leaves of actively growing plants.

The amount of solar energy intercepted by green plants depends a great deal on geographical location. In Britain, this is estimated as approximately 1×10^6 kJ m^{-2} year^{-1}, but at least 95% of this is unavailable to plants for photosynthesis.

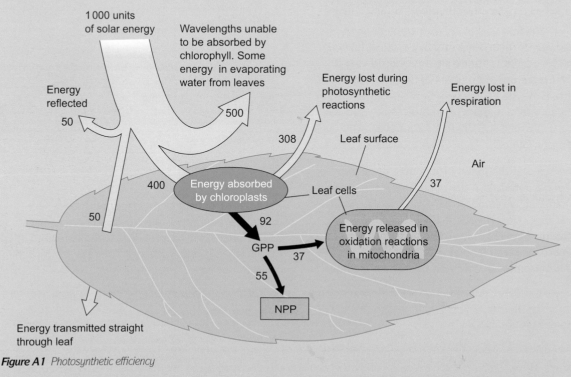

Figure A1 *Photosynthetic efficiency*

Source: adapted from The Open University Science Foundation course and data taken from ABAL, Cambridge University Press

Questions

A1. Calculate the overall percentage efficiency of the use of the solar radiation by the plant to produce materials for growth.

A2. What percentage of the energy absorbed by chloroplasts is actually used to synthesise carbohydrate?

A3. What percentage of the energy in the carbohydrate produced by photosynthesis is incorporated into growth compounds?

A4. Use your knowledge of leaves and chloroplasts to explain the features that:

   a. keep the amount of light transmitted to a minimum

   b. enable the chlorophyll to make use of the green wavelengths of light

   c. maximise the efficiency with which chlorophyll molecules absorb light.

A5. The efficiency of net primary production (NPP) given in the diagram is close to the maximum ever found in nature and is much higher than the mean in most ecosystems. The mean percentage efficiency is rarely more than about one-fifth of this value. Suggest reasons for the efficiency being much lower than the possible maximum.

A6. We make better use of the solar energy falling on an area of land if people feed on crops rather than on animals such as cattle.

   a. Use your understanding of efficiency and energy flow to explain why.

   b. Suggest why it may sometimes be an economical use of land and energy to use animals as a source of food.

Chemical energy store in dry biomass

How do you estimate the energy stored in organic material? How can you estimate the number of calories in your chicken tikka masala? Or the number of kilojoules in your field of wheat? The answer is: **calorimetry**. A commonly used piece of apparatus that is used to measure this is the bomb calorimeter (Figure 8). The process, in a nutshell, consists of drying out the material and then burning it in oxygen. The energy given off is used to heat up water, which surrounds the combustion chamber on all sides. The rise in temperature gives you a measure of the energy that was contained in the material.

Units of energy

The SI unit of energy – and, therefore, the one that we should use and that you will see in examination papers – is the **joule** (J). 1000 joules is a kilojoule (kJ). The joule is defined as the energy required to raise 1 g (1 cm³) of water by 0.24 °C.

The **calorie** is an older, 'unofficial', unit of energy, but it is still widely used to measure food energy. To add to the confusion, there are two different calories:

> The 'small' calorie is defined as the energy required to raise 1 g of water by 1 °C. One of these calories is equal to 4.2 joules.

> The 'large' calorie, the food calorie or the kilocalorie (kcal), is 1000 times larger than the small calorie. The calories on food packaging are actually kilocalories.

As a rough guide, the recommended daily intake for an average adult female is 8400 kJ a day (2000 kcal), while men need on average 10 500 kJ a day (2500 kcal).

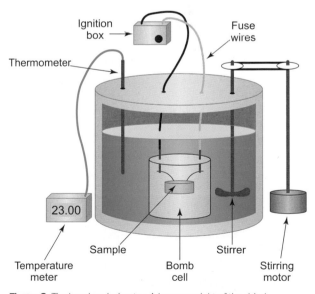

Figure 8 *The bomb calorimeter. A known weight of the dried material is completely oxidised by burning in oxygen. The combustion chamber is surrounded by water, so all the heat is captured. The energy in the sample can be calculated from the increase in water temperature.*

Different types of food have different energy contents. Table 3 shows the amount of energy released when one gram of the pure substance is burned.

	Energy content per gram	
	kJ	kcal
Carbohydrate	17	4.1
Protein	17	4.1
Lipid	37	8.8

Table 3 *The energy content, per gram, of the main food types.*

Worked maths example

A bomb calorimeter contained 1.2 dm^3 of water. Fifteen grams of lean beef was burnt in the calorimeter, and the temperature of the water rose from 20 °C to 86 °C.

> Calculate the energy content of the beef per gram.

> Using your answer, as well as the data in Table 3, suggest which food types the beef may contain.

To calculate the energy content of the beef, we first need to know this data: it takes 4.17 joules of energy to raise the temperature of 1 cm^3 of water by 1 °C.

In our example, 1200 cm^3 of water has been raised by 66 °C (86 − 20).

The total energy required to do that is
1200 × 66 × 4.18 = 331 056 joules.

Converting that into kilojoules, we divide by 1000 (a factor of 10^3) to get 331 kJ.

So, the energy in each gram of beef was $\frac{331}{15} = 22\,kJ\,g^{-1}$

You might expect lean beef to be all protein but that wouldn't give a value of more than about 17. The fact that we got a value of 22 suggests that there was a significant amount of lipid in the sample.

6. If a bomb calorimeter is going to give accurate, reliable readings, it will need to be calibrated.

   a. Explain what is meant by calibration.

   b. Suggest how you calibrate a calorimeter.

7. Although we have standard values for the energy content of each food type, in practice, different animals will obtain different amounts of energy from the same food. A lion, for example, might get less out of 1 kg of meat than a wolf. Suggest two reasons for this.

8. In the worked example, several assumptions were made about the energy transfers in the bomb calorimeter. Suggest what these are and how they will affect the energy values obtained.

How can we make farming more efficient?

We have seen that every step in a food chain results in more than 90% of the available energy being lost. As a result, the simplest way to make food production (in other words, the transfer of energy from producer to us, the consumer) more efficient is to reduce the number of steps in the food chain. This means eating plants.

The food chain:

soya → human

is a lot more efficient than the food chain:

grass → cattle → human

In practice, most farming practices are designed to reduce energy flow into food chains other than the one leading to humans. This includes use of pesticides to remove fungi, bacteria, invertebrates or other mammals that feed upon our crops or herbicides to remove weeds that compete with crops. It could also include animals (such as rabbits) that graze upon the grasses that feed sheep or cattle. Simplifying the food web by eliminating the side chains to which these species belong makes the transfer of energy from producer to humans more efficient.

From the above, it would seem to make sense if we were all vegetarians. However, there are other reasons that people eat meat, not least because they like it and will pay for it. Consequently, meat production will continue to be big business. **Intensive rearing** techniques include several ways in which meat production can be made more efficient.

> Feed the animals concentrated food that contains less un-digestible material. This reduces the amount of energy lost in faeces.

> Keep the animals inside heated barns. Cattle, pigs and chickens are all warm-blooded animals that will increase their metabolic rate (the rate of respiration) to replace lost heat when they are cold. If they are kept warm, more energy is available to be incorporated into new tissue.

> Restrict their movement by keeping them in confined areas. If less energy is expended on muscular contraction, more energy is available for growth.

> Increase growth rate by using hormones and chemicals such as antibiotics.

ASSIGNMENT 2: THE EFFICIENCY OF A GRAZING ANIMAL

(MS 0.1, 0.3, 2.4)

Scientists investigated the efficiency of one individual herbivore. They chose a bullock, because its energy transfer is not complicated by the milk-producing process. Firstly, they needed to estimate the energy contained in the food eaten by the animal, which they did by taking samples of grass from a field. The plot selected was one hectare. One hectare measures 100 m by 100 m. It's about the size of a football or rugby pitch.

Questions

A1. How many square metres are in one hectare?

A2. The scientists selected 20 different plots of area 1 m^2 and collected all of the grass by mowing.

    a. What percentage of the total plot was sampled?

    b. Suggest why mowing was selected as the collection method.

A3. The selected plots were chosen at random. Explain why this was important.

A4. Suggest how these plots could have been chosen.

A5. The grass collected from the plots was first heated in an oven at 105 °C until the weight was constant. Explain why this was done.

A6. The scientists obtained these results:

Mean mass of grass before drying / kg	Mean mass of grass after drying / kg
1.25	0.46

Calculate the percentage water content of the grass.

A7. 100 g of the dry plant material was placed into a bomb calorimeter, which produced a mean value of 85 kJ. Outline how a bomb calorimeter works.

A8. Look at Figure A1. Use the equation $N = I - (F + R)$ to calculate the net production of the bullock, in kJ.

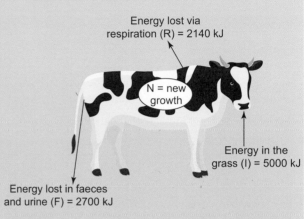

Energy lost via respiration (R) = 2140 kJ

N = new growth

Energy in the grass (I) = 5000 kJ

Energy lost in faeces and urine (F) = 2700 kJ

Figure A1

A9. Calculate the overall efficiency of the energy transfer from producer to primary consumer.

A10. The energy transfer from primary to secondary consumer is genarally higher. Suggest a reason for this.

KEY IDEAS

› Gross primary production (GPP) is the chemical energy store in plant biomass, in a given area or volume, in a given time.

› All organisms use some of the chemical energy in their organic molecules for their own purposes. This energy is released by respiration.

❭ Net primary production (NPP) is the chemical energy store in plant biomass after respiratory losses to the environment have been taken into account:

❭ NPP = GPP − R

❭ Anything that limits the rate of photosynthesis, such as low carbon dioxide concentration, low temperature or low light levels, also limits primary productivity.

❭ The potential energy in dry biomass can be measured by the process of calorimetry, in which a dry sample of the food is burnt in oxygen and the energy released is used to heat up water.

❭ In farming, the efficiency of meat production can be increased by feeding concentrates, using heated accommodation and restricting movement.

PRACTICE QUESTIONS

1. Starfish feed on a variety of invertebrate animals that are attached to rocks on the seashore.

   Figure Q1 shows part of a food web that includes a species of starfish.

   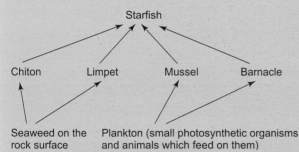

   Figure Q1

   a. Explain why a starfish can be described as both a secondary and a tertiary consumer.

   b. When starfish feed on mussels they leave behind the empty shell. Explain how quadrats could be used to determine the percentage of mussels that had been eaten by starfish on a rocky shore.

   c. Table Q1 shows the composition of the diet of starfish.

	Prey species			
	Chiton	Limpet	Mussel	Barnacle
Percentage of total number of animals eaten	3	5	27	65
Energy provided by each species as a percentage of total energy intake	42	5	38	15

   Table Q1

   i. The percentage of barnacles in the diet is much higher than the percentage of energy that they provide. Suggest **one** explanation for this difference.

   ii. Table Q1 shows that the amount of energy provided by chitons is greater than the amount of energy provided by limpets. Calculate the number of limpets a starfish would need to eat in order to obtain the same amount of energy as it would obtain from one chiton.

   AQA June 2006 Unit 5 Question 4

2. Figure Q2 shows the flow of energy through trees in a woodland ecosystem. The numbers represent mean inputs and outputs of energy in kJ m⁻² day⁻¹.

   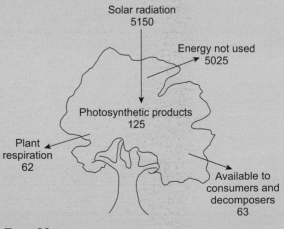

   Figure Q2

   a. Use information in the diagram to

      i. give the amount of energy incorporated into tree biomass

      ii. calculate the percentage of solar energy that is fixed by photosynthesis.

b. Not all the solar radiation reaching the leaves of the tree is used in photosynthesis. Give **two** explanations for this.

c. The graph in Figure Q3 shows the rate of photosynthesis and the rate of respiration in tree leaves at different temperatures.

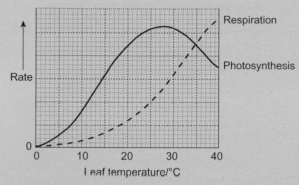

Figure Q2

Give the range of temperatures over which the leaves will show the greatest increase in biomass. Explain your answer.

AQA June 2003 Unit 5 Question 1

3. Figure Q3 shows a pyramid of energy for an ecosystem.

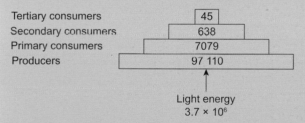

Figure Q3

a. Suggest suitable units for the measurement of energy transfer in this pyramid of energy.

b. i. Calculate the percentage of energy transferred from primary consumers to tertiary consumers.

ii. Give **one** reason why the percentage of energy transferred between consumers is generally low.

c. i. Give **one** reason why all the light energy reaching the producers cannot be used in photosynthesis.

ii. Explain how light energy is used to generate ATP in plants.

AQA January 2007 Unit 5 Question 2

4. Figure Q4 shows the flow of energy through a marine ecosystem.

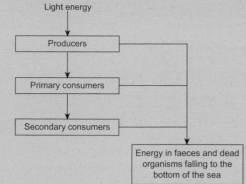

Figure Q4

a. Give **one** reason why not all the light energy falling on the producers is used in photosynthesis.

b. Describe what happens to the energy in faeces and dead organisms that fall to the bottom of the sea.

c. The producers in this ecosystem are seaweeds, which have a large surface area to volume ratio. Give **two** advantages to seaweeds of having a large surface area to volume ratio.

d. Some species of seaweed are submerged in water for most of the time. Explain how being underwater might affect the rate of photosynthesis.

AQA June 2005 Unit 5 Question 2

5. Figure Q5 shows organisms in a food web.

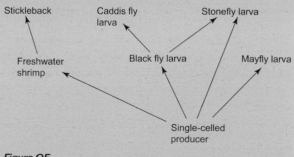

Figure Q5

a. i. Name **all** the secondary consumers in this food web.

ii. Use the diagram to explain the likely effect of a sudden decrease in the stickleback population on the population of mayfly larvae.

(continued)

b. A pyramid of energy for this food web is shown in Figure Q6. The bars are drawn to the same scale.

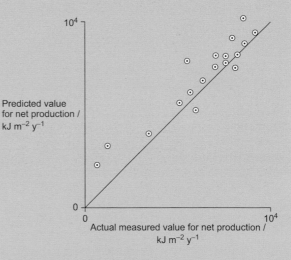

Figure Q6

i. Use the pyramid of energy to calculate the percentage efficiency of energy transfer between producers and primary consumers. Show your working.

ii. The average efficiency of energy transfer between producers and primary consumers in pyramids of energy is around 10%. Suggest why the efficiency of energy transfer from producers to primary consumers in this food web is higher than 10%.

c. Energy from the Sun may ultimately end up in dead plant matter. Describe how.

AQA January 2012 Unit 4 Question 2

6. Scientists constructed a mathematical model. They used this model to estimate the transfer of energy through consumers in a natural grassland ecosystem. Table Q2 shows their results.

Energy transferred as percentage of energy in biomass of producers				
Ingested food (F)	Absorbed from gut (A)	Egested (E)	Net production (P)	Respired (R)
Primary consumers				
Mammals 25.00	12.50	12.50	0.25	12.25
Insects 4.00	1.60	2.40	0.64	0.96
Secondary consumers				
Mammals 0.16	0.13	0.03	0.003	0.127
Insects 0.17	0.135	0.035	0.040	0.095

Table Q2

a. Complete the equation to show how net production is calculated from the energy in ingested food.

P =

b. Describe and explain how intensive rearing of domestic livestock would affect:

i. the figure for A in the first row of the table

ii. the figure for R in the first row of the table.

c. i. Calculate the ratio of R : A for mammalian primary consumers.

ii. The R : A ratio is higher in mammalian primary consumers than it is in insect primary consumers. Suggest a reason for this higher value.

d. The scientists tested their model by comparing the values it predicted with actual measured values. Figure Q7 shows their results.

Figure Q7

Are the values predicted by the model supported by the actual measured values? Evaluate the evidence in the graph.

AQA June 2010 Unit 4 Question 4

7. Explain how the intensive rearing of domestic livestock increases net productivity.

AQA June 2013 Unit 4 Question 8c

4 NUTRIENT CYCLES

PRIOR KNOWLEDGE

You will probably have studied the water cycle and the carbon cycle in earlier years. In the AS year you learnt about enzymes and processes that transport substances in and out of cells. This knowledge is applied several times in this chapter.

LEARNING OBJECTIVES

In this chapter we look at the way in which two vital elements – nitrogen and phosphorus – pass through the bodies of living organisms time and time again.

(Specification 3.5.4)

One of the most spectacular algal blooms ever seen occurred in the build-up to the Beijing Olympics in 2008. The sea at Qingdao, east China, which was to be home to the sailing events, suffered such an algal bloom that, from a distance, the water looked more like a lawn.

In cases like this it is easy to blame farmers for excessive use of fertiliser, but this case seemed more complex. It is thought that the huge algal bloom was indirectly triggered by the rapid expansion of a farmed seaweed called Porphyra almost 200 km down the coast. The problem species is an algae called *Enteromorpha prolifera*, which grows on and around the Porphyra, thriving in the same conditions.

Porphyra is big business. It is farmed on semi-floating rafts made of bamboo and net curtain. The seaweed is mainly sold as food and, ironically, is also grown to prevent eutrophication, as the seaweed takes up nutrients that might otherwise accumulate. It seems that *E. prolifera* broke free from the seaweed farm and, given the right conditions, began to bloom. A clue as to the origins of the pest algae was the bamboo poles and netting caught upon the vast green mats.

Satellite photos showed that, on 15 May 2008, small green patches of algae, covering around 80 km^2, appeared off the coasts of neighbouring provinces. Growth was so rapid that within 10 days, these patches had moved away from the coast and into the Yellow Sea, covering 1200 km^2, and impacting about 40 000 km^2 of ocean, making it the largest algal boom ever recorded. On the 18 June, algae patches began to move towards the coast at Qingdao, landing on the shore on 28 June.

The green tide grew and grew as it moved closer to the regatta city of Qingdao. At one point, it became the largest ever algal bloom recorded anywhere in the world. The massive green tide covered about 600 km^2. In a concerted effort lasting over two weeks, it took more than 10 000 people to clean up, removing over one million tonnes of algae from the beach and coast.

4.1 RECYCLING AND DECAY

The importance of recycling

Your body is made from 'second-hand' chemicals. So is every other organism on the planet. The atoms and molecules that make up your cells and tissues have all been part of other organisms before, probably many times. The simple truth is that these atoms – carbon, nitrogen, phosphorus – are in limited supply. We can't recycle energy – the Sun provides it and it is transferred in various forms through food chains to re-appear as heat – but the elements that make up our bodies are in short supply and are used again and again. It's the Sun's energy that drives the cycles.

Figure 1 *You are what you eat. Some of the atoms in the meat will be incorporated into your body. One way or another, all of the atoms will leave your body and become incorporated into other organisms.*

The process of decay

Broadly, there are just three ways in which an organism can obtain its biological molecules. One is photosynthesis, which we have seen. Another way is to search for food, eat it and digest it in a gut and absorb biological molecules, which is what animals do. The third way is **saprobiotic nutrition**, seen in saprobionts – organisms, such as fungi and bacteria, that live and feed on dead organic matter.

The process of decay is absolutely vital to life. Without it, the vital nutrients would remain locked inside dead organic material. Fungi and most bacteria obtain their

organic material from the process of decay. This is more correctly known as saprobiotic nutrition.

The mechanism of saprobiotic nutrition involves **extracellular digestion**. The cells of bacteria and fungi synthesise and secrete enzymes. These organisms are able to detect the composition of the surrounding dead organic material and activate the genes that make the right digestive enzymes. The enzymes hydrolyse the surrounding material into simple, soluble compounds such as sugars and amino acids, which are then absorbed by the cells. These organisms can digest pretty much anything, as long as they can make the right enzyme. One interesting area of genetic engineering is to develop strains of bacteria that can digest waste material and pollutants such as oil, plastic and pesticides.

Eventually, most organic material will rot: leaves, faeces, dead bodies. When proteins are hydrolysed, the resulting amino acids are absorbed into the cells of the decomposers. When amino acids are metabolised, the amino ($-NH_2$) group is removed, a process called **deamination.** When excreted, the amino group in solution becomes ammonium (NH_4^+) ions, and so the process is called **ammonification**. Saprophytic decay, decomposition, rotting, deamination and ammonification are all carried out by the same organisms.

Figure 2 *Extracellular digestion. The appearance of fruiting bodies such as mushrooms is a sure sign that there is a network of fungal threads underneath, releasing enzymes and digesting the compounds within the wood.*

4.2 THE NITROGEN CYCLE

You have already seen that proteins, DNA, RNA and ATP are all essential for life. All of these compounds contain nitrogen. Producers make carbohydrates via photosynthesis, but they need a supply of nitrogen and phosphorus in order to make these other vital compounds. Nitrogen comes in many different forms – 80% of the atmosphere is nitrogen gas – but generally, producers can only absorb nitrogen in the form of **nitrate** (NO_3^-) ions.

The cycling of nitrogen is rather more complex than that of most ions because digestion of proteins does not release the nitrate ions. There are three main stages in the production of nitrate ions from proteins. These are:

> digestion of proteins to amino acids by decomposers – **saprobiotic digestion**; digestion involves hydrolysis, catalysed by enzymes

> formation of ammonium compounds from amino acids – **ammonification**

> conversion of ammonium compounds to nitrates – **nitrification**.

Ammonification

Following decomposition, the metabolism of many bacteria results in the removal of nitrogen-containing amino groups (–NH_2) from amino acids, converting them into ammonia (NH_3), or ammonium ions (NH_4^+). This is very similar to the process of deamination that

takes place in our livers, and which produces urea. In fact, urea excreted by mammals is also converted to ammonia by some bacteria. If you have ever been in a horse's stable, you may have smelt the pungent ammonia resulting from this reaction.

Nitrification

Nitrification is the process that converts ammonium ions to nitrate ions. This is carried out by **nitrifying bacteria**, in two stages. Different species of bacteria are involved at each stage:

$$NH_4^+ \quad \rightarrow \quad NO_2^- \quad \rightarrow \quad NO_3^-$$

ammonium ions   nitrite ions   nitrate ions

These reactions are oxidations. As we have seen in respiration, oxidation reactions release energy. Nitrifying bacteria use this energy to carry out **chemosynthesis**, in which they synthesise their own organic compounds.

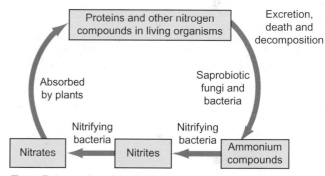

Figure 3 *An overview of the circulation of nitrogen*

Denitrification

In theory, this cycle could maintain the supplies of nitrates for plants indefinitely. However, there is a complication in the real world. Where soils are waterlogged and there is little or no oxygen available for respiration, **denitrifying bacteria** use nitrate ions, instead of oxygen, as electron acceptors during respiration. This reaction produces nitrogen gas, which is released into the atmosphere, thus reducing the amount of nitrates in the soil.

Nitrogen fixation

The air contains enormous quantities of nitrogen – almost 80% of the air is nitrogen gas, N_2. However, molecules of N_2 gas have a triple bond ($N\equiv N$) that is very difficult to break. Nitrogen gas molecules are so unreactive that they are useless to plants. Nitrogen gas diffuses in and out of plant leaves all the time, and in and out of their cells, but it can't be used in any metabolic reactions. As far as the plant is concerned, it might as well not be there.

Some species of bacteria can use nitrogen gas to synthesise nitrogen compounds. These bacteria can reduce nitrogen (N_2) to ammonia (NH_3) in a process called **nitrogen fixation**. In this process, nitrogen gas is combined with hydrogen ions obtained from water. Some of these nitrogen-fixing bacteria live freely in the soil or water, but others can fix nitrogen only when living inside green plants.

For example, *Rhizobium* bacteria live inside small lumps (nodules) on the roots of leguminous plants such as clover, peas and beans (Figure 4). The bacteria have nitrogenase enzymes that fix nitrogen and produce ammonia. This is converted to amino groups that are used to synthesise amino acids inside the cells of the nodules.

An interesting area of genetic engineering research is to insert the gene for nitrogenase into crop plants, which could fix their own nitrogen, so extra fertiliser would not need to be added.

Figure 4 *Nodules on the roots of the pea plant. The nodules contain* Rhizobium *bacteria, which possess the nitrogenase enzyme.*

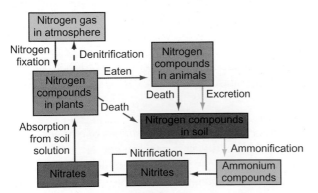

Figure 5 *The complete nitrogen cycle*

Nitrogen fixation is an example of mutualism, because both the bacteria and the plants benefit from the relationship. The leguminous plants obtain amino acids without having to absorb nitrates, which are often in short supply in soil. The bacteria get sugars from the plants, which they use as a source of energy to synthesise the ammonia. They also get a very low oxygen environment, maintained by leghaemoglobin in nodules. This is essential for these bacteria to live and for fixation of nitrogen.

Once these additional processes are added to the nitrogen recycling flow chart in Figure 3, the complete cycle becomes more complex (Figure 5). You can now see the vital role that microorganisms play, and why it is important to maintain healthy populations of microorganisms in the soil.

QUESTIONS

1. With reference to the nitrogen cycle, explain how good soil drainage may help to maintain a high concentration of nitrate ions in the soil.

2. Farmers and vegetable growers may practise crop rotation, which means that they do not grow the same kind of crop in the same area of ground each year. Clover, peas or beans are often grown for one year in the rotation. Suggest how this may help to maintain the fertility of the soil.

Stretch and challenge

3. Use your knowledge of the biochemistry of aerobic respiration to suggest how denitrifying bacteria might use nitrate and nitrite ions as electron acceptors.

Mycorrhizae

Close inspection of many plants, including every tree species yet studied, has revealed a close, beneficial relationship between the plant's roots and certain species of fungi.

The word mycorrhizae means 'fungus-root', and it is a classic example of a mutualism – a relationship between two species in which both benefit. The threads of the mycorrhizal fungus grow in and around the roots (Figure 6a), giving a much greater surface area for absorption than the plant roots could achieve on their own. The fungus benefits from the sugars that the plant provides, while the plant benefits from the enhanced absorption of water and minerals. It may be that, in addition to providing an increased surface area, the fungal threads are able to absorb certain mineral ions more efficiently, possibly due to different membrane proteins and absorption mechanisms.

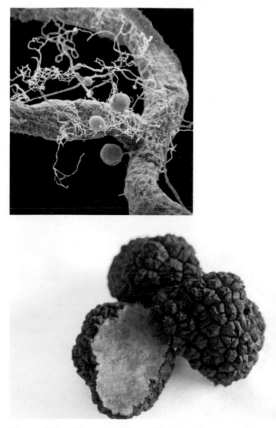

Figure 6 *Top: Close up of microrrhizal threads on a soybean root. The thin fungal threads surrounding the root can be seen in yellow. Bottom: Truffles are the fruiting bodies of certain mycorrhizal fungi – a bit like 'underground mushrooms'. This one is a black Périgord truffle – it is among the most expensive foods in the world.*

The phosphorus cycle

Phosphorus is an essential component of DNA, RNA, ATP and phospholipids (which are the main components of the bilayer of membranes). Phosphorus is also essential for the functioning of several vital enzymes.

The phosphorus cycle is very similar in principle to the nitrogen cycle. The key difference is that the atmosphere plays no part – there are no gases of phosphorus involved – and this makes things a lot simpler.

The first step in the phosphorus cycle is saprobiotic decay. Through extracellular digestion, bacteria and fungi digest large biological molecules and absorb the simple products. The metabolism of these saprobionts then releases ions that contain phosphorus. By far the commonest of these is the phosphate ion; PO_4^{3-}.

But plants don't absorb all the phosphates – some are washed away and end up in lakes, rivers, and oceans. Phosphates in the ocean settle to the ocean floor and become sediment. The phosphates are only returned to the cycle if a geological upheaval exposes sedimentary rocks to weathering once more.

Another reason why the phosphorus cycle is simpler than the nitrogen cycle is that plants and other producers can absorb the phosphate ions directly – there is no equivalent of nitrification. Phosphate and nitrate are two key limiting factors for plant growth, and for this reason they are major components of fertilisers.

KEY IDEAS

> In the nitrogen cycle, saprobiotic (saprophytic) decay releases ammonium ions (NH_4^+). Ammonia (NH_3) is a very soluble gas, and becomes NH_4^+ in solution.

> In a two-stage process called nitrification, ammonium ions are oxidised to nitrate ions (NO_3^-).

> Plant and other producers can absorb nitrate ions and use them to make nitrogen-containing compounds such as proteins and nucleic acids.

> In anaerobic conditions, denitrifying bacteria convert nitrate to nitrogen gas, thus removing it from the cycle and reducing the fertility of soil.

> Nitrogen-fixing bacteria are able to convert nitrogen gas into ammonium ions, thus adding more nitrogen to the cycle. The bacteria that can do this are either free-living or mutualistic in the roots of leguminous plants.

> The phosphorus cycle is similar to the nitrogen cycle, but simpler. Saprophytic decay releases phosphate ions, which can be absorbed by plants and used to make vital phosphorus-containing compounds such as ATP and DNA.

4.3 USING FERTILISERS TO INCREASE PRODUCTIVITY

A limiting factor is defined as one that, if its availability is increased, will increase the rate of growth.

Mineral ions are often limiting factors because when some or all of a crop is harvested, or if livestock is removed from a field, ions are taken from the soil and are not replaced. To continue farming over long periods of time, these mineral ions have to be replaced, otherwise yields begin to fall. That's why we need fertilisers.

Inorganic ions from fertilisers

Plants require many different inorganic ions (sometimes called minerals), which they obtain from the soil by uptake into their root hairs by diffusion or active transport. The ions that are most likely to be in short supply are **nitrate, phosphate and potassium (NPK)**.

We have already seen why producers require nitrate and phosphate. Potassium is important in maintaining the balance of negative and positive ions inside and outside cells, and is involved in protein metabolism. Efficient photosynthesis and active transport rely on an adequate supply of potassium. If it is not available, leaves turn yellow and cereal crops produce less grain.

To achieve high productivity and therefore high yields, farmers apply fertilisers that contain these ions to the soil. They may use an **artificial fertiliser** or a **natural fertiliser**. Artificial, or inorganic, fertilisers consist of inorganic compounds such as ammonium nitrate. Natural, or organic, fertilisers consist of organic materials such as animal manure, compost and sewage sludge.

Good farming practice ideally involves measuring the concentration of inorganic ions in the soil and calculating the amount that will be required by whatever crop is to be grown. Different crops require a different balance of minerals. This is sometimes expressed as the NPK value for the crop – the ratio of nitrogen : phosphorus : potassium that it requires. Spring barley (a cereal crop sown in spring) usually has an NPK value of 2 : 1 : 1. Beans, however, which are legumes, have a value of 0 : 1 : 1. This is because legumes have nitrogen-fixing bacteria in their roots, which make ammonium ions using nitrogen gas from the air spaces in the soil.

When an ion such as nitrate is in short supply, adding some of it to the soil, in a fertiliser, will increase productivity and growth. Up to a point, the more you add the better the growth. However, beyond a certain level, there is no more improvement. Indeed, if you go on adding more and more nitrate, you may actually *reduce*

the productivity of the crop (Figure 7). This can happen for a variety of reasons, one of which is that a very high concentration of inorganic ions in the soil produces such a low water potential that water is drawn out of the plant roots by osmosis.

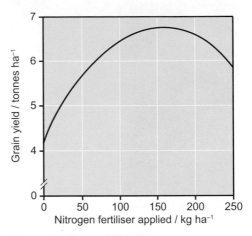

Source: after Cooke, 1980, in Harper, *Principles of Arable Crop Production*, Granada

Figure 7 *Effect of nitrogen-containing fertiliser on grain yield.*

Sometimes, limiting factors interact in terms of their effects on plant growth. For example, if a sugar beet plant is short of phosphorus, it may not be able to make maximum use of the nitrate ions that are available to it (Figure 8). Giving it more nitrate ions will not increase its productivity if the limiting factor is actually phosphate ions.

QUESTIONS

4. With reference to Figure 8, recommend the most appropriate quantity of nitrogen-containing fertiliser to provide for this crop. Explain your decision.

5. Suggest the limiting factor on yield at each of these points on the curves in Figure 8.
   a. Nitrogen fertiliser application of 100 kg ha^{-1}, low phosphorus.
   b. Nitrogen fertiliser application of 21 kg ha^{-1}, high phosphorus.

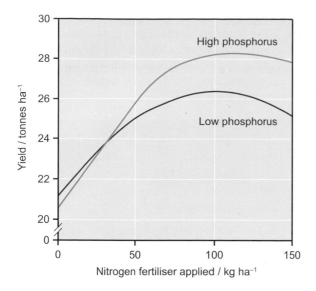

Source: after Cooke, 1980, in Harper,
Principles of Arable Crop Production, Granada

Figure 8 *Effect of nitrogen and phosphorus on yield of sugar beet*

Choosing and applying fertilisers

In an artificial fertiliser made up of a mixture of inorganic ions, the precise amounts and ratios of the different inorganic ions are known, and so they can be matched exactly to the requirements of the crop. Artificial fertilisers are also made in factories and delivered in nice clean containers. In contrast, natural fertilisers often come in great steaming dollops. The nutrient content varies dependent upon the animal species and its diet, and it can be very difficult to match the nutrient needs of the crop. You do not know exactly what you are adding. However, it is cheap.

If soil is very low in nitrogen and a nitrogen-demanding crop is to be grown, then the speed of release of ions from the fertiliser may influence a farmer's choice of fertiliser as much as the quantity of ions that the fertiliser contains. Ammonium nitrate, which is often the major component in artificial fertilisers, is soluble and releases nitrates to the soil easily. Urea, which is found in farmyard manure and other natural fertilisers, gives a much slower rate of release. In most natural fertilisers there are some ions that are in a soluble, readily available form, and others that are released over a longer time period by the decomposition of organic matter by microorganisms. So one application of natural fertiliser can have a much longer-lasting effect than one artificial fertiliser application.

Fertiliser should be added to the soil ready for when the crop's demand for the ions it contains is at its greatest. Nitrate ions and ammonium ions are highly soluble, and during periods of rainfall there is a risk that they will be lost through **leaching** (drainage of nutrients dissolved in water through the soil). This not only wastes money for the farmer, but can also seriously damage nearby aquatic ecosystems. Potassium and phosphates are not so soluble, so problems with losses from the soil by leaching are not as great.

Artificial fertilisers are expensive, so farmers do not want to use more than they need. If the farmer is to make a profit, then the economic value of the increased yield of the crop must be greater than the cost of buying and applying the fertiliser.

Figure 9 *Fertiliser can be applied in controlled amounts.*

Farmers also have to consider the costs of machinery and labour. Many artificial fertilisers are available in granules or pellets, and specialised machinery is needed for spreading them over the land. However, the machinery is light, and the fertiliser is easy to store and clean to handle. If kept in moisture-proof conditions, the fertiliser can be stored for long periods of time.

Natural fertilisers such as farmyard manure are bulky and difficult to store. There may be insufficient organic material available on the farm, so it may have to be transported from livestock areas into arable areas used for crop production. Heavy machinery is needed to handle the manure, and it can be difficult to apply evenly over a field. Weed seeds and fungal spores that cause plant diseases may be present in animal manures. Sewage sludge may contain heavy metals such as lead, zinc and nickel, which can be toxic to plants. On the other hand, organic matter binds the soil particles together. This improves the overall soil structure by improving aeration and drainage in clay soils, and water retention in light, sandy soils. Organic material also acts as a food resource for soil organisms, and the activity of animals such as earthworms also improves soil aeration and drainage. Organic matter releases nutrients over a longer period of time as a result of the action of microorganisms.

Recycling organic waste makes good environmental sense. The nutrients in the organic material are added to soil where they will be used up by crops. If organic material is just left, for example in landfill sites, then there can be problems of uncontrolled leaching.

Figure 10 *Applying farmyard manure can be a 'hit or miss' task, with respect to knowing which nutrients are being added to the soil.*

QUESTION

6. Make lists of:
   a. the advantages
   b. the disadvantages

   of using natural fertilisers (such as farmyard manure) compared with using artificial fertilisers.

ASSIGNMENT 1: HOW MUCH FERTILISER?

Figure A1

Grass seed feeds the world. Wheat, rice, maize ('corn') and barley are all species of grass, and what we refer to as cereals are in fact grass seeds. Worldwide production of cereals runs into billions of tonnes per year.

Table A1 shows the increase in yield when different quantities of nitrogen-containing fertiliser are added to a cereal crop.

Quantity of fertiliser applied / kg ha^{-1}	Mean yield of grain / tonnes ha^{-1}
0	2.9
50	3.4
100	4.3
150	4.7
200	4.8

Table A1

Questions

A1. Draw a graph of the data in Table A1.

A2. Explain why your curve does not pass through the origin.

A3. Explain why the curve does not show a proportional relationship between fertiliser application and grain yield.

A4. The farmer can sell the grain for approximately £200 per tonne. The fertiliser costs approximately £400 per tonne. What quantity of fertiliser would you recommend the farmer should use, in order to obtain a good profit from the crop? (There are 1000 kg in 1 tonne.)

Fertilisers can reduce biodiversity

We have seen how fertilisers are used to increase the productivity of crop plants, but they may be also be added to grassland, in preparation for grazing. Here, they promote the growth of species of grass to such an extent that other species may be out-competed for light. This is one of the main reasons why meadows today tend to contain far fewer species than they would have in the past. A consequence of having fewer plant species is that there are far fewer niches for other species further up the food web. Fewer plant species means fewer insect species, and fewer of the animal species that eat the insects. The use of fertilisers reduces biodiversity (see Figure 11 and *Chapter 12 of Year 1 Student Book*).

Figure 11 *A meadow like this can only continue to support a wide range of species if the use of fertiliser is avoided.*

Eutrophication is 'over fertilization'

Many of the ions contained in fertilisers are highly soluble, and will readily wash out of the soil when it rains. This is called **leaching**. If the ammonium, nitrate and phosphate ions get into water, they can affect the aquatic ecosystems all the way down to the seas and oceans.

The population sizes and rates of growth of aquatic algae and plants are often limited by a shortage of nitrate and phosphate. When these ions are added to the water, these organisms undergo rapid population growth. Often, it is algae that respond most rapidly, turning the water into something looking rather like pea soup (a real-world example is described in the chapter opener). The huge algal population prevents light from reaching plants that live deeper in the water, so these plants may die.

The dead plants – and eventually also the algae – provide a greatly increased supply of food for the decomposers in the water. Many of these are aerobically respiring bacteria. As they have so much more food, their populations also grow rapidly.

These aerobic bacteria use up most of the dissolved oxygen in the water. The lack of oxygen produces anaerobic conditions, in which many invertebrates and almost all vertebrates are unable to live. They move away, or die.

This sequence of events is called **eutrophication**. It is not only caused by pollution from fertilisers, but can also occur if untreated sewage or factory waste containing organic substances gets into the water. The process is summarised in Figure 12.

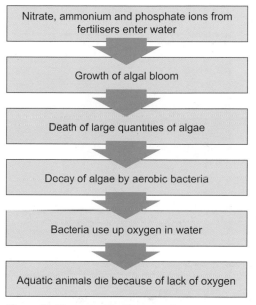

Nitrate, ammonium and phosphate ions from fertilisers enter water

Growth of algal bloom

Death of large quantities of algae

Decay of algae by aerobic bacteria

Bacteria use up oxygen in water

Aquatic animals die because of lack of oxygen

Figure 12 *How eutrophication occurs*

QUESTIONS

7. The concentration of nitrogen compounds in aquatic ecosystems is not just influenced by pollution. There is natural variation in concentration at different times of year. Figure 13 shows the nitrate and ammonium ion concentrations in a small lake over a 12-month period.

   a. Suggest explanations for each of the following:

      i. the decline in nitrate concentration during the spring and summer

      ii. the rise in nitrate concentration during autumn and winter

iii. the steep increase in ammonium ion concentration during early autumn

iv. the slow decline in ammonium ion concentration through the late autumn and winter.

b. From the evidence in the graph, suggest whether this lake is seriously polluted by nitrogen-containing fertilisers from surrounding farms.

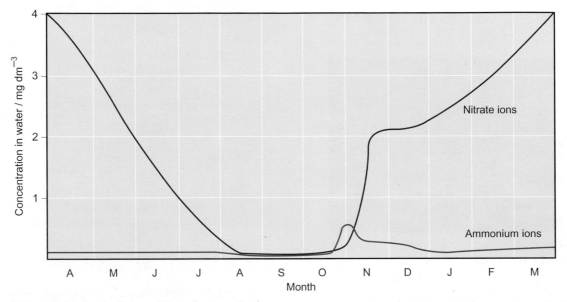

Figure 13 *Annual variations in nitrate and ammonium concentrations*

KEY IDEAS

> Farmers use fertilisers to ensure that crop yield is not limited by a lack of inorganic ions such as nitrate, potassium or phosphate. The quantity of fertiliser to be applied must be judged carefully, as if it is above a certain level the extra crop yield obtained may not outweigh the costs of the fertiliser.

> Natural fertilisers, such as farmyard manure, have some advantages and some disadvantages compared with inorganic fertilisers. They may improve soil structure, and are a good way of dealing with otherwise unused waste materials. However, their ion content is not usually known and cannot be controlled, so it is not possible to calculate exactly how much should be applied for a particular crop growing in a particular soil type.

> Pollution of waterways by nitrogen-containing fertilisers leads to eutrophication, in which excessive growth of the populations of oxygen-requiring bacteria depletes the water of dissolved oxygen.

ASSIGNMENT 2: INDICATOR SPECIES

In the UK, the Environment Agency has the responsibility of monitoring water quality in our rivers. Each year, it takes water samples from each river, and it also responds to reports of pollution incidents. The source of the pollution is tracked down, and the people responsible can be fined. Water pollution incidents decreased significantly between 2000 and 2006. If you would like to find out whether this decrease has continued, visit the Environment Agency's website at: www.environment-agency.gov.uk.

One of the tests that is carried out by Environment Agency scientists is to measure the biochemical oxygen demand, BOD, of the water. The greater the pollution with organic material or fertilisers, the more aerobic bacteria there will be in the water. And the more aerobic bacteria, the faster the oxygen is used up. BOD is a measure of the rate of oxygen use.

To measure BOD:

> Two samples of water are collected from the same site.

> The oxygen content of one sample is measured using an oxygen meter (which uses a sensitive probe).

> The second sample is sealed in an air-free container and incubated in darkness at 20 °C for five days.

> At the end of this time, the oxygen content of the second sample is measured.

> The difference between the oxygen concentrations on the first day and on the last day is used to calculate the BOD.

> Units for BOD are milligrams of oxygen per litre per day. This is written as mg dm^{-3} per day.

Worked example:

A sewage treatment works in Europe claimed that it was treating the water to all required standards, and that there was no difference in the quality of water in the water course upstream of the treatment works, when compared with water quality in the water course downstream of the plant, that is, after it had discharged its treated water. Scientists investigated this claim by measuring the BOD above and below the discharge pipe. Here are their readings:

Water sample location	Initial oxygen reading / mg dm^{-3}	Final oxygen reading / mg dm^{-3}
Sample A upstream	8.60	5.20
Sample B downstream	8.70	3.30

To work out the mass of oxygen used by any bacteria present, subtract the first reading from the second:

> Sample A = 8.6 − 5.2 = 3.4 mg dm^{-3}
> Sample B = 8.7 − 3.3 = 5.4 mg dm^{-3}

Next, we need to work out a BOD value per day.

The samples were both incubated for five days, so, our final BOD readings are:

Sample A = $\frac{3.4}{5}$ = 0.68 mg dm^{-3} day^{-1}

Sample B = $\frac{5.4}{5}$ = 1.08 mg dm^{-3} day^{-1}

The conclusion from the investigation would be that the water from the treatment works is not as clean as was claimed.

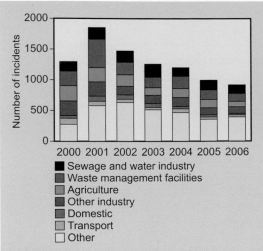

Figure A1 *Water pollution incidents in the UK between 2000 and 2006*

Water pollution can also be detected using an even simpler method, which does not involve using test tubes or water samples at all – just have a look at the species that live there. The organisms that live in a river or stream are greatly affected by the abiotic factors in the water, including the oxygen concentration. Some species, such as rat-tailed maggots and sludgeworms (sometimes called tubifex), have adaptations that allow them to survive in very anaerobic conditions. Others, such as mayfly larvae, can only live in water containing a high concentration of dissolved oxygen. These are **indicator species** – their presence gives an indication of the oxygen concentration in the water, and therefore the degree of pollution.

Each indicator species is allocated a 'biotic index'. The higher the biotic index, the more dissolved oxygen it requires. Researchers can get a good idea of the degree of pollution in a river by collecting

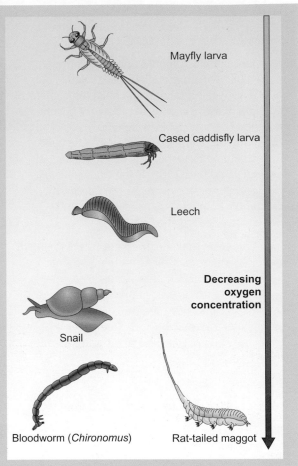

Figure A2 *Some examples of indicator species*

samples in a standard way, and counting the number of each organism that they find. Table A1 shows the species present in samples taken from two points on a river, one upstream of a suspected pollution incident and one just downstream from it.

Species	Biotic index	Number of individuals at site 1	Number of individuals at site 2
Stonefly larvae			
Species 1	10	4	0
Species 2	10	7	0
Species 3	10	7	0
Mayfly larvae			
Species 1	4	2	8
Species 2	10	7	0
Caddisfly larvae			
Case made of stones	10	2	0
Case made of leaves	7	1	0
Freshwater shrimp	6	35	0
Leeches			
Species 1	3	11	1
Species 2	3	3	2
Snails			
Species 1	3	45	30
Fly larvae			
Species 1	2	0	30
Species 2	2	0	65
Worms	1	0	120

Table A1 Data from two sites on a river

Questions

A1. Use the data from the Environment Agency (Figure A1) to determine the relative importance of water pollution from agriculture compared with other sources. Did this change between 2000 and 2006?

A2. Explain how measuring BOD can give a good indication of whether pollution has occurred.

A3. Explain the importance of each of the following measures that must be taken when measuring BOD:

  a. ensuring that there are no air bubbles in the water samples or air spaces in their containers

  b. keeping the second sample in the dark, not in the light, for five days.

A4. Suggest how BOD measurements could be used to help to track down the source of pollution.

A5. Using the data in Table A1, determine which of the two sites was above the source of the pollution. Explain how you used the data when making your decision.

A6. Discuss the advantages and disadvantages of using indicator species to detect water pollution.

A7. Bloodworms and rat-tailed maggots are perfectly able to survive in a relatively high oxygen concentration, but they are almost never found in well-oxygenated water. Suggest which types of environmental factors might cause their absence in well-oxygenated streams and rivers.

PRACTICE QUESTIONS

1. a. Name the type of bacteria that convert:

    i. nitrogen in the air into ammonium compounds

    ii. nitrites into nitrates.

  b. i. Describe and explain how **one** farming practice, other than spreading fertilisers, results in the addition of nitrogen-containing compounds to a field.

    ii. Describe and explain how **one** farming practice results in the removal of nitrogen-containing compounds from a field.

AQA June 2006 Unit 5 Question 1

2. a. Nodules on the roots of some plants enable them to survive in soils that have a low concentration of nitrate ions. Explain how.

  b. Waterlogged soil may have a low concentration of nitrate ions. Explain why.

AQA June 2007 Unit 6 Question 1

3. Arctic tundra is an ecosystem found in very cold climates. Figure Q1 shows some parts of the carbon and nitrogen cycles in arctic tundra.

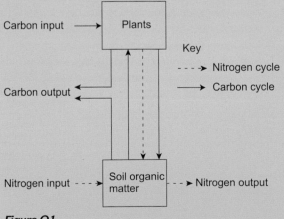

Figure Q1

  a. Name the process represented by:

    i. carbon output

    ii. nitrogen input.

b. An increase in temperature causes an increase in carbon input. Explain why.

c. Fungi obtain their nutrients from the organic matter in soil. Explain how.

AQA June 2007 Unit 5 Question 2

4. Figure Q2 shows part of a river into which raw sewage is discharged. Table Q1 shows the results of a chemical analysis of water samples taken at sites X, Y and Z along the river.

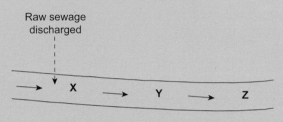

Figure Q2

	Site X	Site Y	Site Z
BOD (biological oxygen demand) / mg dm^{-3}	38.0	17.0	3.0
Ammonium ions / mg dm^{-3}	0.3	0.7	0.1
Nitrate ions / mg dm^{-3}	4.0	6.0	7.0

Table Q1

  a. Explain the decrease in BOD from site X to site Z.

  b. Explain the increase in the concentration of ammonium ions and nitrate ions from site X to site Y.

AQA June 2007 Unit 5 Question 8

5. a. The availability of nitrogen-containing compounds in the soil is often a limiting factor for plant growth. Explain **two** ways in which a shortage of nitrogen-containing compounds could limit plant growth.

b. Farmers apply nitrate fertilisers to improve crop growth.

   i. Explain why plants may fail to grow if high concentrations of nitrate are applied to the soil.

   ii. Streams and rivers running through farmland can also be adversely affected by the application of high concentrations of nitrate fertiliser. Fish cannot survive when the oxygen levels of water are reduced. Explain how high concentrations of nitrate applied to farmland may result in a reduction in the numbers of fish that are present in aquatic ecosystems.

c. Malonate is a substance that inhibits the enzymes of the Krebs cycle. In an investigation, plant roots were placed in a solution containing nitrate and malonate. The solution had air bubbled through it. Explain why these plant roots took up nitrate more slowly than those that were placed in a control solution that contained nitrate but no malonate.

AQA June 2003 Unit 5 Question 8

6. Pea plants are leguminous and have nodules on their roots that contain bacteria that are able to fix nitrogen. Figure Q3 shows some of the processes that are involved in nitrogen fixation by these bacteria.

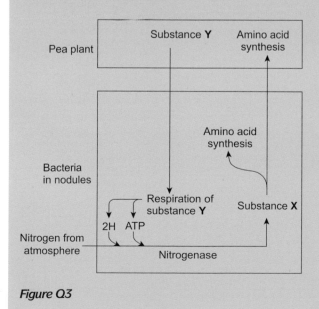

Figure Q3

a. Name:

   i. substance X

   ii. substance Y.

b. Pea plants respire aerobically, producing ATP that can be used for amino acid synthesis. Describe the role of oxygen in aerobic respiration.

c. The bacteria respire anaerobically. This produces hydrogen and ATP used in nitrogen fixation. The hydrogen comes from reduced NAD. Explain how the regeneration of NAD in this way allows ATP production to continue.

d. The enzyme nitrogenase is specific to the reaction shown. Explain how one feature of the enzyme would contribute to this specificity.

e. Sodium ions act as a non-competitive inhibitor of the enzyme nitrogenase. Explain how the presence of a non-competitive inhibitor can alter the rate of the reaction catalysed by nitrogenase.

AQA June 2005 Unit 5 Question 3

7. Figure Q4 shows a river system in an area of farmland. The numbers show the nitrate concentration in parts per million (ppm) in water samples taken at various locations along the river. Concentrations above 250 ppm encourage eutrophication in the river.

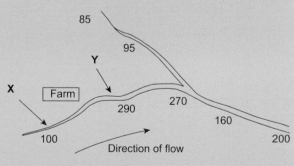

Figure Q4

a. i. Explain how farming practices might be responsible for the change in nitrate concentration in the water between point X and point Y.

   ii. Describe the effect that the nitrate concentration may have in the river at point Y.

(continued)

b. Single-celled organisms were cultured from samples of river water. Give **three** characteristics of the cells that would enable you to distinguish prokaryotes from eukaryotes.

AQA June 2005 Unit 5 Question 7

8. Figure Q5 shows the nitrogen cycle.

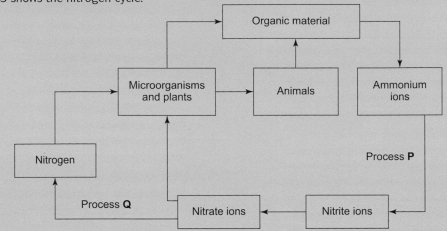

Figure Q5

a. i. Name process P.

ii. Name process Q.

b. Leguminous crop plants have nitrogen-fixing bacteria in nodules on their roots. In soils with a low concentration of nitrate ions, leguminous crops often grow better than other types of crop. Explain why.

c. Applying very high concentrations of fertiliser to the soil can reduce plant growth. Use your knowledge of water potential to explain why.

AQA January 2013 Unit 4 Question 1

5 SURVIVAL AND RESPONSE

PRIOR KNOWLEDGE

You will probably remember that 'sensitivity' is one of the seven signs of life. All organisms are able to detect changes in their surroundings to some extent, and this is essential to their survival.

LEARNING OBJECTIVES

In this chapter we look at some of the ways in which organisms detect their surroundings, and at some simple responses and behaviour patterns in both animals and plants. We also look at receptors and responses in humans, including the skin, vision and reflexes.

(Specification 3.6.1.1, 3.6.1.2, 3.6.1.3)

There are several examples of plants that catch and digest animals. This is impressive, considering that most plants are rooted to the spot and none of them have muscles or intestines. Several species of plant seduce their insect prey with a scent that promises rotting meat, and some have clever structures – pitchers – that condemn unfortunate insects, and some larger species, down a slippery slope into a vat of digestive juices.

The venus fly trap is one of the best known and most dramatic examples of a carnivorous plant – it can actually move fast enough to catch a fly, a feat that eludes many humans. How is a plant able to move so quickly, and how does it detect that there's an insect there, not just a raindrop?

Venus fly traps have sensory hairs. An insect needs to touch two separate hairs within about 20 seconds in order to trigger the trap.

When an object touches two sensory hairs, there is – by plant standards – a very rapid transfer of an electrical signal that is similar to a nerve impulse in animals. The mechanism by which the trap closes has been the subject of much research but, as yet, there is no definitive answer. It must be due to a rapid change in the turgor of the hinge cells in the midrib that connects the two leaves of the trap.

The *acid growth theory* states that H^+ ions are pumped into the cell walls of the hinge cells, making the cellulose softer and allowing the rapid expansion of the cell by osmosis. Another hypothesis states that ions are pumped out of the hinge cells, causing water to follow, so that the cells lose turgor. Both mechanisms have evidence to support them and it may be that the actual mechanism is a combination of the two.

5.1 SIMPLE RESPONSES

All organisms – even the simplest bacteria – are sensitive to their environment to some extent. They are able to detect certain stimuli and then seek them out or avoid them.

This leads us to some basic terms:

Stimulus – a change in an organism's external or internal environment that brings about a response. Examples of stimuli include light, sound, chemicals and pressure.

Receptor – detects the change (stimulus) and (transduces) transforms this energy change into a form that the cell or organism can process – such as nerve impulses in animals. Examples of human receptors include rod cells in the retina, chemoreceptors on the tongue and in the nose, and pressure receptors in the skin.

Coordinator – formulates a response.

Effector – a structure that produces a response.

Invertebrates rely on innate behaviour (behaviour that is encoded in the genes, rather than learned) for many aspects of their lives, such as escaping danger, finding a suitable habitat and locating food. They do this by using three types of behaviour pattern: a **taxis**, a **kinesis** and a **reflex escape response**.

Taxis

A taxis is a directional response. An animal performs a taxis (plural: taxes) when it moves towards or away from a stimulus, such as light, which is coming from a particular direction.

For example, maggots are the larvae of flies. Their innate behaviour includes avoiding bright sunlight, which might harm them, dry them out or make them visible to predators (Figure 1). Maggots display a negative phototaxis – they move away from light. Adult flies have a more protective exoskeleton and many species move towards the light – a positive phototaxis – a behaviour that warms up their bodies.

Kinesis

A kinesis is a non-directional response. How can an animal find suitable conditions when it cannot detect the direction in which they lie? A kinesis is a simple tactic by which an animal that finds itself

Negative phototaxis

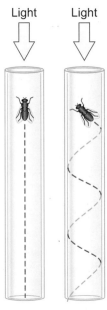

Maggots have light receptors at each side of their heads. As they crawl, they turn their heads alternately to right and left, comparing the light intensity from each side. They always turn towards the darker side, and this takes them away from light.

Positive phototaxis

Adult fruitflies move towards the light by keeping the light intensity the same in each eye. This can be demonstrated with a normally sighted fly and a fly that is blind in one eye. Each fly is placed in a glass tube with the light shining directly down from above. The normally sighted fly moves straight up the inside wall of the tube towards the light whereas the fly that is blind in one eye moves up the tube in a spiral. The attempt to keep the light intensity the same in each eye leads to the fly always having its blind eye turned towards the light.

Figure 1 *Phototaxis*

in unfavourable conditions will move about rapidly, making many turns until, by chance, it finds more favourable conditions. When it does so it slows down and makes tighter turns or stops – thus increasing the chances that it will stay in that favourable environment – and makes small adjustments so that the environment is the best possible.

A classic example of this is seen in woodlice, which are one of the few truly terrestrial (land-living) crustaceans. They live in damp places beneath logs and stones where they are not easily found by predators such as blackbirds and magpies, and where they are not likely to dry out. At high humidity levels woodlice remain inactive, but any slight drying of the environment is detected and they respond to this harmful stimulus by starting to move about. Once it has started moving, a woodlouse keeps on moving until it reaches somewhere sufficiently moist, then it slows down or stops completely.

A slightly different kind of kinesis is seen in flatworms: they respond to chemicals given off by food in the water by increasing their rate of turning, though not in any set direction. For example, if a piece of meat is placed in a pond, you might find several flatworms feeding on it within minutes (Figure 2).

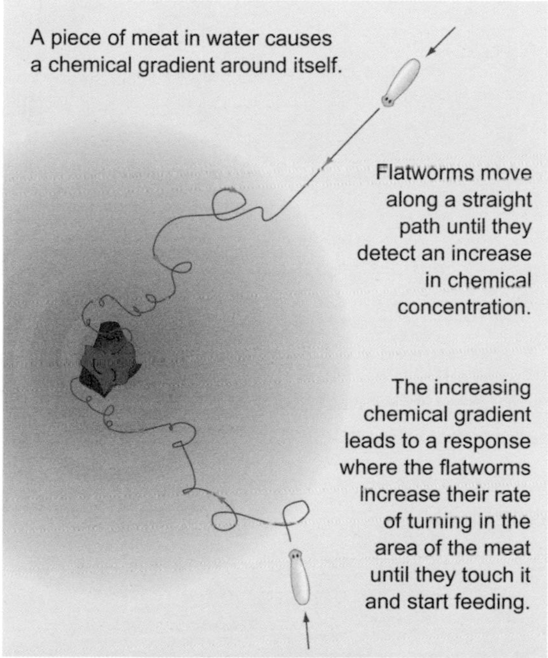

A piece of meat in water causes a chemical gradient around itself.

Flatworms move along a straight path until they detect an increase in chemical concentration.

The increasing chemical gradient leads to a response where the flatworms increase their rate of turning in the area of the meat until they touch it and start feeding.

Figure 2 *Kinesis*

QUESTIONS

1. Twenty flatworms were placed in a dish of water in a well-lit room. Eventually the flatworms became evenly spread around the dish. A light-proof cover was then placed over half of the dish. One hour later, all the flatworms were in the dark half of the dish.

Explain how the flatworms would move to and remain in the dark half of the dish if they were using:

a. a taxis

b. a kinesis.

Reflex actions

A **reflex action** is a rapid, automatic response to a stimulus. A particular stimulus leads to the same response, time after time. For example, earthworms come to the surface of the ground on warm, damp nights to defecate (producing a worm cast) or mate. They respond to the slightest vibration by retreating down into their burrows. This is a reflex escape response and it helps them to avoid being taken by a predator such as a shrew or hedgehog. In a similar way, marine fanworms (Figure 3) will rapidly draw back into their tubes if they perceive a shadow overhead, suggesting a potential predator.

Figure 3 *A Mediterranean fanworm, Sabella spallanzanii*

The simple reflex (arc) in humans

Much behaviour in more complex animals, such as mammals, is learned. But reflexes are still important. Looking at a simple reflex (arc) is a good place to begin a study of more advanced nervous systems.

Two important functions of reflexes are

> to protect from danger – such as blinking or snatching your hand away from a hot object

> to maintain posture – we constantly make minute adjustments to our body position without the need for conscious thought.

Figure 4 shows the essential features of a reflex arc. They are:

1. A **receptor** to detect the stimulus.

2. A **sensory neurone** to transmit changes in frequencies of impulses into the central nervous system (brain and spinal cord).

3. A **relay neurone** acts as the coordinator, and causes nerve impulses in the motor neurone.

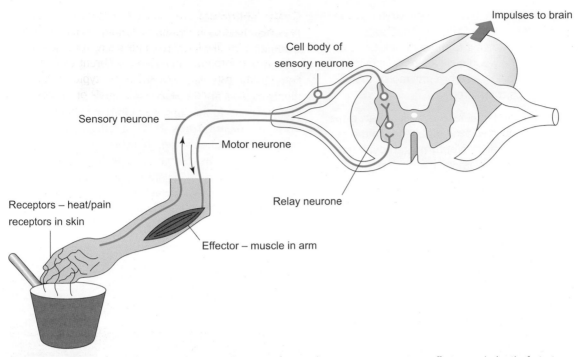

Figure 4 *The simple reflex arc represents the most direct way of connecting up a sense organ to an effector, producing the fastest possible response.*

4. A **motor neurone** to the effector.

5. An **effector** (muscle or gland) that brings about the response, such as rapid movement.

Simple reflexes

› Simple reflexes are specific – one stimulus leads to one response.

› The fewer the number of neurons involved, the fewer the number of synapses needed to connect them, and so the faster the response.

› Simple reflexes do not involve the conscious parts of the brain.

KEY IDEAS

› Invertebrates rely on innate (in-built) behaviour patterns to find favourable conditions, which usually involves finding food and avoiding predation or desiccation (drying out).

› In a taxis, the animal detects the direction of a stimulus, such as light, and moves towards or away from it.

› In a kinesis, the animal moves randomly, exploring new environments, until it finds favourable conditions. It then responds by either slowing down

or increasing its rate of turning until exactly the right conditions are found.

› In a reflex escape response, invertebrates move rapidly away from a stimulus that indicates immediate danger – for example, an approaching predator.

› The simple vertebrate reflex arc generally involves three neurones and brings about the fastest possible response. Reflex arcs are useful for maintaining posture and avoiding danger.

REQUIRED PRACTICAL ACTIVITY 10: APPARATUS AND TECHNIQUES

(ATh)

Investigation into the effect of an environmental variable on the movement of an animal using either a choice chamber or a maze

This practical activity gives you the opportunity to show that you can:

> safely and ethically use organisms to measure plant or animal responses, or physiological functions.

Apparatus and techniques

This practical is about investigating taxes and kineses, or other simple behaviours, in invertebrates such as maggots or woodlice (Figure P1).

Figure P1 *Woodlice are crustaceans, like shrimp and crabs, but they are unusual in being terrestrial (land-living). They excrete ammonia through their exoskeleton. Their exoskeleton is permeable and loses water. Woodlice seek out humid conditions to minimise water loss.*

Choice chambers are usually simple devices that provide animals with different conditions (Figure P2). They are a bit like large petri dishes with the lower half divided into four quadrants. Different conditions can be established in each quadrant, typically light/dark and dry/humid. Individual animals or groups can be placed in the centre and the direction of their movement is recorded.

Mazes are simple devices – often T-shaped pieces, made from cardboard (Figure P3) – that allow you to give an animal a range of different stimuli. For example, a piece of rotting meat in one end of the T can be used to investigate a taxis.

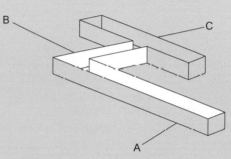

Figure P3 *A simple cardboard maze can be used to investigate taxes, kineses and alternation of turns.*

Alternation of turns

Many species explore their environment by a simple behaviour known as alternation of turns. This can be investigated by a simple maze such as the one shown

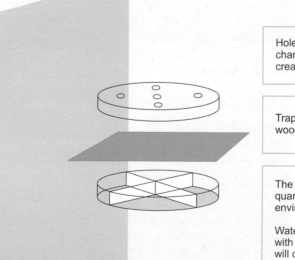

Holes in the lid allow woodlice to be put into the chamber. Covering the top and sides with card can create light and dark areas.

Trap the fabric between the lid and the base. The woodlice can move freely on this surface.

The base of choice chamber is divided into four quarters. Each one can have a different environment.

Water in one half of the base will create an area with a moist environment. Silica gel in the other half will create a dry environment.

Figure P2 *The name 'choice chamber' is misleading because it implies choice, which is beyond the simple nervous systems of species like the woodlouse. It is easy to be anthropomorphic – give human emotions to non-human things – but woodlice neither 'seek out' the best conditions, nor are they 'happy' in rotting vegetation.*

in Figure P3. If a maggot is forced to turn right (at B in Figure P3), its next turn will usually be left, even when given the choice at a T-junction (C in Figure P3). Of course, if a species constantly turned left or right, they would go round in circles, which is not the most effective behaviour for finding food, or for finding ideal conditions.

Carrying out behaviour practicals using the methods described is very straightforward and the investigations produce simple sets of data. The higher level skills come in the analysis of results.

Investigating the effect of light and humidity

A choice between light and dark can be created by simply covering half of the choice chamber with black paper. A choice between dry and humid can be created by placing water into two quadrants and having a desiccant (water-absorber) such as silica gel in the other half. If the two halves with the different conditions are arranged at right angles to each other, you can create four quadrants with conditions that are light/dry, light/damp, dark/dry and dark/damp.

Control experiment

1. Set up the choice chamber with nothing in the base quarters.

2. Use a teaspoon to place 12 maggots in the central hole.

3. Wait four minutes and record the number of maggots in each quadrant.

The hypothesis and the null hypothesis

In science, we are interested in what causes what. Scientific investigations begin with observations. In this case, someone would have noticed that woodlice are always found in particular places. Then we speculate: "could it possibly be that…?" Following this speculation comes a testable idea, known as a hypothesis. In this investigation, our hypothesis could be that woodlice always seek out dark, humid conditions.

So, we carry out investigations and gather data. It is vital to appreciate that, in science, we never prove anything – we can disprove a hypothesis or gather support for it. The sum total of our scientific knowledge is made of the best hypotheses with the strongest evidence to support them.

Statistics can help us to gather support and evidence for our hypothesis. For this, we need a **null hypothesis** – something along the lines of 'there is no difference between the distribution of woodlice in light and dark/dry and humid conditions'.

It's an 'innocent until proven guilty' approach: the null hypothesis is assumed valid until invalidated by a statistical test.

Using statistical tests

Suppose that you did the choice chamber investigation and every woodlouse ended up in the dark, moist quadrant. You might reasonably conclude that there is a clear preference. And if you had even numbers in each quadrant, you might conclude that there was no preference. But what about the grey area in-between? This is where statistics help. Statistical tests are used to decide whether the difference between the observed results (e.g. in genetic crosses) and those predicted from the null hypothesis, are **significant** or simply due to chance.

Chi-squared (χ^2) is one type of statistical test. The chi-squared test gives you a result in terms of probability. This probability (p) will have a value between 0 and 1. If $p = 0.5$, there is a 50% probability that the difference between the observed and expected results is significant, and a 50% probability that the difference is due to chance. You would, therefore, conclude that the difference between the observed and expected results is not significant. If $p = 0.01$, on the other hand, the probability is 1%, meaning that you can be 99% certain that the difference is significant. By convention, if the probability that the difference due to chance is less than 5% (or 0.05 as a decimal), you can say that the difference is significant and so you would **reject the null hypothesis**.

Applying a chi-squared test to the choice chamber investigation

The χ^2 test is suitable if you can answer 'yes' to these questions:

› Do the data fall into particular categories?

› Is there an expected outcome? This is where the null hypothesis has a direct use. There will be no significant difference between the categories if the null hypothesis is correct.

For example... **What conditions will woodlice seek out?**

A choice chamber was set up. Sixteen woodlice were places in the centre hole, and after four minutes, the number of woodlice that were in each quadrant was recorded. The experiment was repeated three times. The results are shown in Table P1.

Conditions	Mean number of woodlice per quadrant after four minutes
Dry, light	0
Dry, dark	3
Damp, light	4
Damp, dark	9

Table P1 *Raw data from a choice chamber investigation*

The chi-squared test is based on calculating the value of χ^2 from the equation:

$$\chi^2 = \frac{\Sigma(O-E)^2}{E}$$

where O represents the observed results and E represents the results that we would expect if there was no significant difference in the number of woodlice in each quadrant.

The results in the table give us the observed results (O). They are 0, 3, 4, and 9. We have to calculate the expected results (E). If the behaviour of the woodlice was purely a matter of chance, we would expect equal numbers in each quadrant. So the expected number in each quadrant is $16 \div 4 = 4$.

We now use the equation to calculate the value of χ^2. The best way to approach it is to write the values in a table such as Table P2, so that each column is the next step in working out the formula.

	Observed results (O)	Expcted results (E)	$(O-E)^2$	$\frac{O-E^2}{E}$
Dry, light	0	4	16	4
Dry, dark	3	4	1	0.25
Damp, light	4	4	0	0
Damp, dark	9	4	25	6.25

Table P2 *Calculating χ^2*

In the equation, the symbol Σ means 'the sum of all' so we have to add together all the separate values of $\frac{(O-E)^2}{E}$. In this example our χ^2 value is therefore 10.5.

We now need to look up our value on a table of values of χ^2. We must first work out the number of **degrees of freedom** in order to look in the right row of the table. The number of degrees of freedom is one less than the number of categories. This investigation has four categories so the number of degrees of freedom is 3.

We now have a χ^2 value (10.5) and a number of degrees of freedom (3). So what next?

We really want to know whether our χ^2 value is above or below the critical 5% value. So we need to use Table P3.

Degrees of freedom	Probability (p)					
	0.50	0.25	0.10	0.05	0.02	0.01
1	0.45	1.32	2.71	3.84	5.41	6.64
2	1.39	2.77	4.61	5.99	7.82	9.21
3	2.37	4.11	6.25	7.82	9.84	11.34
4	3.36	5.39	7.78	9.49	11.67	13.28

Table P3 *Table of chi-squared values*

QUESTIONS

P1. State the null hypothesis for this investigation.

P2. Between which two values does the chi-squared value of 10.5 fall?

P3. What is the probability that the difference between the observed and expected results is due to chance?

P4. What is the conclusion about the whole investigation?

Chi-squared in examinations

You will not be asked to work through any full examples of chi-squared in examinations – it is far too time-consuming. However, you will be expected to know the basic principles and uses of chi-squared, and you may also be asked to interpret values of p, state the null hypothesis and determine degrees of freedom.

5.2 TROPISMS

Rapid movement, by our standards, is almost always brought about by muscles. However, only animals have muscles. Plants can detect stimuli and respond to them, but they usually do so by growing in a particular direction, which they do by a combination of cell division and cell enlargement. Plants' growing responses are called tropisms. There are several different types, including phototropism (light) and gravitropism (gravity; also called geotropism).

Here we will look at phototropism and geotropism in more detail.

Phototropism

Light is essential for photosynthesis and so most plants are able to alter their growth so that their leaves catch the maximum amount of available light. The lentil sprouts in Figure 5 are growing near a window. They respond by growing towards the direction of light, so this response is known as **positive phototropism**.

Roots usually behave in the opposite way to stems: they grow away from the direction of light. They exhibit **negative phototropism**.

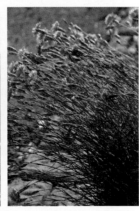

Figure 5 Two examples of phototropism

Geotropism

The tree in Figure 6 originally grew at the top of the hill. Because of erosion, the soil has moved slowly down the hill. Stems usually exhibit **negative gravitropism**: they grow away from the direction of the force of gravity. This normally results in stems growing vertically. As the position of the tree changed, so did the direction of growth of the stem, resulting in the curved growth seen in the photo.

Figure 6 This tree is displaying a gravitropism.

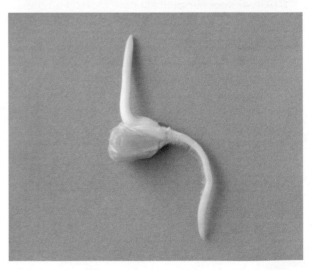

Figure 7 Seeds often germinate deep in soil, where a response to light would be no use. This maize seed (sweetcorn) shows that by detecting gravity the roots can grow downwards while the shoot grows upwards.

QUESTIONS

2. Explain the advantage of positive phototropism to plants that are growing in shaded conditions, such as the pink-flowered plants in the right-hand photograph in Figure 5.

QUESTIONS

3. Explain the advantage to a plant of:
   a. roots exhibiting positive gravitropism
   b. stems exhibiting negative gravitropism.

How tropisms happen

Tropisms happen due to unequal cell growth. In the case of positive phototropism, the cells on the darker side of the stem will divide and elongate faster than those on the illuminated side, so growth is faster on the dark side and the stem bends over. The question is: what is stimulating, or inhibiting, this cell growth?

The answer lies with auxins. These are one type of specific growth factor found in plants. (These growth factors are often also referred to as plant hormones.) The main auxin involved in tropisms is **indoleacetic acid (IAA)**.

IAA and phototropism

There is still much debate among scientists about the mechanism of phototropism, but the most widely accepted hypothesis is as follows:

> The tip of the shoot detects the direction of the light stimulus.

> The molecule that detects light (the photoreceptor) is a protein called **phototropin**.

> IAA is synthesised by cells in the tip and moves down the stem.

> **IAA transporter proteins** are moved into the plasma membrane at the sides of cells of the shoot.

> IAA moves through these transporter proteins and accumulates in the cells on the shaded side.

> This stimulates elongation of the cells on the shaded side, causing the shoot to grow towards the light.

IAA and geotropism

The mechanism for geotropism cannot involve a photoreceptor, but must involve a structure that is sensitive to the force of gravity. Again, there is still much debate among scientists about the mechanism of geotropism, but the most widely accepted hypothesis is as follows:

When a root is placed on its side:

> **Amyloplasts** (organelles containing starch grains) settle by gravity to the bottom of cells in the root tip.

> The amyloplasts cause IAA transporter proteins to be inserted in the plasma membrane of the root cells.

> The IAA transporter proteins move IAA in the direction of the pull of gravity out of the cells.

> IAA accumulates in the cells on the under-side of the root.

> This inhibits root cell elongation.

> The cells at the top surface of the root elongate, causing the root to grow down.

ASSIGNMENT 1: THE DISCOVERY OF AUXINS AND IAA

The story of the discovery of IAA and how it works is a classic piece of science.

Most of the experiments that have led to an understanding of the mechanism of tropisms have been done using oat seeds. The oat seed, like other grass seeds, germinates to produce a cylindrical **coleoptile**. The coleoptile encloses the primary (first) leaf of the young oat plant. Think of it as a shoot.

Charles Darwin and his son Francis performed some of the first experiments on phototropism. In one experiment (A of Figure A1) they placed tinfoil caps on coleoptiles. The coleoptiles were then placed in unidirectional light.

The capped coleoptiles continued to grow vertically, whereas a control group of coleoptiles grew towards the direction of the light stimulus.

In a second experiment (B of Figure A1) they placed sand around the coleoptile, leaving only the

tip exposed to unidirectional light. This coleoptile showed a normal phototropic response.

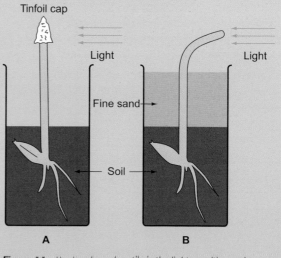

Figure A1 *The tip of a coleoptile is the light-sensitive region.*

The response of the coleoptiles to unidirectional light is caused by the cells on the shaded side of the coleoptile growing faster than those on the illuminated side.

In the early 20th century, a scientist called Boysen-Jensen hypothesised that a chemical messenger carried information from the tip of a coleoptile to the growing cells. Figure A2 shows one of his experiments. Mica is a material that is totally impermeable (today we would use plastic). He inserted wafers of mica just below the tips of coleoptiles, as shown in Figure A2.

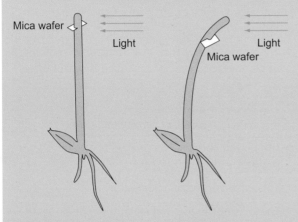

Figure A2 *Mica prevents the translocation of auxins.*

Boysen-Jensen's explanation of the results was that a substance from the tip caused the cells on the shaded side of the coleoptile to grow faster than those on the illuminated side.

The next step was to isolate this chemical substance. A scientist called Frits Went cut the tips off of coleoptiles (he decapitated them) and placed them on agar blocks. After a few hours he placed these agar blocks on the decapitated coleoptiles, as shown in Figure A3.

A control group of decapitated coleoptiles showed no growth in the period of the experiment. His conclusion was that a growth-promoting substance had diffused from the coleoptile tips into the agar blocks, and then from the agar blocks into the decapitated coleoptiles.

Went then repeated the experiment, but this time he placed the agar blocks partially on decapitated coleoptiles, as shown in Figure A4. The amount of the growth-promoting substance was too

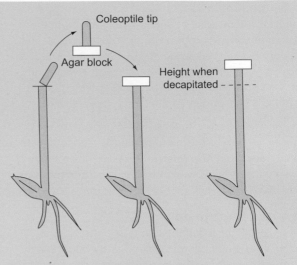

Figure A3 *Auxin diffuses into agar blocks.*

small for it to be analysed at that time, but Went coined the term **auxin** for this substance, from the Greek term, *auxein*, 'to increase'.

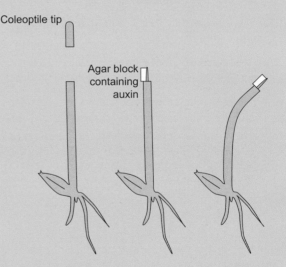

Figure A4 *An eccentrically placed agar-auxin block causes curvature.*

In a further experiment Went illuminated coleoptiles from one side for a few hours, then decapitated them and placed the tips on agar blocks, as shown in Figure A5.

On average, twice as much auxin diffused into the agar block under the non-illuminated side of the coleoptile tip than diffused into the block under the illuminated side.

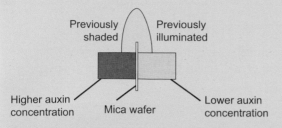

Figure A5 *Differential auxin distribution in an unequally illuminated coleoptile tip*

Similar techniques have been used to investigate gravitropism (sometimes called geotropism). Figure A6 shows an experiment to investigate the effect of gravity on auxin distribution.

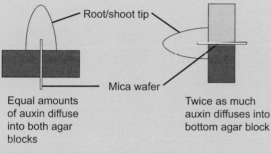

Figure A6 *Movement of auxin in geotropism*

The increased concentration of auxin on the lower side has different effects on roots and shoots. The cells at the lower side of shoots are stimulated to grow by the increased auxin concentration, but the growth of root cells is inhibited. Figure A7 shows that root cells and shoot cells have very different sensitivities to auxins.

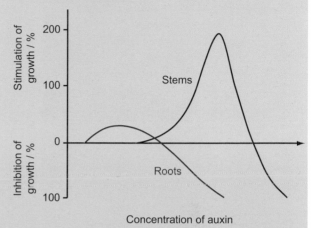

Figure A7 *Differential effect of auxin on growth of roots and stems*

Questions

A1. Look at Figure A1. What can you conclude from Darwin's two experiments, A and B, about:

    a. the position of the photoreceptor in an oat coleoptile?

    b. the effector region of the coleoptile?

A2. Look at Figure A2. Do the results of Boysen-Jensen's experiment support his hypothesis? Explain the reasons for your answer.

A3. Explain the results of Frits Went's first experiment (Figure A3).

A4. Went used the same method (Figure A4) to compare the amount of auxin that diffuses from coleoptile tips into agar blocks. Suggest how this could be done.

A5. What was the function of the mica wafer in the experiment shown in Figure A5?

A6. Suggest two possible explanations for this unequal distribution of auxin found in the experiment shown in Figure A5.

A7. Use Figures A6 and A7 to help explain, in terms of auxins and cell growth, why stems are negatively geotropic.

ASSIGNMENT 2: USING SKYLAB TO INVESTIGATE TROPISMS

(PS 2.1, 2.3)

Figure A1 *Skylab, an orbiting space laboratory*

Skylab is an orbiting space laboratory. As part of its science education programme, NASA allows students to suggest experiments to be performed in Skylab. A student, Donald W. Schlack, suggested an experiment for Skylab that would investigate the effects of light on a seed developing in zero gravity.

With the help of engineers he constructed eight compartments arranged in two parallel rows of four (Figure A2). The growth container was similar to the multi-compartment cardboard potting containers found at plant nurseries. Each compartment had two windowed surfaces, which allowed periodic photography of the developing seedlings from both a front and side view.

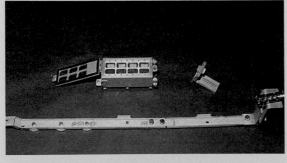

Figure A2 *Donald W. Schlack's growth container*

The study of light intensities on plants was accomplished by using light filters. For this purpose:

❯ Five windows were covered with special filters that allowed different degrees of light transmittance.

❯ Two windows were blocked to prevent any light from reaching the seeds.

❯ The remaining window had no filter, allowing 100% transmission of light.

Three rice seeds were inserted into each compartment through covered holes. Photographs of the apparatus were taken at regular intervals for 30 days.

Of the 24 seeds planted, only 10 developed. This is close to the germination ratio of 12 out of 24 observed in the control group planted on Earth.

The three largest plants grew in the container in compartments 1, 4 and 6 with light transmission of 100%, 3%, and 2%, respectively.

Plant growth was extremely irregular and inconsistent. Some plant stems made 180-degree turns away from the light and many plant tips demonstrated curled patterns.

The longest stems to develop in testing on Earth were approximately 2 inches (5 cm) long. The stem on the plant grown on board Skylab grew to 4.2 inches (10.7 cm).

Questions

A1. Evaluate the design of the experiment.

A2. Did the experiment produce valid results? Explain the reason for your answer.

A3. Use the results to explain the plants' response to light in zero gravity.

KEY IDEAS

> Tropic movements maintain the roots and shoots of plants in favourable environments.

> Most plant stems grow towards directional light; they are positively phototropic.

> Most plant roots grow away from directional light; they are negatively phototropic.

> Most plant stems grow away from the direction of the force of gravity; they are negatively geotropic.

> Most plant roots grow towards the direction of the force of gravity; they are positively geotropic.

> IAA affects the growth of plant cells.

> IAA is produced at the tips of the stems and the roots.

> IAA is moved away from the tips to the rest of the root/shoot.

> Shoot and root cells have different sensitivities to IAA.

> Unidirectional light results in IAA moving towards the shaded side of a vertical shoot, causing the cells there to elongate.

> The force of gravity results in IAA moving towards the underside of a horizontal root, inhibiting the growth of root cells there.

5.3 RECEPTORS

Mammalian skin is wonderful; it allows us to identify a variety of different sensations such as heavy pressure, light pressure, vibration, pain, heat and cold.

So what is it that allows us to make these distinctions? Human skin contains different kinds of **sensory receptors**. These are specialised cells that respond to various mechanical, thermal or chemical stimuli. Receptors are specific; each type will only detect one particular stimulus. All of these receptors are **energy transducers**: they convert the energy of the stimulus into a frequency of impulses, or action potentials. These impulses then travel along sensory neurones to the brain. A vast amount of sensory information is channelled into the brain. Our brains make sense of the world by means of a vastly complex processing job that takes account of which nerves the impulses arrive in, their frequency, other impulses arriving at the same time and past experience. It is mind-bendingly complex.

Each square centimetre of skin averages about 200 pain receptors, 100 pressure receptors, 12 cold receptors and two warmth receptors, although there is variation in the actual numbers of each. Table 1 lists the characteristics of the five types of pressure receptors found in human skin.

The Pacinian corpuscle

From the list in Table 1, the Pacinian corpuscle is the receptor that we need to look at in detail. It is a type of **mechanoreceptor** that is sensitive to physical stimuli. Pacinian corpuscles in the skin are very large receptors, almost 1 mm in diameter. Each corpuscle is basically an extension of a sensory nerve (a nerve is a bundle of many axons and dendrons from many neurones) in which the terminal part has become a receptor surrounded by layers of gel, so that the whole thing is a bit like an onion in structure. Each layer is composed of thin, flat cells called lamellae, and fibrous connective tissue separated by gelatinous material (Figure 8).

Pacinian corpuscles detect large pressure changes and vibrations. Vitally, they do not respond to prolonged stimuli. This is an important concept – most receptors respond to changes in stimuli but then stop responding if the stimulus remains constant. This is one way by which the nervous system tries to avoid overloading the brain with constant, irrelevant stimuli.

Receptor	Stimulus	Sensation
Merkel nerve endings	Steady indentation	Pressure
Meissner's corpuscle	Low-frequency vibration	Gentle fluttering
Ruffini endings	Rapid indentation	Stretch
Pacinian corpuscle	Vibration and pressure	Vibration
Hair receptor	Hair deflection	Brushing

Table 1 Skin pressure receptors

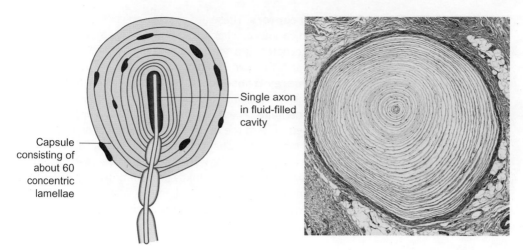

Figure 8 *Internal structure of a Pacinian corpuscle (left) and a light micrograph of a Pacinian corpuscle (right).*

The Pacinian corpuscle works as follows:

> Pressure or vibration causes compression of the capsule. The pressure is transferred through the gel to the receptor.

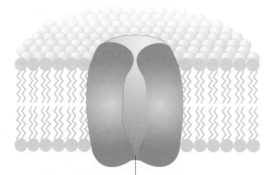

Channel closed. Na⁺ ions unable to pass through

Stretching of membrane causes sodium ion channels to open, allowing Na⁺ ions to pass through

Figure 9 *Gated sodium ion channels. These specific membrane proteins are, by definition, controlling facilitated diffusion. You may remember from the AS course that changing the tertiary structure of a protein can alter its function.*

> The membrane of the receptor has **stretch-mediated sodium channels**. The more physical pressure is applied to these proteins, the more permeable they are to sodium ions (Figure 9).

> Sodium ions flood into the receptor, building up a charge known as a **generator potential** (Figure 10).

> If the generator potential reaches a **threshold** (critical level), an action potential will be generated.

> The action potential passes down the neurone to the brain.

> Even if the stimulus persists, the gel repositions itself to relieve the pressure, a bit like a shock absorber, so that the pressure is no longer transferred to the receptor. Result: no more impulses.

QUESTIONS

4. Name the process by which sodium ions pass through the gated channels.

5. Use information from Figure 10 to describe the relationship between a stimulus and the generator potential.

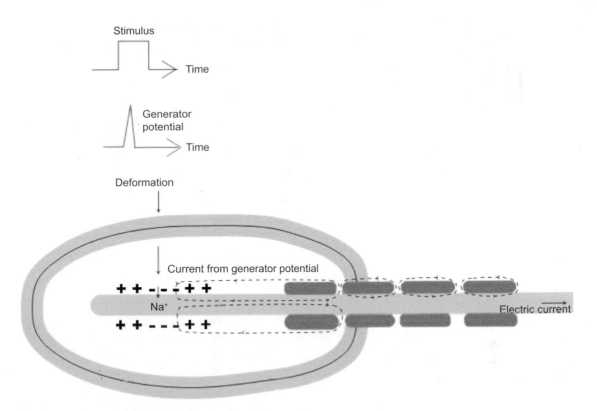

Figure 10 *Production of a generator potential by a Pacinian corpuscle*

KEY IDEAS

› A receptor responds to a specific type of stimulus.

› Pacinian corpuscles are sensitive to vibrations and to large changes in pressure.

› Stimulation of the membrane of the axon in the Pacinian corpuscle leads to deformation of stretch-mediated sodium ion channels.

› As sodium ions pass through the sodium ion channels into the neurone, a generator potential is produced. If the threshold is reached, an impulse passes down the sensory neurone to the brain, and we perceive the sensation of vibration or pressure.

5.4 LIGHT RECEPTORS IN THE HUMAN EYE

There are two types of light receptors in the human retina: **rods** and **cones**. Figure 11 shows the detailed structure of these two specialised cells, while the micrograph (Figure 12) shows how they are arranged in most of the retina – all the areas apart from the fovea.

Rods and cones are receptor cells that detect light and generate action potentials. Both have the same basic structure, but they differ in shape and in the pigment that they contain. Rod cells are relatively thin and contain **rhodopsin**, while cone cells are thicker and have **iodopsin**. Rhodopsin and iodopsin, like many pigments, are chemically changed by light – this is known as **bleaching**. In rods and cones, bleaching is rapid and reversible, and this leads to the generation of a nerve impulse.

Rods

Each rod cell is packed with about 180 molecules of the light-sensitive pigment rhodopsin arranged on discs called **lamellae**. When a photon of light hits a rhodopsin molecule, it breaks down into a pigment called **retinal** and the protein **opsin**. This brings about a series of chemical reactions that results in the release of a transmitter substance by the rod cell. The transmitter substance stimulates a chain of events that may eventually result in nerve impulses being passed to the brain along a neurone in the optic

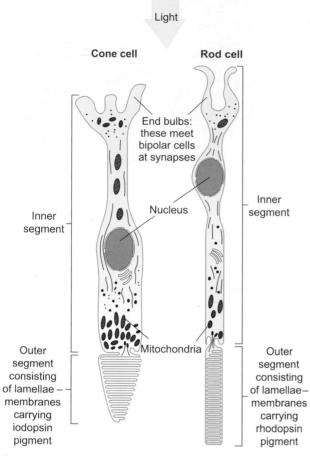

Light

Cone cell   **Rod cell**

End bulbs: these meet bipolar cells at synapses

Inner segment

Nucleus

Inner segment

Outer segment consisting of lamellae – membranes carrying iodopsin pigment

Mitochondria

Outer segment consisting of lamellae – membranes carrying rhodopsin pigment

Figure 11 A cone cell and a rod cell. Note: in an examination, you will not need to recall the structure of these cells – only the differences in optical pigments and connections.

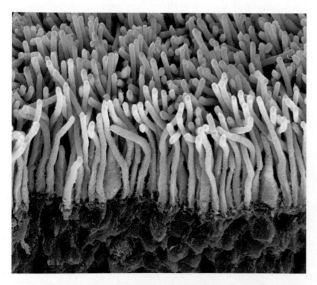

Figure 12 False-colour scanning electron micrograph (SEM) of rods (yellow) and cones (green) in the retina of the eye. The outer nuclear layer is purple.

nerve. The body needs a supply of vitamin A in order to make retinal.

Rhodopsin is a very light-sensitive pigment. Most of the time, when we are in the light, rhodopsin is continually bleached and has to be resynthesised. When we enter a dimly-lit room, the light-bleached pigment is restored to its unbleached form, rhodopsin. This effect is called **dark adaptation** and explains why we are gradually able to see more as we 'get used to' the dim light. In dim light, it takes about 30 minutes to resynthesise all the rhodopsin from the retinal and opsin.

Rod cells are connected to neurones called **bipolar cells**. The rod cell and its bipolar cell work in a different way to most other receptors. Other receptors produce a transmitter substance only when they are stimulated. But a rod cell produces a transmitter substance when it is not being stimulated, and stops production when it is stimulated. Rod cells allow us to perceive shape and movement in dim light, but do not contribute anything to colour vision.

Cones

Cones work on the same principle as rods, except that their pigment is iodopsin. Cones have a higher threshold; the pigment is only broken down by high intensity light, so they operate in daylight. Most of the impulses passing to the brain in bright light come from the cones, where iodopsin is resynthesised much more quickly than rhodopsin in the rods.

QUESTIONS

6. Why can't we see very well when we first enter a poorly lit room from a brightly lit area?

7. It is often very sunny in winter ski resorts. Skiers wear dark goggles to prevent snow 'blindness'. Explain what causes snow blindness.

Sensitivity and acuity

› **Sensitivity** describes the strength of a specific stimulus required for the receptor to detect it. In this case, it is the intensity of light required for a rod or cone cell to be able to detect it.

> **Acuity** is the ability to see detail; in other words, resolution.

> **Convergence** is the idea that several rod cells can feed information into one sensory neurone in the optic nerve.

Overall, the rods are more sensitive but their acuity is relatively poor. It is the cones that allow us to perceive detail – to read, for example – but they only function in relatively bright light.

Figure 13 shows a section through the retina. It may look complex, but it is a lot simpler than the situation in real life. Strangely, light has to pass between several layers of cells before it reaches the rods and cones. The rods and cones form synapses with neurones called bipolar cells. The bipolar cells in turn synapse with ganglion cells, which synapse with the sensory neurone fibres. These transmit impulses to the brain via the optic nerve.

There is maximum acuity at the **fovea** because here there are many densely packed cones, and each bipolar cell is (synaptically) connected to a single cone cell – there is very little convergence. This means that more sensory information goes to the brain per unit area of retina, and consequently we can perceive more detail. Elsewhere in the retina there are fewer cones, and each bipolar cell is

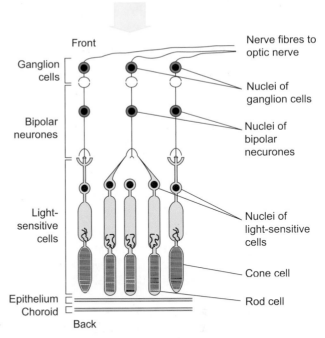

Figure 13 Light penetration into the retina.

synaptically connected to several rods – it may or may not be 'stimulated' by any number of these – depending on where photons hit (Figure 14).

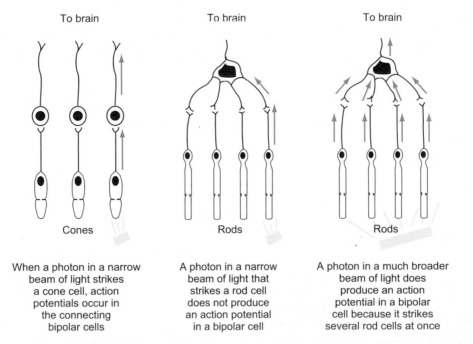

| When a photon in a narrow beam of light strikes a cone cell, action potentials occur in the connecting bipolar cells | A photon in a narrow beam of light that strikes a rod cell does not produce an action potential in a bipolar cell | A photon in a much broader beam of light does produce an action potential in a bipolar cell because it strikes several rod cells at once |

Figure 14 Differences in convergence in rods and cones help to explain the differences in acuity. If one (or a few) rod cells in a cluster receive enough light to send impulses to bipolar cell, then impulses will be sent down the optic nerve to the brain. However, it is only possible to perceive that light fell somewhere on that cluster, which results in low acuity. Cones each have their own bipolar cell, and so the brain perceives where light fell with a high degree of accuracy, resulting in high acuity.

Bright light is needed for cones to work well. Conversely, rods are more effective in dim light. There are two reasons for this:

1   The pigment in the rods is more easily bleached by low-intensity light.

2   There is a lot more convergence. Overall, 126 million receptors (rods and cones) connect to one million ganglion cells in the optic nerve. There are 120 million rods in the retina and only six million cones. So, on average, 120 rods send their signals to one ganglion cell, whereas six cones connect to one ganglion cell.

Convergence leads to higher sensitivity by a process known as **summation**. Dim light results in the production of only a small amount of transmitter substance by each rod. Individually, this is insufficient to overcome the threshold of the bipolar cell, but the total amount of transmitter substance produced by several rods is sufficient to overcome the threshold and depolarise the bipolar cell. The result of several rods causing depolarisation of one bipolar cell is to give less acuity, but better **sensitivity**.

When we look directly at something in bright light, light from the object is focused on cones in the fovea, and we see it clearly. But when there is not much light, for example when we look at a faint star, we can see the object more easily if we look slightly to one side of it. This is because light is then focused to one side of the eye where there are more rods, rather than on the fovea where there are more cones.

A comparison of rods and cones is given in Table 2.

Figure 15 shows how the relative numbers of rods and cones vary in different parts of the retina.

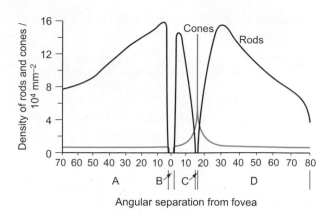

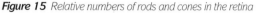

Figure 15 *Relative numbers of rods and cones in the retina*

QUESTIONS

8. a. Why can't we see colours in dim light?

    b. Why do rods give us greater sensitivity in dim light?

    c. Why do cones give us greater acuity in bright light?

    d. Light from the centre of our field of vision is focused on the cones at the fovea. What evidence is there, from what we see, that we have cones in other parts of the retina?

9. a. Look at Figure 15. Which region, A to D, is the fovea? Give the reason for your answer.

    b. Which regions would be most sensitive to dim light?

    c. What would we see of an image focused at B? Give the reason for your answer.

	Rods	Cones
Distribution	Periphery of retina	All over retina but concentrated at fovea
Pigment	Rhodopsin	Iodopsin
Number per eye/millions	120	Six
Retinal convergence	120+ rods to one ganglion cell	In fovea, one cone to one ganglion cell
Sensitivity	Good; one photon gives response	Poor; several hundred photons needed
Acuity	Poor	Good

Table 2 *Rods and cones compared*

ASSIGNMENT 3: THE TRICHROMATIC THEORY OF COLOUR VISION

There is only one type of rod and this responds most strongly to bluish-green light. Cones are divided into three types, each of which has a different sensitivity to different wavelengths of light. There are red-light receptors, green-light receptors and blue-light receptors, but the ranges of sensitivity overlap and most wavelengths of light stimulate at least two types of cone, as Figure A1 shows.

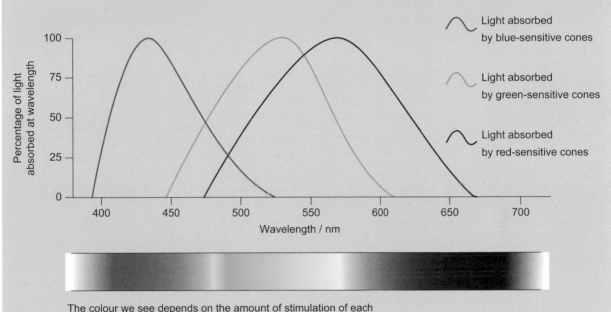

Light absorbed by blue-sensitive cones

Light absorbed by green-sensitive cones

Light absorbed by red-sensitive cones

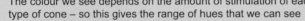

The colour we see depends on the amount of stimulation of each type of cone – so this gives the range of hues that we can see

Figure A1 *Wavelengths of light absorbed by different cones*

The discovery of three types of cone supports the trichromatic theory of colour vision. This theory states that we see all the colours of the visible spectrum by mixing the three primary colours – blue, green and red. A white object stimulates all three types of cone, so the brain interprets the impulses as white light. The brain interprets any combination of messages from the three types of cone as a particular colour. Look at Figure A2. Yellow light stimulates the red-light receptors and the green-light receptors and the brain interprets the impulses from the receptors as yellow. Different colours will stimulate the three cone types to different extents.

A good insight into the way our colour vision works is given by creating an after-image. If you look at, say, a triangular piece of red card on a white background for a few seconds, and then look at the white surface, you will see an after-image of a cyan triangle. This is because you have bleached the pigment in the red-sensitive cones. When you look at a white surface, you are stimulating all three cones but the red ones won't work so well, because their pigment has been bleached, so you will see the colour cyan – a result of stimulating the blue and green cones equally. See Figure A2.

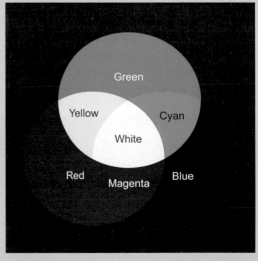

Figure A2

Questions

A1. Which cones are stimulated by light of wavelength 600 nm?

A2. Why do you see an orange/yellow colour when light of 600 nm stimulates the cones?

A3. Which cones are stimulated by the white paper and black letters of this question?

Colour blindness

Colour blindness is the name given to a range of conditions that result in an individual not being able to perceive red, blue and green in the usual way. Apart from a few exceptional cases, it doesn't mean that they will see things in black and white, however.

The genes for making the green-sensitive and red-sensitive pigment (but not the blue-sensitive pigment) are located on the X chromosome, so red–green colour blindness is a sex-linked condition. A faulty allele results in abnormal pigments – males have only one copy of each sex-linked allele so if it is the mutated form, they will have the condition. Females have two copies of the allele and both need to be faulty to cause colour blindness. As a consequence, about 8% of males, but fewer than 1% of females, have faulty colour vision.

Many colour-blind males lack either the red-sensitive cones or the green-sensitive cones and so confuse red, blue-green and grey. For example, bright red roses can appear to be the same colour as the leaves, and scarlet clothes may appear to be dark grey. Complete colour blindness in which all cone pigments are absent is very rare.

The genes for the cone opsins have now been isolated and sequenced. Their base pair sequences show that the three cone opsins differ only slightly from one another. Since the cone opsins are also similar to rhodopsin, it may be that cone opsins are a mutated form of rhodopsin that were selected for during evolution.

Look at the left part of Figure A3. If you have normal colour vision you will see a 7 in reddish brown dots.

Figure A3 *Assessment of colour vision*

Stretch and challenge

A4. People with red–green colour blindness will not see a 7 in Figure A3. Explain why.

A5. Use a genetic diagram to explain how a male inherits red–green colour blindness from two normal-sighted parents.

A6. Suggest how opsins might have been derived from rhodopsin.

A7. Stare at the shape on the right-hand side of Figure A3 for 20 seconds and then look at a white surface. What colours do you see? This is called an after-image. How does the trichromatic theory explain after-images?

KEY IDEAS

» Rods and cones are photoreceptors. They contain pigment that is broken down by light. This breakdown generates products that initiate processes leading to impulses in neurones in the optic nerve.

» Rods are the principal receptors in dim light, cones in bright light.

» Up to 120 rods converge with one bipolar cell, giving low visual acuity.

» At the fovea, one cone converges with one bipolar cell, giving high visual acuity.

5.5 THE AUTONOMIC NERVOUS SYSTEM

Autonomic means 'self-governing'. The autonomic nervous system is part of the nervous system that controls many bodily functions that do not normally need conscious thought.

The ANS has two parts: **sympathetic** and **parasympathetic**.

Generally, impulses triggered along sympathetic neurones have similar effects to the hormone adrenaline; they prepare the body for action. The parasympathetic nervous system generally acts antagonistically to the sympathetic system, so has opposing effects. So while sympathetic stimulation can be thought of as 'fight or flight', the parasympathetic system calms the body down and can be thought of as 'rest and digest'.

You do not need to know much about the autonomic nervous system, apart from its role in the control of heartbeat.

The control of heartbeat

> The **sinoatrial node (SAN)** is the 'natural' pacemaker of the heart.

> The SAN generates an impulse that spreads over and causes the atria to contract.

> The impulse cannot pass directly through to the ventricles.

> The impulse reaches the **atrioventricular node (AVN)** where it is delayed for a fraction of a second; this delay ensures that the ventricles can fill, and then channels the impulse down the **bundle of His**.

> The bundle of His transmits the impulse down the septum of the heart to the apex. It does not cause ventricular contraction.

> The impulse spreads up from the apex of the heart in the **Purkinje fibres**, causing ventricular contraction from the base of the ventricles towards the aorta and pulmonary arteries.

The SAN gives the heart its amazing property of being myogenic; it can contract on its own, without the need for external nervous stimulation. A heart removed from a living body will continue to beat as long as it is supplied with glucose and oxygen. The SAN acts a bit like the cox of a rowing crew, making sure that all the cells contract when they should. The SAN does not require impulses from the nervous system to initiate electric impulses in the heart tissue.

Although the heart can beat on its own, nerve impulses can change the rate of the heartbeat. The heart of a healthy adult beats roughly 70 times per minute. During exercise the rate may increase to as high as 200 beats per minute – the maximum that you should exercise at is generally taken to be 220 minus your age. During sleep it may fall to as low as 50 beats per minute.

The rate at which the heart beats is modified by nerve impulses from two areas of the brain (Figure 16). One is the **cardioacceleratory centre**; the other is the **cardioinhibitory centre**. Both are located in the **cardiovascular centre** in the **medulla oblongata** of the brain (often just called the medulla). Neurones carry nerve impulses from these centres to SAN.

QUESTIONS

10. What are the advantages to an athlete of a rise in heart rate during a race?

How does the heart rate speed up?

We know that heart rate can be adjusted to the needs of the body. It speeds up when we exercise, or when we are anxious, but how are these changes brought about?

Receptors that are sensitive to chemical change are called **chemoreceptors.** There are two patches of chemoreceptors in the walls of blood vessels, which are sensitive to the chemical composition of the blood. They are located:

> in the **aortic body** in the aorta, just above the heart

> in the **carotid body** in the wall of the carotid artery in the neck.

At both sites the receptors are sensitive to carbon dioxide concentration in the blood. It is tempting to think that when carbon dioxide concentrations rise, impulses are relayed straight to the CV centre in the medulla, which responds by increasing the number of sympathetic nerve impulses, causing heart rate to increase. In practice, the situation seems less straightforward. We know that if the oxygen concentration of the blood is low, or if the carbon dioxide concentration is high, ventilation rate increases. This somehow also causes the rate of heartbeat to increase, but the exact mechanism is not clear.

Another set of receptors, **baroreceptors**, are sensitive to blood pressure. Baroreceptors are found in various arteries but are particularly concentrated in the **carotid sinus**, close to the carotid body in the

95

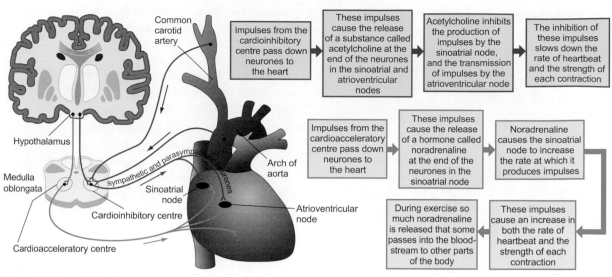

Figure 16 *Control of heartbeat*

neck. They are stretch receptors: the higher the blood pressure, the higher the frequency of nerve impulses to the medulla (in the brain). These receptors form part of a negative feedback system that prevents blood pressure getting too high.

Impulses produced by the cardioacceleratory centre pass down **sympathetic neurones** to the SAN and the AVN. Impulses that arrive at the ends of the sympathetic neurones stimulate the release of **noradrenaline** from the synapses. Noradrenaline causes the SAN to increase heart rate and increases the strength of each contraction.

Impulses produced by the cardioinhibitory centre pass down **parasympathetic neurones** to the SAN and the AVN. When the impulses arrive at the ends of the parasympathetic fibres, they stimulate the release of **acetylcholine**. Acetylcholine causes the SAN to reduce the rate of heartbeat and inhibits the transmission of impulses by the AVN. The actions of the sympathetic and parasympathetic fibres are therefore **antagonistic**.

Overall, there are two ways to increase heartbeat: more impulses down the sympathetic neurones or fewer impulses down the parasympathetic neurones. Obviously, the converse will slow the heart rate down. Overall, heartbeat is adjusted by changing the balance of the impulses down the sympathetic and parasympathetic neurones.

QUESTIONS

11. **a.** What effect would an increase in blood pressure have on the rate of heartbeat?
    b. How would this change in heart rate affect blood pressure?
    c. How do sympathetic impulses affect the heart?
    d. How do parasympathetic impulses affect the heart?

KEY IDEAS

> The rate at which the sinoatrial node sends out impulses can be modified by the nervous system and by hormones.

> The cardiovascular centre in the medulla of the brain is influenced by impulses from pressure receptors and chemoreceptors in the walls of the aorta and carotid sinuses.

> Sympathetic and parasympathetic neurones pass from the cardiovascular centre to the heart.

> Impulses via sympathetic neurones speed up the rate at which the sinoatrial node sends out impulses.

> Impulses via parasympathetic neurones slow down the rate at which the sinoatrial node sends out impulses.

PRACTICE QUESTIONS

1. The highland midge is a tiny blood-sucking insect that is the scourge of people on fishing holidays on the west coast of Scotland. Scientists are investigating claims that an extract from bog myrtle plants acts as a natural midge-repellent. Figure Q1 shows apparatus used in one of their investigations. In a series of tests more than 80% of the midges flew into branch Q.

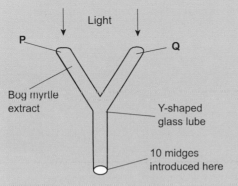

Figure Q1

   a. Suggest why the apparatus was illuminated only from above.

   b. What type of behaviour did the midges exhibit in response to the bog myrtle extract?

   c. Outline an investigation to test the effectiveness of bog myrtle extract in preventing human volunteers from being bitten by midges.

   AQA B March 2000 Unit 4 Question 3

2. a. The times taken in the various stages of a complete cardiac cycle are shown in Table Q1.

Stage of cardiac cycle	Time taken / s
Contraction of the atria	0.1
Contraction of the ventricles	0.3
Relaxation of both atria and ventricles	0.4

Table Q1

   i. Use the information in Table Q1 to calculate the heart rate in beats per minute.

   ii. If the same rate of heartbeat were maintained throughout a 12-hour period, for how many hours would the ventricular muscle be contracting? Show your working.

   b. Although the heart does have a nerve supply, the role of the nervous system is not to initiate the heartbeat but rather to modify the rate of contraction. The heart determines its own regular contraction.

   i. Describe how the regular contraction of the atria and ventricles is initiated and coordinated by the heart itself.

   ii. Describe the role of the nervous system in modifying the heart rate in response to an increase in blood pressure.

   c. An interventricular septal defect is an opening in the wall (septum) that separates the left and right ventricles. Suggest and explain the effect of this defect on blood flow through the heart.

   AQA B June 2002 Unit 3 Question 7

3. Figure Q2 shows a section through a human eye. Figure Q3 shows the distribution of rods and cones in the retina of the human eye.

   a. Use Figures Q2 and Q3 to explain why:

   i. no image is perceived when rays of light strike the retina at the point marked P

   ii. most detail is perceived when rays of light strike the part of the retina labelled Q.

   b. Rod cells allow us to see objects in dim light. Explain how the connections of rod cells to neurones in the retina make this possible.

   AQA January 2003 Unit 6 Question 1

(continued)

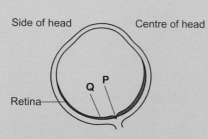

Figures Q2

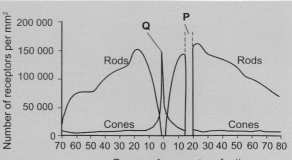

Figures Q3

4. Chitons are small animals that live on the seashore. When the tide is out they are found on the lower surfaces of stones. When the stones are turned over, the chitons move to the new lower surface, as shown in Figure Q4.

   a. Suggest two advantages to the chitons of this response.

   b. Give two factors, other than light, to which the chitons might be responding.

   c. A student investigated the response of chitons to light. Three covered dishes, X, Y and Z, were arranged as shown in Figure Q5. One half of the top of each dish was painted black; the other half was transparent. The dishes were placed on a table outside at noon on a bright day with light clouds in the sky. Ten chitons were placed in the light half of each dish. The number of chitons in each half of each dish was recorded every five minutes for the next hour.

   i. Suggest why the dishes were arranged as shown in Figure Q5.

   ii. The results of the investigation are shown in Table Q2.

Time / minutes	Number of chitons					
	Dish X		Dish Y		Dish Z	
	Light	Dark	Light	Dark	Light	Dark
0	10	0	10	0	10	0
5	9	1	7	3	8	2
10	6	4	7	3	7	3
15	5	5	7	3	6	4
20	3	7	5	5	5	5
25	3	7	4	6	5	5
30	3	7	3	7	5	5
35	3	7	3	7	5	5
40	2	8	3	7	4	6
45	1	9	3	7	4	6
50	1	9	2	8	4	6
55	1	9	3	7	2	8
60	1	9	1	9	1	9

Table Q2

   What conclusions may be drawn from these results?

   iii. Explain how kinesis could account for the results shown in Table Q2.

AQA June 2000 Unit 4 Question 1

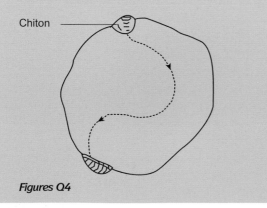

Figures Q4

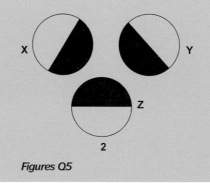

Figures Q5

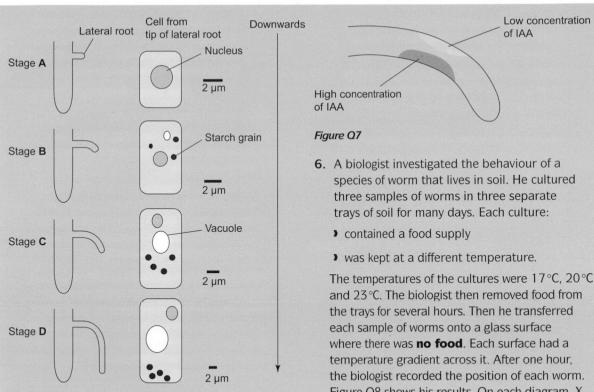

Figure Q6

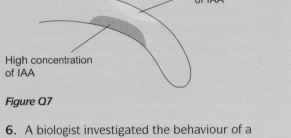

Figure Q7

5. Scientists investigated the response of lateral roots to gravity. Lateral roots grow from the side of main roots. Figure Q6 shows four stages, A to D, in the growth of a lateral root and typical cells from the tip of the lateral root in each stage. All of the cells are drawn with the bottom of the cell towards the bottom of the page.

a. Describe **three** changes in the root tip cells between stages A and D.

b. The scientists' hypothesis was that there was a relationship between the starch grains in the root tip cells and the bending and direction of growth of lateral roots. Does the information in the diagram support this hypothesis? Give reasons for your answer.

c. Figure Q7 shows the distribution of indoleacetic acid (IAA) in the lateral root at stage B.

Explain how this distribution of IAA causes the root to bend.

AQA June 2013 Unit 5 Question 3

6. A biologist investigated the behaviour of a species of worm that lives in soil. He cultured three samples of worms in three separate trays of soil for many days. Each culture:

❯ contained a food supply

❯ was kept at a different temperature.

The temperatures of the cultures were 17 °C, 20 °C and 23 °C. The biologist then removed food from the trays for several hours. Then he transferred each sample of worms onto a glass surface where there was **no food**. Each surface had a temperature gradient across it. After one hour, the biologist recorded the position of each worm. Figure Q8 shows his results. On each diagram, X (in a circle) marks where he released the worms onto the glass surface.

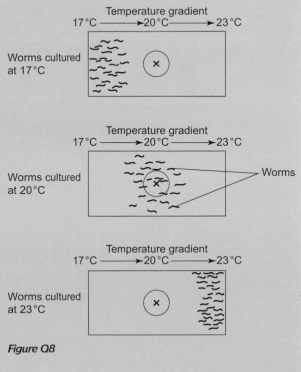

Figure Q8

(continued)

a. The biologist concluded that the worms' behaviour demonstrated taxis. How do these results support this conclusion?

b. Using the information provided, suggest an explanation for the worms' behaviour on the glass surfaces in the absence of food.

c. In each experiment, the biologist exposed the surfaces to light that was dim and even, so that he could see where the worms went. Apart from seeing where the worms went, suggest two reasons why it was important that the light was dim and even.

AQA June 2014 Unit 5 Question 2

7. a. Increased intensity of exercise leads to an increased heart rate. Explain how.

b. Scientists investigated the effect of taking omega-3 fatty acids in fish oil on heart rate during exercise. They recruited two large groups of volunteers, A and B. For each group, they measured the mean heart rates at different intensities of exercise. The volunteers were then given capsules to take for eight weeks.

Group A was given capsules containing omega-3 fatty acids in fish oil.

Group B was given capsules containing olive oil.

After eight weeks, they repeated the measurements of mean heart rates at different intensities of exercise. Figure Q9 shows their results. The bars represent the standard deviations.

  i. Group B was given capsules containing olive oil. Explain why.

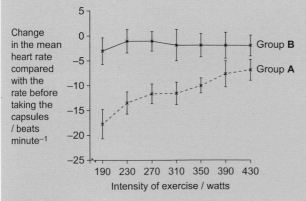

Figure Q9

ii. The scientists concluded that omega-3 fatty acids lower the heart rate during exercise. Explain how the information in the graph supports this conclusion.

AQA June 2012 Unit 5 Question 4

8. IAA is a specific growth factor.

a. Name the process by which IAA moves from the growing regions of a plant shoot to other tissues.

b. When a young shoot is illuminated from one side, IAA stimulates growth on the shaded side. Explain why growth on the shaded side helps to maintain the leaves in a favourable environment.

NAA is a similar substance to IAA. It is used to control the growth of cultivated plants. Plant physiologists investigated the effect of temperature on the uptake of NAA by leaves. They sprayed a solution containing NAA on the upper and lower surfaces of a leaf. Figure Q10 shows their results.

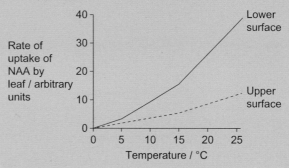

Figure Q10

c. Explain the effect of temperature on the rate at which NAA is taken up by the lower surface of the leaf.

d. There are differences in the properties of the cuticle on the upper and lower surfaces of leaves.

  i. Suggest how these differences in the cuticle might explain the differences in rates of uptake of NAA by the two surfaces.

  ii. In this investigation, the physiologists investigated the leaves of pear trees. Explain why the results might be different for other species.

AQA June 2011 Unit 5 Question 3

6 NERVES AND SYNAPSES

PRIOR KNOWLEDGE

You have already seen that the nervous system is a complex network of specialised cells that allows us to sense our surroundings and to react to it. Receptors gather information about the external and internal environment and then pass this information into the central nervous system for processing. The CNS decides on a response, which is then put into action via our muscles and glands.

LEARNING OBJECTIVES

In this chapter we take a brief look at the structure of the central nervous system before looking in detail at an individual nerve cell, known as a neurone. We look at the way in which nerve impulses are transmitted along a neurone, and finally we look at synapses, which are the junctions between neurones that allow us to select certain pathways.

(Specification 3.6.2.1, 3.6.2.2)

Brain tissue is the most complex material in the known universe. With a volume of about 1300 cm^3, the human brain consists of around 100 billion neurones, along with many glial cells that nourish and protect them. Each neurone has thousands of synapses with other neurones, and the number of different routes that nerve impulses can take through the brain is impossible to calculate.

Thinking about thinking is always a challenge. Your thoughts are neural pathways through the brain. If someone asks you "What is the capital city of France?" synapses will select a pathway that leads you (hopefully) to the answer of Paris, because at some time in the past it was stored away as a memory.

What makes us unique individuals is the sum total of our memories and experiences. A big tragedy is that as they grow older, many people can be robbed of their mental abilities, despite having an otherwise healthy body.

The word *dementia* describes a set of symptoms that may include memory loss and difficulties with language, thinking or problem-solving. Dementia is caused when the brain is damaged by diseases such as Alzheimer's disease, or by a stroke. Dementia is progressive, meaning that the symptoms will gradually get worse. It is estimated that there will be one million people with dementia in the UK by 2025.

The underlying cause of Alzheimer's is a combination of tangled protein filaments (neurofibrillary tangles) within nerve cells, and the build-up of beta-amyloid protein that forms plaques around cells. There is currently no cure for Alzheimer's but there are several very promising lines of research.

Look at Figure 1. It shows a computer-processed vertical slice through the brain of an Alzheimer's disease patient (left) compared with a normal brain (right). The Alzheimer's brain is considerably shrunken, due to the degeneration and death of nerve cells. As well as having a decrease in brain volume, the surface of the Alzheimer's brain is often more deeply folded.

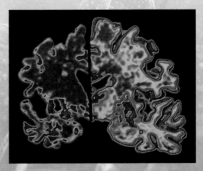

Figure 1 *Computer-processed vertical slice through the brain of an Alzheimer's disease patient (left) compared with a normal brain (right).*

6.1 OVERVIEW OF THE CENTRAL NERVOUS SYSTEM

Here is a reminder of some basic terms:

> A **neurone** is a nerve cell, which is specialised to carry impulses along elongated threads of cytoplasm.

> **Sensory neurones** carry impulses from a receptor into the central nervous system.

> **Motor neurones** carry impulses from the central nervous system to an effector.

> **Effectors** are muscles and glands; tissues that produce a response.

> **Synapses** are junctions between neurones.

The nervous system comprises two regions: the **central nervous system** and the **peripheral nervous system**. The central nervous system consists of the brain and the spinal cord (see Figure 2). The peripheral nervous system consists of nerves – the sensory and motor nerves – which are made up of neurones that carry information to and from the central nervous system.

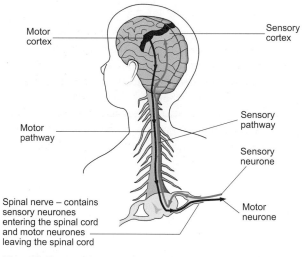

Figure 2 *The central nervous system. Note: you do not need to remember the detail of this illustration for the examination.*

General features of nerve cells

Overall, there are four basic types of tissue in the animal body: nerve, muscle, epithelia and connective. Of these, nerve and muscle are known as **excitable tissues**. We look at nervous tissue in this chapter and muscle in the next chapter.

There is a wide variety of neurones, but all have the following basic features:

> A **cell body** that contains the nucleus and other organelles, such as mitochondria.

> One or more threads of cytoplasm (or 'processes') leading towards the cell body. These are **dendrites**.

> One or more threads of cytoplasm leading away from the cell body. These are **axons**.

Individual neurones can be incredibly long. In humans the longest ones pass from the ends of the toes, up the legs into the spinal cord. In larger animals, such as whales, they can be many metres long.

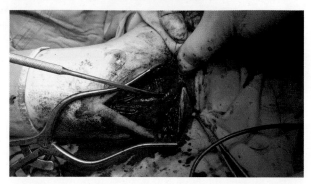

Figure 3 *Surgery on the ulnar nerve. When you bump your elbow, this nerve sometimes gets momentarily trapped between skin and bone and causes a feeling a bit like an electric shock; sometimes we say you "bumped your funny bone".*

The motor neurone

Motor neurones show typical features of neurones. Figure 4 shows the structure of a motor neurone that carries a nerve impulse from the spinal cord to a muscle. If the nerve supply to a muscle is damaged, that muscle will be paralysed.

A neurone consists of a cell body, containing the nucleus of the cell, with one or more long thin structures called processes. These processes are extensions of the cytoplasm, surrounded by a cell-surface (plasma) membrane. The processes that conduct nerve impulses towards the cell body are called **dendrons**, while those that conduct impulses away from the cell body are called axons.

Dendrons have very fine processes called **dendrites**. The dendrites on the cell body of the motor neurone receive impulses from other neurones in the spinal cord. The motor neurone in Figure 4 has one long axon which carries nerve impulses to a muscle.

You will notice that the motor neurone has an insulating cover over the axon, called a **myelin sheath**. This sheath is formed by **Schwann cells**, which twist around the axon several times as they grow, as shown in Figure 5. Most of the myelin sheath is composed of the cell-surface (plasma) membranes of Schwann cells. The junctions between adjacent Schwann cells are called **nodes of Ranvier**.

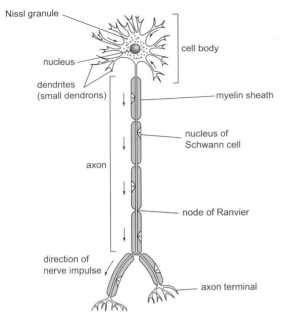

Figure 4 *The motor neurone*

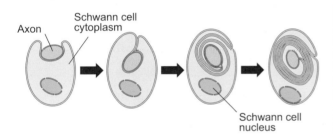

Figure 5 *Schwann cell growing round an axon*

Figure 6 *False-colour transmission electron micrograph of part of the myelin sheath (orange and green layers) of the human auditory nerve.*

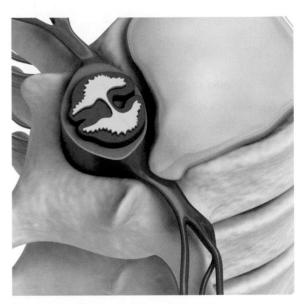

Figure 7 *A slipped disc. The intervertebral cartilage can rupture and put pressure on spinal nerves, causing pain and interfering with nerve function.*

QUESTIONS

1. The myelin sheath is made up mainly of the cell-surface (plasma) membranes of Schwann cells. These cell-surface (plasma) membranes contain phospholipid molecules that contain fatty acids. These fatty acids prevent the movement of charged water-soluble ions. There are several layers of membranes in the sheath. Suggest the function of the sheath.

Nerves

Nerves are bundles of nerve fibres, as shown in Figure 8.

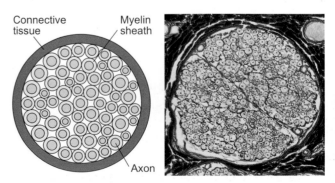

Figure 8 *Left: Cross-section through a nerve. Right: Light micrograph of a cross-section through the human sciatic nerve, showing myelinated nerve fibres of different sizes (yellow circles). The nerve is surrounded by loose connective tissue (dark brown).*

Spinal nerves are mixed nerves, they contain both sensory and motor nerve fibres. Myelin sheaths insulate the plasma membranes of the fibres from tissue fluid. This enables myelinated fibres to transmit impulses much faster than non-myelinated fibres. The outside of a nerve is made up of connective tissue – a tissue adapted for binding structures together.

QUESTIONS

2. **a.** What is the difference between a nerve and a neurone?

    b. Which type of neurone in a spinal nerve is damaged when:

    i. a person cannot feel a pin prick on the leg?

    ii. a person cannot move a leg?

ASSIGNMENT 1: MYELINATED AND NON-MYELINATED NERVES

(MS 0.2)

The graph in Figure A1 shows the relationship between nerve impulse conduction speed and axon diameter in myelinated and non-myelinated nerve fibres.

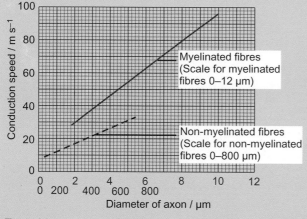

Myelinated fibres (Scale for myelinated fibres 0–12 μm)

Non-myelinated fibres (Scale for non-myelinated fibres 0–800 μm)

Figure A1

Questions

A1. Give three trends shown by the graph.

A2. What is the maximum conduction speed of a non-myelinated nerve fibre?

A3. Calculate the percentage increase in conduction speed when the diameter of a non-myelinated fibre increases from 200 μm to 400 μm.

A4. How much faster is the myelinated fibre conducting at maximum speed than the non-myelinated fibre transmitting at maximum speed?

A5. Vertebrate animals possess myelinated fibres in many parts of the nervous system, but invertebrates do not have myelinated nerve fibres. Suggest two advantages to vertebrates of having myelinated nerve fibres, in addition to conduction speed.

KEY IDEAS

> A nerve cell is called a neurone.

> All neurones have the same basic structure:

> a cell body containing the nucleus

> dendrons that carry impulses towards the cell body

> an axon that carries impulses away from the cell body.

> Many neurones have a myelin sheath, made up of Schwann cells, which acts as an insulator of the nerve fibres.

> The junctions between neurones are called synapses; transmission across synapses is by movement of chemical substances.

> A nerve is a collection of nerve fibres (the axons of the neurones).

ASSIGNMENT 2: CAN WE REVERSE PARALYSIS?

Roger Fenn fell and broke his neck. The accident damaged his spinal cord above the point where spinal nerves branch off to the arms. Nerve tissue, unlike bone, cannot repair itself easily, so Roger's arms and legs are permanently paralysed. Fortunately, he can still move the muscles in his shoulders normally and this has given him the chance to be much less dependent on the help of others.

Electronics and biology came together and, using a thorough understanding of the structure of the nervous system, designers came up with an electronic grip system, shown in Figure A1. The electronics mimic the natural impulses that pass along nerve cells to operate the muscles. Roger had an operation to implant the system in his right arm.

After 14 years of living without the use of his hands, Roger now uses his shoulder muscles to operate his lower arms and hands and he can feed himself, clean his teeth, comb his hair, and let himself in and out of the house with an ordinary door key.

Questions

A1. In what form is the electric current carried along the wires in the electronic grip system?

A2. What structure in the nervous system does the joystick mimic?

A3. What type of neurone has the same function as the wires that take electronic signals to Roger's muscles?

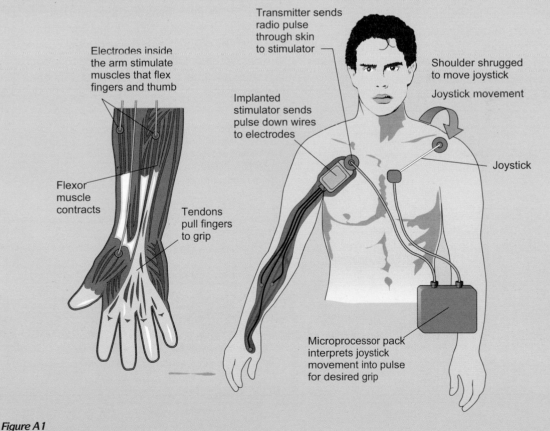

Electrodes inside the arm stimulate muscles that flex fingers and thumb

Flexor muscle contracts

Tendons pull fingers to grip

Transmitter sends radio pulse through skin to stimulator

Implanted stimulator sends pulse down wires to electrodes

Shoulder shrugged to move joystick

Joystick movement

Joystick

Microprocessor pack interprets joystick movement into pulse for desired grip

Figure A1

6.2 THE NERVE IMPULSE

In this section we will will look at at how nerve impulses are transmitted down the axon of a neurone. But first we need to find out what is happening inside a nerve cell at rest, when no impulse is being transmitted.

The resting potential

The resting potential is a voltage (potential difference) across the axon membrane, and this keeps the neurone in a state of readiness. The potential difference is due to an unequal distribution of charge on either side of a cell-surface (plasma) membrane. Fluid on the inside of the axon is negatively charged compared with the fluid that bathes the outside. This difference is caused by an unequal distribution of positive and negative ions.

Measuring potential differences

How can we study individual nerve cells when they are so small? Scientists first observed electrical activity in nerves over 200 years ago, but it is only in the last 50 years that the underlying mechanisms have been understood. During the 1950s, scientists developed micropipettes with points as narrow as 0.5 μm. (You would have to split a human hair at least a hundred times before it would fit into this pipette.) These can be used to insert microelectrodes into individual axons. Two electrodes – one in the neurone and one immersed in the fluid outside the axon – are needed to measure the potential difference (the voltage) between the outside and inside of an axon.

QUESTIONS

3. From your Year 1 studies, which are the commonest positive and negative ions in tissue fluid?

4. Non-myelinated fibres are usually used in experiments that investigate electrical activity in neurones. Suggest why.

Figure 9 shows how electrodes can be used to investigate electrical activity in a giant squid axon. When both electrodes are positioned in the bathing fluid there is no potential difference between them. When the micropipette is inserted into the axon there is a potential difference of −70 mV between the inside of the axon and the outside. This difference in potential is called the resting potential.

Positively charged ions such as sodium (Na^+) are called cations because they move towards a negative electrode called a cathode. Negatively charged ions such as chloride (Cl^-) are called anions because they move towards an anode. The resting potential is caused by the movement of cations through the cell membrane of the axon. Since the inside of the axon is negatively charged with respect to the outside, the net movement of cations required to produce a resting potential must be *outwards* through the cell membrane.

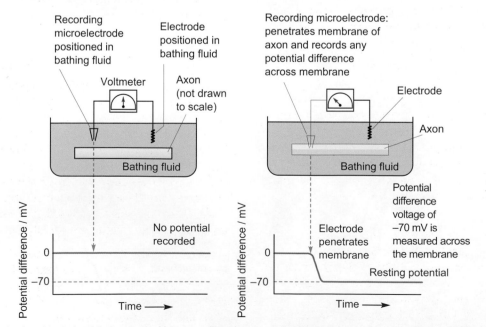

Figure 9 *Investigating electrical activity in an axon. Note: you will not be expected to know and recall this method in an examination.*

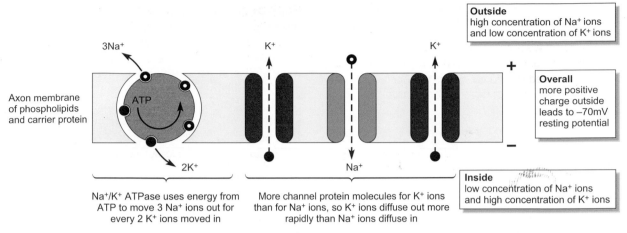

Outside
high concentration of Na⁺ ions
and low concentration of K⁺ ions

Overall
more positive
charge outside
leads to −70mV
resting potential

Inside
low concentration of Na⁺ ions
and high concentration of K⁺ ions

Na⁺/K⁺ ATPase uses energy from
ATP to move 3 Na⁺ ions out for
every 2 K⁺ ions moved in

More channel protein molecules for K⁺ ions
than for Na⁺ ions, so K⁺ ions diffuse out more
rapidly than Na⁺ ions diffuse in

Figure 10 *Producing the resting potential*

How is the resting potential produced?

Figure 10 shows that two mechanisms are involved in setting up the resting potential:

› active transport by Na⁺/K⁺ carrier proteins (called pumps)

› unequal facilitated diffusion.

Active transport in the axon membrane involves a carrier protein known as the **Na⁺/K⁺ ATPase pump.** It uses the energy obtained from the splitting of ATP to pump positive ions either into or out of the axon, against their concentration gradients. More precisely, three Na⁺ ions are pumped out, while two K⁺ ions are pumped in. Every square micrometre of the axon membrane contains up to 200 of these pumps. Each one moves about 200 Na⁺ ions out of the axon and about 130 K⁺ ions into the axon, every second.

The facilitated diffusion occurs through **gated channel proteins**, which can alter their shape and therefore their permeability. The axon membrane contains both Na⁺ and K⁺ channels, allowing Na⁺ to diffuse in and K⁺ to diffuse out. However, in the resting state, the Na⁺ channels are less permeable than the K⁺ channels, so that K⁺ ions diffuse out faster the Na⁺ ions diffuses in. Often the channels are just described as open or closed, though there is a range of permeability from fully open to fully closed.

So, overall, both processes result in cations accumulating outside the axon. This unequal distribution of ions results in the resting potential having a value of about −70 mV. Contributing to the overall ionic situation are the negatively charged chloride ions and charged proteins retained inside the cell. The axon uses ATP to maintain this electrochemical gradient across its membrane. If respiration stops, so will the active transport; the gradient will be lost and the axon will be unable to transmit an impulse.

QUESTIONS

5. Why do the Na⁺ ions and K⁺ ions move in opposite directions through the channel proteins?

6. Dinitrophenol (DNP) is a metabolic poison that inhibits respiration. If DNP is added to the solution bathing an axon, the axon does not develop a resting potential. Explain why.

The action potential

The terms 'nerve impulse' and 'action potential' are often used interchangeably, but there is subtle difference. An action potential is a change in the membrane potential, while a nerve impulse is a self-propagating action potential that moves along a neuron membrane. When a neurone is stimulated, information passes down the length of its axon. It is not an electrical current, it is a reversal of the resting potential – often described as a **wave of depolarisation** – that moves rapidly along the axon.

An action potential is initiated with one simple action: the sodium channels open. As a result, Na⁺ ions diffuse rapidly into the axon through the channels (by facilitated diffusion), reversing the resting potential. This is known as **depolarisation**.

107

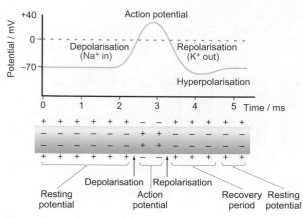

Figure 11 *An action potential*

An action potential will only be generated if the stimulus is greater than a certain intensity – known as the **threshold**. If a stimulus exceeds the threshold level, the sodium ion channels in the axon membrane open fully. If the stimulus is below the threshold level, they remain closed and no depolarisation occurs.

Depolarisation of the membrane takes about a millisecond, but it can be studied by attaching microelectrodes to an axon and connecting the microelectrodes to a cathode ray oscilloscope (CRO) (Figure 12). The CRO can show electrical changes as a trace on a screen. It can show these changes in real time, and it can also freeze a moment in time, which is very useful when studying events that take milliseconds. These events are faster than we can imagine, because they are the processes *by which* we imagine. 'Thinking about thinking' really is a challenge.

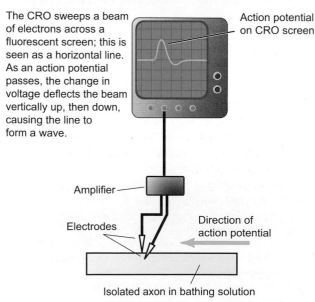

The CRO sweeps a beam of electrons across a fluorescent screen; this is seen as a horizontal line. As an action potential passes, the change in voltage deflects the beam vertically up, then down, causing the line to form a wave.

Action potential on CRO screen

Amplifier

Electrodes

Direction of action potential

Isolated axon in bathing solution

Figure 12 *Observing an action potential*

Repolarisation

After the membrane has been depolarised, it recovers. Depolarisation only occurs in a short part of the axon, which then recovers its resting potential while the action potential moves on down the axon. The membrane recovers its negative resting potential because of the gated potassium channels. Shortly after the gated sodium channels in the axon opened to let Na$^+$ ions in and depolarise the membrane, the gated potassium channels also open fully (Figure 13).

Because there is a greater concentration of K$^+$ ions inside the membrane than outside, they move down their concentration gradient to the outside, through the gated channels, by facilitated diffusion. This movement of K$^+$ ions results in the net positive charge outside the membrane being restored, once again producing a resting potential. Restoration of the resting potential is called **repolarisation**. The overshoot following repolarisation is called hyperpolarisation and results from the fact that the potassium ion diffusion out of the axon continues, due to the increased permeability of the potassium channels, until the resting potential equilibrium is established again. For a short period after repolarisation, both the gated channels for sodium ions and the gated channels for potassium ions remain closed. During this period the membrane cannot be depolarised and therefore no impulse can pass. This period is known as the **refractory period**.

The refractory period has two parts:

1 **The absolute refractory period**, during which it is impossible to generate another action potential

2 **The relative refractory period**, during which time it is possible to generate another action potential, but the stimulus must be of greater intensity than normal.

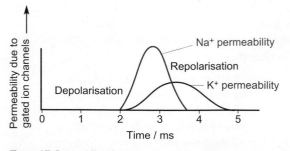

Figure 13 *Permeability of membrane to sodium ions and potassium ions*

The refractory period is important for the following reasons:

> Each action potential is kept discrete – there is no overlapping of potentials.

> It ensures that the action potentials travel in only one direction.

The all-or-nothing principle

It is tempting to think that the greater the stimulus, the greater the size of the action potential, but this is not the case. All action potentials are the same size – this is known as the **all-or-nothing principle**. Looking at Figure 14, all impulses are of the same amplitude (the 'height' of the spike). We can tell the difference between stimuli of different intensity because the *frequency* of impulses varies. A more intense stimulus results in a greater frequency: more impulses per second. Looking at the trace, the height of the spikes remain the same, but the interval between them gets smaller. The refractory period puts a limit on the frequency of impulses that can be generated, and once that limit has been reached, a stronger stimulus will not increase the frequency any further.

QUESTIONS

Figure 14 shows changes in potential across an axon membrane during and after an action potential.

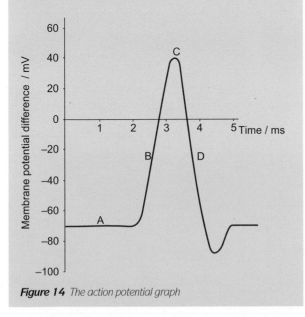

Figure 14 *The action potential graph*

7. Which section of the graph labelled A to D shows:
   a. repolarisation?
   b. action potential?
   c. resting potential?
   d. depolarisation?

8. By how much did the potential difference change when the action potential was produced?

9. How long is the refractory period?

Worked maths example

(MS 0.2)

1. What is the maximum frequency of impulses that can be transmitted down the neurone represented by the graph in Figure 14?
   > The frequency is measured in impulses per second.
   > From the graph we can see that it takes three milliseconds to fully re-establish the resting potential, so the maximum possible frequency is one impulse every three milliseconds.
   > As there are 1000 milliseconds in a second, the maximum frequency is $\frac{1000}{3}$ which is 333 s^{-1}

2. Impulses travel along myelinated neurones at a speed of 100 m s^{-1}. How long will it take the impulse to travel 10 mm?
   > 100 metres per second is fast. It is the length of one football pitch in one second, or ten times faster than the fastest sprinter. It is just over 220 miles per hour.
   > With calculations like this it is important to get the units in the same order of magnitude. Here we have metres and millimetres. A millimetre is 10^{-3} m, or one thousandth of a metre.
   > So a speed of 100 metres per second is 100 000 mm per second,
   > So to travel 10 mm takes $\frac{10}{100\,000}$ of a second, which is 0.0001 second. This would be better expressed in milliseconds, which makes the answer 0.1 ms.

Transmission of impulses along nerve fibres

In non-myelinated fibres, the impulse is transmitted along the fibre when each short length of the membrane causes the next segment to depolarise. Transmission is relatively slow since the whole membrane must be depolarised in successive sections.

Depolarisation in myelinated fibres occurs only at the nodes of Ranvier, since the sheath cells are pressed tightly against the axon (Figure 15). In these myelinated nerve fibres, the impulse 'jumps' from one node of Ranvier to the next, resulting in very rapid conduction. This is known as **saltatory conduction** ('saltere' means jump).

The myelin sheath is an adaptation that gives rapid transmission of nerve impulses. Non-myelinated fibres are not adapted in this way and therefore transmit impulses much more slowly.

Overall, the speed of transmission of impulses from one region of the body to another depends on three factors:

1. whether the nerves are myelinated or not
2. the distance involved (greater distance = slower transmission)
3. the number of synapses involved – synapses slow down the transmission of impulses.

Non-myelinated axon

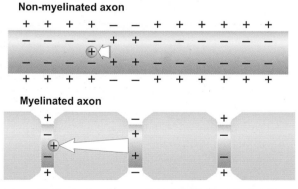

Myelinated axon

Figure 15 *Conduction along myelinated and non-myelinated fibres*

Transmission speed is also influenced by the diameter of the axon. The wider the axon, the greater the speed of conduction. Squid do not have myelinated fibres, but these animals have evolved fibres with giant axons, up to 1 mm in diameter, which conduct impulses very rapidly.

In invertebrates transmission speed is affected by temperature – the higher the temperature, the greater the transmission speed. Mammalian nerve fibres are at body temperature, so these fibres do not normally experience changes in temperature.

QUESTIONS

10. Suggest why increasing temperature increases the rate of conduction in invertebrate nerve fibres.

KEY IDEAS

> - A resting potential makes a neurone ready to transmit a nerve impulse.
> - The resting potential is produced by a combination of two processes: active transport and unequal facilitated diffusion.
> - The active transport is carried out by the $Na+/K+$ ATPase pump, a carrier protein in the axon membrane. As sodium ions are pumped out of the cell, potassium ions are pumped in, but at a slower rate.
> - The unequal facilitated diffusion results because, in the resting state, the gated potassium channels are more permeable than the gated sodium channels.
> - Together, these two processes result in more positive ions outside the axon. This electrochemical gradient is the resting potential.
> - An action potential, or nerve impulse, occurs when closed sodium channels in the membrane suddenly open. The concentration of sodium ions is higher outside than inside the axon, therefore sodium ions move into the cell by facilitated diffusion. This causes depolarisation – a reversal of the resting potential.
> - After depolarisation, the membrane is repolarised by the outflow of potassium ions through the potassium channels. The resting potential is then restored by the sodium/potassium (Na^+/K^+) pump.
> - While the membrane is being repolarised, the membrane cannot be depolarised again, so no new action potential can form. The period when this happens is called the refractory period.

> ❭ Conduction along myelinated fibres is very rapid since the impulse 'jumps' from one node of Ranvier to the next. This is known as saltatory conduction.
>
> ❭ Conduction speeds are increased by increased diameter of axons and by increased temperature.

6.3 SYNAPSES

The junction where two neurones meet is called a synapse. In all but the most powerful electron micrographs, neurones appear to be actually touching, but there is in fact a very narrow gap between them called the **synaptic cleft**. Information is carried across the synaptic cleft by chemicals called **neurotransmitters**. Many drugs exert their effects by interfering with this chemical transmission; it is by studying the effects of drugs on synapses that we have obtained much of our understanding of how synapses work.

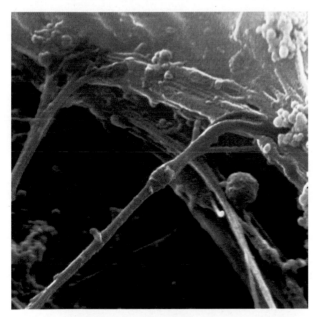

Figure 16 *False-colour SEM of the junction sites (synapses) between nerve fibres (purple) and a neurone cell body (yellow).*

The scanning electron micrograph (SEM) in Figure 16 shows several nerve fibres forming synapses with a cell body. A neurone may have synapses that connect with up to 10 000 other neurones. That's a lot.

Transmission of an impulse across a synapse

An action potential passing along an axon will come to one or more synapses. Figure 17 shows the main stages in the transmission of impulses across the junction between two neurones.

> ❭ An action potential arrives at the synapse. The presynaptic part consists of a swelling called the synaptic bulb or knob, which contains vesicles of neurotransmitter e.g. acetylcholine.

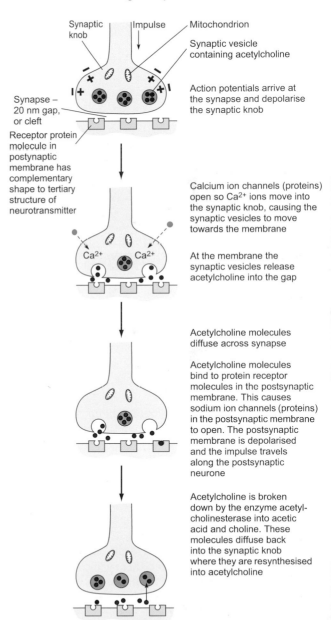

Figure 17 *Transmission of an impulse across a synapse*

> ❭ An action potential arriving at the synaptic knob causes calcium ion channels in the membrane to

open, resulting in an influx of calcium ions. The calcium ions bind to the synaptic vesicles, causing them to move to the membrane and release the neurotransmitter substance into the synaptic cleft. This is an example of exocytosis.

> The neurotransmitter diffuses across the synaptic cleft to the postsynaptic membrane.

> The neurotransmitter molecules bind to specific protein receptor molecules in the postsynaptic membrane.

> This causes the postsynaptic membrane to become more permeable to sodium ions, which diffuse in.

> This causes depolarisation of the postsynaptic membrane.

> If the depolarisation reaches a threshold, an action potential is generated in the postsynaptic neurone.

> There is a delay of about half a millisecond at a synapse. This is the time needed for the neurotransmitter to diffuse across the gap, bind to a receptor protein and lead to the increase in the postsynaptic potential.

The neurotransmitter is removed quickly from the synaptic cleft; otherwise the neurone would keep on firing uncontrollably. A very fast-acting enzyme called **acetylcholinesterase** breaks down acetylcholine into acetic acid and choline. These substances are reabsorbed through proteins in the presynaptic membrane. ATP from mitochondria is used to provide the energy to resynthesise acetylcholine, which is then returned to the vesicles.

The significance of synapses

It is impossible to overestimate the importance of synapses. Acting as junctions between neurones, they allow the selection of different pathways, leading to different sensory experiences, thoughts and actions.

The description of how impulses are transmitted across synapses might seem to indicate that an action potential arriving at a synapse automatically generates an impulse in all connecting neurones, but this cannot be the case – the result would be chaos. A synapse can be either **excitatory** (increasing the activity of the next cell) or **inhibitory** (decreasing the activity of the next cell), which enables synapses to either pass information on, or to block information. Thinking about it, synapses must inhibit far more than they stimulate.

Synapses can become **fatigued**. This happens when so many action potentials arrive at a synaptic knob

in so short a time period that the cell runs out of neurotransmitter and cannot resynthesise it fast enough. The impulse can no longer cross the synapse. This loss of response at a synapse is known as **adaptation** and a consequence is that animals ignore stimuli that go on for a long time. For example, once we are used to stimuli such as the tick of a clock or the feel of our clothes brushing against our skin, we do not notice them. Such stimuli are irrelevant to our survival. Sudden changes in our environment, such as the unexpected approach of a car in a quiet lane, are more important.

Synaptic transmission may lead to action potentials/nerve impulses in just one other neurone, or transmission may spread the action potential out to several neurones. Synapses also occur at the junctions between nerves and muscle fibres, where they are called **neuromuscular junctions**.

Different types of neurotransmitter

More than 40 different neurotransmitters have now been identified. One of the most common in voluntary nerves is **acetylcholine**. Synapses that have acetylcholine as their neurotransmitter are called **cholinergic synapses**. The synapses of the sympathetic nervous system secrete noradrenaline and are known as adrenergic. There are many different transmitter substances in the brain, including serotonin, melatonin and dopamine.

QUESTIONS

11. Use information from Figure 17 to explain why transmission across a synapse is unidirectional.

12. Eserine is a drug that is used after eye surgery. It helps to prevent swelling of the eye caused by fluid accumulation. Muscle contractions help to remove excess fluid from the eye. Eserine works by inhibiting acetylcholinesterase. What is the effect of eserine at a cholinergic synapse?

Summation

Sometimes, the amount of neurotransmitter resulting from one impulse in the presynaptic neurone is not sufficient to reach the threshold in the postsynaptic membrane, so an impulse is not generated. Several action potentials might be needed to produce enough neurotransmitter to reach the threshold. This can

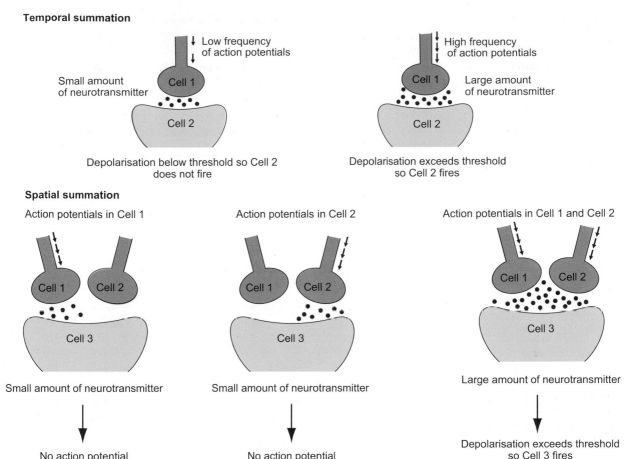

Temporal summation

↓ Low frequency of action potentials

Small amount of neurotransmitter

Cell 1

Cell 2

Depolarisation below threshold so Cell 2 does not fire

↓↓ High frequency of action potentials

Cell 1

Large amount of neurotransmitter

Cell 2

Depolarisation exceeds threshold so Cell 2 fires

Spatial summation

Action potentials in Cell 1

Cell 1   Cell 2

Cell 3

Small amount of neurotransmitter

↓

No action potential

Action potentials in Cell 2

Cell 1   Cell 2

Cell 3

Small amount of neurotransmitter

↓

No action potential

Action potentials in Cell 1 and Cell 2

Cell 1   Cell 2

Cell 3

Large amount of neurotransmitter

↓

Depolarisation exceeds threshold so Cell 3 fires

Figure 18 *Temporal and spatial summation*

be achieved in two ways: temporal summation and spatial summation. Think of it as separated in time or separated in space. Temporal and spatial summation are shown in Figure 18.

In temporal summation, several action potentials arrive at the postsynaptic membrane in rapid succession. As a result, neurotransmitter accumulates and depolarises the post synaptic membrane enough to reach the threshold.

In spatial summation, neurotransmitter released by *different* presynaptic neurones arrives at the postsynaptic membrane at the same time. Spatial summation occurs in the retina of the eye. In dim light an individual receptor cell might not produce sufficient transmitter substance to depolarise a sensory neurone, but several receptors will produce enough, thus enabling us to see, even in low light conditions.

Summation is important for the brain to work properly. For example, it might be better to ignore a weak stimulus, such as mild pressure on the skin, but a stronger stimulus might cause injury and so require

a response. A strong stimulus sends a high frequency of nerve impulses to the brain.

Synapses that use noradrenaline

Synapses that use noradrenaline affect heart rate, breathing rate and brain activity. This is similar to the effect of the hormone adrenaline, which prepares the body for emergencies.

In Chapter 5 you learned that noradrenaline speeds up the rate of heartbeat when it is released by nerve fibres. In some people, the release of too much noradrenaline causes the heart to race. One way to treat this is to use drugs known as beta-blockers. These drugs have molecular shapes similar to noradrenaline.

QUESTIONS

13. Which part of the heart is directly affected by the release of noradrenaline?

14. Suggest how beta-blockers work.

The neuromuscular junction

The neuromuscular junction (Figure 19) is a synapse that forms the junction between a motor neurone and a muscle fibre. Exactly the same sequence of events happens at this synapse as when two neurones connect, but in this case the postsynaptic membrane is the muscle fibre membrane, which is called the sarcolemma. This muscle fibre membrane is depolarised when acetylcholine released from the presynaptic membrane of the neurone diffuses across the synapse and binds to protein receptors. Depolarisation sets in motion a sequence of events that lead to contraction of the muscle fibre. These events are described in Chapter 7.

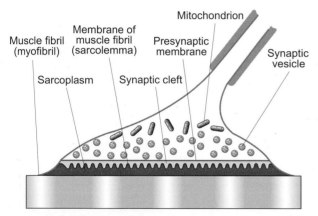

Figure 19 *A neuromuscular junction*

> ▸ Na$^+$ ions diffuse into the postsynaptic membrane, causing depolarisation.
>
> ▸ If the depolarisation reaches a threshold, an action potential is generated in the postsynaptic neurone.
>
> ▸ Acetylcholine is a common transmitter substance but there are many others.
>
> ▸ Neuromuscular junctions are modified synapses that join motor nerves to muscles. The wave of depolarisation in the muscle fibril leads to an influx of calcium ions, and muscle contraction.

6.4 DRUGS AND SYNAPSES

Neurotransmitters are released in tiny amounts: only 500–1000 molecules from each synapse are required to trigger an action potential in the postsynaptic neurone. So, drugs that affect neurotransmitters or their binding sites can have powerful effects, even when given in fairly small doses. Some chemicals, many of them from plants, have a dramatic effect on the nervous system.

The effect of nicotine

A nicotine molecule is a similar shape to acetylcholine, so it can bind with acetylcholine receptors and cause sodium ion channels to open, as shown in Figure 20.

Nicotine receptors are found throughout the nervous system and there are at least five different types. Some of these are more sensitive to nicotine than others. Some activate quickly, and then turn off. Others stay active as long as nicotine is present. Nicotine is a major component of tobacco and is the main reason for smokers becoming addicted to their habit. Once the nervous system gets used to nicotine, going without it creates unpleasant symptoms such as depression and anxiety. The average smoker inhales smoke from about 20 cigarettes per day, which averages at about 200 puffs per day or 80 000 puffs per year. This delivers a constant supply of nicotine to the nervous system – a smoker has to puff on a cigarette every five minutes during waking hours to maintain nicotine concentrations that will keep the nicotine receptors active.

There is a powerful correlation rate between smoking and depression. Do people take up smoking to relieve an underlying depression or anxiety?

KEY IDEAS

> ▸ There is a sequence of events at cholinergic synapses and neuromuscular junctions that uses chemical neurotransmitters to transmit an action potential across the synaptic cleft to the postsynaptic neurone or muscle fibril.
>
> ▸ Action potential arrives at the presynaptic membrane.
>
> ▸ Ca^{2+} channels open and Ca^{2+} ions enter the presynaptic membrane.
>
> ▸ Vesicles containing acetylcholine move towards the presynaptic membrane.
>
> ▸ Vesicles fuse with the membrane.
>
> ▸ Acetylcholine is released from the synaptic vesicles into the synaptic cleft.
>
> ▸ Acetylcholine diffuses across the synaptic cleft to the postsynaptic membrane.
>
> ▸ Acetylcholine binds with specific receptor proteins of the postsynaptic membrane.

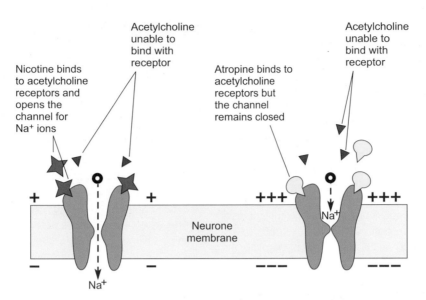

Figure 20 *The contrasting effects of nicotine and atropine on a synapse*

The effect of atropine

The following examples are being used to illustrate ideas. Atropine is a drug that also binds to acetylcholine receptors, but in contrast with nicotine, atropine does not open the sodium channels. It blocks the receptors, and prevents acetylcholine from binding to them, as shown in Figure 20. When this happens in motor neurones, it causes muscle paralysis.

Atropine is extracted from the deadly nightshade plant, *Atropa belladonna* (Figure 21). When atropine eye drops are used, the pupils dilate, giving women what was thought to be a more alluring look. Although now out of favour, using atropine drops in the eyes was once a widespread practice, from as far back as the Renaissance through to the early years of Hollywood films.

The effects of nicotine and of atropine on synapses are shown in Figure 20, but you will not be required to give specific examples.

Figure 21 *The deadly nightshade plant* (Atropa belladonna) *is very poisonous. It contains the alkaloids atropine, solanine and hyoscyamine. 'Atropa' comes from the name of the Greek Fate, Atropa, who severs the strand of life; 'belladonna' means 'beautiful woman' in Italian, referring to the effect on the eyes.*

QUESTIONS

15. **a.** A caffeine molecule has a similar shape to a molecule of an inhibitory brain transmitter called adenosine. How does caffeine increase alertness?
    b. How could someone become addicted to caffeine?

KEY IDEAS

- Drugs that have shapes similar to neurotransmitter substances can affect protein receptors in postsynaptic membranes.
- Some drugs bind to postsynaptic receptors, causing gated ion channels to remain open.
- Some drugs bind to postsynaptic receptors, causing gated ion channels to remain closed.
- Some drugs act on the presynaptic neurone, for example, by preventing calcium ion influx.
- Some drugs inhibit the action of acetylcholinesterase.
- Some drugs inhibit reabsorption of the neurotransmitter substance from the synapse.

ASSIGNMENT 3: MORE THAN YOU THINK

In the introduction to his book, *The Astonishing Hypothesis*, Francis Crick writes:

"The Astonishing Hypothesis is that 'You', your joys and your sorrows, your memories and your ambitions, your sense of personal identity and free will, are in fact no more than the behaviour of a vast assembly of nerve cells. One of the most difficult aspects of the nervous system to explain is: how can ion movements in neurones give us consciousness and self-awareness? Yet we accept that certain other complex structures have qualities that we would not predict by looking at their component parts. For example, the components of a motorcar do very little until they are fitted together – but then the whole assembly can be driven down the motorway at 70 mph."

Conditioning

The pets sharing our homes are quick to learn where food can be found. The sound of a tin being opened brings a cat or dog into the kitchen very quickly, because the animal has learned to associate the sound of the tin opener with food. This type of learning is called conditioning. There are two types of conditioning: classical conditioning and operant conditioning.

Classical conditioning

Conditioning interested the physiologist Pavlov, who worked in Russia at the end of the 19th century. Pavlov wanted to test the effects of different types of food on the salivation reflex. He collected and measured the amount of saliva produced by the dogs when food was placed in their mouths. However, he also noticed that his dogs started to salivate as soon as they heard his approaching footsteps, before he had given them any food. Pavlov then found that by giving the dogs a reward of food, he could train them to salivate in response to a stimulus such as a flashing light or a ringing bell. Pavlov called this type of learning, in which the usual stimulus (food) is replaced by a new stimulus (light or a bell), a conditioned reflex. This was the first type of conditioning to be described, and so it is now known as classical conditioning.

Operant conditioning

Pavlov's work encouraged others to study the way that animals learn. Skinner developed a special apparatus (the Skinner box) for training an animal, usually a rat. By pressing a lever in the box, the rat gains a reward of a food pellet. At first, the rat presses the lever just by accident, but it soon learns to associate lever pressing with a reward. This is called operant conditioning, because the animal is *rewarded* for an operation (movement) that it does naturally from time to time. The food reward makes it more likely that the rat will press the lever again; in other words the food is a positive reinforcement of the behaviour. All kinds of movement can be reinforced in operant conditioning. For example, if a pigeon is rewarded with food every time it preens its feathers, the rate of preening quickly increases. Reinforcers need not be food: monkeys learn for the reward of seeing another monkey, chickens for the reward of straw to nest in, and dogs for the reward of attention from their owner.

Animals can also be conditioned using punishment. A stern telling off works as a punishment and prevents a dog from jumping up to greet people, so long as the training is done consistently for a few months.

Conditioning is part of the natural lives of animals. For example, caterpillars of the mullein moth have a nasty taste and bright orange spots. The bad taste works as a punishment for any bird that attempts to eat the caterpillar, and the bird learns to associate the orange spots with a bad taste. This is an example of warning colouration.

Learned human behaviour

Learning plays a major part in our daily lives. For example, conditioning is used by advertisers. Some advertisements try to familiarise us with a particular sign or logo, so that we are more likely to select it from a range of similar logos. More commonly, advertisements try to make us associate their product with being attractive, successful or intelligent. We are encouraged to think that buying the product will give us these qualities. Parents also employ conditioning tactics; they often use money to reward children for good behaviour. They also use various forms of punishment. This is rather like operant conditioning in rats, although humans can often see the motives behind other people's behaviour and resist being 'conditioned'. Sociologists and psychologists study the effects of reward and punishment on human behaviour, for example, the effects of prison sentences as a deterrent against crime. While most people agree that too much punishment can make a child withdrawn and unresponsive, some think that too many rewards can encourage selfishness. Skilled parents and teachers are good at giving the right amount of control and encouragement to each child in a home or classroom.

Questions

A1. Use information from the extracts above, and your own ideas, to discuss the statement: "99% of our behaviour is automatic".

ASSIGNMENT 4: ILLEGAL DRUG USE

Cocaine is a class A drug. Possession of class A drugs can carry sentences of up to seven years in prison or an unlimited fine. Judges can sentence class A drug dealers to life in prison or give them an unlimited fine. The 'pleasure' that people get from taking cocaine is caused by the accumulation of a substance called dopamine in synapses in a 'reward' centre in the brain.

Figure A1 shows the normal way in which dopamine acts at a synapse in a reward centre in the brain.

The British Crime Survey (BCS) is a large national survey of adults who live in a representative cross-section of private households in England and Wales. In addition to asking respondents about their experiences of crime, the BCS also asks about a number of other crime-related topics. Since 1996, the BCS has included a comparable module of questions on illegal drug use. This examines the prevalence and trends of illegal drug use among 16–59 year-olds.

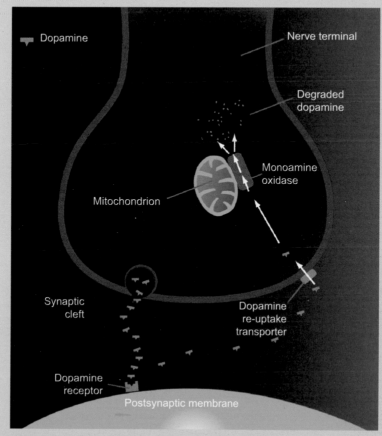

Figure A1 *A dopamine-activated synapse in the brain*

Table A1 shows trends in the use of drugs between 1998 and 2006/07.

Drug	16–24 year olds		16–59 year olds	
Proportion (%) of people in England and Wales reporting to having used drugs in the last year (British Crime Survey)				
	1998	2006/07	1998	2006/07
Cocaine	3.1	6.0	1.2	2.6↑
Crack	0.3	0.4	0.1	0.2
Ecstasy	5.1	4.8	1.5	1.8
LSD	3.2	0.7	0.8	0.2↓
Magic mushrooms	3.9	1.7	0.9	0.6
Heroin	0.3	0.2	0.1	0.1
Methadone	0.6	0.1	0.1	0.1
Amphetamines	9.9	3.5	3.0	1.3
Tranquillisers	1.5	0.6	0.7	0.4
Anabolic steroids	0.5	0.2	0.3	0.1
Cannabis	28.2	20.9↓	10.3	8.2
Ketamine*	n/a	0.8	n/a	0.3
Amyl nitrate**	5.1	4.2	1.5	−1.4
Glues**	1.3	0.6	0.2	0.2
Class A	8.6	8	2.7	3.4
Any drug	31.8	24.1↓	12.1	10.0↓

↑↓ Statistically significant change 1998 to 2006/07
* Only included in BCS since 2006/07
** Not an illegal drug

Table A1 *Trends in the use of drugs between 1998 and 2006*

Many criminologists and social workers complain that the BCS data is very inaccurate. Evidence for this is provided by a Home Office report. Instead of asking people what drugs they have used, an estimate of the number of opiate, crack, cocaine and injecting users was extrapolated from drug treatment, probation, police and prison data. The figures are over six times higher than those from the BCS covering the same period.

Questions

A1. Use information from Figure A1 to describe the cycling of dopamine at a synapse.

A2. Cocaine blocks the dopamine re-uptake transporter. Suggest how this will affect the working of the synapse.

A3. Explain what is meant by 'a statistically significant change'.

A4. Describe the most significant changes in drug use between 1998 and 2006/07.

A5. What conclusions can be drawn from the data about the relationship between illegal drug use and age?

A6. Explain what is meant by 'extrapolated' in this context.

A7. What are the main weaknesses in the method of sampling used by the BCS?

PRACTICE QUESTIONS

1. **a.** The graphs in Figure Q1 show the relationship between the membrane potential of an axon membrane and the numbers of Na⁺(sodium ion) channels and K⁺(potassium ion) channels that are open.

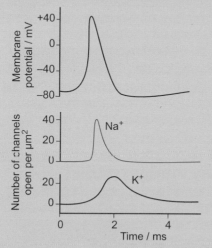

Figure Q1

Using the information in the graphs, explain how:

i. the action potential is generated

ii. the axon membrane is repolarised.

AQA January 2003 Unit 6 Question 8

2. Acetylcholine is a neurotransmitter that binds to postsynaptic membranes and stimulates the production of nerve impulses. GABA is another neurotransmitter. It is produced by certain neurones in the brain and spinal cord. GABA binds to postsynaptic membranes and inhibits the production of nerve impulses. Figure Q3 shows a synapse involving three neurones.

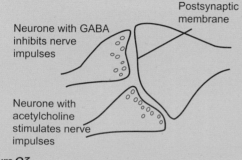

Neurone with GABA inhibits nerve impulses

Postsynaptic membrane

Neurone with acetylcholine stimulates nerve impulses

Figure Q3

a. Describe the sequence of events leading to the release of acetylcholine and the neurotransmitter binding to the postsynaptic membrane.

b. The binding of GABA to receptors on postsynaptic membranes causes negatively charged chloride ions to enter postsynaptic neurones. Explain how this will inhibit transmission of nerve impulses by postsynaptic neurones.

c. Epilepsy may result when there is increased neuronal activity in the brain.

i. One form of epilepsy is due to insufficient GABA. GABA is broken down on the postsynaptic membrane by the enzyme GABA transaminase. Vigabatrin is a new drug that is being used to treat this form of epilepsy. The drug has a similar molecular structure to GABA. Suggest how Vigabatrin may be effective in treating this form of epilepsy.

ii. A different form of epilepsy has been linked to an abnormality in GABA receptors. Suggest and explain how an abnormality in GABA receptors may result in epilepsy.

AQA June 2006 Unit 4 Question 9

3. **a.** The amount of light entering the eye is controlled by a reflex that involves the iris.

i. Where are the receptors for this reflex?

ii. Explain the role of the autonomic nervous system in the control of this reflex.

b. The human retina contains rods and cones. Describe the similarities and differences between the pigments in the rods and cones and the ways in which these pigments respond to light.

c. In dogs, 10–20% of the photoreceptors in the central region of the retina are cones. Two types of cone are present. The graph in Figure Q4 shows their absorption spectra.

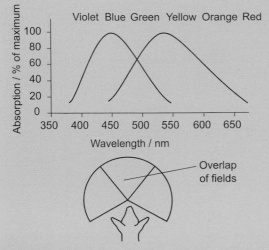

Figure Q4

A dog's eyes are on the sides of its head. This gives the dog a visual field of about 240 degrees, with an overlap of the fields from each eye of about 60 degrees.

i. Apart from the number of types of cone, give one way in which the retina of a dog differs from that of a human.

ii. Using the information given, suggest and explain how a dog's vision differs from human vision.

AQA January 2005 Unit 4 Question 9

4. a. Explain how a resting potential is maintained in a neurone.

b. In an investigation, an impulse was generated in a neurone using electrodes. During transmission along the neurone, an action potential was recorded at one point on the neurone. When the impulse reached the neuromuscular junction, it stimulated a muscle cell to contract. The force generated by the contraction was measured. The results are shown in the graph in Figure Q5.

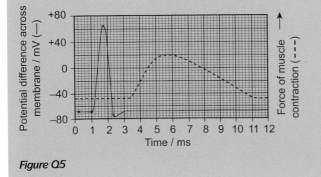

Figure Q5

The distance between the point on the neurone where the action potential was measured and the neuromuscular junction was exactly 18 mm.

i. Use the graph to estimate the time between the maximum depolarisation and the start of contraction by the muscle cell.

ii. Use your answer to part i. to calculate the speed of transmission along this neurone to the muscle cell. Give your answer in mm per second. Show your working.

iii. Give **one** reason why the value calculated in part ii. would be an underestimate of the speed of transmission of an impulse along a neurone.

Acetylcholine is the neurotransmitter at neuromuscular junctions.

c. Describe how the release of acetylcholine into a neuromuscular junction causes the cell membrane of a muscle fibre to depolarise.

d. Use your knowledge of the processes occurring at a neuromuscular junction to explain each of the following.

i. The cobra is a very poisonous snake. The molecular structure of cobra toxin is similar to the molecular structure of acetylcholine. The toxin permanently prevents muscle contraction.

ii. The insecticide DFP combines with the active site of the enzyme acetylcholinesterase. The muscles stay contracted until the insecticide is lost from the neuromuscular junction.

AQA January 2004 Unit 4 Question 7

5. a. Figure Q6 shows the changes in membrane potential at one point on an axon when an action potential is generated.

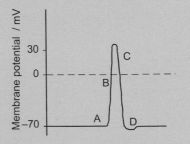

Figure Q6

The changes shown in Figure Q6 are due to the movement of ions across the axon membrane. Complete the table by giving the letter (A to D) that shows where each process is occurring most rapidly.

Process	Letter
Active transport of sodium and potassium ions	
Diffusion of sodium ions	
Diffusion of potassium ions	

b. Figure Q7 shows the relationship between axon diameter, myelination and the rate of conduction of the nerve impulse in a cat (a mammal) and a lizard (a reptile).

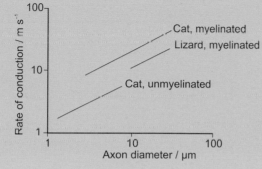

Figure Q7

i. Explain the effect of myelination on the rate of nerve impulse conduction.

ii. For the same diameter of axon, the graph shows that the rate of conduction of the nerve impulse in myelinated neurones in the cat is faster than that in the lizard. Suggest an explanation for this.

c. Figure Q8 shows how a stimulating electrode was used to change the potential difference across an axon membrane. Two other electrodes, P and Q, were used to record any potential difference produced after stimulation. The experiment was repeated six times, using a different stimulus potential each time.

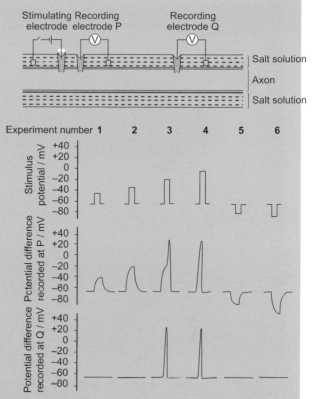

Figure Q8

In experiments 1 to 4, the stimulating voltage made the inside of the axon less negative.

In experiments 5 and 6, it made the inside of the axon more negative.

Explain the results of experiments 1 to 4.

d. Figure Q9 shows two neurones, X and Y, which each have a synapse with neurone Z.

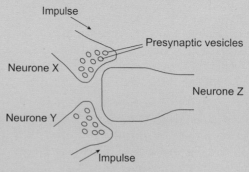

Figure Q9

Neurone X releases acetylcholine from its presynaptic vesicles. Neurone Y releases a different neurotransmitter substance that allows chloride ions (Cl^-) to enter neurone Z. Use this information, and information from Figure Q8, to explain how neurones X and Y have an antagonistic effect on neurone Z.

AQA June 2006 Unit 6 Question 8

6. a. The table shows the membrane potential of an axon at rest and during the different phases of an action potential. Complete the table by writing whether the sodium ion (Na^+) channels and potassium ion (K^+) channels are open or closed.

	Resting	Starting to depolarise	Repolarising
Membrane potential / mV	−70	−50	−20
Na^+ channels in axon membrane			
K^+ channels in axon membrane			

b. Describe how the resting potential is established in an axon by the movement of ions across the membrane.

c. Sodium and potassium ions can only cross the axon membrane through proteins. Explain why.

AQA June 2005 Unit 6 Question 4

7. Serotonin is a neurotransmitter that is released in some synapses in the brain. It is transported back out of the synaptic gap by a transport protein in the presynaptic membrane.

a. Serotonin diffuses across the synaptic gap and binds to a receptor on the postsynaptic membrane. Describe how this causes depolarisation of the postsynaptic membrane.

b. It is important that a neurotransmitter such as serotonin is transported back out of synapses. Explain why.

c. Scientists investigated the effect of a drug called MDMA on movement of mice. They measured the amount of movement of three groups of mice, K, L and M.

Group K, mice not given MDMA.

Group L, mice given MDMA.

Group M, mutant mice that did not produce a serotonin receptor on their postsynaptic membranes and were given MDMA.

The graph in Figure Q10 shows their results.

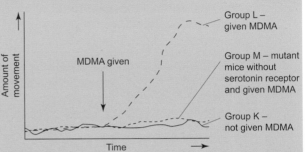

Figure Q10

The scientists concluded that MDMA affects movement by binding to serotonin receptors.

How do these results support this conclusion?

AQA June 2013 Unit 5 Question 7

8. a. A myelinated axon conducts impulses faster than a non-myelinated axon. Explain this difference.

Doctors investigated the relationship between myelin in brain tissue and different types of dementia. All types of dementia involve loss of mental ability. The doctors measured the mean amount of myelin in samples of brain tissue from:

❯ a control group of 12 people without dementia

❯ 20 people with vascular dementia (VaD)

❯ 19 people with Alzheimer's dementia (AD)

❯ 31 people with Lewy body dementia (LD).

The doctors' results are shown in Figure Q11. The vertical bars show standard errors.

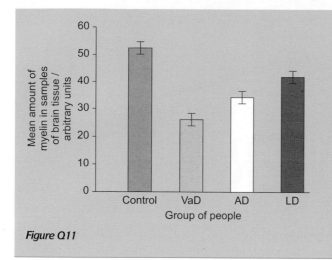

Figure Q11

b. The doctors used a statistical test to compare the results for AD and LD. They obtained a value for P of 0.047. What does this result show about the difference between the means for AD and LD? Use the words **probability** and **chance** in your answer.

c. A student who read this investigation concluded that there was a relationship between the amount of myelin in a person's brain and whether or not they had dementia. Do these data support this conclusion? Give reasons for your answer.

AQA June 2014 Unit 5 Question 3

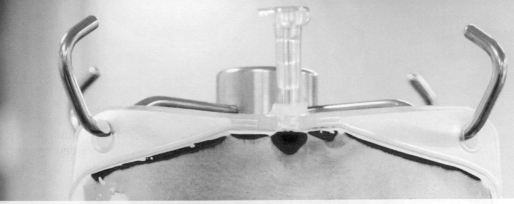

7 MUSCLE POWER

PRIOR KNOWLEDGE

We have already looked at the nervous system, and the way in which receptors gather sensory information and feed it into the central nervous system. We have also seen how, via motor nerves, the CNS allows us to respond by controlling the effectors: the muscles and glands.

LEARNING OBJECTIVES

In this chapter we consider the structure of muscle fibres, the mechanism of muscle contraction and how muscle contraction moves parts of the body. We also look at the different types of muscle fibres, and the ways in which these muscles get their energy.

(Specification 3.6.3)

The issue of cheating athletes has been making the headlines for decades. There is a constant battle between some athletes who use increasingly subtle and harder-to-detect illegal approaches to increasing their chances of winning, and the authorities that must develop ever more sophisticated ways to catch them.

How do athletes cheat? It depends on what they want.

Sprinters, weightlifters, jumpers and throwers are looking for more power. In addition to good technique, their performance depends on the size of their muscles and their power-to-weight ratio. Illegal ways to increase muscle size centre on the use of banned substances such as steroids and human growth hormone.

Endurance athletes, such as marathon runners and long-distance cyclists, do not necessarily want more power. What is more important for them is the capacity to keep the muscles provided with fuel and oxygen, and to prevent the accumulation of waste products. They need a good heart and lungs, and blood that can carry lots of oxygen. Large muscles are a hindrance when you are trying to get materials in and out as fast as possible.

Blood doping is a general term for any illegal technique that increases the volume of red cells. When an individual lives at high altitude, a natural process occurs in which the body detects the lower oxygen levels in the blood, and responds by making EPO. This hormone stimulates the bone marrow to produce more red cells and so, in a matter of weeks, the proportion of blood taken up by red blood cells increases. However, this process is reversed when not at altitude, and takes too long to be of much use to a serious athlete. Blood doping mimics this 'high altitude' process without having to climb a mountain.

Blood doping can take place in two main ways. Firstly, the athlete can take out a certain volume of their blood, often half a litre, concentrate the red cells and store them. When the body has replaced the red cells, the stored cells are put back in. Result: the haematocrit (the volume of the blood occupied by red cells) increases and so does the athlete's oxygen-carrying capacity. The second way to achieve this is simply to inject EPO.

Both of these practices are very difficult to detect. The transfusion involves the athlete's own blood and EPO is a hormone found naturally in the body. The IAAF (International Association of Athletics Federations) tests athletes regularly, to produce a Biological Passport. The testing is looking for abnormal levels, and a profile that fluctuates widely. One of the tests measures the percentage of reticulocytes, which are newly-made red cells. If an athlete has been withdrawing and injecting blood, there will be an increase in reticulocyte count just after withdrawal, and a decrease when the old red cells are put back.

7.1 AN OVERVIEW OF MUSCLES

Muscle is a remarkable tissue because of its primary ability to contract. Try as they might, engineers struggle to produce artificial muscles. Muscle tissue is confined to the animal kingdom and is one of the main reasons for the success of animals. Without muscle, rapid movement is almost impossible.

There are three types of muscle tissue in the body:

) **skeletal muscle** – also called voluntary or striped muscle (this is the one you may need to recall in an examination)

) **smooth muscle** – also called involuntary or unstriped muscle

) **cardiac muscle** – heart muscle.

In terms of distribution, skeletal muscle is found attached to the skeleton where, largely under voluntary control, it is responsible for movement and the maintenance of posture. Cardiac muscle is just found in the heart, while smooth muscle is generally found in tubular organs such as the intestines, blood vessels, airways and reproductive system.

Antagonistic muscle action

Skeletal muscle, as the name implies, is attached to the skeleton. Bone is a tough, incompressible tissue and so movement is brought about when the muscles pull the bones. When muscles contract, they pull but they cannot push. For this reason, they generally work in pairs, or sets, so that when one muscle contracts the other relaxes. For example, to flex (bend) the arm, the biceps muscle contracts and the triceps relaxes, which pulls on the bones in the forearm and bends the arm at the elbow. To extend (straighten) the arm again, the biceps relaxes and the triceps contracts, pulling the forearm bones back down again. A similar arrangement of antagonistic muscle pairs occurs all over the body, although the names of the different muscles are beyond the requirements of the specification.

The gross structure of skeletal muscle

Skeletal muscles are made up of overlapping striped muscle fibres. These are held together by connective tissue, with a tendon at each end. The tendons attach the muscle to bones. When the fibres contract, the muscle shortens, pulls the tendons and moves the bones.

The stripes on skeletal muscle fibres can be seen through a light microscope, as Figure 1 shows.

Skeletal muscles are very different from the rest of the cells in the body. Like other cells, a striped muscle fibre has cytoplasm, called sarcoplasm, and is surrounded by a cell-surface (plasma) membrane, called a sarcolemma. However, in order to build what are, in molecular terms, enormous muscle fibres, the normal cellular structure breaks down. The result is that skeletal muscle fibres have many nuclei in the cytoplasm, which lie near the surface of the fibre.

Skeletal muscle fibres consist mainly of much thinner fibre-like structures called **myofibrils**, which are composed mainly of protein molecules. It is these myofibrils that bring about contraction. They transfer chemical energy from organic molecules into movement.

QUESTIONS

1. Explain how skeletal muscle is different from other body tissues.

Ultrastructure of skeletal muscle

Although it is possible to see the stripes in skeletal muscle using a light microscope, it is only when we use an electron microscope that it becomes clear what the stripes actually are. Each myofibril is made up from a repeated pattern of two protein filaments – thick filaments composed of the protein **myosin** and thin filaments composed of the protein **actin**.

Figure 2 shows the structure of a myofibril as determined by early electron microscopes. The light bands consist of actin filaments only. The dark bands consist of overlapping actin and myosin filaments. Discs hold the groups of actin filaments together.

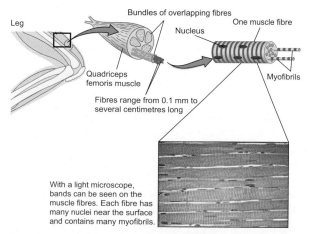

Figure 1 *Structure of skeletal muscle*

(a)

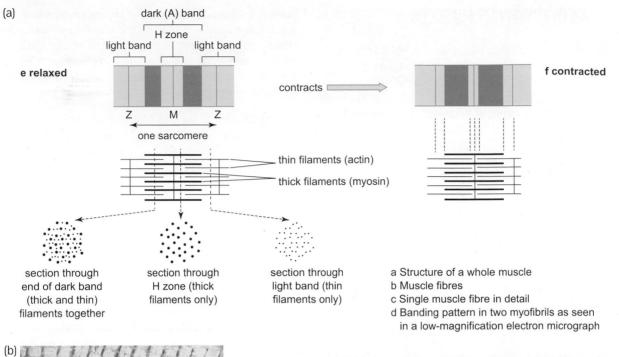

a Structure of a whole muscle
b Muscle fibres
c Single muscle fibre in detail
d Banding pattern in two myofibrils as seen in a low-magnification electron micrograph

(b)

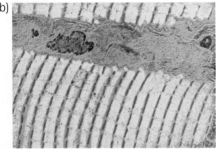

Figure 2 (a) The myofibril.; (b) A false-colour electron micrograph showing that the bands on the myofibrils are lined up to give a banded appearance to the whole fibre.

As the resolving power of electron microscopes increases, more detail can be seen in the myofibril:

❯ Where the two sets of filaments overlap the myofibril appears dark.

❯ The region where there are only myosin filaments is slightly lighter.

❯ The region where there are only actin filaments appears lighter still.

❯ In the centre of each light band is the Z disc, which holds actin filaments in position. Similarly, M discs hold myosin filaments in position.

QUESTIONS

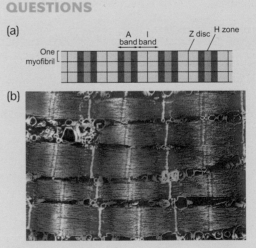

Figure 3 (a) Structure of striped muscle as revealed by electron microscopy. (b) A false-colour electron micrograph. The straight green lines are the Z discs, the myosin filaments are orange-pink and the actin filaments are blue. The green bubble-like structures are sarcoplasmic reticula.

2. Scientists use the letters A, H, I and Z to identify the different parts of a myofibril. Look at Figure 3.

   a. Why do the A bands look dark?

   b. What is found:

      i. in the H zone?

      ii. in the I band?

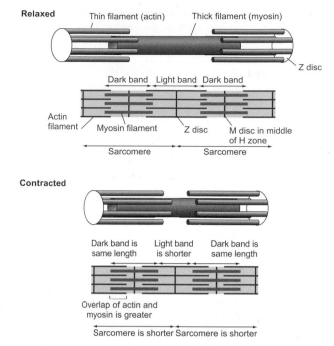

Thin filament (actin)   Thick filament (myosin)

Z disc

Dark band   Light band   Dark band

Actin filament   Myosin filament   Z disc   M disc in middle of H zone

Sarcomere   Sarcomere

Contracted

Dark band is same length   Light band is shorter   Dark band is same length

Overlap of actin and myosin is greater

Sarcomere is shorter   Sarcomere is shorter

Figure 4 The sliding filament theory of muscle contraction

KEY IDEAS

> Muscle is one of the four major types of tissue in the body.

> There are three types of muscle tissue in the body: skeletal (voluntary) muscle, which we use mainly to move our limbs; cardiac muscle, which makes up most of the heart; and involuntary (unstriped) muscle, which is found primarily in tubular organs such as the intestines, ureters and blood vessels.

> Muscles are attached to the skeleton via tendons. Movement results when muscles pull on inflexible bones, acting around joints.

> Muscles can only contract, they cannot push. For this reason, they work in antagonistic pairs, or sets, which combine to bend and flex limbs, and produce other movements such as maintaining posture.

> Skeletal muscle is made from many overlapping muscles fibres. Each fibre is composed of many small overlapping myofibrils.

> Under the microscope these myofibrils can be seen to consist of a repeated pattern of thick and thin filaments.

> The thick filaments are the protein myosin, while the thin filaments are the protein actin.

QUESTIONS

3. a. Do the actin filaments or the myosin filaments change their length when a sarcomere shortens?

   b. Why does the A band widen and the H zone get narrower when a sarcomere contracts?

7.2 HOW A MUSCLE CONTRACTS

Now that you know the structure of skeletal muscle it is possible to go on to look at how muscle fibres are able to contract to bring about movement. When a myofibril contracts:

> the sarcomeres (one repeated unit of actin and myosin) become shorter

> the light bands become shorter

> the dark bands stay the same length.

In the 1950s, Jean Hanson and Hugh Huxley at London University put forward the sliding filament theory of muscle contraction, which suggested that muscular contraction comes about by the actin filaments sliding between the myosin filaments, using energy from ATP. This theory is still accepted. In the region of overlap, six actin filaments are arranged neatly around each myosin filament, as Figure 4 shows.

Meet the cast

There are five basic components involved in muscular contraction:

> **Myosin** – the thick protein with many heads

> **Actin** – the thin protein with the myosin binding sites

> **Tropomyosin** – a thin protein that covers the myosin binding sites on the actin

> **ATP** – provides energy to detach myosin heads, re-cock and attach the heads further along the actin

> **Calcium ions** – initiate the contraction process by moving tropomyosin and causing ATP to hydrolyse.

Partly surrounding each myofibril is a membrane called the **sarcoplasmic reticulum**. It is a modification of the endoplasmic reticulum. Its function is to store calcium ions. When the sarcoplasmic reticulum is depolarised, it releases calcium ions into the myofibril, where they set in motion the events of contraction. The sarcoplasm contains many mitochondria to supply the energy for contraction.

Muscular contraction, step by step

1 An action potential arrives down a motor neurone and terminates at the **neuromuscular junction** (a modified synapse).

2 Acetylcholine is secreted into the synapse.

3 Acetylcholine fits into receptor sites on the postsynaptic membrane (sarcolemma) of the myofibril, known as the motor end plate.

4 The binding causes a depolarisation that spreads from the postsynaptic plasma membrane of the myofibril (the sarcolemma) to the sarcoplasmic reticulum within the fibril, resulting in an influx of calcium ions into the myofilament.

5 The calcium ions bind to the tropomyosin on the actin, moving it out of the way and exposing the myosin binding sites.

6 In the resting state, an ATP molecule is attached to the myosin head. When the actin binding site is exposed, the myosin head attaches.

7 The myosin head pivots and pulls backwards, so that the actin is pulled over the myosin. This is the 'power stroke' that pulls the filaments over each other. The energy for this was stored in the myosin head, transferred when the ATP molecule attached. The radiating heads on one myosin molecule pull on six surrounding actin fibres at the same time.

8 A fresh ATP molecule becomes fixed to the myosin head, causing it to detach from the actin.

9 The splitting of the new ATP molecule provides the energy for repositioning of the myosin head back to its original position, 'cocking the trigger' again.

10 The myosin head becomes attached to the actin once again, but further along, and there is another power stroke.

11 In this way, the actin is quickly pulled over the myosin in a ratchet motion. The actin is pulled towards the centre of the sarcomere, as the myosin heads at both ends of each thick, myosin filament are pulling in opposite directions – towards the centre of the sarcomere. This shortens the sarcomere, the whole filament and the muscle.

Electron micrographs of the dark bands show cross-bridges between the myosin and actin filaments. These bridges are the heads of the myosin molecules, which pull on the actin filaments

to make the myofibril shorten. This is called the ratchet mechanism because the actin molecules are moved along one step at a time by the myosin heads. Figure 5 shows how this mechanism operates.

Myosin cross-bridges point in six different directions and are arranged in the form of a spiral. Each myosin cross-bridge has a wider 'head'. This head attached to the binding site on the actin filament and then

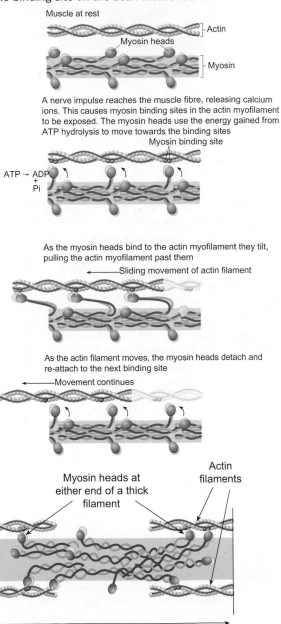

Figure 5 *The diagrams in part (a) show how the myosin heads interact with the actin filaments and pull them using a ratchet mechanism. The diagram in part (b) shows how the myosin heads always perform the power stroke in one direction. The myosin molecules are attached to each other by their tails, and so the myosin heads at either end of a thick filament move actins attached to opposite ends of a sarcomere together.*

performs its 'power stroke' — it moves rather like an oar, remaining stiff and therefore moving the actin filament. The myosin head then disengages and moves through a 'recovery stroke' to engage with the next binding site, rather like returning an oar to the starting position. The cycle is then repeated. Because of their spiral arrangement, cross-bridges will be at different positions in the power stroke/recovery stroke cycle, so muscle contraction is smooth rather than jerky.

The role of tropomyosin, calcium ions and ATP in muscle contraction

Why don't cross-bridges form in resting muscle? The actin filaments in resting muscle do have myosin binding sites, but these are blocked by molecules of a protein called tropomyosin, as shown in Figure 6.

When calcium ions bind to tropomyosin molecules, the shape of the protein is altered and it can no longer block the binding site, so the myosin heads can bind and pull on the actin filaments, making the fibre contract. The calcium ions also activate the enzyme ATPase in the myosin molcules. This hydrolyses ATP, which releases the energy needed to bring about contraction.

The neuromuscular junction

At the ends of motor nerves are modified synapses known as neuromuscular junctions. When an impulse reaches the junction, the events in the presynaptic part are very similar to those of other synapses. The key difference is that the postsynaptic part is a muscle fibre, and an action potential arriving down a motor nerve will bring about the release of calcium ions into the myofibril.

In muscles, calcium ions are stored in the sarcoplasmic reticulum. When the muscle is resting, calcium ions are pumped into the endoplasmic reticulum by active transport. The arrival of an action potential at a neuromuscular junction sets off the chain of events that lead to the contraction of myofibrils, as described and shown in Figure 7.

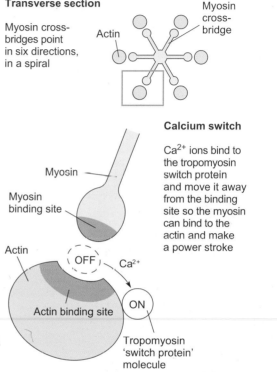

Transverse section

Myosin cross-bridges point in six directions, in a spiral

Actin

Myosin cross-bridge

Calcium switch

Ca^{2+} ions bind to the tropomyosin switch protein and move it away from the binding site so the myosin can bind to the actin and make a power stroke

Myosin

Myosin binding site

Actin

OFF

Ca^{2+}

ON

Actin binding site

Tropomyosin 'switch protein' molecule

Figure 6 *Calcium ions bind to tropomyosin and the myosin binding site on actin is exposed*

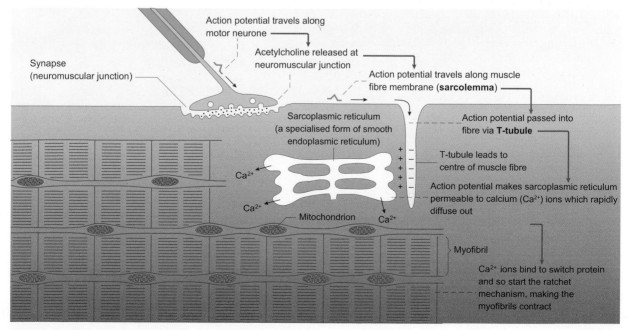

Action potential travels along motor neurone

Acetylcholine released at neuromuscular junction

Synapse (neuromuscular junction)

Action potential travels along muscle fibre membrane (**sarcolemma**)

Sarcoplasmic reticulum (a specialised form of smooth endoplasmic reticulum)

Action potential passed into fibre via **T-tubule**

T-tubule leads to centre of muscle fibre

Action potential makes sarcoplasmic reticulum permeable to calcium (Ca^{2+}) ions which rapidly diffuse out

Ca^{2+}

Ca^{2+}

Mitochondrion

Ca^{2+}

Myofibril

Ca^{2+} ions bind to switch protein and so start the ratchet mechanism, making the myofibrils contract

Figure 7 *The neuromuscular junction*

QUESTIONS

4. a. Look at Figure 7. Draw a flow chart to show how a nerve impulse arriving at a neuromuscular junction triggers events that lead to contraction of the muscle fibre.

b. Why are there large numbers of mitochondria in the muscle fibre?

ASSIGNMENT 1: CONTROLLING MUSCLE CONTRACTION

In order to control movement, the brain can control how strongly a muscle contracts. It does this by changing:

> how much each fibre contracts

> how many fibres contract.

When one action potential arrives at a neuromuscular junction, it causes one brief contraction or twitch of the fibre. If a second action potential arrives before the fibre has fully relaxed, the second twitch adds to the effect of the first, and a greater contraction occurs. The 'adding together' of the effects of action potentials is called **summation**.

A rapid sequence of action potentials causes a continuous strong contraction of the muscle fibre, which is called a **tetanus**. The more nerve impulses there are per second in a motor nerve, the stronger the contraction of each muscle fibre will be.

Each motor neurone serves about 150 muscle fibres. One motor neurone and its associated muscle fibres are together called a **motor unit**. Action potentials in a motor neurone cause all the muscle fibres in its motor unit to contract together. If a stronger contraction is needed, the brain recruits more motor units by sending action potentials along more motor neurones within the motor nerve.

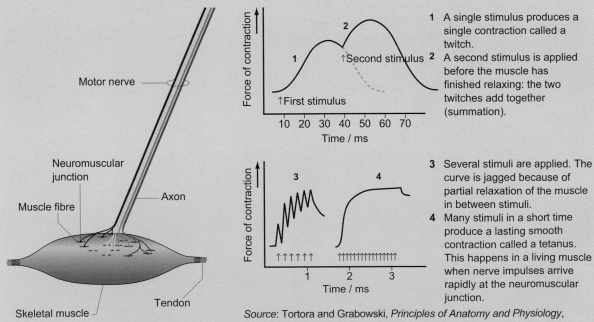

1 A single stimulus produces a single contraction called a twitch.
2 A second stimulus is applied before the muscle has finished relaxing: the two twitches add together (summation).

3 Several stimuli are applied. The curve is jagged because of partial relaxation of the muscle in between stimuli.
4 Many stimuli in a short time produce a lasting smooth contraction called a tetanus. This happens in a living muscle when nerve impulses arrive rapidly at the neuromuscular junction.

Source: Tortora and Grabowski, *Principles of Anatomy and Physiology*, Pearson, 1993

Figure A1 *Controlling muscle contraction*

Questions

A1. In Chapter 6, you learned that two types of summation can occur at neurone–neurone synapses: spatial summation and temporal summation. Which of these types of summation is occurring in a muscle fibre to cause a stronger contraction?

A2. What are the main differences in behaviour between a muscle fibre and a neurone on receiving impulses at increasing frequencies?

A3. What type of summation is this?

KEY IDEAS

> Skeletal muscle is composed of bundles of striped fibres, which are so large that the normal cellular structure breaks down and nuclei are dotted around in the cytoplasm.

> Each myofibril contains thick myosin filaments and thinner actin filaments.

> The sliding filament theory of muscle contraction states that the contraction of myofibrils is brought about by a ratchet mechanism, in which processes from the myosin filaments bind to the actin filaments and 'row' the actin filaments in a spiral manner.

> The events of muscular contraction can be summarised as: action potential arrives → depolarisation spreads along myofibril → calcium ions released → calcium ions cause tropomyosin to move away from myosin binding site on actin → myosin head attaches to actin → myosin head changes angle and pulls actin over myosin, inwards towards Z lines → new ATP molecule attaches to head and is split → myosin head detaches, re-cocks and reattaches further along actin filament. In this way the sarcomere shortens and the muscle. contracts.

7.3 MUSCLES AND ENERGY

Muscles cannot contract without ATP. There are three different sources of ATP for muscles, dependent upon how long contraction needs to last for. These sources are:

(1) The ATP already in the muscles, which was made during periods of less vigorous activity. More ATP can be made almost instantly using a molecule called phosphocreatine. This is the ATP/phosphocreatine system.

(2) ATP from glycolysis – the first stage of respiration. This is anaerobic respiration.

(3) ATP from full aerobic respiration.

Let's look these three systems in more detail.

(1) The ATP/phosphocreatine system

Although ATP is the energy currency for muscle cells, only about 85 grams of ATP is present in the body at any one time. This provides only enough energy for performing intense exercise for several seconds. ATP must therefore be constantly re-synthesised to supply energy for muscle contraction. Some energy for ATP re-synthesis is supplied directly and rapidly by the splitting of a phosphate molecule from another energy-rich compound called phosphocreatine, or creatine phosphate (CP). Phosphocreatine is similar to ATP because a large amount of energy is released when the bond between the creatine and phosphate molecules is split. Re-synthesis of ATP occurs if sufficient energy is available to re-join an ADP molecule with one phosphate (P) molecule. The breakdown of phosphocreatine can supply this energy.

Cells cannot store large amounts of ATP – its too unstable and very quickly used (i.e. a high turnover rate), but they can store phosphocreatine. The mobilisation of phosphocreatine for energy is almost instantaneous, so phosphocreatine is known as a 'reservoir' of phosphate. A low concentration of ADP in a cell stimulates the activity of creatine kinase, the enzyme that breaks down phosphocreatine.

$$\text{Creatine kinase}$$
$$\downarrow$$
$$CP \rightarrow C + Pi + \text{energy}$$
$$\downarrow$$
$$ADP + Pi \rightarrow ATP$$

The energy released from the breakdown of ATP and phosphocreatine can sustain all-out exercise, such as running, for about 8 seconds. In the 100 m race, the body cannot maintain maximum speed for longer than this duration. During the last few seconds of a race the runners are actually slowing down. The winner is usually the one who slows down least.

(2) The glycolytic system

This system provides ATP from the first part of respiration: glycolysis. As we saw in Chapter 2, glycolysis yields two molecules of ATP per glucose, which is not much compared with the full 36 or so from aerobic respiration, but glycolysis doesn't take long and doesn't need oxygen. This anaerobic system can fuel exercise at full power, but is short-lived because of the accumulation of lactate.

Lactate is lactic acid in solution, and its build-up is a big problem. The end product of glycolysis, pyruvate, is converted into lactate in order to re-synthesise the coenzyme (NAD^+). If this did not happen, glycolysis could not continue and there would be no more ATP. The problem is that lactate accumulates in the muscles where it lowers the pH and interferes with muscle activity.

An important concept here is that of the **energy continuum**. This means that one energy system gives way to the next so that there is no flat spot when we have to stop for a rest. So, we have enough ATP and phosphocreatine to allow us to exercise at full power until the glycolytic system can step up and provide more ATP. When the glycolytic system has to stop, due to accumulated lactate, the aerobic system takes over.

The glycolytic system bridges the gap between the ATP/phosphocreatine system and the aerobic system, and fuels activity for a duration of between about eight seconds and one minute. For this reason, sprints such as the 200 m and 400 m get most of their ATP from this system, and the accumulation of lactate is the reason why the 400 m is one of the most painful events.

(3) The aerobic system

The aerobic system provides ATP from the complete oxidation of glucose, or other respiratory fuel (often lipid). As we saw in Chapter 2, this process has four key stages and requires oxygen. The advantage of the aerobic system is that it can provide our muscles with ATP for as long as they have oxygen and fuel. This can be a matter of hours. The disadvantage of the aerobic

system is that it takes about a minute to produce its ATP, and it only allows the muscles to operate at about two thirds of their full power. This is why you can't sprint for long distances.

Figure 8 shows how the different systems for obtaining ATP overlap as duration of exercise extends.

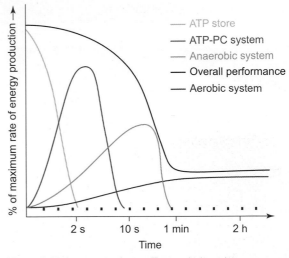

Figure 8 *The energy continuum. The graph shows how one energy system takes over from another to provide a continuous supply of ATP for the muscles. Note that the x-axis is not linear.*

Fast and slow skeletal muscle fibres

You may have noticed that chickens and turkeys have light meat and dark meat. Why is that? A scientist named Ranvier — he of the 'node of Ranvier' fame (*see Chapter 6*) — reported differences in muscle colour in 1873. The explanation for the colour differences has a basis in physiology. The dark meat in turkey is 'red' or **slow skeletal muscle fibres.** The white meat is 'white' or **fast skeletal muscle fibres.** Most animals have some combination of these two fibre types, though the distinctions may be less obvious.

Muscle physiologists use biopsies to study the make-up of muscles from athletes who compete in different types of events. Taking a biopsy involves using a special type of needle to remove about 50 mg of living muscle tissue from a muscle. Studying samples has shown that all skeletal muscles contain the two types of fibres — fast and slow.

Fast skeletal muscle fibres can produce ATP very quickly via glycolysis. Their contraction speed is very rapid. Fast skeletal muscle fibres are used mainly for sprinting and jumping or escaping from danger.

Slow skeletal muscle fibres contract at about half the speed of fast skeletal muscle fibres. These slow skeletal muscle fibres contain more mitochondria than fast skeletal muscle fibres, so they produce ATP mainly via aerobic respiration. They are used mainly during walking or jogging. Middle-distance running, and sports such as football and hockey, use both types.

Table 1 shows some of the properties of fast-twitch and slow-twitch fibres. Most muscles contain a

mixture of the two sorts of fibre, but there are differences in the ratios of the two types between people. This ratio is controlled by genes. Exercise increases the number of both types of fibre in muscles, but in the same ratio. So, you are born either a sprinter or a long-distance runner.

Type	Speed of contraction	ATP source	Respiration	Fatigue	Motor unit
Slow skeletal muscle fibres	Slow	Glucose and lipids for aerobic respiration	Aerobic	Slow	Small
Fast skeletal muscle fibres	Fast	Phosphocreatine (to generate ATP from ADP and P), and glycogen for anaerobic respiration	Anaerobic	Rapid	Large

Table 1 *Features of slow-twitch and fast-twitch muscles*

QUESTIONS

6. It could be helpful to revise the information about respiration in Chapter 2 before answering these questions.

   a. Apart from muscles, where is most of the body's glycogen stored?

   b. Where are triglycerides stored in the body?

   c. i. What is the advantage to a sprinter of having phosphocreatine as the main energy source in muscles?

   ii. What is the main disadvantage?

   d. What is the end product of anaerobic respiration?

   e. Explain how lactic acid contributes to muscle fatigue.

   f. What is the advantage to slow-twitch fibres of having abundant mitochondria?

ASSIGNMENT 2: CAN MUSCLE FIBRE TYPES BE CHANGED?

If you want to win an Olympic medal in the 100 metres sprint, you had better be born with about 80% fast skeletal muscle fibres. Want to win the Olympic marathon? You will need 80% slow skeletal muscle fibres in your leg muscles. We all have a certain balance of fast and slow skeletal muscle fibres – it's genetically determined. The question is: can training change the balance? Can a sprinter be turned into a marathon runner?

Table A1 shows the percentage of slow skeletal muscle fibres in three muscle groups in male athletes.

Consider the two pieces of evidence, **A** and **B**, below.

A Six men participated in a five-month programme of aerobic bicycle training. Muscle biopsy specimens taken from the calf muscles before and after training indicated no change in fibre

composition, although all the men improved considerably in work capacity and aerobic power.

B In another study of four men who took part in 18 weeks of aerobic and 11 weeks of anaerobic training, the anaerobic training caused an increase in the percentage of fast skeletal muscle fibres and a decrease in the percentage of slow skeletal muscle fibres.

Questions

A1. Do the data in table A1 support the hypothesis that there is a relationship between event and the ratio of slow skeletal muscle fibres to fast skeletal muscle fibres in the relevant muscle group? Use data from the table to support your answer.

Event	Mean percentage of slow skeletal muscle fibres in muscle group		
	Shoulder muscles	Calf muscles	Thigh muscles
Long-distance runner		79	
Canoeist	71		
Triathlete	60	59	63
Swimmer	67		
Sprinter		24	
Cyclist			57
Weight lifter	53	44	
Shot putter		38	

Table A1 *Percentage of slow skeletal muscle fibres in three muscle groups in male athletes (the gaps are where no data is available)*

A2. Evaluate the contribution of the evidence from **A** and **B** in supporting the hypothesis that training can affect the proportions of fast-twitch and slow-twitch fibres in muscle.

A3. Table A2 shows the results of a survey into the effects of types of training on skeletal muscle. From the information in the table, evaluate whether the data provides evidence supporting the hypothesis that training influences muscle fibre properties.

Muscle property	Slow skeletal muscle fibres		Fast skeletal muscle fibres	
	Anaerobic training	Aerobic training	Anaerobic training	Aerobic training
Percentage composition	0 or ?	0 or ?	0 or ?	0 or ?
Size	+	0 or ?	+ +	0
Oxidative capacity	0	+ +	0	+
Anaerobic capacity	? or +	0	? or +	0
Glycogen content	0	+ +	0	+ +

0 = no change
? = unknown
+ = moderate increase
+ + = large increase

Table A2 *Results of a survey into the effects of types of training on skeletal muscle*

KEY IDEAS

▸ When exercising at full power, the ATP in the muscles runs out after few seconds. Phosphocreatine is an accessory energy store in muscle cells.

▸ Energy from the breakdown of phosphocreatine is used by muscle cells to synthesise ATP from ADP and phosphate. Together the ATP/phosphocreatine system provides energy for the first 8 to 10 seconds of exercise.

▸ The glycolytic system takes over from the ATP/phosphocreatine system and can continue to provide ATP until the aerobic system takes over. The glycolytic system creates lactic acid.

▸ The aerobic system takes a while to make ATP – around a minute – but can continue to provide power for exercise as long as there is fuel (usually glucose/lipid) and oxygen.

> If you exercise hard enough, the aerobic system cannot supply ATP fast enough. A percentage of anaerobic respiration will then also occur (with glycolysis producing ATP faster). At some point, the build up of lactate will make you stop.

> Slow-twitch muscle fibres derive most of their energy from aerobic respiration, are slow to fatigue and are most useful in long-lasting exercise.

> Fast-twitch muscle fibres derive most of their energy from phosphocreatine and glycogen, are quick to fatigue and are most useful during short bursts of intense activity.

PRACTICE QUESTIONS

1. Figure Q1 shows part of a myofibril from a relaxed muscle fibre.

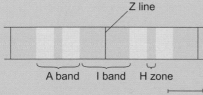

1.0 µm

Figure Q1

a. When the muscle fibre contracts, which of the A band, I band and H zone:
   i. remain unchanged in length?
   ii. decrease in length?

b. Explain what caused the decrease in length in part **a. ii.**

c. The whole muscle fibre is 30 mm long when relaxed. Each sarcomere is 2.25 µm long when contracted. Use the scale given on the diagram to calculate the length of the contracted muscle fibre in millimetres.

d. Table Q1 gives some properties of the two different types of muscle fibre found in skeletal muscle.

i. Copy and complete Table Q1 by writing the words 'high' or 'low' for the remaining three properties of each type of muscle fibre.

ii. The myosin-ATPase in Type 1 muscle fibres has a faster rate of reaction than that in Type 2 fibres. Use your knowledge of the mechanism of muscle contraction to explain how this will help Type 1 muscle fibres to contract faster than Type 2.

iii. The blood leaving an active muscle with a high percentage of Type 1 muscle fibres contained a higher concentration of lactate than that leaving a muscle with a high percentage of Type 2 muscle fibres. Explain why.

AQA A June 2006 Unit 7 Question 7

2. Figure Q2a shows part of a single myofibril from a skeletal muscle fibre as it appears under an optical microscope.

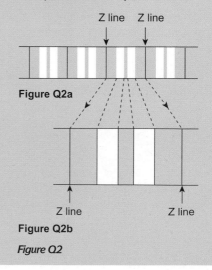

Figure Q2a

Figure Q2b

Figure Q2

| | Type of muscle fibre | |
	Type 1	Type 2
Speed of contraction	high	low
Force generated	high	low
Activity of the enzymes of glycolysis	high	low
Number of mitochondria		
Activity of Krebs cycle enzymes		
Rate of fatigue		

Table Q1

a. i. Copy and complete Figure Q2b to show the arrangement of actin and myosin filaments in this part of the myofibril as they would appear under an electron microscope. Label the actin and myosin filaments.

ii. Why are the details you have drawn in Figure Q2b visible under the electron microscope but not under the optical microscope?

b. The myofibril in Figure Q2a is magnified × 8000. A muscle fibre is 40 μm in diameter. Calculate the number of myofibrils that would fit side by side across the diameter of the muscle fibre. Show your working.

AQA January 2005 Unit 7 Question 2

3. Figure Q3 shows part of a sarcomere.

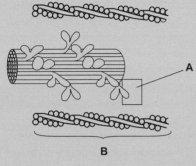

Figure Q3

a. i. Name the main protein in structure B.

ii. Name the structure in box A.

b. i. Describe how calcium ions cause the myofibril to start contracting.

ii. Describe the events that occur within a myofibril that enable it to contract.

Slow-twitch and fast-twitch skeletal muscle fibres differ in a number of ways. Slow-twitch muscle fibres get their ATP from aerobic respiration while anaerobic respiration provides fast-twitch muscle fibres with their ATP. Figure Q4 shows a bundle of fast-twitch and slow-twitch muscle fibres as seen through an optical microscope. The muscle fibres have been stained using a stain that binds to the enzymes that operate in the electron transport chain.

Key:
= Heavily stained fibre
= Lightly stained fibre

Figure Q4

c. i. Describe how you could calculate the percentage of fast-twitch muscle fibres in this bundle.

ii. The figure calculated by the method in part **c. i.** may not be true for the muscle as a whole. Explain why.

d. The muscle fibres in Figure Q5 correspond to those in region X of Figure Q4. They were stained with a substance that binds to enzymes involved in glycolysis. Shade Figure Q5 to show the appearance of the muscle fibres. Use the shading shown in the key.

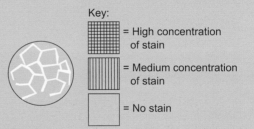

Key:
= High concentration of stain
= Medium concentration of stain
= No stain

Figure Q5

e. Recent research has shown that the difference in muscle fibre types is due in part to the presence of different forms of the protein myosin with different molecular shapes. Explain how a new form of myosin with different properties could have been produced as a result of mutation.

AQA January 2004 Unit 7 Question 7

4. Figure Q6 shows the arrangement of some of the proteins in a myofibril from a skeletal muscle. The myofibril is shown in the relaxed state.

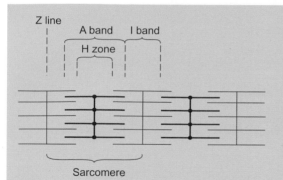

Figure Q6

a. Name the protein found in the H zone.

b. When the muscle contracts, what happens to the width of:

  i. the A band?

  ii. the I band?

c. The distance between two Z lines in a myofibril is 1.6 µm. Calculate the magnification of Figure Q6. Show your working.

AQA January 2003 Unit 7 Question 3

5. Skeletal muscle is made of bundles of fibres.

a. Describe the roles of calcium ions, ATP and phosphocreatine in producing contraction of a muscle fibre.

b. Table Q2 shows some properties of slow-twitch and fast-twitch muscle fibres.

Property of muscle fibre	Type I (slow-twitch fibres)	Type II (fast-twitch fibres)
Number of mitochondria per fibre	Many	Few
Concentration of enzymes regulating glycolysis	Moderate	High
Resistance to fatigue	High	Low

Table Q2

Endurance athletes, such as marathon runners, nearly always have a high proportion of slow-twitch fibres in their muscles. Explain the benefit of this.

c. During exercise, much heat is generated. Describe the homeostatic mechanisms that restore normal body temperature following vigorous exercise.

AQA June 2002 Unit 7 Question 9

6. a. Describe the part played by each of the following in myofibril contraction.

  i. Tropomyosin

  ii. Myosin

b. Table Q3 shows features of fast and slow muscle fibres.

Feature of muscle fibre	Fast muscle fibre	Slow muscle fibre
Type of respiration	Mainly anaerobic	Mainly aerobic
Glycogen	High concentration	Low concentration
Capillaries	Few	Many

Table Q3

Use information from the table to suggest and explain **one** advantage of:

  i. the high glycogen content of fast muscle fibres

  ii. the number of capillaries supplying slow muscle fibres.

AQA June 2013 Unit 5 Question 2

7. Figure Q7 shows two relaxed sarcomeres from skeletal muscle.

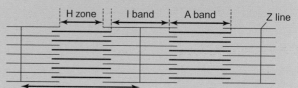

Length of sarcomere = 2.2 µm

Figure Q7

a. When the sarcomeres contract, what happens to the length of

  i. the I band?

  ii. the A band

b. The length of each sarcomere in the diagram is 2.2 µm. Use this information to calculate the magnification of the diagram. Show your working.

c. People who have McArdle's disease produce less ATP than healthy people. As a result, they are not able to maintain strong muscle contraction during exercise. Use your knowledge of the sliding filament theory to suggest why.

AQA June 2012 Unit 5 Question 2

8. a. What is the role of phosphocreatine (PC) in providing energy during muscle contraction?

Scientists investigated the time for phosphocreatine (PC) to be re-formed in arm muscles after the same exercise in healthy people of different ages. The exercise involved brief, rapid contractions of arm muscles. Figure Q8 shows the scientists' results. Each cross is the result for one person.

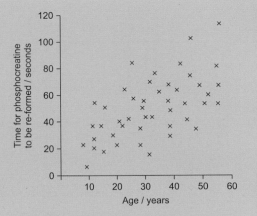

Figure Q8

b. There is a lot of variation in the time taken for PC to be re-formed in people of a very similar age. Suggest **one** reason for this variation.

c. Use your knowledge of fast muscle fibres to explain the data in Figure Q8.

AQA June 2014 Unit 5 Question 6

8 HOMEOSTASIS

PRIOR KNOWLEDGE

You will have encountered the idea of homeostasis in earlier years. It is simply the idea that the conditions within the body need to be kept relatively constant. Examples include temperature, pH and blood glucose levels.

LEARNING OBJECTIVES

In this chapter we look at negative feedback – the basic mechanism behind homeostasis – before looking in more detail at the control of blood glucose and the role of the kidneys in regulating the water potential of body fluids.

(Specification 3.6.4.1, 3.6.4.2, 3.6.4.3)

According to NHS figures, there are 3.9 million people living with diabetes in the UK, though some are borderline and undiagnosed. That's more than one in 16 of the population. This figure has more than doubled since 1996, when there were 1.4 million. It is estimated that by 2025 five million people in the UK will have diabetes.

Diabetics have trouble controlling their blood glucose concentration. If the problem is severe, the person with diabetes may need to check their blood glucose level every few hours, and sometimes up to 10 times a day. This involves the finger-prick test – taking a drop of blood from the finger and placing it on a test-strip that indicates the concentration of glucose in the blood.

Trials are now underway with a new glucose sensor that is implanted under the skin and monitors glucose concentrations constantly. It sends the reading to a smartphone and so, provided you have the right app, in the future it may be possible to check your blood glucose concentrations (and many other physiological factors) in just the same way as you check the time.

It is interesting to speculate where this technology may take us. In the future, it may be possible to check blood hormone concentrations, so that women can tell where they are in their monthly cycle – at ovulation, for example – or to check if a particular contraceptive is working. Even more sensitive tests might be able to detect the early signs of various diseases.

8.1 WHAT IS HOMEOSTASIS?

All cells in the body need to be maintained in the best physical and chemical conditions possible if they are to function properly. Keeping every cell at the optimum temperature, with enough water and nutrients, is a complex task that involves many systems in the body; biologists call this **homeostasis**.

The word *homeostasis* means *steady state* but it is more accurate to say that conditions inside the body need to be maintained within certain limits. Some factors – such as temperature and blood pH – are kept within very narrow limits. Others, such as blood glucose, can vary within a slightly wider range without adversely affecting the individual.

To understand why homeostasis is so important, think about enzymes. Metabolism – the sum total of the chemical reactions in the body – is incredibly complex and relies on an intricate interplay of many different enzymes. As you saw in the first year of your Biology A-level, enzymes are very sensitive to temperature and pH. It is not enough for enzymes simply to work well until they are denatured; in practice they all need to be working at the correct rate, so that products are made as fast as they are needed.

Negative feedbacks

A negative feedback is a mechanism for stability. All negative feedbacks have the same basic structure:

› A physiological factor changes. For example, during exercise, the increased muscle activity causes the blood temperature to rise.

› Receptors detect this stimulus. If blood temperature starts to rise, this is detected by thermoreceptors in the hypothalamus in the brain.

› Mechanisms are activated that correct the change. To reduce the temperature, the body sweats, blood vessels in the skin dilate, and so on.

The extent of the change is monitored, and mechanisms are switched off when the physiological factor returns to within acceptable limits. This is the key feature of a negative feedback.

You can think of negative feedback as 'detection–correction'. In examples of negative feedback in vertebrates, the receptors gather information and channel it into the central nervous system (CNS). In turn, the CNS coordinates the response, usually without the need for conscious thought.

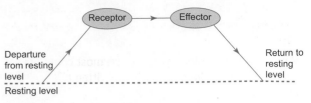

Figure 1 *A negative feedback loop*

Positive feedbacks

In contrast to negative feedbacks, positive feedbacks are mechanisms for change. Examples of positive feedbacks in the body include blood clotting, ovulation and childbirth. They are situations in which change creates more change. For example, when childbirth begins, contraction of the uterus causes the secretion of the hormone oxytocin, which in turn stimulates further contractions. The contractions therefore get more frequent and powerful until the baby is delivered.

Positive feedbacks can result when negative feedbacks break down, and physiological levels deviate outside normal limits. For example, when core temperature exceeds about 40 °C, a positive feedback can develop that makes the temperature rise even further. Enzymes work faster above 40 °C – contrary to popular belief, most are not denatured until about 50 °C – and so we respire more quickly and our general metabolic rate increases. Metabolic reactions generate more heat, which makes the enzymes work faster and so on. Death results at about 42 °C due to a metabolic imbalance, not because all our enzymes have been denatured.

8.2 REGULATION OF BLOOD GLUCOSE

The control of blood glucose is a classic example of homeostasis. The brain is particularly important here. Many tissues can cope with relatively wide variations in blood glucose concentration. They can store glucose as glycogen and can turn to other fuels – such as lipids – when glucose runs out. The brain can do neither.

The blood must contain between four and six millimoles of glucose per cubic decimetre of blood ($4-6$ mmol dm^{-3}) so that it can supply the brain cells. If blood glucose strays outside these limits, even for a few minutes, brain cells can suffer and the central nervous system may not function correctly. In the Year 1 book you learned how small changes in volume affected the functioning of red blood cells. Glucose is an important contributor to the water potential of blood and tissue fluid.

Just how much glucose is circulating in our blood?

When measuring blood glucose, the most commonly used units are millimoles per litre, written as mmol dm^{-3}.

Normal blood glucose concentrations fall between 4 and 6 mmol dm^{-3}.

How much glucose would be needed to make 1 litre of a solution with concentration of, say, 5 mmol dm^{-3}?

A millimole is 10^{-3} (one thousandth) of a mole.

The relative molecular mass of glucose ($C_6H_{12}O_6$) is 180 (rounded down).

So, one mole of glucose has a mass of 180 g

one millimole $= \dfrac{180}{1000} = 0.180$ g

5 mmol is $5 \times 0.180 = 0.9$ g

So, one litre of a 5 mmol dm^{-3} solution contains just 0.9 g of glucose (to make it, you would put the 0.9 g of glucose into a measuring cylinder and top it up to a litre).

Think about that amount the next time you are tempted to polish off two Mars bars and a pint of chocolate milk.

The pancreas

Before we look at the mechanism of blood glucose control, it helps to know a little about the pancreas (Figures 2 and 3). This leaf-shaped organ is found in the abdomen, tucked away between the stomach and the liver. 99% of the pancreas is responsible

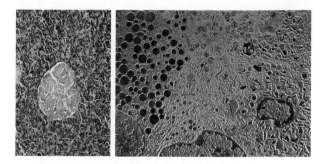

Figure 3 *The light micrograph (left) shows a section through the islets of Langerhans in the pancreas. The electron micrograph on the right shows insulin-secreting beta cells (the green, yellow and brown cells on the right) and glucagon-secreting alpha cells (the red cells on the left).*

for making pancreatic juice. It delivers this digestive juice to the small intestine by means of the pancreatic duct. However, we are interested in the 1% or so of the pancreas that is endocrine (hormone producing) tissue. There are small patches of endocrine tissue called **islets of Langerhans**, which contain three types of cells, each of which makes a different hormone:

➤ Alpha (α) cells produce glucagon.

➤ Beta (β) cells produce insulin.

What happens when blood glucose falls?

Blood glucose concentrations will fall if an individual hasn't eaten anything for a while, or if their activity increases. The receptors for a fall in blood glucose concentrations are the alpha cells in the islets of Langerhans. The control of blood glucose is unusual in mammals because the receptors and effectors *are the same cells*: the CNS is not involved. When

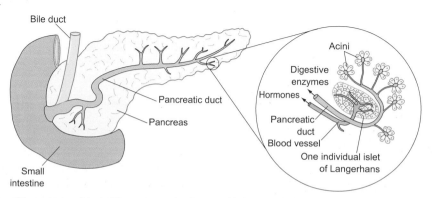

Figure 2 *The structure of the pancreas. Most of the pancreas is taken up with clusters of cells called acini that make pancreatic juice. However, small patches of cells called islets of Langerhans make the hormones that control blood glucose concentration.*

these alpha cells detect a fall in blood glucose, they respond by secreting glucagon. Glucagon is a peptide hormone – a short chain of 29 amino acids. Like all hormones, glucagon travels in the blood to all parts of the body but only has an effect on those cells with specific glucagon receptor proteins in their membranes. These are cells that have significant stores of glycogen inside them, notably the liver and muscles.

Glucagon works, indirectly, by activating enzymes inside cells that convert glycogen into glucose, a process called **glycogenolysis**. The glucose then diffuses into the blood, increasing the blood glucose concentration towards its normal level. When blood glucose concentration start to rise again as a result of glucagon secretion and glycogenolysis, this is also detected by the alpha cells and glucagon secretion is reduced. This overall process is a classic example of negative feedback. The mode of glucagon action is covered in more detail in the next section.

When glycogen supplies begin to run out, glucose can also be formed by **gluconeogenesis**. The word means 'generating new glucose' and basically involves making glucose from non-carbohydrate sources. This new glucose is made from pyruvate, and so is essentially the reverse of glycolysis, but the process involves different enzymes. During starvation, the body's proteins are also hydrolysed into amino acids, which are then used to produce pyruvate for use in gluconeogenesis. Gluconeogenesis ensures that blood glucose does not fall below the critical concentration.

QUESTIONS

1. Will gluconeogenesis require energy or release energy? Give the reason for your answer.

What happens when blood glucose rises?

Blood glucose concentrations rise shortly after we eat, when the digested carbohydrate is absorbed from the small intestine. The beta cells detect this rise and respond by secreting **insulin**. This hormone, like glucagon, travels to all parts of the body in the blood, but it mainly affects cells in the muscles, liver and adipose (fat storage) tissue. Insulin increases the rate at which liver cells, muscle cells and fat cells absorb glucose.

The key to lowering blood glucose levels is facilitated diffusion. Glucose can only pass into cells through specific glucose transport (carrier) proteins in cell membranes. The more proteins there are, the faster glucose leaves the blood and enters cells. Cells with insulin receptors in their membrane also have vesicles (spheres of membrane) that contain extra glucose transport proteins just under the cell-surface membrane.

How insulin works
Look at Figure 4.

1   Insulin fits into specific insulin receptors on cell membranes of target cells.

2   This binding causes vesicles containing glucose channel proteins to join the cell surface membrane, thus increasing the rate of facilitated diffusion into the cells.

3   Insulin also activates enzymes in the liver to convert glucose into glycogen, a process called **glycogenesis**. In some cells, insulin also activates the enzymes that synthesise triglycerides.

Overall, insulin secretion causes a fall in blood glucose concentration, to bring it down to within normal concentration limits. The pancreatic beta cells detect this and reduce insulin reduction. This overall process is another example of negative feedback.

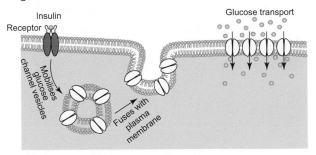

Figure 4 *The mode of action of insulin. When insulin binds to its receptor, vesicles containing extra glucose transport proteins join the surface membrane and speed up the facilitated diffusion of glucose into the cell.*

Figure 5 shows how the rate of glucose uptake into the liver is affected by the presence of insulin. As insulin and glucagon have opposite effects on blood sugar level they are said to be **antagonistic**. In homeostasis, separate mechanisms control departures in different directions from the original state – which gives more control. If insulin secretion drops, then blood glucose concentration would probably drift back up, eventually. The glucagon mechanism allows a more rapid and controlled increase in blood glucose concentration.

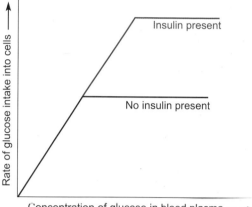

Figure 5 *The effect of insulin on glucose uptake. Insulin works by making more glucose transport proteins available in cell membranes. Note that the graph levels off in both cases. This is because the number of glucose transporters is finite. Once glucose is passing through them as fast as possible, an increase in glucose concentration will not speed up the rate of transport. It's a bit like trying to get a crowd into a stadium more quickly by opening more turnstiles.*

QUESTIONS

2. Write one-sentence definitions for these processes:
   a. glycogenesis
   b. glycogenolysis
   c. gluconeogenesis.

3. a. Only 1% of cells in the pancreas are involved in hormone production. What is the function of the other 99%?
   b. What type of carbohydrate is glycogen?
   c. How is the structure of glycogen related to its function?
   d. What type of reaction causes the breakdown of glycogen into glucose?
   e. What type of reaction converts glucose to glycogen?

f. Glucose enters liver cells by facilitated diffusion. What are the main factors that affect the rate of facilitated diffusion of a substance into a cell?

g. How does an increase in the number of carrier proteins in the cell surface membrane increase the rate of glucose uptake by cells?

Adrenaline, glucagon and the mode of hormone action

The hormone **adrenaline** also affects blood glucose concentration. As you would expect from a hormone that prepares the body for action, it raises blood glucose concentrations.

Adrenaline is secreted by the **adrenal glands**, which are two small glands situated just above the kidneys. This hormone has a similar effect on liver cells as glucagon – it stimulates glycogenolysis. Adrenaline and glucagon do not actually enter their target cells.

So, how do adrenaline and glucagon actually work (Figure 6)?

▶ The hormones bind to receptor proteins on the cell-surface membranes of their target cells.

▶ This changes the shape (configuration) of the protein that spans/crosses the membrane.

▶ This configuration change activates an enzyme on the inside of the membrane: **adenylate cyclase**.

▶ In turn, adenylate cyclase converts ATP into cyclic AMP, which is known as the 'second messenger', meaning that it carries the message of the hormone inside the cell.

▶ Cyclic AMP activates one of several **protein kinases** in the cytoplasm. In the case of adrenaline and glucagon, **protein kinase A** activates the enzymes that hydrolyse glycogen.

Generally speaking, there are two types of hormones: water soluble and lipid soluble. Like all water-soluble hormones, adrenaline and glucagon are the 'first messengers'. They do not enter the cell. As a consequence, they require a second messenger inside the cell – that role is taken by cAMP. Many lipid-soluble hormones are steroids (or derived from steroids) and examples include testosterone, oestrogen and progesterone. Being lipid soluble, these hormones can pass through the phospholipid bilayer into the cell, where they combine with other substances to directly affect the expression of certain genes – *see Chapter 12*.

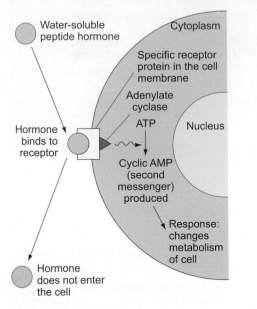

Figure 6 *Water-soluble hormones, such as glucagon and adrenaline, work via a second messenger, which is activated when the hormone fits into a specific receptor in the membrane.*

QUESTIONS

4. Explain how hormones can be specific when they are transported to every cell in the body.

Diabetes: when blood glucose regulation fails

The word diabetes means 'to pass through' and refers to the fact that diabetics were constantly thirsty and constantly needing to urinate. The 'pissing evil' was one common name for the disease during historical times when no treatment was available. The full medical name is **diabetes mellitus**, the latter word meaning 'sugar'.

There are two types of diabetes mellitus:

› Type 1, when the islets of Langerhans fail to produce insulin.

› Type 2, when the body produces insulin but the cells fail to respond to it.

Generally, type 1 diabetics develop the disease at an early age because the beta cells have been destroyed or are inactive. Type 1 diabetics have to inject insulin (Figure 7) for the rest of their lives. Type 2 diabetics develop the symptoms later in life, often as a result of being overweight. Around 90% of diabetics in the UK have type 2 diabetes.

Until insulin treatment was developed in the 1920s, type 1 diabetes was usually fatal. Since then, millions of diabetics have been able to live relatively normal lives – although they do have to inject themselves daily with insulin. The hormone cannot be taken as a pill because it is digested by the enzymes in the gut.

Figure 7 *A modern insulin pen. There are several different types of insulin available, which vary accord to speed of action. Fast-acting insulin works to lower blood glucose levels immediately. Slow-acting insulin needs to be metabolised by the body before it becomes active.*

In order to stay healthy, people with diabetes need to balance very carefully what they eat and the amount of insulin that they inject. If they inject too much insulin, skip a meal or take too much strenuous exercise, their blood glucose level can fall too low. Low blood glucose is known as **hypoglycaemia**, and this is often described as 'having a hypo'. The symptoms include sweating, trembling, hunger, blurring of vision and difficulty in concentration. Eating sugary or starchy foods soon raises the blood sugar concentration and the symptoms disappear. An untreated 'hypo' can lead to unconsciousness.

The opposite can also happen. If the individual is not keeping to their diet, eats too much carbohydrate, or takes too little insulin, blood glucose can rise to dangerously high levels. This is called **hyperglycaemia**. The symptoms include feeling sick, drowsiness and stomach pain. It can also lead to unconsciousness if left untreated.

QUESTIONS

5. **a.** Explain why people with diabetes are encouraged to eat starchy foods rather than sugary foods.

144

b. From your knowledge of diabetes, suggest explanations for the following symptoms:

  i. excessive thirst

  ii. weight loss

  iii. fatigue

  iv. breath smelling fruity (due to ketones, which are a by-product of lipid metabolism)

  v. excessive urination.

KEY IDEAS

> The pancreas monitors and controls blood glucose concentration; the brain is *not* involved.

> Alpha (α) cells in the pancreas detect a fall in blood glucose concentration and respond by secreting the hormone glucagon.

> Glucagon activates enzymes in the liver that convert glycogen to glucose.

> Adrenaline, which is secreted by the adrenal glands, has a similar effect on liver cells as glucagon.

> The action of glucagon and adrenaline is known as the second messenger model, since both hormones stimulate the action of cAMP (the second messenger), which activates protein kinase A, which in turn stimulates the action of the enzymes that break down glycogen.

> Beta (β) cells in the pancreas detect a rise in blood glucose concentration and respond by secreting the hormone insulin.

> Insulin increases the rate of uptake of glucose by body cells, by stimulating the movement of carrier protein molecules from vesicles in the cytoplasm to the cell surface membrane. These carrier protein molecules move glucose into the cells by facilitated diffusion.

> Insulin also activates enzymes in the liver, which catalyse condensation reactions that convert glucose to glycogen.

> The actions of both insulin and glucagon are part of a negative feedback mechanism, bringing the blood glucose concentration back to within normal limits.

> When control of blood glucose fails, diabetes can develop.

> Type 1 diabetes occurs when cells in the islets of Langerhans are damaged and no longer produce insulin.

> Type 2 diabetes is a result of cells in the body becoming resistant to the effects of insulin, and is often associated with being overweight.

ASSIGNMENT 1: MAKING HUMAN INSULIN

After Banting and Best's discovery in the 1920s of the role of insulin, the hormone was purified from the pancreatic tissue of slaughtered animals. However, cow and pig insulin differs from human insulin by just one amino acid, and that is enough to produce an immune reaction that slowly renders the insulin ineffective. So the search was on to find ways of making human insulin.

Insulin is a protein. It consists of 51 amino acids in two polypeptide chains that are joined together by sulfur bridges. The sequence of amino acids that make up insulin was worked out in the early 1950s – the first protein ever to have its primary structure worked out. However, although its structure was known, repeated attempts to synthesise insulin gave very poor yields because it was difficult to get the sulfur bridges to form between the two peptide chains, which are needed to make the functional molecule.

The breakthrough came when a protein called proinsulin was discovered in the pancreas. This longer protein is the molecule from which insulin is formed in the body.

Proinsulin is a relatively simple molecule to synthesise because it is a single chain consisting of 86 amino acids. If the 35 amino acids in the C peptide (a peptide comprises two or more amino acids joined together by peptide bonds) are chopped off (see Figure A1), the remaining parts of the molecule form insulin using the correct sulfur bridges. This mirrors exactly what happens in the beta cells of the pancreas. Today, human insulin is made by genetic engineering – *see Chapter 12*.

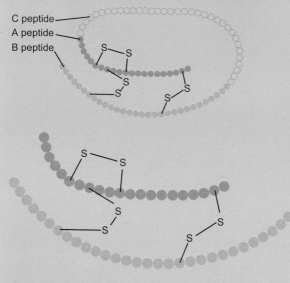

Figure A1 *Scientists first produced the whole proinsulin molecule. They then removed 35 amino acids, the C peptide, as shown. This left two separate peptides, the A and B peptides, joined by sulfur bridges.*

Questions

A1. What is a polypeptide?

A2. What type of enzyme will remove the C peptide from proinsulin?

A3. Apart from length, what other differences are there likely to be between the three proinsulin peptides?

A4. What is the minimum number of nucleotides needed to code for proinsulin?

8.3 THE CONTROL OF BLOOD WATER POTENTIAL

You may have noticed that on a hot day your urine is darker than normal. On the other hand, when you drink a large volume of fluid, your urine looks just like water. What you see results from your kidneys trying to keep the water potential of your blood and tissue fluid as constant as possible, and it's an important aspect of homeostasis.

The control of water potential in the blood and body fluids is called **osmoregulation,** and involves water movement in and out of cells by osmosis. If water potential is maintained, there is less net water flow in and out of cells. The key organs involved are the kidneys, which are paired organs found in the abdominal cavity. Put your hands on your hips, wiggle your thumbs – that is roughly where your kidneys are.

The kidneys have three key functions:

1 Excretion – the removal of metabolic waste from the body.

2 The control of blood volume.

3 The control of blood water potential.

By definition, excretion is removal of metabolic waste – the by-products of the reactions that occur in the cells. Carbon dioxide, water and urea are all metabolic wastes. The kidneys are responsible for **nitrogenous** excretion, which is the removal of nitrogen-containing compounds. In mammals, the main nitrogen-containing compound is urea, formula: $CO(NH_2)_2$. Think of it is as one molecule of carbon dioxide joined to two molecules of ammonia. The ammonia comes from the breakdown of excess amino acids in the liver, a process called **deamination**.

Incidentally, *defecation* is not excretion. It is egestion. It is the removal of the undigested contents of the gut along with bacteria and cells from the gut lining. It is only excretion in the sense that gut contents contain bile pigments, which are the by-products of haemoglobin breakdown that occurs in the liver.

REQUIRED PRACTICAL ACTIVITY 11: APPARATUS AND TECHNIQUES

(MS 0.2, 1.3, 3.2; PS 1.1, 1.2, 3.1, 4.1; AT b, AT c, AT f)

Production of a dilution series of a glucose solution and use of colorimetric techniques to produce a calibration curve with which to identify the concentration of glucose in an unknown 'urine' sample.

This practical activity gives you the opportunity to show that you can:

> use appropriate instrumentation to record quantitative measurements

> use laboratory glassware apparatus for experimental techniques

> use qualitative reagents to identify biological molecules.

Background

This practical involves analytical chemistry. It is a simple method that can be used to estimate the glucose concentration in your urine. It is not particularly ethical (or pleasant) to use real urine, so we use tea or yellow food colouring as a substitute.

There should be no glucose in urine – the kidneys should re-absorb it all. The presence of glucose in the urine is a sign of diabetes, and occurs because there is so much sugar in the blood that the kidneys can't re-absorb it all.

The test for glucose – and other reducing sugars – is the Benedict's test. This is a quantitative test because the more glucose there is in the sample, the greater the amount of precipitate (solid) copper(II) oxide and the deeper the colour.

When you carry out this required practical activity, you will produce a calibration curve using samples of known sugar content, which you can then use to estimate the glucose content of an unknown sample.

Apparatus

You will use a colorimeter (see Figure P1), which measures the transmission (and therefore the absorbance) of light through a solution. You will also need a waterbath for heating the sample.

Basic Technique

You will need to create a series of known glucose solutions, which you will almost certainly do by diluting the glucose solution you are given. Table P1 shows a sample table.

Figure P1 *A colorimeter. The sample solution is placed in a small, clear plastic container called a cuvette. Light is shone through the sample to a light sensor (a photoelectric cell) on the other side, which then reads the percentage transmission and absorbance.*

Once you have made your solutions, you will need to add a standard volume of Benedict's solution and heat in a waterbath to react. Eye protection will be needed. You can then use the colorimeter to measure the absorbance (or transmission) of the different solutions. When you plot a graph of glucose concentration against absorbance, you will have a calibration curve (it's called a curve even if it's a straight line) which you can use to estimate the concentration of your unknown solution.

Concentration of final solution / mmol dm^{-3}	Volume of water / cm^3	Volume of glucose standard / cm^3
0.0		
2.0		
4.0		
6.0		
8.0		
10.0		

Table P1

Drawing the graph

Once you have recorded your results in a suitable table, you can draw the graph. Glucose concentration should go on the *x*-axis and transmission or absorbance should go on the *y*-axis. The resulting graph, when plotted, is a calibration curve.

You can now use the graph to estimate the glucose concentration of your unknown sample or samples. This process is called interpolation, because you are estimating values between the known values you have plotted.

QUESTIONS

P1. Complete Table P1 to show the volumes of glucose solution and water needed to make up the dilutions.

P2. Explain why the 0.0 mmol dm^{-3} glucose solution was used to calibrate the colorimeter.

P3. Identify three sources of error in this method.

P4. This method can be used to estimate the reducing sugar contents of fruit juice, although it will be difficult to see the blue colour disappearing for purple or red fruit juices. Suggest one reason why the reducing sugar content of fruit juices is likely to be different from their glucose content.

P5. When using a graph, explain the difference between *interpolation* and *extrapolation*.

An overview of kidney function

Think about what goes into the kidney and what comes out. One tube enters the kidney – the **renal artery**, and two come out, the **renal vein** and the **ureter**. Blood entering in the renal artery contains urea and other wastes, and varying amounts of water and salt. Blood in the renal vein will contain less urea, water and salt. The fluid leaving in the ureter is urine. Overall, the kidney removes most of the urea, and varying amounts of water and salt from the blood. The solution of unwanted substances produced is urine.

The kidneys operate via two basic processes:

1 **Ultrafiltration** (filtration under pressure). This produces **filtrate**, which is basically the same composition as tissue fluid.

2 **Selective re-absorption and secretion.** The nephron will re-absorb some substances back into the blood, but not others. For example, it will re-absorb all the glucose and amino acids. It will re-absorb a varying amount of water depending on the body's state of dehydration.

It is important to appreciate that the kidney removes some metabolic waste at all times, in solution. This means that some water must be lost no matter how dehydrated you are. A vital aspect of the kidney's role is that it can produce urine that has a lower water potential than the blood. This is sometimes called **hypertonic** urine. Animals that live in dry environments – such as camels and gerbils – can produce urine with an amazingly low water potential, allowing them to excrete while minimising water loss.

QUESTIONS

6. Specifically, what generates the hydrostatic pressure of the blood?

The structure of the kidney

Figure 8a shows the basic structure of the kidney. Each kidney is a collection of about a thousand nephrons that are tightly packed together and surrounded by a dense network of blood vessels. The different regions of the kidney relate to the different regions of the nephrons. The **cortex** (outer part) of the kidney consists of the Bowman's capsules and the tubules (PCT, proximal convoluted tubule; and

DCT, distal convoluted tubule), while the **medulla** (central part) consists of the loops of Henlé and collecting ducts.

The urine made by the kidneys drains into the ureters, which push the fluid by peristalsis (slow rhythmic muscular contractions) to the bladder. As it fills, stretch receptors in the bladder walls make us aware of the situation. When convenient, sphincter muscles (rings of muscle that act as valves) relax and urine is released to the outside via a single urethra.

The nephron

A nephron is a kidney tubule. It is thin but very long, up to 30–40 mm in humans. As shown on the right of Figure 8a, each nephron consists of five main regions:

1 **Bowman's capsule**. The top end of the nephron is shaped like a wine glass, and contains a knot of blood vessels called the **glomerulus**. This is the region where the blood is filtered to produce filtrate.

2 The **proximal (or first) convoluted tubule** (PCT). The name means 'near, twisted tube'. Most of the filtrate is immediately re-absorbed into the blood.

3 The **loop of Henlé** – a hairpin-shaped loop that is the key to water conservation in dry conditions.

4 The **distal (or second) convoluted tubule** ('far, twisted tube'; DCT) – where a lot of the fine-tuning of the filtrate takes place. Substances are re-absorbed or excreted according to the needs of the body.

5 The **collecting duct** – the final part of the nephron that re-absorbs water. The fluid that passes out of the collecting duct is urine.

The blood vessels that come out of the glomerulus wrap around the rest of nephron. It is this close association between the nephron and the blood that allows the exchange of substances according to the needs of the body.

The formation of glomerular filtrate in Bowman's capsule

This is the region of ultrafiltration – filtration under pressure. Blood that enters the Bowman's capsule encounters something of a bottleneck: the entrance to the glomerulus is wider than the exit. As a consequence, hydrostatic pressure forces blood against a filter that consists of three layers,

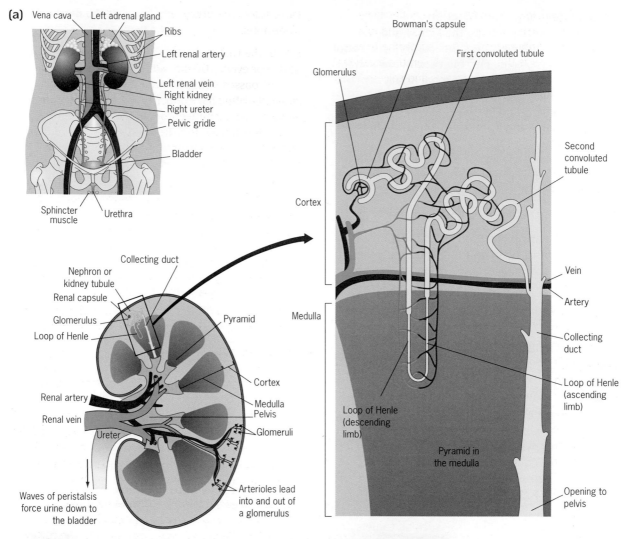

(a)

Vena cava
Left adrenal gland
Ribs
Left renal artery
Left renal vein
Right kidney
Right ureter
Pelvic gridle
Bladder
Sphincter muscle
Urethra

Bowman's capsule
First convoluted tubule
Glomerulus
Cortex
Medulla
Second convoluted tubule
Vein
Artery
Collecting duct
Loop of Henle (ascending limb)
Loop of Henle (descending limb)
Pyramid in the medulla
Opening to pelvis

Collecting duct
Nephron or kidney tubule
Renal capsule
Glomerulus
Loop of Henle
Renal artery
Renal vein
Ureter
Pyramid
Cortex
Medulla
Pelvis
Glomeruli
Arterioles lead into and out of a glomerulus

Waves of peristalsis force urine down to the bladder

(b)

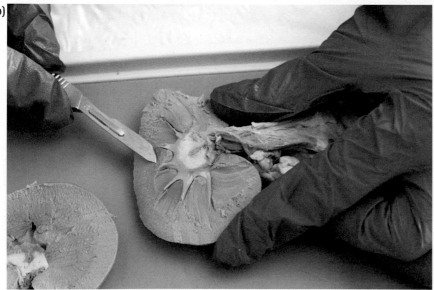

Figure 8 *Gross structure of the kidney*

summarised below. This physical filter effectively removes the barrier of the selectively permeable cell-surface membrane, and filters according to size. The critical layer is the basement layer, the mesh of which is too small to allow proteins and cells through. The three layers of the filter are:

1 The **endothelium** of the capillary. The cells have gaps in between them called **fenestrations** that help the filtration process.

2 The cells lining the tubule. These are called **podocytes** because they appear to have feet.

3 A **basement membrane**. This is a continuous sheet of protein between the other two layers of cells. It forms a continuous mesh and as such is the finest part of the filter.

The fluid that results from filtration through these three layers into the tubule is called filtrate. It has the same composition as tissue fluid: blood plasma without the large proteins. If we simply excreted this filtrate we would become dehydrated very quickly, and would lose large amounts of vital nutrients such as glucose and amino acids. What needs to happen now is that most of the filtrate is re-absorbed, so that we only excrete what we don't need.

Re-absorption by the proximal convoluted tubule

After formation, the filtrate passes immediately out of the Bowman's capsule and into the proximal tubule (Figure 10). This is the main region of re-absorption. Glucose, amino acids, and most ions are re-absorbed

straight into the blood, and water follows these solutes by osmosis.

In fact, the vast majority of the filtrate passes straight back. For every 100 cm^3 of filtrate formed, about 99 cm^3 passes straight back into the blood. This is called **obligate** re-absorption because it always happens. The nephron performs its homeostatic function by adding to or re-absorbing from the fluid that is left. In this way, filtrate is turned into urine.

The role of the loop of Henlé

The loop of Henlé is a hairpin-shaped region of the nephron that takes filtrate deep into the medulla and then returns it to the cortex. The loop effectively creates a region of high salt concentration in the medulla, through which the collecting duct must pass. Dependent upon how permeable the collecting duct is to water – a factor that is largely under hormonal control – the salt will draw water out of the collecting duct by osmosis so that it is conserved in the body.

You can tell a lot about an animal's relationship with water by the length of its loop of Henlé. Animals that live where water is scarce minimise water loss by making urine with a very low water potential. These animals have a longer loop of Henlé, so a section through their kidneys shows a relatively large medulla and a smaller cortex. The longer the loop, the more concentrated a region of salt it can create and the more concentrated the urine it can produce.

The loop of Henlé consists of a **descending limb**, which takes fluid down into the medulla, and an **ascending limb**, which brings it back to the cortex.

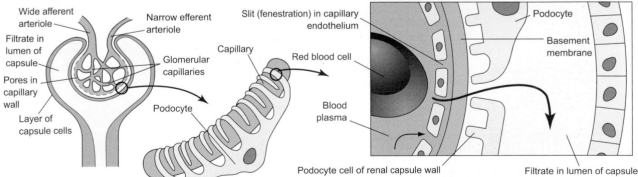

The walls of capillaries in the renal capsule are much more permeable than those of normal capillaries: the cells do not fit tightly together, but have thin slits in between (**fenestrations**), through which all the constituents of the plasma can pass

The renal capsule is lined with unique cells called **podocytes** ('foot-cells'). These cells, like those of the capillary, do not fit tightly together, but form a network of slits that fit over the capillary

Between these two relatively coarse filters is the continuous basement membrane. This finer filter prevents the passage of all molecules with a relative molecular mass greater than about 68 000, so the larger molecules (mainly proteins) remain in the blood

Figure 9 *The fine structure of the renal capsule, a region of the kidney adapted for ultrafiltration of the blood. Note the difference in size between the afferent and efferent arteriole*

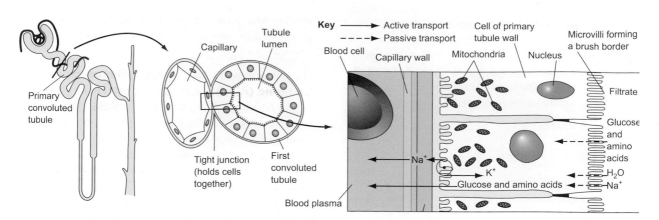

Figure 10 *Section through PCT and blood vessels*

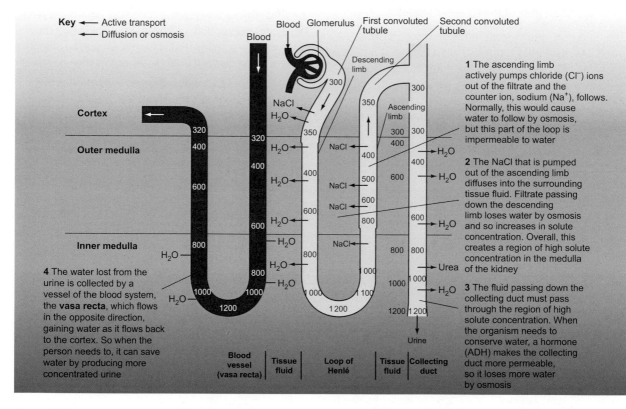

Figure 11 *How the loop of Henlé works. The numbers refer to the solute concentration in mg per 100 cm³*

Surrounding the loop is a network of blood capillaries known as the **vasa recta**.

How the loop of Henlé works (Figure 11):

Step 1 As filtrate passes down the descending limb, water leaves by osmosis due to the higher salt concentration in the surrounding fluid. Water passes through specific membrane channels called **aquaporins**. The longer the loop, the more water flows out of the filtrate and the lower the water potential of the filtrate.

Step 2 As filtrate flows up the ascending limb, sodium, potassium and chloride ions are pumped out of the filtrate by an active transport mechanism, resulting in the high concentration of salt in the surrounding fluid, which was mentioned in step 1. The ascending limb is impermeable to water, otherwise water would simply follow the solute by osmosis and the loop would not be able to function.

The overall point of the loop is that it creates a region of high salt concentration (a 'sodium gradient'), and very low water potential, through which the collecting duct must pass.

The distal convoluted tubule

The distal convoluted tubule has a role in the regulation of the potassium, sodium and calcium ions, along with pH (acid/base) balance. These processes are beyond the specification. The permeability of the tubule to water is, to some extent, under the influence of ADH – see below – though the role of the loop of Henlé and the collecting duct are more significant in controlling water potential.

The control of water potential

A negative feedback system operates to control the water potential of the blood. If water loss exceeds water intake – when we have been sweating and not drinking much, for example – the fall in the blood's water potential is detected by **osmoreceptor cells** in the hypothalamus (Figure 12). In response,

the hypothalamus secretes a **releasing factor** that stimulates the posterior (rear) lobe of the pituitary gland.

The posterior pituitary releases **anti-diuretic hormone (ADH).** Diuresis is the production of urine, so this hormone slows down that process. ADH is a peptide hormone that travels in the blood where its target organ is the collecting duct (and to some extend the DCT) of the nephron. ADH makes the duct more permeable to water, by acting on proteins called V2 **aquaporins**. In a similar way to insulin activating more glucose transport proteins, ADH stimulates more aquaporins to join the membrane of the collecting duct cells, making it more permeable to water.

When the walls of the duct are permeable to water, the low water potential of the surrounding fluid – the region of high salt concentration created by the loop of Henlé – draws water out by osmosis. This results in more water leaving the duct and re-entering the blood. In this way water is conserved, and the urine has a lower water potential, which is why it becomes dark. So ADH acts to return the water potential of the blood to within normal limits. ADH release sets in motion events that eventually lead to a reduction in ADH release – negative feedback.

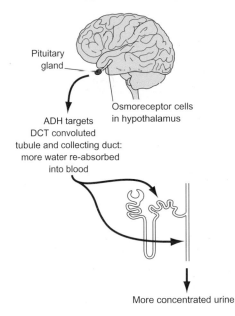

Pituitary gland

Osmoreceptor cells in hypothalamus

ADH targets DCT convoluted tubule and collecting duct: more water re-absorbed into blood

More concentrated urine

Figure 12 *The hypothalamus and the pituitary*

QUESTIONS

7. Individuals who cannot make enough ADH have a condition called **diabetes insipidus**. Suggest what the symptoms of this condition are.

ASSIGNMENT 2: KIDNEY FAILURE

If one kidney stops working, most people can usually live a normal life. If both kidneys stop working, the result is critical. Urea, potassium, phosphate and water can build up rapidly to the point where the patient feels very ill and is unable to carry out most normal activities.

Most people suffering from acute renal failure are waiting for a transplant, but there are not enough suitable donors. To manage the condition while waiting for a transplant, patients are put on the Giovanetti diet and have to have regular dialysis sessions. The essential features of the diet are:

> ❯ low potassium (no foods such as chocolate, bananas or tomatoes)
>
> ❯ low protein, limited to 50 g a day
>
> ❯ fluids limited to half a litre a day.

Dialysis (Figure A1) is a method of separating small molecules from larger ones using a partially permeable membrane. Blood dialysis, or haemodialysis, separates the smaller molecules in plasma, such as urea and glucose, from the larger ones, such as proteins.

Blood is taken from a vein in the patient's forearm and passed into the dialysis machine where it passes into many small artificial capillaries. These are made from plastic and are semi-permeable. While blood flows in one direction inside the tubes, a fluid called dialysate flows outside the tubes in the opposite direction.

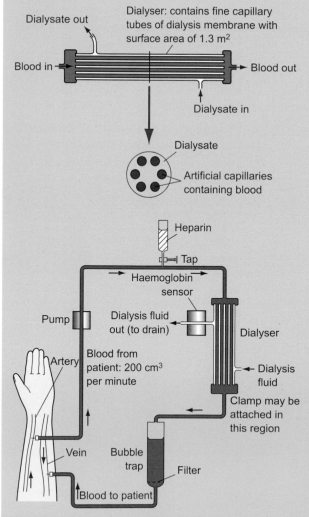

In dialysis, molecules are exchanged between the blood and the dialysate. The composition of the dialysate is carefully controlled so that the urea is filtered out of the blood. The concentrations of glucose and salts in the dialysate are also carefully controlled so that normal concentrations are maintained in the blood.

Questions

A1. Kidney failure often results when there is a significant loss of blood. Explain why the kidneys cannot function when blood pressure drops.

A2. Explain why protein intake needs to be limited in people with kidney failure.

A3. Explain why fluid intake needs to be limited in kidney failure patients.

A4. a. By which physical process do solutes enter or leave the blood during dialysis?

b. Why do the blood and dialysate flow in opposite directions?

c. Suggest two problems that would occur if the dialysate was just pure water.

d. Why does the dialysate contain glucose, amino acids and salts?

e. Why is there no urea in the dialysate?

A5. a. Calculate the volume of blood that is processed by the dialyser in four hours.

b. Why is the anticoagulant, heparin, added to the blood?

c. Why is heparin not given during the last hour of dialysis?

d. Why is a filter included in the circuit?

e. Suggest why the omission of the bubble trap might prove dangerous to the patient.

f. What would a positive reading on the haemoglobin indicator indicate?

g. The dialysing fluid is kept at 40 °C. Suggest two reasons for this.

h. Excess water can be removed from the blood in two ways. One is to increase the amount of glucose in the dialysing fluid. Explain how this method would work.

i. Another method involves partially clamping the tube in the region shown in Figure A1. Explain the principle involved in removing water in this way.

Figure A1 The essential features of a haemodialysis machine

PRACTICE QUESTIONS

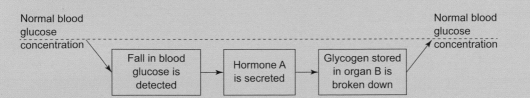

Figure Q1

1. Figure Q1 shows some of the events that maintain blood glucose concentration in a mammal.

   a. Name:

      i. hormone A

      ii. organ B.

   b. Explain why the events shown in Figure Q1 can be described as an example of negative feedback.

   c. Explain how the structure of a glycogen molecule is related to its function in maintaining blood glucose concentration.

   AQA January 2004 Unit 6 Question 2

2. a. When insulin binds to receptors on liver cells, it leads to the formation of glycogen from glucose. This lowers the concentration of glucose in liver cells. Explain how the formation of glycogen in liver cells leads to a lowering of blood glucose concentration.

   People with type 2 diabetes have cells with low sensitivity to insulin. About 80% of people with type 2 diabetes are overweight or obese. Some people who are obese have gastric bypass surgery (GBS) to help them to lose weight.

   Doctors investigated whether GBS affected sensitivity to insulin. They measured patients' sensitivity to insulin before and after GBS. About half of the patients had type 2 diabetes. The other half did not but were considered at high risk of developing the condition.

   Table Q1 shows the doctors' results. The higher the number, the greater the sensitivity to insulin.

Patients	Mean sensitivity to insulin / arbitrary units (± SD)	
	Before GBS	One month after GBS
Did not have diabetes	0.55 (± 0.32)	1.30 (± 0.88)
Had type 2 diabetes	0.40 (± 0.24)	1.10 (± 0.87)

Table Q1

   b. The doctors concluded that many of the patients who did not have type 2 diabetes were at high risk of developing the condition. Use the data in Table Q1 to suggest why they reached this conclusion.

   c. The doctors also concluded that GBS cured many patients' diabetes but that some were not helped very much. Do these data support this conclusion? Give reasons for your answer.

   AQA June 2014 Unit 5 Question 4

3. a. Describe the role of insulin in the control of blood glucose concentration.

   Figure Q2 shows the pathway by which glycogen is broken down in liver and muscle cells.

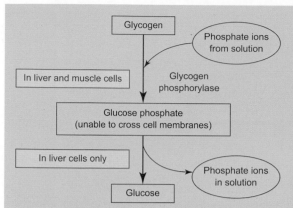

Figure Q2

b. Suggest why it is important that muscle cells do not convert glucose phosphate to glucose.

c. The production of glycogen phosphorylase from an inactive form of the enzyme is triggered by the hormones glucagon and adrenaline, and by calcium ions. Adrenaline is a hormone released when an animal senses danger. This is controlled by the sympathetic nervous system. Figure Q3 shows the receptors for glucagon and adrenaline on liver and muscle cells.

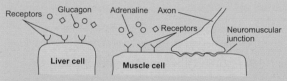

Figure Q3

Use the information in Figures Q2 and Q3 to suggest how glycogen breakdown in liver and muscle cells is increased when an animal runs away from a predator.

AQA January 2003 Unit 4 Question 9

4. Many diabetics inject insulin, because their pancreas has stopped producing it. Attempts have been made to transplant pancreatic cells from human embryos into diabetics, but these foreign cells are often destroyed as a result of antibodies produced by the diabetic's immune system.

Figure Q4 shows a new type of transplant that has been tested in rats.

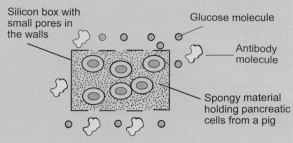

Figure Q4

a. i. Explain why this transplant is not destroyed by the rat but can respond to changes in the rat's blood glucose concentration.

ii. Suggest why there might be controversy if this transplant was used in humans.

b. Explain how the cells in the transplant control the blood glucose concentration of the rat.

AQA June 2003 Unit 4 Question 2

5. a. What is homeostasis?

b. Describe the role of the hormone glucagon in the control of blood sugar concentration.

AQA June 2007 Unit 4 Question 6

6. Read this passage:

Diabetes

Diabetes mellitus is a group of disorders that all lead to an increase in blood glucose concentration (hyperglycaemia). The two major types of diabetes mellitus are type 1 and type 2. In type 1 diabetes there is a deficiency of insulin. Type 1 diabetes is also called insulin-dependent diabetes mellitus because regular injections of insulin are essential. It most commonly develops in people younger than age twenty.

Type 2 diabetes most often occurs in people who are over forty and overweight. Clinical symptoms may be mild, and the high glucose concentrations in the blood can be controlled by diet and exercise. Some type 2 diabetics secrete low amounts of insulin but others have a sufficient amount or even a surplus of insulin in the blood. For these people, diabetes arises not from a shortage of insulin but because target cells become less responsive to it. Type 2 diabetes is therefore called non-insulin-dependent diabetes mellitus.

a. Describe how blood glucose concentration is controlled by hormones in an individual who is not affected by diabetes.

b. Suggest how diet and exercise can maintain low glucose concentrations in the blood of type 2 diabetes.

c. Glucose starts to appear in the urine when the blood glucose concentration exceeds about 180 mg dm^{-3}. Explain how the kidney normally prevents glucose appearing in urine.

AQA June 2000 Unit 3 Question 8

7. In the kidney, ultrafiltration and selective re-absorption are two of the processes involved in the formation of urine.

   a. i. Where does ultrafiltration occur?

      ii. Give **one** component of the blood that is not normally present in the filtrate.

   b. The kidneys remove a substance called creatinine from the blood. The rate of creatinine removal is a measure of the rate of filtration of the blood. In one hour, a person excreted 75 mg of creatinine in his urine. The concentration of creatinine in the blood entering his kidneys was constant at 0.01 mg cm^{-3}.

      Calculate the rate at which the blood was filtered in cm^3 min^{-1}. Show your working.

   c. Re-absorption of glucose takes place in the proximal tubule. Explain how the cells of the proximal tubule are adapted for this function.

AQA January 2008 Unit 1 Question 2

8. a. Mammals control their blood water potential.

   i. Describe how a decrease in the blood water potential is detected.

   ii. Explain how the body responds to a decrease in blood water potential.

The whale is a large mammal that lives in the sea. You probably knew that. Whales take in sea water with their food. They have adaptations that prevent them from dehydrating when they take in sea water. Humans do not have such adaptations. If humans drink sea water they become dehydrated.

Scientists measured the volume of urine produced by whales and by humans when they take in sea water. They also measured the chloride ion content of the urine produced by humans and by whales. Sea water has a chloride concentration of 535 mmol dm^{-3}.

Table Q2 shows the results.

Species	Volume of urine produced per dm^3 of sea water taken in / cm^3	Chloride concentration of urine / mmol dm^{-3}
Human	1350	400
Whale	650	820

Table Q2

   b. Use the data in the table to explain:

      i. why a human who drinks sea water becomes dehydrated

      ii. how a whale is adapted to be able to drink sea water.

   c. Long loops of Henlē enable the whale to produce very concentrated urine. Explain how.

AQA June 2008 Unit 4 Question 5

9 GENES AND INHERITANCE

PRIOR KNOWLEDGE

In Year 1, you looked at the relationship between DNA, genes and chromosomes, before looking at the way in which DNA is used to make proteins. You also saw how meiosis is a special type of cell division that 'shuffles' the genes and makes new allele combinations.

LEARNING OBJECTIVES

In this chapter, we will look at how characteristics can be passed on from parents to their offspring. This branch of biology is called genetics, and it has a weird and wonderful vocabulary all of its own. It is important that you become familiar with these technical terms and are able to use them with confidence.

(Specification 3.7.1)

In 1968, the mother of geneticist Nancy Wexler was diagnosed as having Huntington's disease. Nancy's three uncles, all brothers of her mother, had already died of the distressing condition, the symptoms of which only appear in middle age and include relentless loss of coordination and mental deterioration. Nancy realised that she had a 50:50 chance of developing the disease in later life. However, the Wexler family were not prone to giving in easily.

Nancy's father, Milton, resolved to set up a research foundation to find a cure, if possible in time to save his wife. Sadly, the search was to take much longer than their optimistic hopes. Nancy's mother died 10 years later, but Nancy remained a driving force in the hunt for the elusive gene that causes the disease.

The first breakthrough came when a Venezuelan doctor reported a family in a remote part of his country with large numbers of cases of the disease. Nancy Wexler immediately organised a research team to collect blood samples and eventually traced 11 000 descendants of one 19th-century woman who had carried the fatal gene. Back in the USA, the team analysed the blood samples and discovered that the gene was situated somewhere on chromosome 4.

The gene was much more tricky to find than those of several other genetic disorders, but in 1993, after searching through some five million nucleotide bases on chromosome 4, its position was located (Figure 1). The mutant form of the gene responsible for the disease is nicknamed the 'stuttering gene' because one DNA triplet (CAG) was found to be repeated up to 120 times in people suffering from the disease. Identifying the gene makes it much easier to test, before any symptoms appear, whether individuals in affected families have inherited the disease, and to identify affected children before birth. The next stage is to understand how the mutant form of the gene, which is a dominant allele, affects the brain and causes such devastating results. Then treatment and a cure can become a real possibility.

At the time of writing, there is no still no cure for this invariably fatal disease. Nevertheless, research continues to progress. We now know that the disease is caused by a mutation in the gene that encodes a protein called huntingtin. In people with the normal form of the gene, the huntingtin protein contains fewer than 35 glutamines (one of the 20 types of amino acid), but in people with Huntington's disease the protein has 36 or more glutamines. This appears to make the protein molecules clump together. Some results suggest that the resulting damage to neurones may be caused by the person's own immune system treating the huntingtin as a foreign protein, and making complementary antibodies.

Source: adapted from an article by Susan Katz Miller, New Scientist, 24 April 1993.

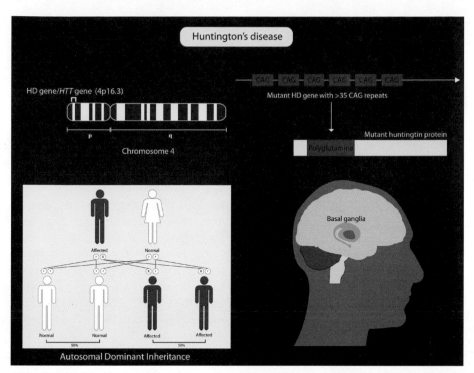

Figure 1 *The Huntington's disease gene has been located on the short arm of chromosome 4. Different alleles have different number of CAG repeats, which translate into proteins with long tails consisting of the amino acid glutamine. These tails make the proteins clump together and prevent the brain cells from functioning properly.*

9.1 GENES AND PHENOTYPES

A reminder of basic terms

Let's start with one of the most obvious – the term **gene**. You probably remember from Year 1 that a gene is a length of DNA that codes for a particular polypeptide or protein. Despite all the discoveries made by the Human Genome Project, we still do not know exactly how many genes there are in a human cell, but we think it is probably just over 20 000. These genes are found on **chromosomes**, of which we have 46. Each chromosome is a very long, supercoiled molecule of DNA. There are hundreds or thousands of genes on most of the chromosomes.

Each human body cell has two complete sets of chromosomes. A cell with two sets of chromosomes is said to be **diploid**. We have 23 chromosomes in each set, making 46 in all. One set came from the father and one set from the mother. Different species have different numbers of chromosomes. Guinea pigs have 64. Chimpanzees have 48, chickens and dogs have 78. There is no relationship between the number of chromosomes and the complexity of the organism.

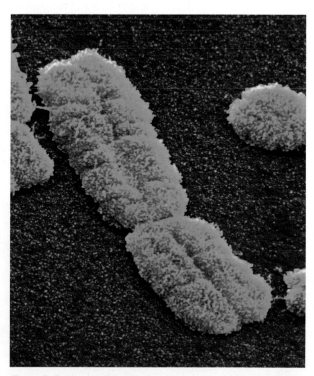

Figure 2 *False-colour scanning electron microscope image of a chromosome just before cell division, showing the two chromatids joined at the centromere. Magnification ×8500.*

Genotypes

An organism's *genotype* is simply the complete set of gene variants, or forms, that it has inherited. Many genes occur in more than one form. Different forms of the same gene are called **alleles**. A simple example would be a gene for flower colour with two alleles, one coding for red flowers and one coding for white flowers.

We all have the same genes, but we don't all have the same alleles unless we have an identical twin. These alleles are responsible for genetic variation, and cause some of the observable characteristics of individuals within a species – their phenotypes. As we shall see, other phenotypic characteristics are due to an interaction of the characteristics determined by the alleles, with the environment.

> It is possible that some genes that code for essential proteins effectively have no alleles, because any change to the DNA sequence of the gene would lead to a non functioning protein. Any diploid inheriting two would fail – in a haploid organism, one would be fatal.

> Some genes have two alleles. We study their inheritance in this chapter.

> Some genes have more than two alleles. For example, the gene that controls the ABO blood group has three alleles. We look at these **multiple alleles** later in the chapter.

A dominant allele is defined as one which, if present, is expressed and therefore can be seen in the phenotype. Recessive alleles are only expressed in the absence of the dominant one.

Figure 3 shows a full set of chromosomes in a human body cell. It is not a 'natural' picture – after the micrograph is taken the chromosomes are cut and pasted so that each is alongside its homologous pair, and arranged in order of size.

The essential facts about homologous chromosomes are:

> they have the same genes

> at the same positions (or loci)

> but they may or may not have the same alleles.

You may remember that if both alleles are the same, the individual is said to be **homozygous** for that gene, and the genotype would be written as, say, AA or aa. If the homologous chromosomes each have a different allele they are said to be **heterozygous**, written as Aa.

It makes things easier if we use shorthand symbols to represent different alleles of a gene. The convention is to use one letter for the two alleles. The upper-case letter is used for the dominant allele, and the lower-case letter for the recessive allele. So, in the case of Huntington's disease, we could use h to represent the normal gene for huntingtin – because it's recessive – and H to represent the abnormal allele.

As there are two copies of each gene in each cell, there are three possible combinations of alleles.

They are: HH   Hh   hh

We do not need to write down hH as well, because this is no different to Hh.

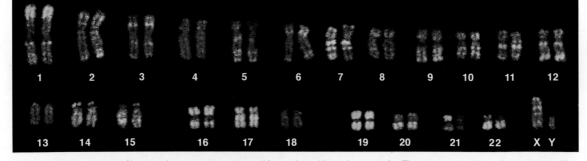

Figure 3 The full complement of human chromosomes arranged in numbered homologous pairs. These are metaphase chromosomes. These pictures are prepared by stimulating cells to divide and then adding a chemical that inhibits spindle movement, thus 'freezing' the cells in mid-mitosis. The cell is then photographed and the chromosomes are arranged by cutting and pasting. Note that this individual is a male, as shown by the X and Y chromosome.

Phenotypes

Phenotype is defined as the observable or measurable features that an organism possesses. 'Dark hair and left handed' would be an example. Most phenotypic features can also be affected by the environment, for example, skin colour going darker in the sun.

Many genetic diseases are causes by mutant alleles that do not code for the required protein. Cystic fibrosis is a classic example (see below). In cases like this, the individual will not have the disease unless they are unfortunate enough to inherit two faulty alleles. Heterozygotes are healthy, because one functioning allele is all you need. This means that the cystic fibrosis allele is recessive. Huntington's disease is different. Here the mutant allele codes for a protein that actively causes damage, and so isn't masked by a normal allele. In the case of Huntington's, individuals only need to have one copy of the allele to have the disease. So with Huntington's disease, a genotype of hh gives the normal phenotype, while a genotype of Hh or HH means that the individual will develop the disease at some stage in their life.

You will often find it helpful when you are answering genetics questions on examination papers to start by quickly jotting down all the different possible genotypes and their corresponding phenotypes, like this:

Genotype	Phenotype
HH	Huntington's disease
Hh	Huntington's disease
hh	normal

Codominance

Not all alleles behave in a simple dominant/recessive fashion. Some are codominant, which means that if two different alleles are present, they will both be expressed. The snapdragon flower is a simple example. Petal colour is controlled by two alleles, one for red and one for white. If an individual plant is heterozygous it will have pink flowers because both alleles are expressed, and therefore shown in the phenotype.

The human ABO blood group system is a good example of codominance. Every individual can be placed into a group: A, B, AB or O, on the basis of the proteins that they carry on their red blood cells. Group A individuals have the A proteins on their red cells, Group B people have B proteins, AB have both, O have neither. This is controlled by one gene with three alleles, as shown.

I^A	The allele that gives blood group A
I^B	The allele that gives blood group B
I^o	The allele that gives blood group O

I^A and I^B are codominant over I^o. When the two alleles I^A and I^B are present together, *both* of them affect the phenotype. The person has blood group AB. This explains why they are written using the same letter with a different superscript. If we used just the letters A and B, this would imply that they were different *genes*, not just different alleles of the same gene. If we used A to represent the allele giving blood group A, and a to represent the allele giving blood group B, this would imply that allele A is dominant and allele a is recessive, which is not true. So, when choosing symbols for codominant alleles, use one symbol to represent the gene, and then different superscripts to code for its different alleles.

If you look very carefully, you may be able to spot that the superscript in I^o is actually a lower-case o, not an upper-case O. This is done because this allele is recessive to both I^A and I^B.

Armed with this information, we can write down all the possible genotypes and phenotypes:

Blood group genotype	Blood group phenotype
$I^A I^A$	group A
$I^A I^B$	group AB
$I^A I^o$	group A
$I^B I^B$	group B
$I^B I^o$	group B
$I^o I^o$	group O

The term used to describe a situation where there are three or more different alleles of a gene is **multiple alleles**.

QUESTIONS

2. A faulty allele of the gene that codes for haemoglobin produces a form of this protein that cannot transport oxygen when oxygen concentrations are low. A person with two of these faulty alleles has a disease called sickle cell anaemia. A person with one copy of the faulty allele and one normal allele has a mild form of the disease called sickle cell trait.

   a. Do these alleles show dominance or codominance? Explain your answer.

   b. Choose suitable symbols for the sickle cell allele and the normal allele.

   c. Write down the possible genotypes and the phenotypes that they produce.

KEY IDEAS

› A gene is a length of DNA that codes for the production of a particular protein.

› The observable characteristics of an organism are known as its phenotype.

› Phenotype = genotype + environment.

› A diploid cell contains two sets of chromosomes. There are therefore two copies of each chromosome in a set, and two copies of the genes that they carry.

› Homologous chromosomes carry the same genes at the same loci.

› Genes often come in different forms, called alleles.

› The alleles of a gene that an organism has are known as its genotype. If the two alleles are the same, it is homozygous. If they are different, it is heterozygous.

› An allele is said to be dominant if it exerts its full effect on the phenotype even when a different allele of the same gene is also present. An allele that only has an effect when no other allele is present is said to be recessive. If both alleles have an effect in a heterozygote, they are said to be codominant.

› Some genes have three or more different alleles, known as multiple alleles.

9.2 INHERITING GENES

Monohybrid inheritance – the inheritance of one gene

As you know, your genes came from your parents. You inherited one complete set of genes from your mother and one complete set from your father. They were passed on to you when the nucleus of a sperm and the nucleus of an egg fused. The two sets of genes became the genes of the **zygote**, and were copied over and over again as the zygote divided by mitosis to form all the billions of cells in your body.

To understand how genes are inherited, you need to think back to what you know about how gametes are produced. You will probably remember that, in animals, gametes are made by **meiosis** – a special kind of cell division in which the normal chromosome number is halved. Meiosis of diploid cells in a woman's ovary or a man's testis produces cells with only a single set of chromosomes. They are said to be **haploid**. Each gamete has only 23 chromosomes, rather than 46.

Because of this, each gamete has only one copy of each gene, not two. Using the example of Huntington's disease, an individual can have the genotype HH, Hh or hh. If a man has the genotype HH, each of his sperm will contain one copy of the H allele. If he has the genotype Hh, approximately half of his sperm will contain an H allele, and the other half will have an h allele. Understanding this enables us to predict the genotypes – and therefore the phenotypes – of the offspring of a couple. Let's take an example of a woman with the genotype hh and a man with the genotype Hh.

Each of the woman's ova (eggs) will contain an h allele. As we have seen, half of the man's sperm will be genotype H, and half will be genotype h. When a sperm fertilises an egg in the woman's oviduct, there is an equal chance that it will be an H sperm or an h sperm. This means that there is an equal chance that the child will have the genotype Hh or hh.

We can show all this in a particular format known as a **genetic diagram**. These may seem a nuisance to write out, especially if you are quick at seeing how things work, but it is important to do it correctly and it is good practice for when things get more complex. The genetic diagram for this Huntington's disease-related cross is shown in Figure 4.

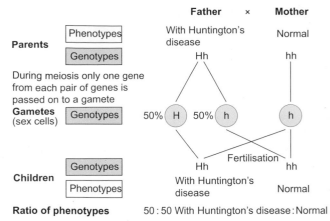

Parents

Phenotypes

Genotypes

Father × Mother

With Huntington's disease — Normal

Hh — hh

During meiosis only one gene from each pair of genes is passed on to a gamete

Gametes (sex cells)

Genotypes

50% H 50% h h

Children

Genotypes

Phenotypes

Hh   Fertilisation   hh

With Huntington's disease — Normal

Ratio of phenotypes   50 : 50 With Huntington's disease : Normal

Figure 4 *Genetic diagram for the inheritance of Huntington's disease.*

Case study: cystic fibrosis

Cystic fibrosis is a genetic disease that is caused by a faulty allele of a gene that controls the formation of an important membrane protein. This protein is called CFTR. Its function is to control the movement of chloride ions out of cells. This is especially important in the cells in the lungs. Normally, chloride ions are moved out of the cells through this protein, and water molecules follow. If the protein is not working, chloride ions cannot move out. This means there is less water outside the cells. This results in the production of sticky mucus, which causes difficulties with getting air into and out of the lungs, as well as problems with gas exchange across the walls of the alveoli. The mucus builds up and is prone to becoming infected with bacteria.

Unlike the allele that causes Huntington's disease, the allele that causes cystic fibrosis is recessive. It's simply a protein that doesn't work. We can use the symbol F for the normal (dominant) allele, and f for the faulty one. (C and c are not a good choice, because you won't be able to tell the difference between them if you are writing quickly.) The genetic diagram in Figure 5 shows

how two parents who do not have cystic fibrosis can have a child who does.

Probabilities in genetics

In the genetic diagram showing the inheritance of cystic fibrosis (Figure 5), we have a list of four genotypes for the offspring. This does not mean that the couple will have four children; it simply shows the possible results of the different gametes fusing together. It indicates the *probability* of each of these genotypes occurring. It shows us that, each time these two parents have a child, there is a one in four chance that the child will get one copy of the cystic fibrosis allele from each parent, and therefore have cystic fibrosis.

There are several ways in which we can write down these probabilities. We can say that:

> The ratio of normal offspring to cystic fibrosis offspring is likely to be 3 : 1.

> The probability of the child having cystic fibrosis is 0.25.

> 25% of the offspring are likely to have cystic fibrosis.

These all mean the same thing.

If you toss a coin 50 times, you'd expect it to fall heads down 25 times and tails down 25 times. But it might not, as we are dealing with chance and probability. If you toss the coin six times, you might get three heads and three tails, but you could also get four of one and two of the other, or even five of one and one of the other. Or, you could get six heads or six tails. The more often you toss the coin, the more likely you are to get to a 1 : 1 ratio of heads to tails.

It's the same with genetics. When there are large numbers of offspring, we tend to see the ratios that we would expect. When there are small numbers, we should not be surprised if these ratios are not achieved. If the couple in Figure 5 had four children, we would be correct in predicting that they would probably have three who were normal and one with cystic fibrosis. But they might have four normal children, or two with cystic fibrosis.

And, of course, they might not have four children. They might have none, or one, or three, or seven. All we can say is that each time they have a child, there is a one in four chance that the child will have cystic fibrosis.

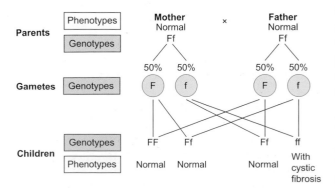

Parents

Phenotypes

Genotypes

Mother Normal × Father Normal

Ff — Ff

Gametes

Genotypes

50% 50%   50% 50%

F f   F f

Children

Genotypes

Phenotypes

FF   Ff   Ff   ff

Normal Normal Normal With cystic fibrosis

Figure 5 *Inheriting cystic fibrosis*

Another important thing to remember is that whenever the couple has a child, the chance of that child having cystic fibrosis is *not affected* by whether or not their other children have the disease. Each time, the probability of the child having cystic fibrosis is 0.25, no matter what the genotype of any brothers or sisters.

Note: the examples given in this book – Huntington's disease and cystic fibrosis – are to aid your understanding of genetics; they are not required knowledge that you will need to recall in an examination.

ASSIGNMENT 1: INHERITANCE OF HUNTINGTON'S DISEASE

The pedigree diagram in Figure A1 shows the incidence of Huntington's disease in three generations of a family. Pedigree diagrams are family trees, though they can feature any species, not just humans. By convention, the oldest are at the top, males are squares and females are circles. The lines below shows their children/offspring. This diagram shows three generations; the grandparents are at the top, grandchildren at the bottom.

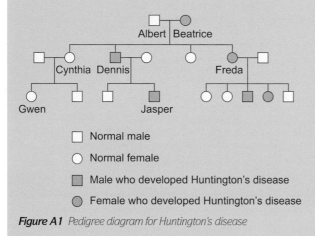

▢ Normal male

◯ Normal female

▨ Male who developed Huntington's disease

◉ Female who developed Huntington's disease

Figure A1 *Pedigree diagram for Huntington's disease*

Questions

A1. Describe the evidence in the family tree that Beatrice was heterozygous for Huntington's disease.

A2. Gwen goes on to have three children. She is worried that they might develop Huntington's disease. What advice would you give her? Construct a genetic diagram as part of your explanation.

A3. What are the chances that a child of Jasper's will develop Huntington's disease?

A4. It would be possible to test each of Jasper's children when they are young, or even before birth, to find out if they have the allele for Huntington's disease. If you were Jasper or his wife, would you want to have this test done? Do you think it would be right to offer this test to parents? Discuss your reasons – both scientific and ethical – and explain the possible problems that might result from the use of such a test.

A5. Although Huntington's disease is always fatal, it has not been removed by natural selection and continues to be passed on from parents to offspring. Look back at the introduction to this chapter, and explain why this is so.

QUESTIONS

3. Construct a genetic diagram to show the possible genotypes and phenotypes of the offspring of a man with the genotype $I^A I^A$ and a woman with the genotype $I^B I^o$. Complete your genetic diagram with a statement about the expected ratios of each genotype and phenotype in their offspring.

4. A woman with blood group A has a child with blood group O. The paternity of the child is not known. One possible father has blood group AB and another has blood group A.

   Construct genetic diagrams to show which of these men could definitely not be the father of the child.

ASSIGNMENT 2: BREEDING PEDIGREE CATS

The study of genetics is extremely useful when it comes to breeding domestic animals and improving the quality of crop plants. Most of the animals that we commonly use for food or have as pets are very different from their wild ancestors – they are the result of generations of selective breeding.

In cats, a gene (C) is associated with the colour of the animal's coat. There are three alleles. The normal allele, C^C, makes the cat's coat blackish and is dominant. Siamese cats have a recessive allele, C^s, and they must be homozygous for this allele. Burmese cats have a different allele of the gene, C^b, which makes the coat colour dark brown instead of pale cream. The extremities are black as in Siamese cats. Burmese cats are homozygous for the C^b allele, while Tonkinese cats are $C^b C^s$.

Why do Siamese cats have dark extremities? The C^s allele codes for an enzyme that synthesises black pigment, but this enzyme is very temperature sensitive and only works at below body temperature. The mutant allele codes for an enzyme with a tertiary structure that is slightly different from that of the normal enzyme, but molecules of this enzyme happen to unfold (denature) at about 37 °C. The Siamese cat is therefore only black in the cooler parts of the body, such as the tail, ears and lower legs. The rest of the coat is pale cream

coloured. This shows how both the genotype and the environment can affect the phenotype.

Questions

A1. **a.** What are the genotypes of a Siamese cat and of a Burmese cat?

b. Most cats have the normal allele, C^C. What will the kittens be like if a Siamese cat mates with an ordinary homozygous black cat? Explain your answer with a genetic diagram.

A2. When a cat breeder mated a Siamese cat with a Burmese cat, all the kittens in the litter had pale brown coats.

a. What is the genotype of this breeder's pale brown kittens?

b. Are the alleles in this genotype codominant? Explain your answer.

c. What results would you expect if two of these pale brown cats interbreed, producing large litters?

d. The breeder wants to sell kittens with the pale brown coat colour. How should she obtain litters of kittens with this coat colour?

Figure A1 (Left to right) A Siamese cat, a Burmese cat and a Tonkinese cat

A3. a. When the two alleles of a gene are dominant and recessive, crossing heterozygotes gives a 3 : 1 ratio of phenotypes in the offspring. What is the ratio of phenotypes when the two alleles are codominant?

b. Manx cats are tail-less. When bred together they produce an apparently odd ratio of two tail-less : one normal tailed kittens. This is because embryos that are homozygous for the Manx allele fail to develop in the womb and are never born. Figure A2 shows how the ratio arises. What proportion of kittens will have tails if a Manx cat mates with a tailed cat? Explain your answer.

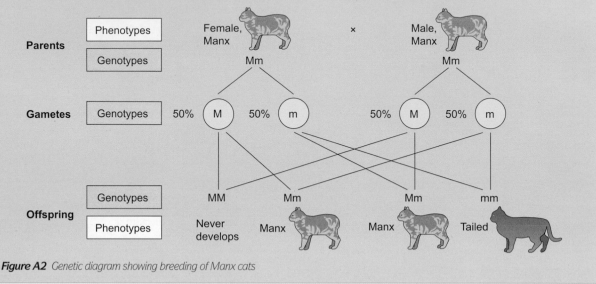

Figure A2 *Genetic diagram showing breeding of Manx cats*

Autosomes and sex chromosomes

In humans and many other animals, specific chromosomes determine sex. There are different types of sex-determination chromosome systems. In humans, each cell has 46 chromosomes: 22 pairs of **autosomes** and one pair of **sex chromosomes**. The autosomes all come in homologous pairs. Women have two X chromosomes, which are also homologous. Men have one X and one Y, which are not homologous. Hence in humans, sex is determined by the X and Y chromosomes. However not all organisms have XX females and XY males. In some insects females are XX and males are X – the absence of an extra chromosome is associated with maleness. In birds it is the male that has two of the same chromosomes – males are ZZ and females are ZW. In the following examples we will use the human system to illustrate sex-linked genes.

Genes that are found on the sex chromosomes are said to be sex-linked. In humans, those that are carried on the X chromosome are X-linked, and those on the Y chromosome are said to be Y-linked. Currently, it is estimated that there are about 2000 genes on the human X chromosome, compared with just 78 on the Y chromosome.

Women have two copies of each gene on the X chromosomes, but men only have one. So, if a man has a faulty allele on his X chromosome, he will have whatever trait or disease that allele codes for, because there isn't another one to mask its effect. It is important to remember that as far as X-linked genes are concerned, men can't be carriers.

A classic example is red/green colour blindness. A particular X-linked gene affects a pigment in the retina of the eye. A mutant allele of this gene causes red/green colour blindness. A person with this allele cannot distinguish between red and green. Since males have only one X chromosome, they have only one copy of this gene. If this gene is the mutant allele, they will be red/green colour blind. Females will only be red/green colour blind if they inherit the allele on both chromosomes. This explains why this type of colour blindness is much more common in men than women.

Males have a one in two chance of inheriting the condition if their mother carries the mutant allele, as shown in Figure 6.

Notice how the alleles are written. For sex-linked genes, you need to show the chromosome as well as the allele. This is done writing an X plus a superscript – such as X^H – to indicate the particular allele carried. The Y chromosome is written as Y or Y^-, to show that it does not contain that gene.

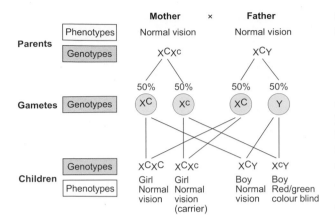

Figure 6 The inheritance of red/green colour blindness

QUESTIONS

5. **a.** What percentage of children from the cross shown in Figure 6 are colour blind? What percentage of girls and what percentage of boys?

   b. What parental genotypes could produce a red/green colour-blind girl?

   c. Explain why a son never inherits red/green colour blindness from his father.

Worked example

Examination questions often feature pedigree diagrams, or family trees. The pedigree diagram in Figure 7 shows the pattern of inheritance of one type of myopia (short-sightedness) in a family.

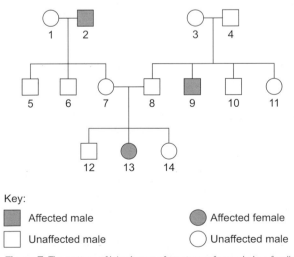

Key:

■ Affected male   ● Affected female

□ Unaffected male   ○ Unaffected male

Figure 7 The pattern of inheritance of one type of myopia in a family

Give one piece of evidence from the diagram that suggests:

▶ that the allele for myopia is recessive

▶ that the allele is not sex-linked.

As a general point, always try to name individuals in your answer, rather than stating vague generalities. In this case, affected individuals 9 and 13 are both born to unaffected parents. In both cases, the parents must be carrying the alleles. Therefore, it is recessive by definition.

The key to these questions is that males get their Y chromosome from their fathers (otherwise they would not be males) and so must get their X chromosome from their mothers. Using the notation N for the dominant allele and n for the recessing allele, individual 13 must be X^nX^n. However, her father (8) only has one copy of the allele and he isn't affected. He must be $X^N Y$ in order to be unaffected, so he hasn't got an n allele to pass to his daughter. Therefore, it can't be X-linked

Haemophilia as an example of a sex-linked disorder

Haemophilia is an inherited disease in which the blood fails to clot easily. This causes internal bleeding, especially in the joints. The most common reason for haemophilia is shortage of a blood-clotting protein known as Factor VIII. The gene for Factor VIII is located on the X chromosome, so it is X-linked. Males are much more likely to inherit haemophilia because they have only one copy of the X chromosome. Females can carry the faulty allele, and pass it on to their sons, but they themselves show no signs of haemophilia. A female zygote that is homozygous for this allele usually dies soon after fertilisation, so women with haemophilia are rare.

The normal dominant allele that produces Factor VIII is written as X^H, and the recessive allele that results in failure to produce Factor VIII is X^h.

Genetic counselling can help people to decide whether or not to have children. Couples whose babies are at risk from a serious genetic disorder, such as haemophilia, may choose to have tests during the early stages of pregnancy and perhaps opt for a termination if the embryo is affected. (IVF and embryo screening can be used in some cases to ensure that only embryos that do not carry specific genetic disorders are implanted into the mother.) When a haemophiliac man marries a woman who does not have haemophilia, the couple may opt for genetic testing to find out if the woman is carrying the allele for haemophilia. This would be very unlikely, but if it were the case, a boy child born to the couple would have a 50:50 chance of having haemophilia (dpending on whether the X chromosome inherited from his mother carris the allele for haemophilia). Under these circumstances, the couple may make an informed decision not to have children at all.

If the woman is not carrying the allele, none of their children will have the disorder, because sons will inherit an X chromosome with a normal allele from their mother. None of the boys will carry the gene for haemophilia so they cannot pass it on to their children. However, the girls will carry the haemophilia allele, because they inherit one of their X chromosomes from their father and this must carry the recessive allele. Later in life, they should be aware that if they have children, there is a 50% chance of their sons having haemophilia, and this is assuming that the father does not have haemophilia.

QUESTIONS

6. **a.** What is the genotype of a male with haemophilia?
    b. Females with haemophilia are rare. What would be the most likely genotypes of the parents of a girl born with haemophilia?

Dihybrid inheritance

We have looked at the inheritance of one gene with two alleles. Things get more complex when we look at two genes, each with two alleles. We start by looking at genes on different chromosomes – they are all on separate ones – and so, as a result of meiosis, they can pass into the gametes in any combination. If the

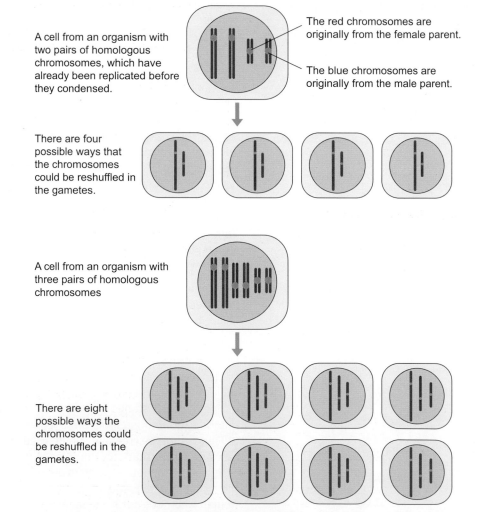

A cell from an organism with two pairs of homologous chromosomes, which have already been replicated before they condensed.

The red chromosomes are originally from the female parent.

The blue chromosomes are originally from the male parent.

There are four possible ways that the chromosomes could be reshuffled in the gametes.

A cell from an organism with three pairs of homologous chromosomes

There are eight possible ways the chromosomes could be reshuffled in the gametes.

Figure 8 An overview of meiosis, showing independent segregation (also called independent assortment). The basic laws of genetics were worked out by a monk, Gregor Mendel, in the 1860s. However, his work wasn't appreciated until the process of meiosis was discovered around 1900. The vital point here is that any one of a pair of chromosomes can pass into the gamete with any from another pair. This means that an individual with a genotype of AaBb can produce gametes of AB, aB, Ab or ab.

genes are on the same chromosome they are said to be **linked**. That is a different situation, which is covered later in this chapter.

The vital steps in working out the outcomes of a dihybrid cross are:

1. **Work out the parents' genotypes**, if they haven't been given to you. Sometimes you have to figure out the genotype from a description of the phenotype.

2. **Work out the possible gametes**. This is where your knowledge of meiosis can be applied. You need to understand what is meant by independent segregation. It's a good idea to make the gametes clear by putting a circle round them.

3. **Work out the outcomes of all possible fertilisations**. Fertilisation is always random, so any male gamete can combine with any female gamete.

4. **Translate the genotypes into phenotypes and work out the ratios/probabilities**.

Worked example of dihybrid inheritance

Consider the following traits in mice. Coat colour is controlled by one gene with two alleles: B for black fur is dominant to b for brown fur. A second gene controls hair length. The allele A for short hair is dominant to allele a, for long hair.

What happens when a homozygous black, short-haired mouse of genotype AABB mates with a homozygous brown, long-haired mouse of genotype aabb? Will these characteristics always be inherited together, or can they be separated, so you get mice with long black fur, or short brown fur? This short answer is yes, because that's the magic of meiosis and sexual reproduction – meiosis produces new combinations of alleles. Figure 9 shows the process.

The F1 generation is very straightforward because all the gametes are the same (AB and ab) and

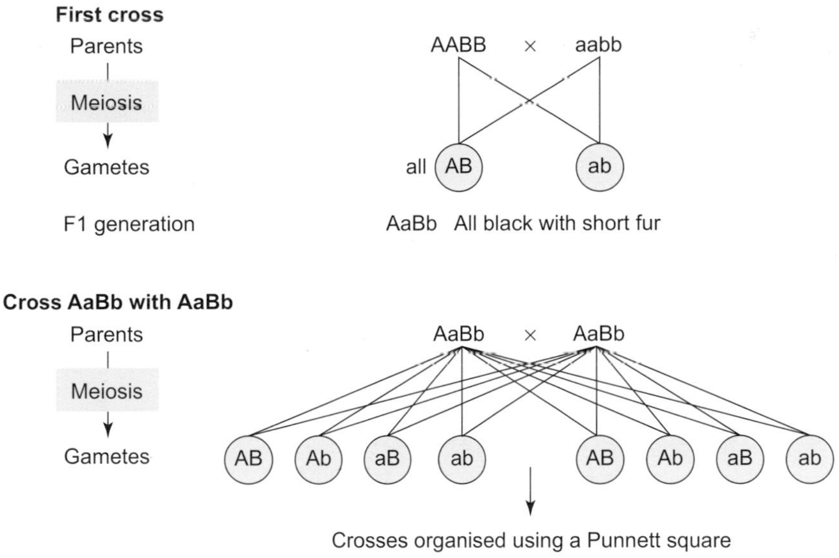

First cross

Parents — Meiosis → Gametes

AABB × aabb

all (AB) (ab)

F1 generation   AaBb   All black with short fur

Cross AaBb with AaBb

Parents — Meiosis → Gametes

AaBb × AaBb

(AB) (Ab) (aB) (ab)   (AB) (Ab) (aB) (ab)

Crosses organised using a Punnett square

	Female gametes			
	AB	Ab	aB	ab
AB	AABB	AABb	AaBB	AaBb
Ab	AABb	AAbb	AaBb	Aabb
aB	AaBB	AaBb	aaBB	aaBb
ab	AaBb	Aabb	aaBb	aabb

Male gametes (label on left for rows AB, Ab, aB, ab)

F2 generation

Black, short fur	Black, long fur	brown, short fur	Brown, long fur
9	3	3	1

A 9 : 3 : 3 : 1 ratio is typical for the F2 generation in a dihybrid cross

Figure 9 A dihybrid cross

so all fertilisations produce genotypes of AaBb. They all look the same – black with short fur. The fun starts when mice with genotype AaBb start reproducing together.

If you start with a genotype of AaBb, you have four different alleles, each of which is on a separate chromosome. By independent segregation in meiosis, either of the first two can go into the gamete with either of the second two. This gives gametes of AB, Ab, aB and ab from both male and female. Fertilisation gives a total of 16 (4 × 4) different possibilities. To organise your thoughts, you can use a Punnett square, as shown in Figure 9.

QUESTIONS

7. When both parents are heterozygous for both alleles, as in Figure 9, that's as complicated as dihybrid inheritance gets. All other genotypes produce simpler combinations.

   Work out the ratio of phenotypes you would expect from the following crosses:

   a. AABb × AaBB

   b. aaBb × AAbb

   c. Aabb × aaBb

Use of the chi-squared test in genetics

Chi-squared is a statistical test that can be used to see whether there is a significant difference between the observed results (what you got) and the expected results (predicted from theory). We covered the use of the test in Chapter 5. The chi-squared test can also be used in genetics to compare the goodness of fit of observed phenotypic ratios with expected ratios. For example, if a particular cross is made, and the ratios of offspring are not as expected, are the differences simply due to chance or is there some other interaction at work, for example, epistasis, where the expression of one gene is affected by and dependent on the expression of another gene (this is described in more detail later in this chapter)?

Genetic crosses in plants

A yellow-flowered plant was crossed with a red-flowered plant. The resulting offspring (F1) were all orange. This would suggest that there is one gene with two alleles. These alleles codes for different proteins – probably enzymes – that make different pigments that lead to differently coloured flowers. Allele R codes for red and r codes for yellow flowers. It seems that these alleles are codominant, and a genotype of Rr results orange flowers. If this hypothesis is true, you would

expect a ratio of 1 red : 2 orange : 1 yellow in the F2 generation. However, when these flowers were selfed (bred together) the results in Table 1 were obtained.

Phenotype	Observed numbers	Expected numbers
Red	77	80
Orange	162	160
Yellow	61	80
Total	320	320

Table 1

There were 320 individual plants in this F2 generation so you would expect something close to 80 : 160 : 80. These results might seem to be close enough to the expected ratio to support the hypothesis, but 320 is a good number of crosses – more than enough to minimise sampling error – and so a trained geneticist might look for another explanation.

A second hypothesis is that there is epistasis occurring – a situation where the expression of one allele depends on the possession of another allele of a different gene. See page 170. Often, these alleles code for enzymes in a metabolic pathway. Without both enzymes, the end product – in this case a pigment – cannot be made. The situation is more complex than one gene with two alleles. Perhaps there are two genes, each with two alleles. Alleles R and r both code for red flowers, but allele R needs to be present in order for the Y/y gene to be expressed. It both R and Y are present, flowers are orange. If R is present but Y is not, flowers are yellow. In the absence of allele R, all flowers are red.

If this second hypothesis is true, we would expect the following numbers in the F2 generation (Table 2):

Proportion	Genotype	Phenotype	Expected numbers
9/16	Y–R–	Orange	180
3/16	yyR–	Yellow	60
3/16	Y–rr	Red	80
1/16	yyrr		

Note: a dash – means that the other allele doesn't matter

Table 2

So, which hypothesis is best supported by the observed results? The chi-squared test can be used to find out. Chi-squared is always calculated from actual numbers and not percentages, proportions or fractions. Sample size is therefore very important.

The formula for chi-squared, χ^2, is:

$$\chi^2 = \sum \frac{(O - E)^2}{E}$$

where O represents the observed results and E represents the results that we get by calculation,

using the expected ratio from theory and the number of offspring.

For hypothesis 1 (one gene, two alleles, codominant), the calculation is as in Table 3:

Phenotype	Observed (O)	Expected (E)	$(O - E)^2$	$(O - E)^2/E$
Orange	182	160	484	3.0
Yellow	61	80	361	4.5
Red	77	80	9	0.1
				$\chi^2 = 7.6$

Table 3

For hypothesis 2 (two genes, two alleles, epistasis), the calculation is as shown in Table 4:

Phenotype	Observed (O)	Expected (E)	$(O - E)^2$	$(O - E)^2/E$
Orange	182	160	4	0.02
Yellow	61	60	1	0.02
Red	77	80	9	0.11
				$\chi^2 = 0.15$

Table 4

We now need to look up the values on a table of values of χ. We must first work out the number of **degrees of freedom** in order to look in the right row of the table. The number of degrees of freedom is one less than the number of categories. This

investigation has three categories so the number of degrees of freedom is 2.

We really want to know whether the χ^2 value is above or below the critical 5% value. So we need to use Table 5.

Degrees of freedom	Probability (p)							
	0.975	0.9	0.50	0.25	0.10	0.05	0.02	0.01
1	0.000	0.016	0.45	1.32	2.71	3.84	5.41	6.64
2	0.051	0.211	1.39	2.77	4.61	5.99	7.82	9.21
3	0.216	0.584	2.37	4.11	6.25	7.82	9.84	11.34
4	0.484	1.064	3.36	5.39	7.78	9.49	11.67	13.28

Table 5 *Table of chi-squared values*

For hypothesis 1, the χ^2 value of 7.6 and 2 degrees of freedom gives us a probability between 0.05 (5%) and 0.02 (2%). This means that you would expect results to differ by as much as this between 2% and 5% of the time.

For hypothesis 2, the χ^2 value of 0.15 and 2 degrees of freedom gives us a probability between 0.9 (90%) and 0.975 (97.5%). This means that you would expect the results to differ by this much more than 90% of the time.

From this we can conclude that hypothesis 2 (epistasis) is much more likely.

Adapted from An Introduction to Genetic Analysis, 7th Edition, Published by Freeman.

Autosomal linkage

When genes occur together on the same autosome, they are said to be **linked**. This means that they will always be inherited together, unless they are separated by crossing over between (non-sister) chromatids on homologous chromosomes during meiosis. You may remember that crossing over occurs during the first meiotic division, when homologous chromosomes lie alongside each other and points of crossover – called **chiasmata** – are formed at random points along the chromosome. The result is that blocks of genes are swapped between the homologous chromosomes, and the result is new allele combinations.

If two genes are located at opposite ends of the chromosome, they will almost always be separated by crossing over. The closer they are together, the more rarely they will be separated by crossing over. This fact can be used to figure out the relative positions (loci) of genes on chromosomes.

Evidence that genes are linked comes by looking at the offspring. Taking the example of the rats above, we saw that if two black, short-haired rats of genotype AaBb were crossed, you would expect a ratio of 9 : 3 : 3 : 1. However, that assumes that the genes are on different chromosomes, and so can be separated by independent segregation in meiosis. It's a different matter if the genes are on the same chromosome. The tell-tale sign of linkage is when greater numbers of offspring have the same phenotypes as their parents, and fewer are phenotypically different to their parents.

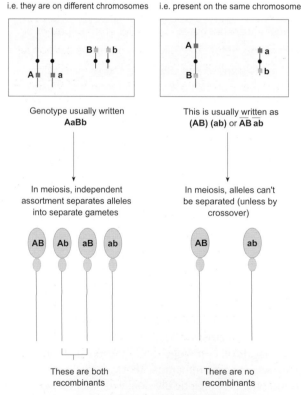

Figure 10 *When two genes are close together on the same chromosome, they are almost always inherited together. They can only be separated by crossover. The chance of being separated by crossover depends on the distance between them.*

Worked example of linkage

In the sweet pea plant, the allele for purple flowers is dominant to the allele for red flowers, and the allele for elongated pollen is dominant to round pollen (which develops into the plant's male gamete).

If pure breeding (in other words, homozygous) plants with purple flowers and elongated pollen grains are crossed with plants with red flowers and round pollen grains, the F1 are all purple with elongated pollen grains. When the F1 are selfed (bred together), you would expect a 9 : 3 : 3 : 1 ratio. This does not happen because the genes for flower colour and pollen grains are found on the same chromosome. There are more plants like the 'parents' – purple/elongated and red/round – and fewer recombinants (offspring that have different allele combinations to their parents). The actual results are shown in Table 6:

Phenotype	Approximate numbers expected if no linkage (9 : 3 : 3 : 1 ratio)	Observed numbers
Purple, elongated	405	336
Purple, rounded	135	31
Red, elongated	135	28
Red, rounded	45	325
Total	720	720

Table 6

The purple/rounded and red/elongated plants are known as recombinants, because they have new combinations of alleles – produced by crossing over. Of the 720 offspring, 59 (31 + 29) are recombinants. This is 8% and so we can say that the loci for flower colour and pollen shape are eight genetic units apart. If they were further apart, there would be more opportunities for chiasmata to form between them, and there would be more recombinants.

Epistasis

Epistasis is a situation where the expression of one gene depends on (and is affected by) the expression of another gene. A classic example of this is seen in coat colour in Labrador dogs. Generally, there are three colour varieties, golden (or yellow), brown and black (Figure 11).

Figure 11 *The three colour varieties of Labrador dog – the most popular pedigree dog in the UK.*

A first gene controls the colour of the pigment in the fur.

› Allele B codes for black pigment.

› Allele b codes for brown pigment.

However, without the presence of an allele from a second, controlling gene, the pigment cannot be deposited in the fur. When there is no pigment, the coat appears yellow.

› Allele E causes the pigment to accumulate in the hairs.

› Allele e prevents the pigment from accumulating in the hairs.

As a consequence, all dogs that do not inherit the E allele will be yellow.

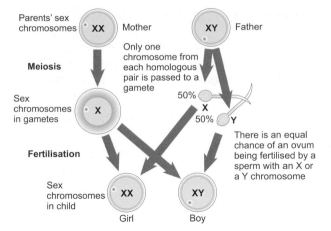

Figure 12 *How sex is determined*

The full details that explain how the chromosomes actually determine the sex of the child are not yet known. The Y chromosome is much smaller than the X, so many of the genes that are present on the X chromosome are missing from the Y. However, there is one gene on the Y chromosome, the SRY gene, which is thought to be the key to maleness. It seems that all babies begin life as females – that's why males have nipples – but then activation of the SRY gene imposes maleness on the developing foetus. The SRY gene causes the developing reproductive organs to become testes rather than ovaries. It is probable that the hormones that the testes produce then stimulate other male features to develop. However, other genes may well be involved.

QUESTIONS

8. Give all the possible genotypes of Labradors with coat colour that is:

   a. yellow

   b. brown

   c. black

Sex inheritance

In mammals, whether a baby develops as a male or as a female depends not on a single gene but on a pair of chromosomes. Look back at Figure 3 – the full complement of human chromosomes was taken from a male; it has one X chromosome and a much smaller Y chromosome. A female has two X chromosomes.

Figure 12 shows how the sex of a human baby is determined. The proportion of males and females in the population is more or less equal.

QUESTIONS

9. a. Does the egg or the sperm determine whether a baby is a boy or a girl? Explain your answer.

    b. Dairy farmers may want all their calves to develop into cows for milk production. The cows in the herd are artificially inseminated, that is sperm is collected from a bull and injected into each cow's vagina. Suggest how, in principle, it would be possible to ensure that only cows and not bulls were produced. (Hint: it is possible to use cell sorting techniques on semen samples to separate sperm containing a Y chromosome sperm from those containing an X chromosome.)

    c. What problems do you think could arise if parents were able to choose the sex of their child?

ASSIGNMENT 3: SEX CAN BE CONFUSING

We can often tell whether a cell is from a man or from a woman by looking for a tiny structure called a Barr body. Although a woman has two X chromosomes, in each cell one of these is inactivated early in development. It forms a distinctive dark blob, called the Barr body (see the photograph in Figure A1). If we can see a Barr body, then the cell is from a woman. This is quicker and easier to do than looking to see whether the person has two X chromosomes or an X and a Y, because the chromosomes only become visible just before a cell is about to divide. Barr bodies are visible – if the cell is suitably stained – at all stages of the cell cycle.

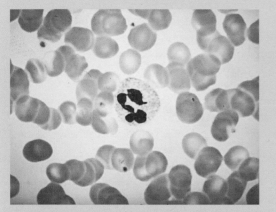

Figure A1 *A light micrograph of a white blood cell, surrounded by red blood cells. The white blood cell has a large nucleus with five lobes. On the right of the top lobe, you can see a drumstick sticking out. This is the condensed X chromosome, or Barr body. It is sometimes called the drumstick chromosome.*

A variety of chromosomal abnormalities can obscure the distinction between the sexes. For example, about one girl in 3000 has only one X chromosome in each body cell. This is called Turner's syndrome. The condition often results in late or non-development of secondary sexual characteristics and infertility. Extra sex chromosomes may be present in other conditions. In Klinefelter's syndrome, for example, an individual has a chromosome complement of XXY. People can also have XXX, XXXY, XYY and various other combinations of sex chromosomes, although they are rare.

It is possible for females with XX chromosomes to have abnormally masculine bodies and muscle strength because their adrenal glands do not respond to female hormones in the usual way. Conversely, there are people with XY chromosomes who have a female body shape and muscle strength because their cells do not respond to male hormones as normal. This is called androgen insensitivity syndrome (AIS). The person has all the characteristics of a woman, and will always think of herself as female (Figure A2).

Figure A2 *Santhi Soundarajan won a silver medal in the 800 m race at the 2006 Asian Games but later failed a gender test. It is thought that she has androgen insensitivity syndrome (AIS).*

Questions

A1. How many chromosomes would a person with Turner's syndrome have in her body cells? Explain your answer.

A2. For each of the following chromosome complements, would you expect the person to show male or female characteristics?

  a. XXY

  b. XXX

  c. XYY

  d. XXXY

  Explain your answers.

A3. Women competing at events such as the Olympic Games may be checked to ensure that they really are female. Do you think that someone with the genotype XY, but who has androgen insensitivity syndrome (AIS), should be allowed to compete as a woman? Discuss your reasons.

KEY IDEAS

> In many organisms, body cells are diploid – they contain two sets of chromosomes and therefore two copies of every gene. Gametes are haploid, and therefore contain only one copy of each gene. If a person is homozygous for a particular gene, both alleles are the same. If they are heterozygous, the alleles are different.

> In animals, but not all organisms, gametes are produced by meiosis. In independent segregation, one chromosome from each homologous pair passes into the gamete.

> There is an equal chance of any gamete from one parent fusing with any gamete from the other. We can show this in a genetic diagram. The genetic diagram shows the different genotypes that can arise in the offspring, and the relative chances of each genotype occurring.

> It is important to remember that the offspring ratios expected by genetic diagrams are only probabilities, and the observed (actual) results may not be exactly the same, especially if small numbers of offspring are involved.

> In a situation involving dominance, if two heterozygous organisms are crossed we would expect a ratio of three offspring showing the dominant characteristic to one showing the recessive characteristic in their phenotype (a 3 : 1 ratio). If a heterozygous organism were crossed with a homozygous recessive organism, then we would expect a 1 : 1 ratio of dominant : recessive characteristic in the offspring.

> In dihybrid inheritance, two genes are inherited. If both parents are heterozygous for both alleles, giving a genotype of, say, AaBb, there will be gametes of AB, Ab, aB, and ab. This gives 16 different combinations and, typically, a phenotypic ratio of 9 : 3 : 3 : 1.

> In humans, sex is determined by the X and Y chromosomes. Genotype XX produces females, and XY produces males. The process of meiosis results in half of the sperm containing an X chromosome and half containing a Y chromosome. The sex of a baby is determined by whichever sperm fertilises the egg.

> Numerous genes that are found on the X chromosome are not found on the Y chromosome. A man has only one copy of each X-linked gene. A recessive X-linked allele will therefore always show up in a man, whereas it will often be masked by a dominant allele in a woman. Examples of sex-linked conditions are haemophilia and red/green colour blindness.

> Genes that are located on the same chromosome are said to be linked. When this is the case, a dihybrid cross will produce far more offspring with the same genotypes as their parents, and fewer recombinants (offspring with new combinations of parental alleles).

> Any recombinants produced are the result of crossing over in meiosis.

> The chi-squared test can be used to assess the 'goodness of fit' of the results of genetic crosses.

PRACTICE QUESTIONS

1. IQ test scores have been used as a measure of intelligence. Genetic and environmental factors may both be involved in determining intelligence. In an investigation of families with adopted children, the mean IQ scores of the adopted children were closer to the mean IQ scores of their adoptive parents than to the scores of their biological parents.

   a. Explain what the results of this investigation suggest about the importance of genetic and environmental factors in determining intelligence.

   b. Explain how data from studies of identical twins and non-identical twins could provide further evidence about the genetic control of intelligence.

   AQA June 2006 Unit 4 Question 2

2. a. Mutation may produce multiple alleles of a gene. Explain how.

   b. An allele may be present in the genotype but its effects are not seen in the phenotype. In terms of protein production, explain why.

   c. Independent assortment of homologous chromosomes might result in several different phenotypes among the offspring of two parents.

      i. Explain what is meant by *homologous* chromosomes.

      ii. Explain how independent assortment might result in several different phenotypes in the offspring of two parents.

   AQA June 2008 Unit 4 Question 4

3. In a breed of cattle the H allele for the hornless condition is dominant to the h allele for the horned condition. In the same breed of cattle the two alleles C^R (red) and C^W (white) control coat colour. When red cattle were crossed with white cattle all the offspring were roan. Roan cattle have a mixture of red and white hairs.

   a. Explain what is meant by a *dominant* allele.

   b. Name the relationship between the two alleles that control coat colour.

   c. Horned, roan cattle were crossed with white cattle that were heterozygous for the hornless condition. Compete the genetic diagram (Figure Q1) to show the ratio of offspring phenotypes that you would expect.

Parental phenotypes	Horned, roan	×	Hornless, white
Parental genotypes			
Gametes			
Offspring genotypes			
Offspring phenotypes			
Ration of offspring phenotypes			

Figure Q1

   d. The semen of prize dairy bulls may be collected for in-vitro fertilisation. The sperm cells in the semen can be separated so that all the calves produced are of the same sex. The two kinds of sperm cells differ by about 3% in DNA content.

      i. Explain what causes the sperm cells of one kind to have 3% more DNA than sperm cells of the other kind.

      ii. Suggest **one** reason why farmers would want the calves to be all of the same sex.

   AQA June 2006 Unit 4 Question 6

4. a. A protein found on red blood cells, called antigen G, is coded for by a dominant allele of a gene found on the X chromosome. There is no corresponding gene on the Y chromosome.

The members of one family were tested for the presence of antigen G in the blood. The antigen was found in the daughter, her father and her father's mother, as shown in the genetic diagram in Figure Q2. No other members had the antigen.

Figure Q2

	Grandmother	Grandfather (has antigen G)	Grandmother	Grandfather
Genotypes	.... or	....	....	....
Gomete genotypes	.... or	....	....	....
	Father (has antigen G)		Mother	
Genotypes	....		....	
Gomete genotypes	....		....	
	Daughter (has antigen G)			
Genotype	....			

Figure Q2

i. One of the grandmothers has two possible genotypes. Write these on the genetic diagram, using the symbol X^G to show the presence of the allele for antigen G on the X chromosome, and X^g for its absence.

ii. Complete the rest of the diagram.

iii. The mother and father have a son. What is the probability of this son inheriting antigen G? Explain your answer.

b. During meiosis, when the X and Y chromosomes pair up, they do not form a typical bivalent as do other chromosomes. Explain why.

AQA June 2004 Unit 4 Question 5

5. In a species of fruit fly, females have two X chromosomes, and males have an X and a Y chromosome. A gene controlling eye shape in fruit flies is sex-linked, and is found only on the X chromosome. This gene has two alleles, R for round eyes and B for bar eyes. A homozygous, round-eyed female ($X^R X^R$) was crossed with a bar-eyed male. In the offspring (Offspring 1), all the female offspring had wide bar eyes (intermediate in size) and all the males had round eyes.

Figure Q3 shows the heads of three fruit flies.

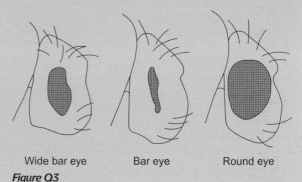

Wide bar eye   Bar eye   Round eye

Figure Q3

a. Name the relationship between the two alleles that control eye shape.

b. Give the genotype of the male parent.

c. Offspring 1 were allowed to interbreed. Copy and complete the genetic diagram (Figure Q4) to show the phenotypic ratio that you would expect in the resulting Offspring 2.

Parental phenotypes	Round-eyed female	Bar-eyed male
Parental genotypes	$X^R X^R$	
Offspring 1 genotypes	Wide bar-eyed female	Round-eyed male
Gametes		
Offspring 2 genotypes		
Offspring 2 phenotypes and ratio		

Figure Q4

AQA January 2002 Unit 4 Question 4

6. A sex-linked gene controls fur colour in cats. Ginger-coloured fur is controlled by the allele G, and black-coloured fur is controlled by the allele g. Some female cats have ginger and black patches of fur. They are described as tortoiseshell. Male cats cannot be tortoiseshell.

a. What is meant by a *sex-linked* gene?

b. A male cat with the genotype X^g Y mates with a tortoiseshell female.

   i. Give the phenotype of the male.

   ii. Give the genotype of the tortoiseshell female.

iii. Complete the genetic diagram (Figure Q5) to show the genotypes and the ratio of phenotypes expected in the offspring of this cross.

Parents	Male	Tortoiseshell female
Parental genotypes	$X^B Y$	....
Parental gametes		
Offspring genotypes		
Offspring phenotypes		
Ratio		

Figure Q5

AQA January 2004 Unit 4 Question 5 (a)–(b)

7. Hair type in dachshund dogs is controlled by two genes that are on different chromosomes. Dogs with the H allele have wiry hair and dogs with the genotype hh have non-wiry hair. The length of wiry hair is always the same. Dogs with non-wiry hair have either long or short hair. The length of non-wiry hair is controlled by another gene. Dogs with the D allele have short hair and those with the genotype dd have long hair.

a. Give all the possible genotypes for dachshunds with non-wiry, short hair.

b. What type of interaction is occurring between the two genes? Explain your answer.

c. A wiry-haired male with the genotype HhDd was mated with a non-wiry, long-haired female with the genotype hhdd. Complete the genetic diagram (Figure Q6) to show the ratio of offspring phenotypes expected in this cross.

Parental phenotypes	Wiry-haired male	Non-wiry, long-haired female
Parental genotypes	HhDd	hhdd
Gametes		
Offspring genotypes		
Offspring phenotypes		
Ratio of offspring phenotypes		

Figure Q6

AQA June 2007 Unit 4 Question 5

8. The production of pigment in rabbit fur is controlled by two genes. One gene controls whether any pigment is made. This gene has three alleles. Allele A codes for the production of one form of the enzyme tyrosinase, which converts tyrosine into a black pigment. Allele a^h codes for the production of a second form of the enzyme, which becomes inactive at temperatures close to a rabbit's core body temperature, so only the face, ears, legs and tail are pigmented. A third allele, a, fails to code for a functional tyrosinase. The other gene controls the density of pigment in the fur. This gene has two alleles. Allele B is dominant and results in the production of large amounts of pigment, making the fur black. Allele b results in less pigment, so the fur appears brown.

a. How do multiple alleles of a gene arise?

b. Table Q1 shows some genotypes and phenotypes.

Genotype	Phenotype
A–B–	All fur black
aaB–	All fur white (albino)
a^habb	White body fur with brown face, ears, legs and tail (Himalayan)

Table Q1

i. What do the dashes represent in the genotype of the black rabbit?

ii. Give all the possible genotypes for a Himalayan rabbit with black face, ears, legs and tail.

iii. Suggest an explanation for the pigment being present only in the tail, ears, face and legs of a Himalayan rabbit.

c. Using the information given, explain why the phenotypes of rabbits with AABB and AahBB genotypes are the same.

AQA June 2005 Unit 4 Question 7

10 POPULATIONS

PRIOR KNOWLEDGE

In earlier years you will have studied the basic structure of ecosystems, including food chains and food webs. Earlier in this book we looked at the energy flow through food chains, and at the recycling of nutrients such as nitrogen and phosphorus. We also looked at the genetics of individual organisms, and at the chi-squared statistical test.

LEARNING OBJECTIVES

In this chapter we look at the genetics of populations rather than individuals. We consider the way in which individual organisms and populations are affected by their environment. We also look at the way in which an ecosystem develops, and the way in which ecosystems can be studied.

(Specification 3.7.2, 3.7.4)

Badgers and hedgehogs are two of Britain's most loved animals. Badgers are not commonly seen, as they are generally nervous of people, and they tend to live outside urban areas and well away from villages. On the other hand, until recently, most people would have been familiar with hedgehogs – they have been regular visitors and residents in gardens, where they are usually welcomed because they will eat slugs and snails as an (albeit small) proportion of their diets.

But recently, things have been changing. The sight of a hedgehog in a garden – either in the town or in the country – is becoming increasingly rare. Even the number of hedgehogs killed on the roads has decreased, which is probably a sign that there are fewer of them around rather than that they have developed better road sense. Although there has not been a definitive count of the hedgehog population in Britain, some researchers think that it has decreased from about two million in the mid-1990s to less than half of that now.

Over a similar time period, the population of badgers has been steadily increasing. At least part of the reason for this is the increased protection for badgers that has been provided by the Badgers Act of 1973 and the Protection of Badgers Act of 1992. It is now illegal to disturb badgers, let alone kill them.

Badgers are predators of hedgehogs – indeed, probably the only significant predator, as no other animal is prepared to deal with the prickles. Badgers simply tip over the hedgehog, force it to uncurl using their hugely strong forepaws and claws, and scoop out the hedgehog from its prickly covering. People have frequently reported finding the remains of scooped-out hedgehogs in their gardens, shortly after badgers have appeared in the area. A research paper into the relationship between hedgehog populations and badger populations, published in 2006, showed that hedgehogs were far less common where badgers were abundant (for example, in pasture fields in rural habitats) than where badgers were rare. There appears to be a strong negative spatial relationship between badgers and hedgehogs. Lots of badgers mean few hedgehogs.

So, do we have to make a choice? Save the hedgehogs or save the badgers? The situation is probably more complex than it seems. Many people do not accept that badgers are the main cause of hedgehog decline. For example, they cite the warmer winters that we have experienced recently, which make it difficult for hedgehogs to hibernate in their normal way. Some people feel strongly protective about furry animals such as badgers, and cannot accept that perhaps we do need to control their numbers to maintain some kind of balance between different species. What we do need is to find out more about what is affecting hedgehog numbers. And if we are going to act to save them, we need to do it quickly. Some ecologists are predicting that, if things continue as they are, there will be no hedgehogs in Britain by 2025.

10.1 GENES IN POPULATIONS

Gene pools and allele frequencies
Two vital definitions:

> A **population** is a group of organisms of the same species occupying a particular space at a particular time that can potentially interbreed. Examples of populations include all of the elephants in a game reserve, all of the water fleas in a pond or all of the bluebells in a woodland.

> All the genes and alleles in a population are known as the **gene pool** of that population.

By definition, members of the same population are able to breed with each other. The different alleles of all the genes in the gene pool are constantly being passed from parents to offspring within the population, theoretically in any possible combination.

Within most species, there may be different populations. For example, meadow brown butterflies tend not to move very far from where they were born. The meadow brown butterflies in one meadow may never meet the meadow brown butterflies from a nearby meadow. They are therefore two different populations, because they don't often interbreed with each other. Each population has its own gene pool. There may be particular alleles of genes that are present in one population's gene pool, but not in the other. As we shall see in Chapter 11, this is a very important feature in the development of new species.

Figure 1 *Meadow brown butterflies may spend their whole lives in one field.*

Allele frequency
It can be helpful to know something about how common a particular allele is in a population. We call this the **frequency** of that allele. Any particular allele will have a frequency somewhere between 1 (meaning 100%) and 0 (0%).

For any one gene, the frequencies of all its different alleles add up to 1. If there is only one allele, then the frequency is 1. If there are two different alleles, A and a, for example, and they are equally common, then the frequency of each allele is 0.5. If the frequency of one allele is 0.32, you know that the frequency of the other is 0.68, assuming that there are just two alleles.

Almost all the organisms you will study at this level are diploid, meaning that their body cells contain two sets of chromosomes and therefore two copies of each gene. So, in a population of 1000 individuals, there will be 2000 copies of any particular gene (assuming that the gene is not sex-linked). If there are two alleles, R and r, and you know that 400 alleles are r, then 1600 alleles must be R.

The Hardy–Weinberg principle
The English mathematician G H Hardy and the German medic Wilhelm Weinberg give their names to two important (and inter-related) ideas:

1   The **Hardy–Weinberg principle** states that allele frequencies in a population *will not change* from one generation to the next, provided that certain conditions are met (see below). If allele frequencies are changing, it might be evidence that the population is evolving.

2   The **Hardy–Weinberg equation** allow us to calculate the frequencies of alleles and genotypes in a population, starting from the simple observation of the number of recessive phenotypes.

Imagine that there is a population of 100 moths. Their wing colour is controlled by one gene with two alleles. Allele B codes for the normal speckled colour while allele b codes for a black colouration.

> BB moths are speckled

> Bb moths are speckled

> bb moths are black.

In this population there are 16 black individuals – they are easy to see and we know their genotype. But how many of the 84 speckled individuals are BB and how many are Bb? That's where the Hardy–Weinberg equations can be used.

If p stands for the frequency of the B allele, and q stands for the frequency of the b allele, then $p + q = 1$. This simply means that if you add up all the B alleles and all the b alleles, they must add up to 1, or 100%, because there are no other alternatives.

Each individual has two copies of this gene, and so their genotype can only be BB, Bb or bb.

This gives rise to the equation:

$p^2 + 2pq + q^2 = 1$

- In this equation, p^2 is the frequency of the BB genotype.

- $2pq$ is the frequency of Bb, because there are two ways of generating that genotype (Bb or bB).

- And q^2 is the frequency of the bb genotype.

- So this equation is simply saying that when you add up all the genotypes, you must get the whole population.

Hardy–Weinberg worked example

In our moth example, if 16 individuals were black, 16 out of 100 is 16%, or 0.16 as a decimal.

So, we know that q^2 is 0.16

And, therefore, q is $\sqrt{0.16}$, which is 0.4

We know that $p + q = 1$, so $p = 0.6$

The frequency of the Bb genotype is $2pq$, so that is $2 \times 0.4 \times 0.6$, which is 0.48 (or 48%)

So, 48 of the population of 100 moths will have genotype Bb and, therefore, 36 will have the genotype BB.

Figure 2 *The frequency of the recessive allele can be worked out by counting the number of individuals who are homozygous recessive. In this case, it's the specked moth.*

Conditions for the Hardy–Weinberg principle

The Hardy–Weinberg principle states that the allele frequency *will not change* from one generation to the next. However, this makes several assumptions:

- The organisms are diploid, and reproduce sexually.

- The alleles are not sex-linked, so that they are equally distributed between both sexes.

- There is no migration in to or out of the population.

- The gene does not mutate to create new alleles.

- The population is large. In small populations, chance plays a large part in determining allele frequency (The name given to a change in allele frequency due to chance is **genetic drift** – which is covered in Chapter 11).

- There is no mating between individuals from different generations.

- Mating is random: all genotypes are equally likely to mate.

- Selection isn't taking place. If one genotype produces a phenotype with a selective advantage it will, be more likely to reproduce more successfully than others. This is **selection**. In this case, the frequency of one allele will increase at the expense of the other.

QUESTIONS
Stretch and challenge

2. The process of working out the allele frequencies using the Hardy–Weinberg equation is just the same as already described, but the numbers are smaller.

    About one in every 3300 children in Britain is born with cystic fibrosis caused by a recessive allele.

    a. Work out the frequency of the cystic fibrosis allele in the whole population of Britain.

    b. Work out the percentage of people who are carriers of the cystic fibrosis allele.

    PKU stands for phenylketonuria. This is a genetic disease caused by a recessive allele, p. About one in every 15 000 babies born in the UK has PKU.

    c. Calculate the frequency of carriers of PKU in the UK population.

KEY IDEAS

> The gene pool is all the alleles of all the genes that are present in a population.

> A population is a group of organisms of the same species occupying a particular space at a particular time that can potentially interbreed. A species may contain many different populations, which interbreed within their population but not often with other populations.

> The Hardy–Weinberg equation allows us to calculate the frequency of a particular allele in a population, assuming that allele frequencies do not change from generation to generation. It is:

$$p^2 + 2pq + q^2 = 1$$

where:

p^2 is the frequency of the homozygous dominant genotype (for example, FF)

$2pq$ is the frequency of the heterozygous genotype (Ff), and

q^2 is the frequency of the homozygous recessive genotype (ff).

10.2 POPULATIONS AND ECOSYSTEMS

In this section, we will be looking at some of the many factors that influence population size. This is important to us for numerous reasons — not only so that we can understand what is happening to species that share our world with us, but also so that we can take control of our own population, which expanded hugely during the 20th century and continues to do so (although at a decreasing rate) today.

There are several terms that we will be using throughout this chapter, and it is important that you know exactly what they mean, especially as many of them have other, broader meanings in everyday language.

Ecosystem: a definable area with its own community of organisms and physical environment, all interacting as a relatively self sustaining unit.

Habitat: the part of an ecosystem in which particular organisms live. The mud on the bottom of a pond and the surface layer of water are both habitats.

Population: all the interbreeding organisms of one species living in a particular habitat at the same time, such as all the pond snails or water lilies in a pond.

Community: all the populations of all the species that live together in a particular ecosystem. The pond community comprises all the plants, snails, insects, frogs and fish living there, as well as the microscopic algae, bacteria and so on. Think of it as the living part of the ecosystem.

Abiotic factors: the non-living, physical conditions in an ecosystem, such as temperature, light, soil conditions (sometimes called **edaphic factors** and **topographical factors**) and pH.

Biotic factors: the effects of the activities of living organisms on other organisms. Food availability, predation and competition are examples of biotic factors.

The pond community shown in Figure 3 contains many different species of plants and animals, many more

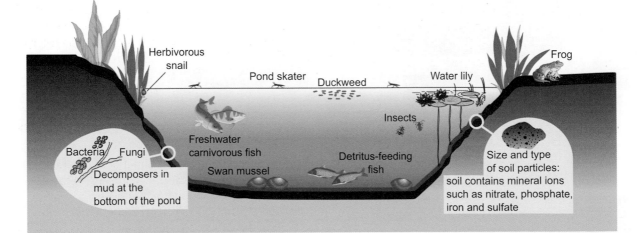

Figure 3 A pond ecosystem

than can be shown in the illustration. Each species is a specialist in some way. There are examples of every trophic (feeding) level in the food chain, some producers, some primary consumers, and so on.

The total size and richness of the community depends on the resources available to the producers. A pond that has few mineral nutrients dissolved in the water will support a limited amount of plant life, and hence relatively few consumers.

QUESTIONS

3. Which term correctly describes:
   a. all the oak trees in a wood
   b. the surface of the bark of an oak tree
   c. the Siberian tundra
   d. the salt concentration of a rock pool
   e. the organisms living in a rock pool
   f. the effect of snails grazing on pondweed?

Different species are not evenly distributed throughout the pond. The greater the variety in the physical environment – such as shallow edges, deep water, shaded banks and so on – the greater the diversity is likely to be. Those plants that must have their roots in the soil can grow only near the margins and in shallow water. Others, such as the duckweed, float and can therefore extend across the surface of the pond. Swan mussels (Figure 4) lie on the bottom and filter food particles from the water that they suck through their bodies, whereas pond skaters (Figure 5) are fast-moving predators that can literally walk and run on water.

Figure 4 *A freshwater swan mussel; the frilly edge of the siphons can be seen projecting between the valves (shell).*

Figure 5 *A pond skater, Gerris lacustris, on the surface of water*

The concept of the ecological niche

Each species in the community is adapted to a set of conditions, and a species is only successful where the abiotic and biotic factors in an ecosystem are suited to its way of life.

The way of life of a particular species in a habitat is called its **ecological niche**. The organism can only live where the abiotic and biotic factors fulfil its requirements. As an example, we can look at the ecological niche of the swan mussel, which lives predominantly on the bed of shallow ponds.

The body structure of the swan mussel obviously rules out a similar lifestyle to the pond skater; it would be hopeless at chasing insects across the surface of the water. Instead, it uses its siphon and cilia to draw a current of water through its body and filter out microscopic organisms for food. This may seem very lazy, but it is an energy-efficient way of obtaining food, as long as the pond water contains a good supply of microscopic food particles. This is more likely in shallow ponds than in deep ponds, since microscopic plant plankton need light. Very deep water could also contain less oxygen and more silt, which could clog the delicate filter system of the mussel. All these factors contribute to the specific requirements of the mussel and determine its niche in the pond.

Niches within a habitat

In a particular habitat, every species has its own niche. The niche is governed by the adaptation of the species to both biotic and abiotic factors.

Organisms of different species that have different niches are able to coexist in a community because they do not compete for exactly the same resources. Even species that live in the same habitat and that appear to be very similar often have different ways of life. For example, several snail species live in pond habitats, but different species are part of different food chains, and the smaller and lighter snail species can live on the more delicate plants that cannot be exploited by their heavier snail neighbours. Similarly, different species of the hummingbird (Figure 6) have very slightly different-shaped beaks that enable them to feed from one type of flower but not another (Figure 6). If they had identical niches, then competition would be likely to result in all but one of the species becoming extinct in that habitat. We will look at competition in more detail later in this chapter.

Competing for the same niche

If two species were to try to occupy the same niche, one would out-compete the other, perhaps by being better able to use the food supply, or more effectively protecting itself from predators. Eventually, the less successful competitor disappears from the habitat.

Interestingly, similar niches in different ecosystems in other parts of the world may be occupied by different species. Australia used to have numerous marsupial species that grazed on the vegetation, but when rabbits were introduced some of the marsupial species were out-competed because of the rabbits' more efficient method of reproduction. Similarly, when the grey squirrel was introduced to Britain from North America, it was able to exploit woodland food sources such as nuts and acorns more effectively than the native red squirrel and has largely supplanted it.

Figure 6 *A Rufous hummingbird drinks nectar from a flowering currant bush, pollinating it at the same time.*

KEY IDEAS

> A community is all the populations of different species, all living in the same place at the same time. A population is all the members of one

species, living together at the same time. The community and its non-living environment make up an ecosystem, in which the living and non-living components interact.

> Abiotic factors are those resulting from non-living parts of an ecosystem. Biotic factors result from living organisms.

> Each species has its own ecological niche – its role in the community. The niche is determined by the adaptations that the species has evolved, so that it is able to be successful in a particular range of abiotic and biotic conditions.

> No two species can occupy exactly the same niche in a community, although niches do often overlap. However, in different ecosystems there may be different species that have evolved similar adaptations that make them successful in similar niches to one another.

10.3 SAMPLING POPULATIONS

When an ecologist begins to study an ecosystem, there are almost always three basic questions that need to be answered. These are:

> What organisms live there?

> Where do these organisms live?

> How many of them are there?

In order to answer these questions, numerical data must be collected from the ecosystem. The data that you collect, and the way in which you collect them, will be determined by the precise questions that you want to answer.

When studying an ecosystem, it is not possible – or necessary – to count and record every individual that lives there. Instead, we use various **sampling techniques**, attempting to do so in such a way that the results we obtain are genuinely representative of the habitat.

Ethical fieldwork

Whichever of the following techniques you are able to use in your own fieldwork, you must never forget that your studies do not take precedence over the lives of the animals and plants that you are investigating. Take great care not to disturb the habitat any more than necessary. For example, if you are working on a seashore, turning over rocks to see what lives beneath them, always replace the rock in the same position and orientation in which you found it. If you are working in a meadow, avoid trampling all over the plants – tread carefully, and retrace your steps rather than making new paths in all directions. If you are trapping beetles, check traps regularly and release your captives as soon as you can.

Random and systematic sampling

There are many ways of collecting information about the organisms living in a particular habitat, some of which are described below.

Sampling at random means that you do not make a conscious decision about exactly where the samples are taken. Sampling at random ensures that each part of, say, a meadow has an equal chance of being sampled. This is often the best thing to do where the distribution of species within the area you are interested in is fairly uniform. For example, you may want to know what species of plants are present in a meadow, and determine the relative areas of ground that are covered by each species. If it looks as though the meadow has fairly similar vegetation growing all over it, then samples taken at random should give you data that are representative of the whole meadow.

One method of sampling at random is to use a set of random numbers, either taken from a book or generated by a computer, to tell you where to put the quadrat (the area within which you collect data – described below). The numbers are used as coordinates on a pair of imaginary graph axes along two edges of your sampling area, as shown in Figure 7a. You place your quadrat at the intersection of these coordinates.

Systematic sampling means that you decide where to take your samples, and take them at regular spatial intervals within the area you are interested in. You might decide, for example, to make a map of the meadow and to draw a set of grid lines on it, intersecting each other at right angles at regular intervals, as shown in Figure 7b. You then count and record what is growing at each intersection. This could be useful if you were planning to come back and sample the same area again to find out if any changes had taken place, as you would then be sure that your second sample would be taken in the same places as the first one.

Another reason for deciding on systematic rather than sampling at random is if you can see a change of some kind in the habitat, and you want to know more about it. For example, it may be apparent that the species growing in the meadow gradually change as you move from a dry part to a wetter part, or from the meadow into the edge of adjoining woodland. In these instances, you might choose to sample along a line that runs through these changing areas. This will allow you to collect data about any changes in the species present, and their numbers, as the habitat changes. Such a line is called a **transect**, and is described more fully below.

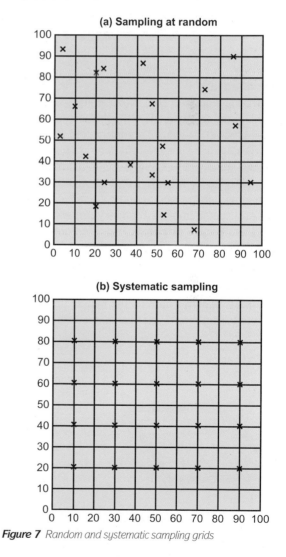

Figure 7 *Random and systematic sampling grids*

Figure 8 *Using a wire quadrat to collect data*

Frame quadrats

A **quadrat** is a defined area within which you collect data. The quadrat is placed on the ground, and you then identify and record the organisms inside it (Figure 8). Quadrats are the usual way of collecting data about which plants are growing in a habitat. They can also be used for **sessile** animals – that is, animals that are immobile for long periods of time, such as limpets and sea anemones. You have probably used some type of **frame quadrat**, a square frame that you place on the ground, then identify and count the organisms inside it (Figure 9).

Exactly what you record in your quadrats, and how you record it, depends both on the kind of organisms that are there, and what you intend to do with the data. A very simple, yet useful, count is of the **species frequency**. For this, you simply record in how many of your quadrats you found a particular species, no matter whether there was just one specimen or 20. For example, if you placed your quadrat on a lawn 50 times and found one or more dandelions in 12 of these quadrats, then the frequency of dandelions is $12/50 \times 100 = 24\%$.

Another set of data that can be recorded is the number of individuals of each species inside the quadrat. This could be appropriate if, for example, you wanted to know what animals were living on a seashore and the sizes of their populations.

It can sometimes be possible to record data about plants in this way, for example, on an area of disturbed soil in a garden that has weeds growing on it. However, in many cases it is simply not possible to tell where one individual plant ends and another starts. In this instance, it is better to estimate the percentage of the area inside the quadrat that is occupied by each species. This is known as **percentage cover**. To help you to judge this, it is useful to divide a quadrat into several smaller ones (Figure 10).

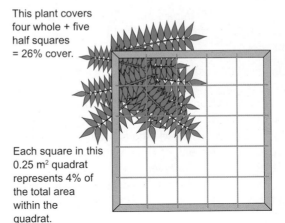

This plant covers four whole + five half squares = 26% cover.

Each square in this 0.25 m² quadrat represents 4% of the total area within the quadrat.

To measure percentage cover:
- Lay a frame quadrat over the selected area.
- Count the number of whole and half squares occupied by the species.
- Calculate this as a percentage of the whole area of the quadrat.
- Repeat for all the other species in the quadrat.

Figure 10 *Percentage cover*

Quadrats can be made from wood, wire or plastic.

50 cm

50 cm

A quadrat with sides of 0.5 m has an area of 0.25 m². Wire fixed at 10 cm intervals gives 25 smaller units, each of 0.01 m², to make counting easier.

Figure 9 *A frame quadrat*

Larger quadrats, for example, for sampling in woodland, can be laid out with string and pegs.

All the species within a quadrat can be counted, or the abundance of each species estimated.

QUESTIONS

4. **a.** The dimensions of a quadrat are 25 cm × 25 cm. Calculate its area in m².

   b. A student uses this quadrat to survey the plants in 20 positions in a habitat. What is the total area surveyed?

   c. The total area of the habitat being studied is 220 m². What percentage of the habitat has the student surveyed?

5. A student is studying the distribution of clover in a field, using a 50 × 50 cm quadrat.

   a. He placed the quadrat 30 times, and found clover growing in 25 quadrats. What is the frequency of clover in this habitat? Round your answer to the nearest whole number.

   b. Figure 11 represents one quadrat, showing the parts where clover is growing. Estimate the percentage cover of clover in this quadrat.

   c. The student notices that the grass growing near the patches of clover is a darker green than in other areas. Clover contains nitrogen-fixing bacteria in its roots. Suggest a reason for the student's observation.

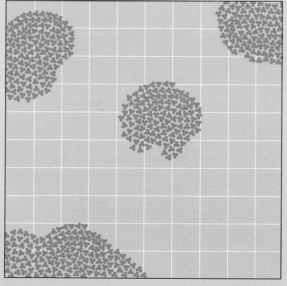

Figure 11 *Estimating the percentage cover of clover in a quadrat*

A third method is to use some kind of **abundance scale**. The ACFOR scale is a frequently used example by which you record each species as being abundant,

common, frequent, occasional or rare. You can make an abundance scale semi-quantitative by relating it to percentage cover, for example, by making A equal to 80%–100% cover, C equal to 60%–80% cover and so on down the scale.

QUESTIONS

6. Suggest the advantages and disadvantages of using the ACFOR scale, compared with estimating percentage cover.

Point quadrats

Estimating percentage cover, even in a quadrat that is divided into many smaller ones, is not easy to do accurately; and the larger the quadrat, the more difficult it gets. One solution is to make the quadrat so small that its area is a single point. Such a quadrat is known as a **point quadrat**. Figure 12 shows a frame that can be used for sampling with point quadrats.

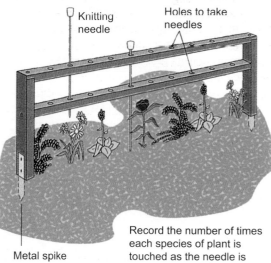

Figure 12 *Point quadrats*

Point quadrats are an excellent way of determining the percentage cover of all the different plant species in an area of relatively short vegetation. You can use random numbers to determine where to place the point quadrat frame. Then you drop the first needle through its hole, and count what it touches on its way to the ground – that is, the species that are present in the tiny quadrat represented by the end of the needle. If the vegetation is quite thick, with a mix of tall and short plants, the point may touch more than one species. You repeat this with all the other needles in the frame, and then repeat the whole exercise over and over again in the habitat. You can then work out the percentage of times you scored a 'hit' for any particular species, and this gives you the percentage cover of that species in that habitat. As leaves can lie above one another and you can hit more than one plant with each point, the percentage cover will probably add up to more than 100%.

Compared with frame quadrats, point quadrats can be a much more objective and repeatable way of collecting data from which to calculate percentage cover, especially in relatively short vegetation. However, they are not so useful where the vegetation is long and thick or where there are overhead trees, because the needle may touch so many leaves on its way to the ground that you have difficulty in determining what it did hit and what it did not.

Line and belt transects

If you have decided to use a transect to collect data, then you need to consider whether it is better to use a **line transect** or a **belt transect** (Figure 13). In either case, you begin by running a tape or piece of string along the line you are going to sample. If you are using a line transect, you then count and record individual organisms that are touching the tape. If the vegetation is very sparse, you could record every single individual. More usually, however, this is impractical, and you will need to choose a suitable interval along the tape — say, every 10 cm — at which to do this.

For a belt transect, you place frame quadrats so that one edge lies against the tape, and record the organisms within each quadrat. Once again, in some cases you might decide to record all along the tape, not missing out anything. Alternatively, if this would be too time consuming, you can place the quadrats at equal intervals along the tape, perhaps every two metres. This is known as an **interrupted belt transect**.

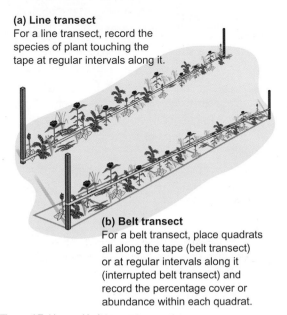

(a) Line transect
For a line transect, record the species of plant touching the tape at regular intervals along it.

(b) Belt transect
For a belt transect, place quadrats all along the tape (belt transect) or at regular intervals along it (interrupted belt transect) and record the percentage cover or abundance within each quadrat.

Figure 13 *Line and belt transects*

QUESTIONS

7. Different species of seaweed live at different heights above the low tide line. Use Figure 14 to find the range of heights at which the different seaweeds live.

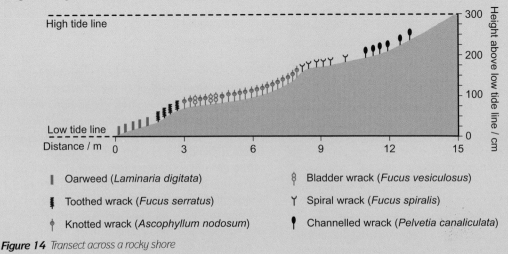

	Oarweed (*Laminaria digitata*)		Bladder wrack (*Fucus vesiculosus*)
	Toothed wrack (*Fucus serratus*)		Spiral wrack (*Fucus spiralis*)
	Knotted wrack (*Ascophyllum nodosum*)		Channelled wrack (*Pelvetia canaliculata*)

Figure 14 *Transect across a rocky shore*

8. A transect was placed across a path on chalk grassland. Fifteen quadrats, each with an area of 400 cm², were placed at regular intervals along the transect. The presence or absence of eight plant species in each quadrat was recorded. The results are shown in Table 1.

Species	Rough grass					Trampled path					Rough grass				
	1	2	3	4	5	6	7	8	9	10	11	12	13	14	15
Daisy					×	×		×	×	×		×			
Hoary plantain						×	×	×	×	×	×				
Ribwort plantain	×	×	×	×	×							×		×	×
Rock rose		×	×	×										×	×
Salad burnet	×	×	×	×	×			×		×	×	×		×	×
Meadow grass						×	×	×	×	×	×				
Sheep's fescue grass		×	×	×	×	×	×	×	×	×	×	×	×	×	×
Tor grass	×	×	×	×	×							×	×	×	×

Table 1 *Transect results; × indicates that the species was present.*

a. Calculate the length of the side of each quadrat.

b. Which species appear to have been seriously affected by people walking along the path?

c. Suggest why some species are better able to grow on the trampled path than in the area on either side. (You may be able to think of several factors, some abiotic and some biotic.)

Judging the results of quadrat studies – interpreting means

After using quadrats to survey an area, you may want to find the mean numbers of different species. For example, if you are investigating the earthworm populations in two different areas of grassland, you might extract the worms from the soil beneath 10 quadrats in each area, and then calculate the mean number of worms per quadrat. Suppose that the numbers of worms in the 10 quadrats in one area were: 12, 14, 11, 15, 13, 12, 16, 11, 14 and 12. The mean number is 13, and you could be reasonably sure that if you count a lot more quadrats in the same area the mean would be roughly similar.

Suppose that in the other area the results were: 2, 1, 0, 112, 5, 2, 3, 0, 4 and 1. The mean is again 13. If you count another 10 quadrats in this area it is quite unlikely that you would get the same again. To suggest that the populations in the two areas were similar would obviously be silly. It is much more likely that there happened to be something odd about the quadrat with 112 worms – maybe it was the site of a recently deposited large cowpat.

You therefore need to be careful when comparing means, but the differences will not always be so obvious as in this case. More commonly, the individual pieces of data that are collected will be fairly evenly distributed about the mean, as shown in the graphs in Figure 15.

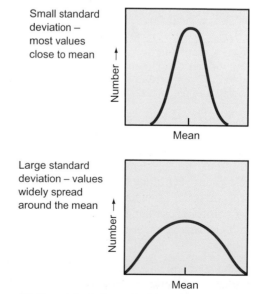

Small standard deviation – most values close to mean

Large standard deviation – values widely spread around the mean

Figure 15 *Normal distributions with different ranges*

In the two graphs in Figure 15, the mean values are the same, but one has a much greater **standard deviation** than the other. Standard deviation is a measure of the spread of the data about the mean. The larger the standard deviation, the larger the spread of the data. One standard deviation is defined as the range of data that includes 68% of the sample, and two standard deviations includes 95% of the sample. We only use the middle values to avoid the data being distorted by extreme values. *Chapter 13 of your Year 1 Student Book* explains in more detail how standard deviations are calculated and used.

The mark–release–recapture technique

The **mark–release–recapture** technique is used for estimating the size of a population of mobile animals (Figure 16).

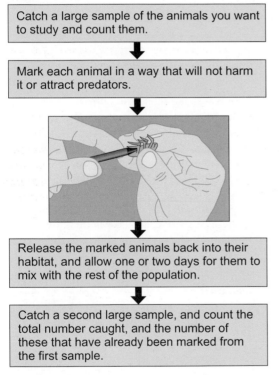

Catch a large sample of the animals you want to study and count them.

Mark each animal in a way that will not harm it or attract predators.

Release the marked animals back into their habitat, and allow one or two days for them to mix with the rest of the population.

Catch a second large sample, and count the total number caught, and the number of these that have already been marked from the first sample.

Figure 16 *The mark–release–recapture technique*

First, a large number of the animals are caught. The method you use for this depends on the species you are investigating. For aquatic insects such as water boatmen, you could use nets. For small mammals in a meadow, you could use Longworth traps. For woodlice, you could just search under stones and pieces of decaying wood.

The animals that you have caught are counted and then marked. The method of marking also depends

on the species you are working with. Water boatmen or woodlice could be marked with a spot of red paint; small mammals by clipping their fur. Whatever method you choose, you need to try to ensure that it will not harm the animals or increase the likelihood of the marked animals being eaten by predators.

The marked animals are then released back into their original habitat. You need to give them enough time to mix thoroughly with the rest of the population, and then you catch another large sample using the same method. Count the total number of marked and unmarked animals in the second sample.

You can now calculate the size of the population using this formula (called the Lincoln index):

$$\text{Total number of animals in population} = \frac{\text{number in sample 1} \times \text{number in sample 2}}{\text{number of marked animals in sample 2}}$$

An easy way of remembering this is that you multiply the two biggest numbers together, and divide by the smallest one.

This method only gives you relatively reliable results if:

> the original number of animals caught and marked is large

> there is no significant immigration into, or emigration out of, the population between the collection of the first sample and the collection of the second sample

> the marked animals are no more or less likely to die than the unmarked ones

> the marked animals do mix fully and randomly into the population after they have been released

> the population does not change significantly in size as a result of births or deaths between the capture of the first sample and the capture of the second sample.

It is probably almost impossible to be certain that your data meet all of these criteria, but nevertheless this method can give a useful approximation of population sizes for many small, mobile animals.

QUESTIONS

9. In an attempt to measure the size of a population of woodlice under a large piece of dead wood, a student captured and marked

54 animals. She released them and waited 48 hours before capturing another sample of 63 animals. Of these, 18 were marked. Use the formula:

$$\text{Total number of animals in population} = \frac{\text{number in sample 1} \times \text{number in sample 2}}{\text{number of marked animals in sample 2}}$$

to estimate the number of woodlice in the population.

KEY IDEAS

> An area can be sampled to find out which species live there, and to estimate the size of their populations. Quadrats are used to delineate an area within which data will be collected.

> Quadrats may be placed at random, using random numbers as coordinates. The percentage of quadrats in which a species occurs gives the species frequency. The mean percentage area that a species covers in all the quadrats gives the mean percentage cover. An abundance scale can be used where it is difficult or too time-consuming to determine percentage cover.

> Quadrats may be of different sizes, including point quadrats, which have a tiny area.

> A transect is a line along which sampling takes place. Quadrats may be placed all along the line, or at intervals. This is useful to get an indication of species distribution across a range of conditions, for example, at different heights on a rocky shore, or in the context of investigating stages in a succession.

> The mark–release–recapture technique can be used to estimate the size of a population of mobile animals. Animals can be caught using a suitable technique, then marked and released. The proportion of marked animals in a second sample can be used to calculate the population, using the Lincoln index.

10.4 POPULATION SIZE

What determines which species live in a particular habitat, and the sizes of their populations? It may simply be that a species has never arrived at that habitat. For example, although all polar bears live in the Arctic, and all penguins live south of the equator, it is likely that polar bears could thrive in the Antarctic, and penguins could live successfully in high northern latitudes. The reason that they do not is that they have never dispersed into those regions.

Often, however, the reasons for the absence of a species from a particular habitat are that certain features of that habitat make it unsuitable for the species to live there. Features such as availability of food and range of temperatures are known as **ecological factors**, and they have a great influence on the distribution and abundance of organisms. Within any ecosystem, a very large number of ecological factors can be identified. As we have seen, we can classify these into abiotic and biotic factors.

Abiotic factors
Abiotic factors result from non-living parts of the ecosystem. They include temperature, light intensity, availability and sodium chloride in water, and availability of gases such as carbon dioxide and oxygen. Most features of the soil, known as **edaphic factors**, are abiotic factors and include the mineral content of the soil, its pH and its water-holding and drainage capacities.

Figure 17 *Many organisms are very sensitive to the pH of their environment. Not many plant species can survive the acid soils found on peat moorlands like these. Cotton grass and sphagnum moss are typical of the few species that are adapted to a pH below 5. High rainfall causes basic ions, such as calcium, to be washed out of the soil. Waterlogging reduces the rate of decay, and organic acids are released from partially decayed peat. These factors both contribute an excess of hydrogen ions to the soil, resulting in the low pH.*

QUESTIONS

Stretch and challenge

10. a. Low pH can affect the activities of cells in two ways. The hydrogen ions may affect enzymes directly, and they may cause an increase in the concentration of heavy metal ions, due to a change in solubility. Use your knowledge of enzymes to explain why each of these factors affects cell activity.

b. Figure 18 shows a rock pool on a rocky shore. Abiotic factors in the rock pool vary considerably at different times. For part of the day it is covered by sea water. When the tide goes out it is exposed to air, and some of the water evaporates. Figure 19 shows variations in the temperature of the water in the pool on a summer's day.

Figure 18 *A rock pool in Port Renfew, Canada*

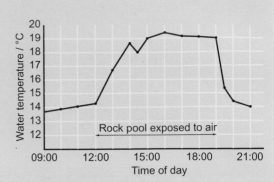

Figure 19 *Variations in rock pool temperature*

i. Explain how a rise in temperature could affect the oxygen concentration in the water of the rock pool. How would this affect the animal life?

ii. Explain how the presence of seaweeds in a pool can affect the concentration of dissolved oxygen in the water while the tide is out, during the daytime, and at night.

iii. The concentration of sodium chloride in the water is an abiotic factor that may vary considerably in a rock pool. Suggest what might cause the salt concentration in the pool to rise above the normal salinity of sea water and what might cause it to fall below normal. How could changes in concentration affect living organisms in the pool?

Within any particular habitat, abiotic factors can vary hugely from place to place and from time to time. In a hedgerow, for example, light intensity is relatively high at the top of the hedge, much lower at the base, and practically zero beneath a stone lying among the hedgerow shrubs. Variations in temperature are highest at the top of the hedge, and much lower under the stone. Humidity, too, will vary most at the top of the hedge, but will remain much more constant – and will often be higher – beneath the stone.

The different areas within a habitat each have their own **microclimate**. Differences between microclimates within a habitat influence the distribution of the species within the habitat. For example, invertebrates such as woodlice, which are not very efficient at preventing water loss from their bodies, would not survive for long if they perched on a leaf at the top of a hedge, in full sunlight, fully exposed to drying winds. The microclimate beneath the stone, however, is ideal for them, and this is where you are most likely to find them.

QUESTIONS

11. Suggest which abiotic factors are likely to be most important in limiting the growth of plants in each of the following habitats:

a. desert

b. the summit of a high mountain in Scotland

c. a mountain stream

d. a sandy shore

e. peat moorland.

Biotic factors

Biotic factors result from living components of the ecosystem. They include availability of food, competition, predation, parasitism and disease.

For consumers, one of the most important resources is food supply. The population size of primary consumers (herbivores) may be strongly affected by the availability of plants to eat. And this, of course, is strongly influenced by abiotic factors such as water supply, light intensity, temperature and edaphic factors such as the mineral content of the soil. This is true for most biotic factors – they are themselves directly or indirectly affected by abiotic factors.

If any one of the resources that an organism requires is in short supply, then organisms requiring that resource have to compete with one another in order to obtain it. **Competition** is frequently a major factor that affects the distribution and the population size of organisms.

Imagine a grassy meadow. The plants in the meadow all need light. The taller a plant is, the more light it is able to obtain. Shorter plants are shaded by taller ones, and receive less light. If the soil is rich in nutrients, then the taller plants, such as some of the more vigorous grasses, thistles and docks, will grow so large and shade the smaller plants so much that these are unable to thrive. Small, less vigorous plants such as orchids or cowslips may disappear completely from the meadow. The result of this competition has been to affect the distribution of the smaller plants. In this example, the resource in short supply is light. The plants competing for it belong to different species, so this is an example of **interspecific competition**.

Competition also occurs between individuals of the same species, known as **intraspecific** competition. Figure 20 shows the results of sowing different numbers of seeds into small pots of soil. You can see that the more seeds that are sown in the pot and therefore the larger the numbers of plants that grow in it, the fewer seeds these plants manage to produce. The plants are probably competing with one another for water and mineral ions from the soil and also for

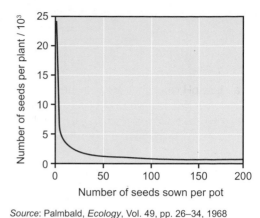

Source: Palmbald, *Ecology*, Vol. 49, pp. 26–34, 1968

Figure 20 *An example of intraspecific competition*

light. The effect of this competition has been to reduce the reproductive capacity of each individual plant.

Intraspecific competition increases as the size of a population grows and gets nearer to the maximum that can be supported sustainably in a particular habitat. This maximum number is known as the **carrying capacity** for that species in that habitat. Interspecific competition occurs whenever two different species living in the same habitat require the same resource, and this resource is in short supply. The more similar the niches of the two species, the more likely it is that interspecific competition will occur between them. If niches of two species are extremely similar, then it is probably impossible for the two species to coexist. This is known as the 'competitive exclusion principle'.

The severity of **predation** on a population is, like interspecific competition, an example of a biotic factor acting between species. For example, hedgehogs are predators of slugs. If there are large numbers of hedgehogs in a garden, this could help to keep the population size of the slugs smaller than it would otherwise be. On the other hand, the size of a predator population may be influenced by the size of the prey population. Records for the number of skins of Canadian lynx (predator) and snowshoe hare (prey) sold to the Hudson Bay Company go back to 1845. They show regular fluctuations with changes in the lynx population lagging behind changes in the hare population (Figure 21).

Figure 21 *A Canadian lynx (left) and a snowshoe hare (right).*

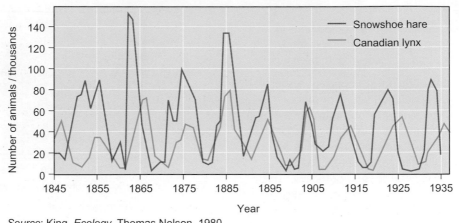

Source: King, *Ecology*, Thomas Nelson, 1980

Figure 22 *Population fluctuations in Canadian lynx and snowshoe hare*

Parasitism and **disease** are very similar to predation in the ways in which they affect population sizes. Imagine a rabbit population living on a grassy hillside, where the rabbits spend much of their time resting inside burrows and hiding from predators. As their population increases, the rabbits become more and more crowded in their burrows. It becomes much easier for parasites or diseases, such as the virus that causes myxomatosis, to spread from one animal to another. Moreover, the individual rabbits may be less able to fight disease or parasites, because competition for food means that some of them may be undernourished. Therefore, as the rabbit population size increases, so the incidence and severity of disease and infection with parasites also increases. The rabbit population falls. When it reaches a lower level, disease and parasitism become less common and less severe, allowing the population to rise again.

Population growth

Imagine that a pair of rabbits is put on an island. Assuming they are a pair, and can find each other, and have suitable food, the population growth curve will follow a predictable pattern.

1   Period of slow growth, often called a **lag phase** as there is a delay before the start of rapid growth. There are many possible reasons for this, such as organisms having to synthesis the correct enzymes to digest a particular food source, or simply that individuals need time to reach sexual maturity,.

2   A period of rapid growth, known as a **log** (for logarithmic) **phase** because the growth is **exponential** (2, 4, 5, 16, 32 and so on) rather than arithmetic (2, 4, 6, 8). When a female rabbit has six litters of 10 kits a year that's exponential growth. Growth is rapid because there are no limiting factors.

3   Growth slows down. No population can go on expanding at the log rate. Sooner or later there will be limiting factors, sometimes known as **environmental resistance**. Examples of limiting factors include a shortage of food, increased predation or accumulation of waste.

4   The population usually stabilises. It may not be steady, but may fluctuate according to different biotic and abiotic factors. The maximum population that can be supported in any particular situation at any one time is called the **carrying capacity**.

Figure 23 shows the results of an experiment in which a culture of single-celled algae was grown in a laboratory beaker. At first, the population grows slowly but then, after a few days, the rate of growth increases rapidly. During this phase, the rate of growth of the population is approximately exponential – that is, the population repeatedly doubles per unit time, such as over an hour. The graph only shows exponential growth between 3 and 12 days.

However, in a small beaker, this rise in numbers is soon restricted by a shortage of resources. Once the surface is covered by algae, there is less light lower down for other cells to photosynthesise. Also, the algae are likely to have absorbed most of the mineral ions that they need for the synthesis of proteins and chlorophyll. In the beaker, population growth stops and starts to fall. This happens when more cells are dying than are being replaced by new ones.

REQUIRED PRACTICAL ACTIVITY 12: APPARATUS AND TECHNIQUES

(AT a, AT b, AT h, AT k, AT l)

Investigation into the effect of a named environmental factor on the distribution of a given species

This practical activity gives you the opportunity to show that you can:

> use appropriate apparatus to record a range of quantitative measurements

> safely and ethically use organisms to make measurements

> use sampling techniques in fieldwork

> use ICT such as computer modelling.

Apparatus

There is a lot of scope for different investigations here, but most will involve measuring the distribution of a particular plant species in two different areas. It is a good idea to choose a species that is easily identified and counted, such as dandelions, daisies, nettles, plantain or ragwort. Bear in mind that ragwort is a toxic plant and should not be touched unless wearing gloves as toxins can be absorbed by skin contact or ingestion. Also be mindful of potential hazards such as litter, dog faeces, broken glass etc. that may be on the grassed area to be investigated. 'Grass' is much more of a problem because there are several different grass species and it is almost impossible to count individual plants. Environmental factors commonly investigated include mowing, use of fertilisers, use of pesticides, trampling and light intensity.

Techniques

All the investigations will involve sampling techniques, usually quadrats and/or transects. One example:

Investigation using a point quadrat into the distribution of dandelions in a lawn not treated with herbicide and a lawn treated with herbicide

Method

You will need a point quadrat (or pin frame) and two tape measures.

1. Before going to the lawn, generate 10 sets of random coordinates. This can be done using a random number generator on a computer or calculator.

2. Go to the site where one area of lawn has been treated using the herbicide, and another area of lawn has been left untreated. (Your teacher will tell you which area is treated.) Make sure that you can identify a dandelion plant by the shape of its leaves.

3. Lay out the tapes at right angles and place the point quadrat at the first set of coordinates.

4. Lower the pointers in the frame one at a time. As each pointer is lowered, record in the tally chart any dandelion that is 'hit' by the pointer.

   Look at the other plants that have been touched by the pointers and attempt to identify them.

   Repeat this at the positions determined by each set of coordinates.

5. Take 100 pointer samples at each site – herbicide-treated, and untreated – that is, 10 placements of the point quadrat.

6. Collect the data from the two sites and add up the total number of dandelion plants at each.

7. Percentage cover of dandelions =
$$\frac{\text{no. of dandelion plants hit}}{\text{total number of pointer samples}} \times 100$$

Alternative practical

An equivalent investigation using dandelion sampling can be carried out very simply using two grass verges: one treated with lawn weedkiller and the other left untreated.

QUESTIONS

P1. What is random sampling?

P2. Why is random sampling necessary?

P3. State the null hypothesis for the dandelion investigation.

P4. Apart from herbicide, suggest five different abiotic factors that could be affecting distribution of the dandelions.

ASSIGNMENT 1: RED GROUSE POPULATIONS

The population size of red grouse (Figure A1) tends to swing up and down, varying widely over a period of about four or five years. Several theories have been put forward to try to explain what is causing the fluctuations. Whatever it is must be a density-dependent factor – that is, a factor that acts more strongly when the population is high than when it is low. As the grouse population increases, this factor increases too and causes the population to decrease. As the population decreases, the factor decreases, allowing the population to increase again.

Figure A1 *Red grouse, Lagopus lagopus, live on heather moorland. They spend much of their time on the ground, where they feed on young heather shoots.*

Suggestions for this density-dependent factor have included food supply and predation. However, neither of these seems to be the answer. Grouse eat only 2% to 3% of the available heather, so supply of heather is very unlikely to be affecting them. And predators such as foxes and birds of prey do not seem to take enough grouse to have such large effects. Two more likely possibilities are intraspecific competition for space, and interactions between the red grouse and a parasite.

Competition for space arises during the autumn, when each breeding male takes control of an area of moorland. Territorial behaviour in autumn determines the number of breeding birds the following spring: the more aggressive the male grouse, the bigger its territory, the greater the emigration rate and the lower the number of breeding pairs. It is possible that male aggression is related to population density – the bigger the population, the more aggressive the males become, thus reducing the population size next year.

The second theory is to do with a parasite of red grouse, a nematode worm called *Trichostrongylus tenuis*. This parasite reduces the growth of grouse populations by decreasing breeding rates. Both the rate and intensity of infection by the parasite increase as the population density of the birds increases. Evidence for this comes from studies showing that:

- both grouse and *T. tenuis* have similar cyclical population densities
- higher levels of parasite infection match greater losses from the grouse population
- some grouse populations do not have any parasites, and their numbers do not oscillate.

During the 1980s and 1990s, six different grouse populations, living on six different areas of moorland in northern England, were investigated. First, using long-term data about grouse populations, predictions were made about when the next population 'crashes' would occur: 1989 and 1993. In 1989, the grouse in four of the six populations were caught and treated with a worm-killing drug. Two of the treated populations were then treated again in 1993. Figure A2 shows the results for three of the six populations.

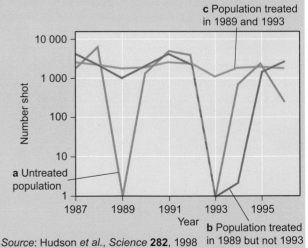

Source: Hudson *et al.*, *Science* **282**, 1998

Figure A2 *Results for three of six grouse populations*

Questions

A1. Explain how these results support the hypothesis that the parasite is responsible for the cyclical fluctuations in red grouse populations.

A2. What evidence is there from these results that the nematode parasite may not be the only cause of these fluctuations?

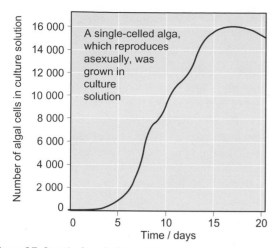

Figure 23 *Growth of an algal population*

In real situations, changes in population size are much more complex, because a species would hardly ever live in total isolation from other species. Figures 25, 26 and 27 show the results of an experiment originally done by a Russian ecologist to investigate competition between two species. The species chosen were both single-celled organisms: *Paramecium aurelia* and *Paramecium caudatum*. Both feed on bacteria and yeast cells.

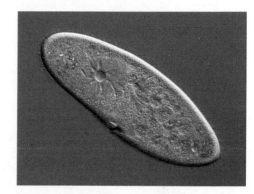

Figure 24 *Paramecium caudatum*

As Figure 27 shows, when both species were grown together in the same culture, both species grew equally well at first. Then, once the food became more scarce, *P. caudatum* was less successful at obtaining food: it was *out-competed*. The numbers of *P. caudatum* declined while those of its competitor species, *P. aurelia*, increased. Interspecific competition is strongly affecting the population size of *P. caudatum*, causing it to be smaller than it would otherwise be.

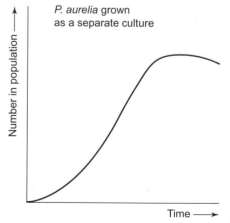

Figure 25 *Growth of a Paramecium aurelia population*

QUESTIONS

12. Yeast is a single-celled fungus. There are many different species. *Saccharomyces cerevisiae* is baker's yeast and *Saccahromyces carlsbergensis* is brewer's yeast. (Yes, it's named after Mr Carlsberg.)

    Suppose that 10 baker's yeast cells were originally put into a beaker and that they all survived after every division.

    a. How many cells would there be in each of the first 10 generations? Show your results in a simple table.

    b. Draw a graph showing the growth of this population. Label the *x*-axis 'Number of generations', and the *y*-axis 'Number of cells in population'. Describe the shape of the curve.

    c. The *y*-axis showing population growth could have a log scale. What is a log scale and why would it be suitable for this graph?

    d. How does the theoretical population growth in your graph compare with the actual growth shown in Figure 23?

    e. Which abiotic factors probably limited the actual growth?

    f. The cloudiness of a liquid is known as the *turbidity*. Suggest a suitable piece of apparatus that could measure turbidity as a means of estimating population growth.

    g. Suggest two reasons why measuring turbidity could lead to inaccurate estimates of population growth.

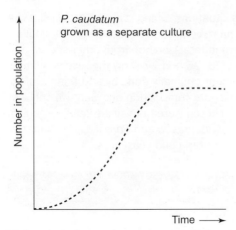

Figure 26 *Growth of a Paramecium caudatum population*

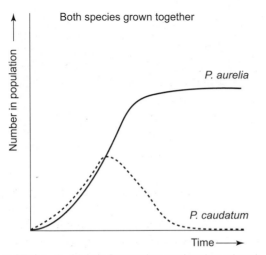

Figure 27 *Growth of the two Paramecium species when cultured together*

Reaching a balance

Given time, most ecosystems reach a balanced situation in which the populations of the majority of species remain within certain limits. However, the interactions between organisms in an ecosystem are highly complex, and quite small changes can alter the balance fairly rapidly.

Obviously, animals that feed on plants damage the plants, but most plants have a remarkable capacity to withstand damage without individuals being killed off. An oak tree in summer may have thousands of insects of many different species feeding on its leaves. Yet it can generate enough new growth to maintain itself for hundreds of years.

The most successful herbaceous plants, the grasses, are adapted to tolerate almost continuous grazing, because the growing point of the stem is tucked away at the base of the leaves, very close to the ground.

Grasses will only suffer serious losses if the number of herbivores escalates excessively, as occurred with rabbits in Australia.

Normally, excessive growth of the herbivore populations is kept under control by predators. If the number of herbivores starts to increase, there will be more food for predators, so predator numbers will also increase. The increase in predation then brings down the population of herbivores again. If the herbivore population falls too low, the predators fail to find enough prey, so the predator population falls again.

QUESTIONS

13. Grazing rabbits are in constant danger from predators. One way in which they are protected is by living in underground burrows. When feeding above ground, their acute hearing and 'all-round' eyesight enables them to sense danger and escape quickly. However, narrow-bodied predators such as the weasel and polecat can follow the rabbits into their burrows.

    Table 2 shows the results of a study of rabbit numbers in a particular colony.

Number of adult rabbits at start of the study	70
Number of breeding females	36
Total number of young emerging to feed during the time period of the study	280
Number of young in the colony at the end of the first season	28
Number of adults in colony at the end of the first season	11

    Table 2 *A study of a colony of rabbits*

    a. Suggest why the number of young surviving in the colony at the end of the first season is so much lower than the number of young that were counted during the study.

    b. What would you expect to happen to the rabbit population in this colony if the same level of loss carried on? Explain your answer.

    c. Suggest how the colony's numbers might be restored by natural means.

KEY IDEAS

> Factors that influence the distribution and abundance (population size) of organisms can be categorised as abiotic and biotic factors.

> Abiotic factors result from the non-living part of the environment, such as temperature or water supply. Biotic factors result from the living parts of the ecosystem, such as competition and predation.

> Abiotic factors can vary greatly in a habitat, forming different microclimates that are important in determining the distribution of a species within the habitat.

> Biotic factors include food supply, predation, parasitism, disease, intraspecific competition and interspecific competition.

> In some cases, one particular factor has a very strong influence on population size. For example, if a predator depends on one species of prey for food, and if that predator kills that prey primarily, then the population of one may be largely determined by the other. This can result in repeated oscillations of the population sizes of both species.

Figure 28 *Gardens tend to be small areas of land where we attempt to control the natural development of ecosystems. If we stopped cultivating this garden, this house would become surrounded by woodland once again.*

Figure 29 *Oak woodland is the natural vegetation in wetter parts of Britain. This one is in Exmoor, Somerset.*

10.5 HOW ECOSYSTEMS DEVELOP

Colonisation and succession

What would happen if your school playing fields, your garden or the local park were suddenly abandoned? If no one mowed the grass anymore? If no one ever killed the weeds? If no one ever walked there?

It would not take long for nature to take over. First, the grass and other plants would grow taller and taller. Seedlings of shrubs would begin to appear. In a few years' time, it would probably be covered with bushes and young trees. It would not be long before there was no trace of any human activities. Eventually, the land would probably develop into a wood.

The natural vegetation in most parts of Britain is deciduous woodland (Figure 29). Given a chance, this is what would grow on the land. Human activities prevent this from happening. We cover things with concrete, dig up allotments, pull up weeds, mow grass, cut hedges, plough fields, and allow sheep and cattle to graze on hillsides.

Our activities, over thousands of years, have greatly changed the appearance of our landscape. Without this, there would be less variety of habitats in Britain. If we want to keep all of these varied habitats – chalk downlands, flower-rich meadows, freshwater ponds – we have to take steps to stop them all gradually turning into woodland. Conservation of habitats has to be active. If we just let things be, we would live in a land covered by oak, ash and beech trees.

The change from a grassy park to an oak wood is an example of **succession** (Figure 30). Succession is a gradual change in the communities in a particular place. At the end of the process, the final community is called the **climax community**. The climax community tends to be fairly stable. In Britain, most places develop woodland as their climax community. Exceptions are areas that are especially wet, have very poor soil or are exposed to very high winds. The woodland will not change very much over time. Individual trees will die, and new ones will grow, but the overall composition of the community will remain pretty much the same over long periods of time.

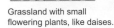

As grazing is reduced ⟶

Grassland with small flowering plants, like daisies.

Taller herbaceous plants, like willowherb and foxgloves, grow and cut off light to small plants, allowing tree seedlings to take root.

Bushes and shrubs, such as hawthorn and bramble, grow. Most herbaceous plants die out.

Fast-growing trees, such as birch, grow up, forming dense, low forest.

Larger, slower growing, but stronger oak trees grow above the birch and establish the climax community.

Figure 30 *Succession: a grassy park gradually turning into woodland*

Why succession occurs

Succession occurs because the species present at any one time cause habitat change. Abiotic factors and biotic factors are altered, so that new and different species – which are better adapted – will out-compete the old species and establish themselves.

As each species takes possession of the habitat, it changes many different factors – for example, the amount of light reaching the ground, the quantity of nutrients in the soil, the food sources for animals. New species are able to move in once the habitat becomes suitable for them. They in turn change the habitat, making it suitable for yet more species. We generally find that, during succession, the number of different species, known as **species richness**, steadily increases.

Sometimes, we are able to study succession occurring on a completely blank canvas – a piece of ground where there are absolutely no living things to start with. This can happen on a new island that has appeared as a result of volcanic eruption beneath the sea, as happened when Surtsey suddenly appeared off the coast of Iceland in November 1963. In 1980, a massive volcanic eruption of Mount St Helens took place, destroying all life over huge areas – the succession that subsequently took place there is described in Assignment 2.

The first organisms to live on bare ground are called **pioneer species**. They are often lichens (Figure 31) – strange mutualistic combinations of an alga and a fungus that are able to grow in the harshest of conditions, such as on bare rocks with no soil. They arrive as spores, carried by the wind or perhaps on the feet of a briefly visiting bird or insect. Their presence begins to provide small amounts of humus in which wind-dispersed plant seeds can be trapped, and which hold water and minerals. After

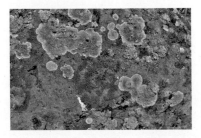

Figure 31 *Lichens are often the first species to grow on empty ground. They are a combination of a photosynthetic alga and a fungus that is able to extract inorganic ions from even the most inhospitable substrates.*

Figure 32 *These yellow verbascums and pink willow herbs have managed to colonise the abandoned railway track. They are pioneer plants. Their seeds blew in on the wind and they are able to cope with the lack of water and minerals in the almost non-existent soil between the rails.*

some years, plants may be able to grow. These pioneer plants generally have adaptations that allow them to survive in difficult conditions (Figure 32).

At the early stage of succession, abiotic factors tend to be the most important factors in determining which species can live there. There is little or no soil, so plants have access to very few minerals, and have difficulty in anchoring themselves to the ground. Water runs off the bare ground, because there is little or no humus able to hold water for a time after rainfall. There is no shelter from wind or the hot sun.

However, as soil gradually builds up over the years, conditions become suitable for other species to survive. Conditions are much less hostile. After a while, many different species will live there, all competing with each other for food, water, light and living space. This is when biotic factors such as competition, predation and grazing become very important in determining which species live there, and how big their populations will be.

Succession on sand dunes

We don't need to stand in one place for a few hundred years to study succession. If we can find a place where succession has been happening for a while, we may be able to see different stages of succession at one glance.

Sand dunes give us a good opportunity to see the stages. This example is used to *illustrate* important concepts and ideas. You do not have to learn this example, or the names of the organisms.

Next to the sea, the sand is an inhospitable place for plants to live. It is sharp-draining, so it does not hold water for any length of time. It is constantly shifting, giving no opportunity for plants to establish their roots. It holds very few nutrients, so plants cannot get the inorganic ions – nitrates, for example – that are essential for their growth. In addition, these coastal areas are often very windy and plants get sprayed with salty water that has a lower water potential than the cytoplasm in their cells.

Not much further away from the sea, however, we can often see sand dunes that have been there for a short while. And further behind these, we can find older dunes. If we set out a transect from the sea to behind the inland dunes, we can study what species live in this environment at different stages of succession – the earliest stages nearest the sea, and the latest stages furthest away from the sea. Figure 33 illustrates the process of succession on sand dunes.

The pioneer plant on the developing sand dunes is often marram grass, which is superbly adapted for life on shifting sands (Figure 34). Marram grass has a dense network of branching underground stems, which hang on tightly to the sand and help to stabilise it. It has tough leaves and is able to withstand the high winds to which it is often exposed. The leaves can roll up, sheltering the stomata and reducing water loss by transpiration. Figure 35 shows the many adaptations of marram grass for reducing water loss by transpiration.

Once the marram grass has taken root, wind-blown sand tends to collect around it, which is how dunes form. Within 10 years, the dunes may be up to three metres high, and well covered by marram grass.

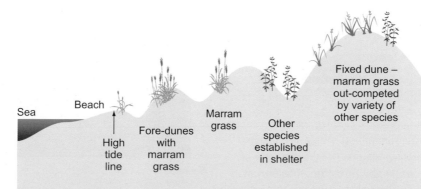

Figure 33 Succession on sand dunes

Figure 34 *A sand dune on a beach, with marram grass growing on it. Once they have been stabilised by marram grass, sand dunes can become several metres high.*

Now a few other species are able to set up home in the shelter that the marram provides. Humus builds up in the dry sand, so that it begins to look rather more like soil. Water retention is improved and mineral nutrients do not drain away so quickly. Other grasses and plants adapted for living in grassland colonise the dunes (Figure 36). Eventually, as conditions begin to improve, the marram grass is out-competed and dies out.

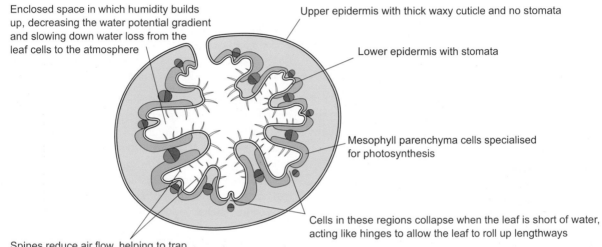

Enclosed space in which humidity builds up, decreasing the water potential gradient and slowing down water loss from the leaf cells to the atmosphere

Upper epidermis with thick waxy cuticle and no stomata

Lower epidermis with stomata

Mesophyll parenchyma cells specialised for photosynthesis

Cells in these regions collapse when the leaf is short of water, acting like hinges to allow the leaf to roll up lengthways

Spines reduce air flow, helping to trap humid air inside the leaf

Figure 35 *Transverse section of a rolled-up leaf of marram grass, Ammophila arenaria*

Figure 36 *On the oldest dunes, furthest from the sea, other plants such as Calluna vulgaris can grow.*

If left undisturbed for long enough, these old dunes will eventually become woodland. The precise type of woodland depends on the abiotic factors that prevail in that place. If it is very wet, then the climax community may be willow carr (Figure 37) – woodland containing

willow and other trees, where water often lies between them. In drier places, oak, beech or ash woodland may develop.

Figure 37 *Willow carr is often the climax community in ground that floods regularly.*

QUESTIONS

15. List four abiotic factors that make colonisation by plants particularly difficult in the sand just above the high tide line. (Some have been mentioned in the text, and you should be able to think of others.)

16. Explain the adaptations of marram grass that enable it to colonise sand dunes next to the sea.

17. Suggest how grassland plants reach the dunes that they colonise.

ASSIGNMENT 2: SUCCESSION ON MOUNT ST HELENS

In May 1980, snow-capped Mount St Helens, in southwest Washington State, USA, exploded (Figure A1). The north side of the mountain collapsed, creating a debris avalanche – a mixture of ice blocks from the shattered glaciers, hot rocks and mud. Two and half square kilometres of material plunged down the mountainside. When it eventually came to rest, it formed a layer with an average depth of 45 m. Temperature measurements in the deposits, taken 10 days after the eruption, varied from 68 °C to 98 °C. Not surprisingly, every living thing beneath the avalanche was killed.

Figure A1 *The unexpected and devastating eruption ripped away huge areas of Mount St Helens.*

It wasn't long before literally hundreds of researchers turned up, eager to take this opportunity to study how life would recolonise the barren ground. Different teams worked in different areas. One group chose to study a huge area of the debris avalanche. They set out markers surrounding 103 circular plots, each with an area of 250 m², and recorded the species that they found there.

The same group returned to the site on numerous occasions for 20 years following the eruption.

Some of their results are shown in the graphs. Figure A2 shows how the percentage cover in the plots changed over time. Figure A3 shows the mean number of species per plot.

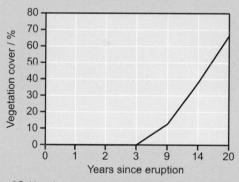

Figure A2 *How the percentage cover in the plots changed over time.*

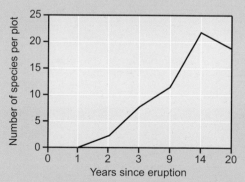

Figure A3 *Mean number of species per plot*

The most common species during the very early stages of the succession were those with light, wind-dispersed seeds, which were fast growing and able to mature quickly. These included a small plant called pearly everlasting, which grows close

(continued)

to the ground, where it escapes most of the wind. As other plants, including grasses, colonised, the little pearly everlastings disappeared. Within a few years, lupines had begun to grow. These are much larger plants than the everlastings, and they have nitrogen-fixing bacteria in their roots. Other nitrogen-fixers, including white clover and bird's-foot trefoil, also took residence in the area.

The first trees to make a substantial showing were alders, which are also nitrogen-fixers In fact, a few of these – and also some western hemlocks – were present very early on in the succession as small seedlings. But most of the western hemlock seedlings soon died, and it took some time before the numbers of alder trees really began to increase, as shown in Figure A4.

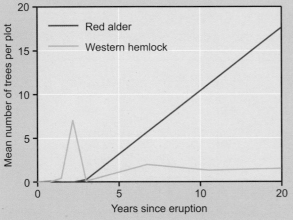

Figure A4

Today, the shattered sides of Mount St Helens are no longer grey and barren. The communities that live there are still changing and it will take many more years before the climax community – western hemlock forest – will become established. Before that happens perhaps there will be another eruption of this active volcano, and the whole process will start over again.

Questions

A1. Describe the abiotic factors making it difficult for plant life on the debris avalanche soon after the Mount St Helens eruption.

A2. Suggest the adaptations of pearly everlasting that make it a successful pioneer plant. (You could look this up on the Internet. The Latin name for this plant is *Anaphalis margaritacea*.)

A3. Describe, and then suggest explanations for, the changes in vegetation cover over time shown in Figure A2.

A4. Describe, and then suggest explanations for, the changes in species diversity over time shown in Figure A3.

A5. Explain why lupines were not able to grow on the site in the first year or so but became quite common later on.

A6. Explain why nitrogen-fixing plants made up a large part of the early communities during this succession.

A7. Suggest why western hemlock is only likely to be able to grow well on this site after alders have been growing there for some years.

KEY IDEAS

> Succession is a gradual change in communities over time. Each community changes the environment so that it becomes suitable for new species to live there. The final community is known as the climax community.

> In the early stages of succession, abiotic factors are most important in determining which species can survive. Pioneer species have adaptations that allow them to colonise these hostile environments. As succession proceeds, biotic factors become more significant.

> Species diversity tends to increase as succession proceeds.

10.6 CONSERVATION

As most of us are only too well aware, human activities can do great damage to the environment. We cut down forests to provide us with wood for building and for fuel, or to clear the land so that it can be used for housing or agriculture. We pollute the land, air and water, making it impossible for some species to live there. The more people on Earth, the more effects that we have on the other organisms with which we share our planet.

Conservation aims to maintain the biodiversity around us. Biodiversity is a difficult term to define but it is often taken to mean the variety of different habitats in an area, the variety of different species living there, and the genetic diversity within those species. Conservation attempts to ensure that we do not allow a decline in the number and range of different ecosystems and species, or the genetic diversity within species.

Planning conservation programmes

Before conservation can begin, we need as much information as possible about what we are trying to conserve. Imagine, for example, that a small woodland has been recognised as an important wildlife habitat, and that an environmental organisation wants to conserve it. They would need to sample and collect data about the species present and the sizes of their populations (which we already covered in this chapter), and about the abiotic factors in the woodland. Then they would need to identify which species or features are most under threat and identify the threats as precisely as possible. It would also be helpful to monitor the woodland over time to look for any changes that may be taking place in the community. Armed with this information, the environmental organisation could then draw up a management plan stating the aims of the conservation programme, and giving details of how to carry it out, including sources of funding.

You might think that a better way of conserving such a woodland would be to put a strong fence around it to keep everyone out, and then just to leave it alone. Cases where such an approach is useful are relatively rare, however. The 'leave it alone' method is most likely to maintain biodiversity if the area is truly wild and untouched by humans. Such wild lands still do exist in places; for example, deep in the Amazonian rainforests in some parts of Brazil, some of the rainforests in Papua New Guinea, the hearts of deserts such as the Sahara and the icy lands of Antarctica. But even in areas such as these, pressures from human activities including forestry and mining make it difficult to be sure that these special places will remain unspoilt in the future.

In many cases, what we want to conserve is something that is the result of previous human activity. Many of the habitats that we think of as special only exist because human activity has prevented them from undergoing succession. If we stop grazing sheep on chalk downland, or stop clearing silt from freshwater ponds, they will undergo succession and end up as woodland. The woodland in our example may contain species that would be lost if we allowed natural succession to occur. Just leaving things alone will not be enough to maintain biodiversity in this area – we need to intervene actively.

Figure 38 *Until recently, sheep had been grazing on this chalk downland.*

Figure 39 *Volunteers clearing scrub from chalk downland.*

KEY IDEAS

❯ Conservation attempts to maintain biodiversity. This involves maintaining a variety of different habitats, which between them can support a wider range of species than a single type of habitat could do.

❯ Conservation frequently involves preventing succession from occurring, or the careful management of succession. Without intervention, many habitats in Britain would gradually turn into woodland. There is generally more diversity in the stages leading up to the climax community than there is in the final stage. This is because there are more niches for the different species to occupy.

ASSIGNMENT 3: BLUE BUTTERFLIES RUN OUT OF THYME

The large blue butterfly, *Maculinea arion* (Figure A1), became extinct in Britain in 1979 (but is now slowly making a comeback through being re-introduced). It lives on chalk grasslands where there are colonies of a particular species of red ant, *Myrmica sabuleti*, and plenty of the low-growing herb, thyme.

Figure A1 *The large blue butterfly, Maculinea arion*

The caterpillars of this beautiful butterfly feed exclusively on wild thyme, burrowing into the flower heads to feed on the flowers and then the developing seeds. When the larvae reach about 4 mm in length, they leave the flower and drop to the ground – and wait.

If they are in a suitable place, the larvae are found by worker ants. The caterpillars have a 'honey gland', which attracts the ants to them. The ants pick up the caterpillars and take them into their underground nests.

The caterpillars are not good guests. They eat the ant grubs, growing fat themselves and eventually pupate. They hatch into adult butterflies the following summer. It is a strange sight to see a crumpled blue butterfly crawling up out of the ground, before spreading its wings in the sun and preparing for its first flight.

Wild thyme (Figure A2) has short stems and grows as mat-like clumps in short grass. The chalk downs used to be heavily grazed by sheep and rabbits, but the numbers of sheep have been reduced as a result of changes in farming practices. Then the viral disease myxomatosis spread through the rabbit population, reducing their numbers. As a result, the downland grass was no longer cropped short. Thyme was unable to compete with the tall grasses for light.

Figure A2 *Wild thyme, Thymus serpyllum*

With the loss of the short grass and thyme came the loss of the butterflies. However, conservationists are determined not to let this butterfly become permanently extinct in Britain. In several areas, including some in Cornwall, areas of downland are being managed to provide perfect conditions for thyme, red ants and the large blue butterfly. The aim is to produce a turf 2–5 cm tall, well sheltered from wind and on well-drained soil – enabling red ants to make thriving underground nests. Sheep or cattle are being grazed on the sites. As bushes start to grow, threatening to turn the grassland into scrub, they are cut down or dug up. However, some bushes, such as gorse, are left so that they can provide shelter. Thyme seeds have been sown, taking care to use seed harvested from plants growing locally.

Large blue butterflies have now been successfully re-introduced at several different sites. With constant attention and careful management, it is hoped that the populations of this globally endangered species will once again increase.

Questions

A1. Explain how the large blue butterfly became extinct in Britain.

A2. Suggest how the specialised niche of this butterfly has contributed to its status as a globally endangered species.

A3. With reference to succession, explain how and why the sites for re-introduction of this butterfly are being managed.

A4. Suggest why the thyme seeds being sown are collected from locally growing plants.

PRACTICE QUESTIONS

1. a. What does the Hardy–Weinberg principle predict?

Table Q1 shows the frequencies of some alleles in the populations of cats in three cities.

City	Frequency of allele			
	White	Non-agouti	Blotched	Long-haired
Athens	0.001	0.72	0.25	0.50
Paris	0.011	0.71	0.78	0.24
London	0.004	0.76	0.81	0.33

Table Q1

b. White cats are deaf. Would the Hardy–Weinberg principle hold true for white cats? Explain your answer.

c. What is the evidence from the table that non-agouti and blotched are alleles of different genes?

d. Hair length in cats is determined by a single gene with two alleles. The allele for long hair (h) is recessive. The allele for short hair (H) is dominant.

Use the information in Table Q1 and the Hardy–Weinberg equation to estimate the percentage of cats in London that are heterozygous for hair length. Show your working.

AQA June 2010 Unit 4 Question 3

2. Sea otters were close to extinction at the start of the 20th century. Following a ban on hunting sea otters, the sizes of their populations began to increase. Scientists studied the frequencies of two alleles of a gene in one population of sea otters. The dominant allele, T, codes for an enzyme. The other allele, t, is recessive and does not produce a functional enzyme.

In a population of sea otters, the allele frequency for the recessive allele, t, was found to be 0.2.

a. i. Use the Hardy–Weinberg equation to calculate the percentage of homozygous recessive sea otters in this population. Show your working.

ii. What does the Hardy–Weinberg principle predict about the frequency of the t allele after another 10 generations?

b. Several years later, scientists repeated their study on this population. They found that the frequency of the recessive allele had decreased. A statistical test showed that the difference between the two frequencies of the t allele was significant at the $p - 0.05$ level. Use the terms *probability* and *chance* to help explain what this means.

AQA June 2011 Unit 4 Question 6b

3. Algae are photosynthesising organisms. Some algae grow on rocky shores. A scientist investigated succession involving different species of algae. He placed concrete blocks on a rocky shore. At regular intervals over two years, he recorded the percentage cover of algal species on the blocks. His results are shown in Figure Q1.

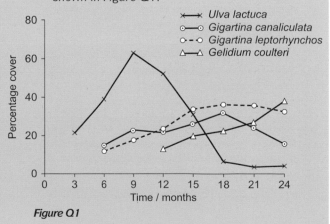

Figure Q1

(*continued*)

a. Name the pioneer species.

b. i. The scientist used percentage cover rather than frequency to record the abundance of algae present. Suggest why.

 ii. Some scientists reviewing this investigation were concerned about the validity of the results because of the use of concrete blocks. Suggest **one** reason why these scientists were concerned about using concrete blocks for the growth of algae.

c. Use the results of this investigation to describe and explain the process of succession.

AQA June 2013 Unit 4 Question 2

4. Ecologists studied a community of fish in a lake.

a. Explain what is meant by a community.

b. i. The ecologists could have used the mark–release–recapture method to estimate the number of one species of fish in the lake. Describe how.

 ii. This species of fish breeds at a certain time of the year. During this fish-breeding season, the mark–release–recapture technique might *not* give a reliable estimate. Suggest **one** reason why.

c. The ecologists found that each species of fish had adaptations to its niche. One of these adaptations was the shape of its mouth. Suggest how the shape of mouth is an adaptation to its niche.

AQA January 2012 Unit 4 Question 1

5. The pH of soil affects the growth of plants. Scientists tried to grow two species of plants on large areas of bare soil of different pH. They grew each species on its own.

In a different investigation, the scientists recorded the growth of the same two species in natural communities. They also measured the pH of the soil where each species grew.

The graphs in Figure Q2 show the results of both investigations.

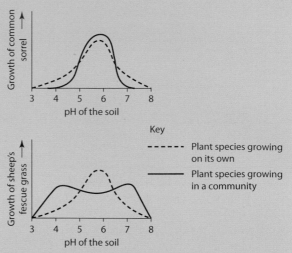

Figure Q2

a. The results are very similar when common sorrel and sheep's fescue were growing on their own. Suggest **one** explanation.

b. The results obtained when these plants were growing in communities are different from when they were growing on their own. Suggest **one** explanation for the difference in the results.

AQA June 2007 Unit Question 3

6. Tree and canyon lizards are found in desert areas in Texas. Both species eat insects. In an investigation the population densities of both species of lizards were measured over a four-year period in:

 ❱ control areas, where both species lived

 ❱ experimental areas, from which one of the species had been removed.

The results for tree lizards are shown in Figure Q3a and the results for canyon lizards are shown in Figure Q3b.

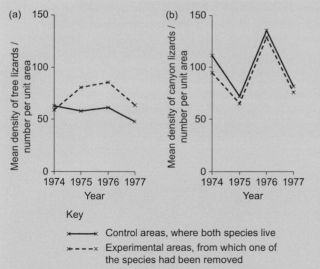

Key

×——————× Control areas, where both species live

×----× Experimental areas, from which one of the species had been removed

Figure Q3

a. Name the type of interaction being studied in the control areas.

b. Describe how the population density of each lizard species is affected by the presence of the other. Give evidence from Figures Q3a and Q3b to support your answer.

i. Tree lizard

ii. Canyon lizard

c. The investigators concluded that, during the four-year period, an abiotic factor had a greater effect on the canyon lizards than on the tree lizards. What evidence from Figures Q3a and Q3b supports this conclusion?

d. Adult tree lizards were found to have shorter lives in experimental areas than in control areas. Using Figure Q3a, suggest an explanation for this.

AQA January 2007 Unit 5 Question 8

7. Figure Q4 shows the stages in a succession from colonisation of bare soil to the formation of woodland.

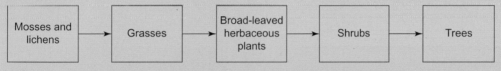

Figure Q4

a. What name is used to describe the final stage in a succession?

b. Explain **one** way in which farming practices prevent the formation of woodland.

c. Clover plants are able to reproduce by vegetative propagation. Suggest **three** advantages of this form of reproduction when clover colonises a new habitat.

AQA January 2007 Unit 5 Question 1

8. A study was made of a transect through sand dunes, from dunes near the seashore to woodland. Samples of quadrats at five positions along the transect were analysed. The results are shown in Table Q2.

	Dunes near seashore	Mobile dunes	Fixed dunes	Heath and scrub	Woodland
Mean percentage plant cover	2	25	90	100	100
Number of plant species per unit area	12	36	95	140	92

Table Q2

a. i. Woodland is the final stage in this ecological succession. Give the term used to describe the final stage in an ecological succession.

ii. The number of plant species per unit area in the woodland is less than that in the heath and scrub. Suggest an explanation for this.

(*continued*)

b. Several of the species of plants living on the dunes have small leaves and their stomata are located in grooves on the underside of the leaves. What do these features suggest about the soil conditions where they live? Explain your answer.

AQA June 2003 Unit 5 Question 3

9. When coal is mined by open-cast mining, the top layer of soil is first scraped off and stored in a large heap. Once mining has finished, the area can be reclaimed. Soil from this store is then spread back over the surface. Some of the bacteria living in the soil store respire aerobically and some respire anaerobically.

Table Q3 shows the numbers of aerobic and anaerobic bacteria found at different depths in a soil store.

	Mean number of bacteria per gram of soil ($\times 10^7$)			
	Aerobic bacteria		Anaerobic bacteria	
Depth / cm	After one month	After six months	After one month	After six months
0	12.0	12.1	0.6	0.8
50	10.4	8.6	0.8	1.3
100	10.1	6.1	0.7	4.1
150	10.0	3.2	0.7	7.9
200	11.6	0.8	0.7	8.4
250	11.9	0.7	0.8	8.8
300	11.0	0.8	0.6	9.1

Table Q3

a. Some of the soil used to determine bacterial numbers was collected from the surface of the soil store. Describe how you would ensure that this soil was collected at random.

b. i. Describe how the numbers of aerobic bacteria after six months change with depth.

ii. Explain the difference in the numbers of aerobic bacteria at a depth of 300 cm between one and six months.

c. Explain how the changes in bacterial numbers that take place at 150 cm illustrate the process of succession.

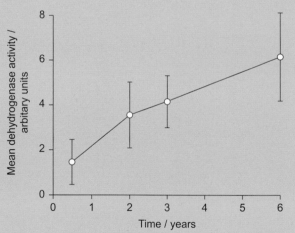

Figure Q6

Dehydrogenase is an enzyme involved in aerobic respiration. Dehydrogenase activity in a soil sample can be used as a measure of the activity of aerobic bacteria. The graph (Figure Q6) shows the mean dehydrogenase activity of soil samples taken from the same depth in a soil store at different times. The bars on the graph represent two standard errors above and below the mean.

d. i. From what depth in the soil store would you expect these soil samples to have been taken? Use information from Table Q3 to explain your answer.

ii. How would you expect dehydrogenase activity to vary with depth after six months? Use information from Table Q3 to explain your answer.

e. What do the error bars tell you about the difference between the mean dehydrogenase activity at six months and at three years? Explain your answer in terms of probability and chance.

f. Table Q4 shows the dehydrogenase activity and the number of aerobic bacteria present in some soil samples.

Dehydrogenase activity / arbitrary units	Number of aerobic bacteria per gram of soil ($\times 10^7$)
13.1	12.7
9.2	8.7
5.5	6.5
3.0	4.6
2.2	2.7
0.4	0.6

Table Q4

A sample of soil was found to have dehydrogenase activity of 8.7 arbitrary units. Explain how you would use the data in Table Q4 to predict the likely number of aerobic bacteria in 1 g of this soil sample.

AQA January 2004 Unit 9 Question 1

11 NATURAL SELECTION AND SPECIATION

PRIOR KNOWLEDGE

At Year 1 and AS level we looked at DNA, genes and chromosomes. We saw that new alleles arise from the process of mutation. We also saw that variation within a species is caused by a combination of mutation and meiosis, and environmental factors. Earlier in this book we looked at inheritance: the ways that genes and alleles are passed on from one individual to another. We also looked at the genetics of populations.

LEARNING OBJECTIVES

In this chapter we build on existing knowledge of population genetics to look at evolution as a change in the allele frequencies in a population. The process of natural selection is one of the most powerful and important processes in science and can lead to the formation of new species. We also look at the other forces that can change allele frequencies.

(Specification 3.7.3)

In September 2013, while exploring a cave system in South Africa, cavers Rick Hunter and Steven Tucker came across the remains of human-like ancestors. There were thousands of bones and bone fragments, including teeth and skulls. They took film of their findings to Professor Lee Berger at the University of Witwatersrand. A full excavation took place a little later, once Professor Berger had assembled a team of scientists who were not claustrophobic, and who were slim enough to fit through the narrow gaps in the cave system. Most of the volunteers were women.

Our knowledge of early humans is very sketchy, and is largely based on partial skeletons, teeth and the occasional skull. However, this remarkable discovery of 15 partial skeletons included both males and females and a variety of ages, from infants to elderly. It also seemed as if the bodies had been placed there deliberately which, if true, was evidence that these early humans were capable of ritual behaviour – burying their own dead.

It seems that every time early human remains are discovered, journalists rush to use the term 'missing link' and so the scientists were at pains to avoid this cliché. However, this new discovery – given the name *Homo naledi* – did seem to fit into a timeline between more primitive bipedal (walking) hominids and humans. Dating techniques have placed the remains at about three million years old, and they could be the first to belong to the genus *Homo*, the same as modern humans.

Professor Berger is determined to find out as much as possible about the remains, using all the latest technology: he has said, "We are going to know when the children were weaned, when they were born, how they developed, the speed at which they developed, the difference between males and females at every developmental stage from infancy, to childhood, to teens, to how they aged and how they died."

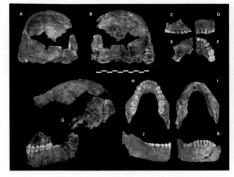
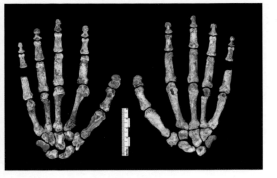

Figure 1 *Fragments of fossil skull and hand of Homo naledi*

11.1 NATURAL SELECTION

Sources of variation

Organisms of the same species carry the same genes, but vary genetically because they have different alleles. The ultimate source of all new alleles is mutation. Once there are different alleles, sexual reproduction can create *new allele combinations* in three ways:

1. Crossing over in meiosis: blocks of genes are swapped between homologous chromosomes, creating new allele combinations on the chromosomes.

2. Independent assortment in meiosis – one chromosome from each homologous pair passes into the gamete at random.

3. Random fertilisation.

This concept has been likened to a pack of cards: mutation creates new cards, and sexual reproduction shuffles the pack.

Variation can also be caused by effects of the environment. For example, an individual is born with a particular skin colour, but this can be altered by the amount of exposure to sunlight.

In recent years a new branch of science, called **epigenetics**, has begun to investigate the way in which the environment can affect gene expression. We look at this idea further in Chapter 13.

Natural selection – the most powerful idea in science?

We covered natural selection in the Year 1 and AS book, but a quick recap of the basics is an essential introduction to the topic of evolution.

In his remarkable book, *On the Origin of Species*, Charles Darwin (Figure 2) put forward the idea of evolution by natural selection. Here's a basic outline of the central idea:

1. Reproduction creates more individuals than can possibly survive.

2. As a consequence, there is competition for resources such as food, nutrients, mates, nesting sites, light.

3. All individuals are different; there is variation within every species.

4. In such conditions, individuals that are fortunate enough to possess a favourable phenotype will have an advantage. Those individuals will have more of a chance of passing their alleles onto the next generation.

A common misconception about natural selection is that it is a matter of life and death – the best adapted survive and the less well adapted die. In practice it is more subtle than that. In biology, a 'fit' organism is one that has more reproductive success. This is also known as **differential reproductive success**; the fortunate individuals in a population whose phenotype gives them a selective advantage will have a higher probability of reproducing. As a result, their combinations of alleles are more likely to be passed on to the next generation. This may lead to changes in the allele frequencies in a population.

Figure 2 *Charles Darwin. Darwin didn't know about DNA, genes or alleles, but all of the research done since has simply served to support and reinforce his ideas.*

QUESTIONS

1. Using the biological definition of fitness, explain why biologists do not use the expression 'survival of the fittest'.

Darwin's finches

The Galapagos Islands (Figure 3) are an isolated group of volcanic islands in the Pacific Ocean, about 600 miles west of South America. Darwin visited these islands in 1835 and was impressed by the fact that on each island the animals and plants were slightly different. Darwin collected many of the small birds he found there and brought them back to the UK for study. He wondered whether one single species of finch had found its way from the mainland, and then had somehow become adapted to take advantage of the different foods available. He said in his journal: "One might really fancy that, from an original paucity (lack) of birds in this archipelago, one species had been taken and modified for different ends."

The finches of the Galapagos Islands have been closely studied for many years. Many of them feed on seeds. Birds with large beaks tend to feed on hard seeds that need to be cracked before they are eaten. Birds with small beaks tend to feed on smaller, softer seeds.

One hallmark of a good scientific theory is that it allows us to make predictions. One prediction that follows from the theory of natural selection is that a population will adapt to changing conditions within the limits of its range of variation. Is there any evidence among Darwin's finches to support this prediction?

In 1983 a significant climate change occurred when a warm ocean current brought prolonged rainfall to the normally dry islands. Many of the cacti died in the wet conditions. This reduced the supply of large, hard seeds. On the other hand, plants that produced small, soft seeds flourished. So, the range of food available to the seed-eating finches changed considerably. There was a remarkably rapid response in the population. Whereas birds with large beaks had been particularly successful in dealing with cactus seeds, they could not pick up the smaller seeds of other plants very easily.

The particular population studied was the medium ground finch, *Geospiza fortis*. As in all populations, there was variation: in this case beak size was vital. Those with small beaks had a selective advantage. Within a few generations the mean size of beak in the population had decreased appreciably. Mathematicians predicted the change in beak size on the basis of the estimated selective advantage. The actual results closely matched their predictions. Moreover, as the climate became drier again in the following years, the trend was reversed in precisely the expected way. This adaptation to changing conditions was only possible because of the rapid reproductive rate and because there was continuous variation in beak size in the population, and this variation could be inherited.

QUESTIONS

2. Another species of ground finch on the islands has a much larger beak, and is specialised to eat cactus seeds. Numbers of this species fell sharply during the very wet years. There was no adaptation affecting beak size such as occurred in the population of medium ground finches. Suggest why the population of this species was unable to adapt to the changing conditions.

Figure 3 *A medium ground finch in the Galapagos Islands*

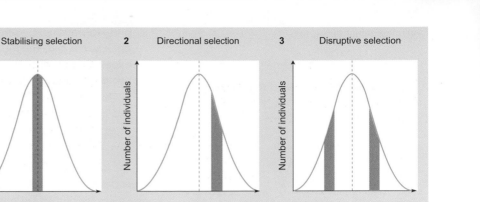

Figure 4 *The three types of selection. The coloured bars represent the range of favourable phenotypes.*

Three different types of selection

There are three basic types of natural selection (see Figure 4), two of which are forces for change, while the other is a force for stability:

> **Directional selection**, in which one extreme of phenotype has an advantage

> **Stabilising selection**, in which phenotypes with middle values have an advantage

> **Disruptive selection**, in which individuals with both extremes of a phenotypic characteristic have an advantage over those in the middle.

A good example of directional selection has been observed in the peppered moth, *Biston betularia* (seen in the Year 1 and AS book). There were two phenotype traits of the moth – the normal speckled phenotype and the much rarer black (melanic). The speckled variety of the moth was common all over England until soot and smoke from the Industrial Revolution made many trees and other surfaces very dark. In these areas the melanic (black) variety was at a selective advantage because it was more hidden from predators. As a consequence, the alleles for black colouration became more frequent with every generation until the black form dominated. When the soot disappeared, directional selection worked in the other direction, favouring the speckled variety once again.

To illustrate disruptive selection, we could return to Darwin's finches. Imagine that a particular species has a range of beak sizes from large to small. The birds with the large beaks might be better adapted to opening seeds, while those with smaller beak sizes might be better at extracting insects from cracks in bark. The birds with medium-sized beaks are adapted for nothing in particular and so are out-competed by the two extremes.

Both directional and disruptive selection lead to a change in allele frequency. Most of the time, however, natural selection does not do this. If the environment does not change, and if the population is already well adapted to its environment, then selection tends to keep things as they are. This is called **stabilising selection**. In Devon and Cornwall, for example, where there was no air pollution during the Industrial Revolution, the peppered moth population remained almost entirely of the speckled phenotype.

Figure 5 shows how stabilising and directional selection acted on the medium ground finches in the Galapagos islands at different times. Beak size in this population shows a normal distribution, with the middle of the range representing the beak size that has the greatest selective advantage. Birds with beaks that are similar in size usually have the best chance of getting plenty to eat, and therefore of surviving

Stabilising selection

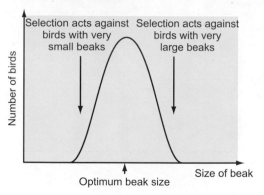

Directional selection

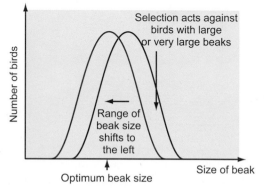

Figure 5 *Stabilising and directional selection in Darwin's finches*

and reproducing. Generation after generation, this beak size is selected for. The frequency of the different alleles that produce different beak sizes stays the same. The position and shape of the graph stay the same. This is stabilising selection.

But during the very wet year described earlier, the birds with smaller beaks had the advantage. The selection pressure shifted. Now the birds towards the lower end of the range had the best chance of survival. They reproduced more than other members of the population with larger beaks. The frequency of the alleles that produce smaller beak sizes increased, while the frequency of the alleles that produce larger beaks decreased, so the next generation had a range of beak sizes that shifted to the left. This becomes an example of directional selection.

ASSIGNMENT 1: SELECTION AND SICKLE CELL ANAEMIA

Red blood cells contain the protein haemoglobin (see Figure A1). This is a soluble, globular protein, made up of four interlinked polypeptides. There are two alpha polypeptides and two beta polypeptides. Each one contains a haem group, which is capable of combining with oxygen when oxygen concentrations are high, and releasing it when oxygen concentrations are low. This allows red blood cells to pick up oxygen in the lungs, carry it in the blood to the tissues, and release it where oxygen concentrations are low, such as in respiring muscles.

A mutation has produced an allele of the gene coding for the beta polypeptide of haemoglobin that has just one incorrect base in it. This results in a different amino acid being present in the polypeptide. This amino acid makes the haemoglobin molecules less soluble, and also causes them to stick together. This happens especially when oxygen concentrations are low. Normal red cells are flexible and can slide over each other without causing blockages. Abnormal

haemoglobin molecules inside the red blood cells of people homozygous for the allele for sickle cell anaemia clump together, pulling the cell into a kind of sickle crescent shape.

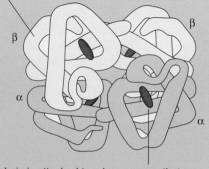

Four polypeptide chains make up the haemoglobin molecule. Each chain contains 574 amino acids.

Each chain is attached to a haem group that can combine with oxygen.

Figure A1 *Haemoglobin*

In this condition, the haemoglobin cannot carry oxygen and the red blood cells are too rigid to squeeze through capillaries, so blockages form. The person's tissues are starved of oxygen, and he or she also experiences pain caused by the blood cells stuck in their capillaries. The person is said to be having a sickle cell crisis. Without treatment this can be fatal.

The allele that causes this disorder is known as the sickle cell allele, and we can use the symbol H^S to represent it. The normal allele is H^A. A person with genotype H^SH^S has sickle cell anaemia (Figure A2), and suffers crises as described. A person with genotype H^SH^A has a mixture of the normal and the abnormal haemoglobin in the blood. Usually the person is fine, but problems may arise if he or she is doing something very strenuous, such as climbing at high altitude where oxygen concentrations are low. The person is said to have sickle cell trait.

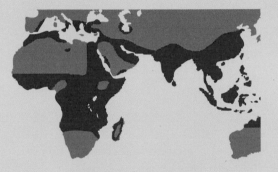

■ Areas with endemic *P. falciparum* malaria

Percentage of population that has the sickle cell allele (haemoglobin S)

■ 14+   ■ 6–8
■ 12–14   ■ 4–6
□ 10–12   ■ 2–4
□ 8–10   ■ 0–2

Figure A3 *The distribution of malaria and sickle cell anaemia in Africa and the Indian subcontinent.*

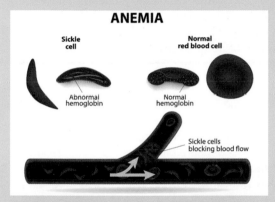

Figure A2 *Sickle cell anaemia*

Why hasn't this harmful allele been eliminated by natural selection from the human population? The reason is that, in the heterozygous state, it confers a selective advantage to the affected person. In many parts of the world, malaria is a common and frequently fatal disease. Many children die from this disease in sub-Saharan Africa and in tropical Asia (see Figure A3). It is in populations here that we find the highest frequencies of the sickle cell allele. There is a direct connection between them. If these populations did not have a high incidence of the sickle cell allele, even more people would die.

Malaria is caused by a protozoan, called *Plasmodium*, that gets inside red blood cells where it feeds and breeds. The most dangerous kind is *P. falciparum* malaria, which can affect the brain and frequently kills. But the malarial parasite doesn't seem to be able to thrive if the haemoglobin in the cells is the sickle variety.

So, when considering the three possible genotypes and the relationship with malaria:

▶ H^AH^A individuals have normal haemoglobin, don't have any sickle cells but are much more prone to contracting malaria, and it is often in a more serious form.

▶ Individuals with genotype H^SH^S have the most severe form of sickle cell. They rarely get malaria but the sickle cell disease means that many do not survive to reproductive age.

▶ Those with H^SH^A may get malaria, but it is a much milder form and rarely fatal. Few people die from it and are therefore able to reproduce.

So, overall, the H^S allele hasn't been removed by natural selection because, in areas where malaria is endemic, those individuals who are H^SH^A have a selective advantage over the H^SH^S and H^AH^A homozygotes.

Questions

A1. In one area of Africa, 2% of children have sickle cell anaemia.

   a. Use the Hardy–Weinberg equation (*see Chapter 10*) to calculate:

      i. the frequency of the sickle cell allele in the population

      ii. the percentage of people in the population who have sickle cell trait.

   b. What assumptions must we make if we are using the Hardy–Weinberg equation in this way?

A2. A couple both have sickle cell trait. Draw a genetic diagram to show the probability that their first child will have sickle cell anaemia.

A3. Many black people in the USA are descended from people who lived in Western Africa. The sickle cell allele is still relatively common in the black population in the USA, but is becoming rarer. Suggest why:

   a. the allele is relatively common

   b. the allele is becoming rarer.

KEY IDEAS

> In all species, individuals show variation in phenotypes, which is due to a combination of the alleles they have inherited and the environment.

> Individuals with advantageous phenotypes are more likely to survive and reproduce – passing on their allele combinations to the next generation. The frequency of the advantageous alleles in the gene pool increases. The change in frequency of alleles is evolution – the process that brings this about is known as natural selection.

> There are three types of selection: directional, stabilising and disruptive.

> Normally, when a species is already well adapted to its environment, and that environment is fairly stable, natural selection keeps things as they are. The frequencies of alleles in the population stay very much the same from generation to generation. This is known as stabilising selection.

> If the environment and therefore selection pressures change, or if a new allele arises by mutation, then there may be a shift in the allele frequencies in subsequent generations. This is due to either directional or disruptive selection.

> Evolution is defined as a change in allele frequency in a population from one generation to the next.

11.2 SPECIATION

In your Year 1 and AS course, you learnt that a species is a group of organisms that share similar features, and that can interbreed to produce fertile offspring. They do not normally breed with other species, and – if they do – then any offspring are not fertile.

How do new species arise? We have seen how natural selection can cause a shift in the frequency of alleles in a population. But our examples so far haven't actually produced a new species. The melanic and speckled forms of the peppered moth are still peppered moths and can interbreed successfully. The medium ground finches with small beaks and large beaks are still medium ground finches.

Looking at the definition of a species, we can see that the crucial feature of a species is that it can breed within itself, but not with other species. So, in order to create a new species from an existing species, a population must somehow become unable to breed with members of other populations of the original species. There must be some kind of barrier which prevents gene flow between them, a mechanism for the population to become **reproductively isolated** from all the members of the original species. Isolation is the key to understanding speciation.

There are two basic models to describe the effects of isolating mechanisms in the process of speciation: **allopatric** and **sympatric**. Allopatric speciation occurs when two populations are physically separated, and this type of speciation is easiest to understand. Sympatric speciation occurs when populations become reproductively isolated despite living in the same geographical area. It is thought to happen when two populations begin to occupy different niches in the same habitat.

QUESTIONS

4. The dog (*Canis familiaris*), the wolf (*Canis lupus*) and the coyote (*Canis latrans*) are classed as separate species. However, they can all interbreed and produce fertile offspring.

Figure 6 *A dog, a wolf and a coyote*

a. What evidence is there in the question that scientists class them as different species?

b. Suggest a reason why they can interbreed successfully.

c. Suggest why hybrids between the three species are relatively rare.

Geographical isolation

Geographical isolation is a key feature of allopatric speciation. Imagine that you could watch what happens to a species of animal over many years. The species is spread over a large area. Part of a population becomes separated from the rest by a river in flood, or by a volcanic eruption, or because part of the land dries out and turns to desert. Over the thousands of years that you keep watch, major geological upheavals cause areas of land to split away and volcanic activity produces new islands. The separated populations do not experience the same environment – the climate, the food supply, the competition, the physical environment could all be significantly different. Some adaptations would be successful on one side of a mountain range, others would be favoured on the opposite side and so the separated populations would evolve in different ways.

Because the selection pressures are different, the processes of natural selection go in slightly different directions on opposite sides of the mountain. In the separated populations there will be a range of variation. Individuals will have different combinations of alleles, and gene mutation may produce new alleles. The animals with phenotypes that favour survival in their local environment will be more likely to pass on the alleles to their offspring. As the allele frequency changes, the phenotypes of the two populations will become more and more different.

After a while, the animals in the two locations might be quite dissimilar, both from each other and from their ancestors. They may be so different that they can no longer interbreed successfully, even if brought together again. If this happens, then they have become reproductively isolated.

How long does this process take? It could take hundreds, thousands or even millions of years. It's very rare to be able to see a new species developing within a person's lifetime, so we usually have to work out how it is happening by looking at what we can see at one moment in time. For example, in the Galapagos Islands, we can see that there are different species of finches on the different islands. They look very similar to one another. This could be explained if one species of finch arrived on one of the islands from the mainland. Some spread to different islands, where the selection pressures were different. They were separated from other members of their species by the water between the islands, so each evolved along its own path, eventually becoming reproductively isolated from each other. There are now 13 different species of finch on the islands.

For new species to develop, separated populations must be genetically isolated. If they live close together and can still interbreed regularly, the populations will continue to exchange alleles. Then they will not separate into populations with distinct sets of alleles. Their gene pools will remain as one, rather than each population having its own gene pool.

Other methods of reproductive separation

Geographical isolation isn't the only way that two populations can become reproductively separated from each other. Reproductive isolation results in genetic isolation. If individuals from two populations become reproductively isolated, then no allele/gene flow occurs between them.

Imagine a field with a species of plant that flowers all day. A new mutation produces an allele that causes some plants to flower only in the morning. These may attract a species of insect that gathers pollen only in the early part of the day. Another mutation in other plants may produce an allele that results in plants that flower only in the evening or at night. These attract a different species of insect for pollination. Both alleles are successful, but the plants form separate populations that are pollinated by one species of insect only. They no longer exchange alleles. Their gene pools are separated.

Further changes in phenotype can occur in both groups – slightly altered petals or stigmas could make pollination by the insect concerned even more efficient. There would then be selection for these alleles and, gradually, the two sets of plants could develop into two distinct species.

So, to summarise, new species arise as a result of:

> Isolation – two populations are separated, for example, geographically or reproductively.

> Genetic variation – each population contains a wide variety of alleles as a result of different mutations and has a range of phenotypes among its members.

> Natural selection – in each population the most successful phenotypes are more likely to pass on their combinations of alleles. This leads to accumulated differences between gene pools.

> Time – over many generations, the populations become so different that successful interbreeding is no longer possible.

An example of sympatric speciation

Figure 7 *An apple maggot fly*

Two hundred years ago, in the USA, the ancestors of apple maggot flies laid their eggs only on hawthorns.

But today, these flies lay eggs on hawthorns (which are native to America) and on domestic apples (which were introduced to America by immigrants from Europe). Females generally choose to lay their eggs on the type of fruit that they grew up in, and males tend to look for mates on the type of fruit that they grew up in. So hawthorn flies generally end up mating with other hawthorn flies and apple flies generally end up mating with other apple flies. This means that gene flow between parts of the population that mate on different types of fruit is reduced. This host shift from hawthorns to apples may be the first step toward sympatric speciation; in fewer than 200 years, some genetic differences between these two groups of flies have evolved.

Sympatric speciation is much more difficult to demonstrate than allopatric speciation, and is the subject of much debate amongst scientists. Many scientists think that it is rare, if it happens at all. To remember the differences between sympatric and allopatric speciation, think 'allo = apart' and 'sym = together'.

Changes in allele frequency

Natural selection is not the only process that can change allele frequency. The Hardy–Weinberg principle (*see Chapter 10*) states that allele frequencies will not change from one generation to the next provided that certain conditions are met. However, it is quite rare that these conditions are met. The following situations can all change allele frequency:

> **Mate-selection** – sometimes, individuals of one particular genotype are more likely to mate with individuals of a similar genotype.

> **Migration** – individuals with different genotypes move into or out of the population.

> **Natural selection** – better adapted phenotypes are more likely to pass on their alleles – the phenotype is a result of interactions between the genotype and the environment.

> **Genetic drift** – random changes in allele frequency due to chance. This sampling error (see below) can be very significant when the population is small.

> **Mutation** – the random process that creates all new alleles and sometimes new genes. It can even result in changes to whole chromosomes.

These causes are summarised in Figure 8.

Genetic drift

One of the conditions of the Hardy–Weinberg principle is that the population must be large.

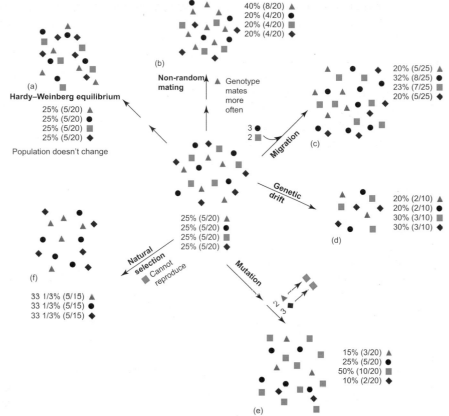

Figure 8 *Summary of the different forces that can lead to a change in allele frequency*

What if the population is not large?

Figure 8 illustrates **genetic drift**, which is basically the idea that allele frequencies can change simply due to chance. In terms of alleles, all offspring are 'samples' of the previous generation, and chance can play a large part if the sample is small. Some individuals fail to reproduce simply due to bad luck, not because they were poorly adapted. Imagine, for example, that there is a population of 1000 beetles with the genotypes HH, Hh and hh, and both alleles are of equal frequency 0.5. If a disaster or predation wipes out all but four of the beetles, chance can play a large part in determining allele frequency. If all four beetles are genotype HH, the h allele will be completely lost from the population. If, on the other hand, the remaining four beetles are HH, HH, Hh and Hh, the frequency of the h alleles has been halved. Over a very small number of generations, genetic drift can see some alleles wiped out – as shown in the worked example "How genetic drift can affect allele frequencies".

A *genetic bottleneck* is the name given to a situation when a population experiences a severe decline in numbers, and then recovers from just a few individuals.

The allele frequencies in the new, recovered population will reflect those found in the original few, not in the large population from where they came. This is known as the founder effect (Figure 9).

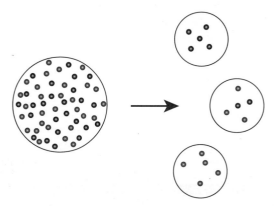

Figure 9 *A simple illustration of the founder effect. The original population is on the left with three possible founder populations on the right. These are all very different from each other, and from the parent population.*

The classic example of this is the cheetah. There is very little variation in the cheetah population – a very small gene pool. It is thought that all the cheetahs in the world are descended from one small family that survived in Africa about 10 000 years ago. As a consequence of passing through a bottleneck, all cheetahs are almost identical and show many of the problems associated with inbreeding – see Figure 10.

Figure 10 *Poor sperm quality, dental problems, susceptibility to the same infectious diseases, and kinked tails are all evidence that the cheetah population has very little genetic diversity.*

QUESTIONS

5. Explain how the genetic problems listed in Figure 10 can be a result of low genetic diversity.

How genetic drift can affect allele frequencies

The random nature of genetic drift can be demonstrated with a few coloured beads or counters. Imagine a population has just six individuals. They possess a particular gene that has two alleles, R and r. Each organism has two copies of these alleles, making a total of 12. You can model this population by using different coloured counters, one for each allele – say, red for R and blue for r. So the population starts with six red counters and six blue counters.

1. Put the 12 counters into a bag/container.

2. Pick out two counters at random. This represents the genotype of the first individual of the next generation. Record the genotype and *put the counters back*. For example, one red and one blue would be recorded as genotype Rr.

3. Repeat the process until you have the genotypes of six new individuals. Record the genotypes and the number of alleles in each generation.

4. Start the next generation with the number of alleles/counters that you had at the end of the last generation. So, for example, if the first generation has genotypes of RR, RR, Rr, Rr, Rr and rr, the number of counters in the container for the next generation would be seven red (R) and five blue (r).

5. Repeat steps 2 to 4 for several more generations, recording your results each time.

Some sample results are shown in Table 1.

Generation	Number of R alleles	Number of r alleles
1	6	6
2	7	5
3	8	4
4	7	5
5	6	6
6	4	8
7	3	9
8	1	11
9	1	11
10	Extinct	12

Table 1 *The effect of genetic drift on allele frequency – possible results.*

The effects of genetic drift are most potent in small populations. When the population is large, it may take many more generations.

KEY IDEAS

> Speciation occurs when two or more populations evolve along different lines. To do this, the populations must be unable to interbreed for some reason or another. This is called reproductive isolation.

> Allopatric speciation occurs when two populations are apart. Sympatric speciation occurs when populations become isolated despite occupying the same area.

> The clearest example of allopatric speciation is seen when a population of organisms becomes geographically isolated from the rest of the species. The selection pressures on this population may be different from those on the other populations of the species, and so the allele frequencies begin to diverge.

> Over many generations, genetic differences accumulate due to a combination of selection and random mutations. A point is reached when individuals are unable to breed successfully with the rest of the species, even if the geographical barrier is removed. When reproductive isolation has been achieved, new species have been formed.

> Forces that can change allele frequency include mutation, migration, non-random mating, natural selection and genetic drift.

> Genetic drift is the name given to a change in allele frequency due to chance rather than selection. It's effectively random sampling of the gene pool. It is most significant when the population is small.

ASSIGNMENT 2: SPECIATION IN ANOLIS LIZARDS

The Caribbean islands and Florida in the USA have many different species of *Anolis* lizards. These lizards usually have green or brown bodies, and the males have large, colourful, inflatable dewlaps ('chin flaps'), which they use in display. These displays help the males to defend their territories, and are also used in courtship.

Researchers are interested in how so many different species of *Anolis* lizards have arisen (see Figure A1). Several teams have been working on the DNA sequences of the different species. The species *Anolis carolinensis* has the distinction of being the very first reptile whose DNA has been completely sequenced.

Earlier research had suggested that the original home of the *Anolis* lizards was in Cuba, and that they had spread from there. Data collected in previous studies suggested that each of the different lizard species on the various islands had developed following separate colonisations from Cuba.

The researchers made a prediction that – if this hypothesis were true – the relationships between the different species of lizards would be closer to the Cuban species than to each other. They tested this hypothesis by analysing the base sequence of the mitochondrial DNA in each of the five species. Table A1 shows the researchers' results. The larger the number, the greater the differences between the two species. The smaller the number, the closer the relationship between the two species.

Figure A1 *Anolis oculatus, Anolis sagrei, Anolis sagrei sagrei, Anolis carolinensis (the first reptile whose DNA has been completely sequenced), and Anolis equestris.*

Species	Species name	Mean difference between mitochondrial base sequences of species				
		Species 1	Species 2	Species 3	Species 4	Species 5
1	A. longiceps		0.125	0.137	0.175	0.119
2	A. maynardi	0.125		0.119	0.168	0.114
3	A. brunneus	0.137	0.119		0.167	0.113
4	A. carolinensis	0.175	0.168	0.167		0.152
5	A. porcatus	0.119	0.114	0.113	0.152	

Table A1 *Mean pairwise divergence for the mitochondrial DNA*

Questions

A1. **a.** Use the data in Table A1 to work out the species to which each of the following is most closely related:

   i. *A. longiceps*

   ii. *A. maynardi*

   iii. *A. brunneus*

   iv. *A. carolinensis.*

A2. Suggest how the lizards on the different islands evolved different features.

A3. The dewlaps of male lizards of different species may be different colours. Suggest how this could make one population of lizards reproductively isolated from another population.

A4. How could the researchers determine whether the five types of lizards that they tested really do belong to different species?

A5. Suggest further investigations that could test the hypothesis that the various species of *Anolis* lizards arose from separate colonisations of islands by lizards originating from Cuba.

Stretch and challenge

A6. In animal cells, DNA is found in both the nucleus and the mitochondria. Suggest an advantage of using mitochondrial DNA rather than nuclear DNA to assess the relationships of the lizard species.

PRACTICE QUESTIONS

1. Great tits are small birds. The graph (Figure Q1) shows the relationship between the number of breeding pairs in the population in a wood, and the mean number of eggs per nest, in different years.

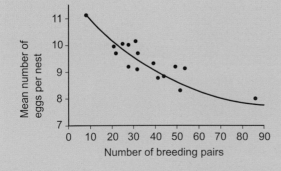

Figure Q1

a. Explain the relationship shown by the graph.

b. Female great tits usually lay between three and 14 eggs in a nest.

   i. In the same year, the birds do not all lay the same number of eggs. Explain how **one** factor, other than the number of breeding pairs, could influence the number of eggs laid by a great tit.

   ii. Natural selection influences the number of eggs laid. Explain why great tits that lay fewer than three eggs per nest or more than 14 eggs per nest are at a selective disadvantage.

AQA June 2006 Unit 5 Question 5

2. In an investigation, the tolerance to copper ions of the grass *Agrostis tenuis* was determined. Samples were taken of plants growing in waste from a copper mine and from nearby areas just outside the mine. The mean copper tolerance of plants from the mine waste was found to be four times higher than that of plants in the surrounding area.

   a. Explain how natural selection could produce a copper-tolerant population in the mine waste.

   b. Copper-tolerant *Agrostis tenuis* plants flower at a different time from those that are not copper tolerant. Explain how this might eventually lead to the emergence of a new species of *Agrostis*.

   AQA January 2005 Unit 4 Question 7

3. Lake Malawi in East Africa contains around 400 different species of cichlids, which are small, brightly coloured fish. All these species have evolved from a common ancestor.

   a. Describe **one** way in which scientists could find out whether cichlids from two different populations belong to the same species.

   b. During the last 700 000 years there have been long periods when the water level was much lower and Lake Malawi split up into many smaller lakes. Explain how speciation of the cichlids may have occurred following the formation of separate, smaller lakes.

   c. Many species of cichlids are similar in size and, apart from their colour, in appearance. Suggest how the variety of colour patterns displayed by these cichlids may help to maintain the fish as separate species.

   AQA January 2006 Unit 4 Question 5

4. The land snail, *Cepaea nemoralis*, is found in a number of different habitats. It is prey to birds such as thrushes. The shells of the snail show variation in colour and in the number of dark bands around them. They may be brown, pink or yellow, and they may have one, three or five bands or none at all (Figure Q2).

Shell with no bands   Shell with five bands

Figure Q2

   a. What type of variation is shown by the banding of the shells? Explain your answer.

   b. The graph (Figure Q3) shows the frequency of yellow, unbanded snails in three habitats. The frequencies were found to be consistent over a period of time.

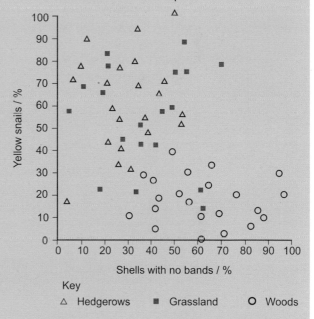

Key
△ Hedgerows   ■ Grassland   O Woods

Figure Q3

   i. Describe what the graph shows about the relationship between the habitats and the phenotypes of the snails.

   ii. Suggest an explanation for this relationship.

   AQA June 2005 Unit 4 Question 6

5. a. Maize seeds were an important food crop for the people who lived in Peru. The seeds could be kept for long periods.

(continued)

Each year, some were sown to grow the next crop. Archaeologists have found well-preserved stores. The graph (Figure Q4) shows the lengths of seeds collected from three stores of different ages.

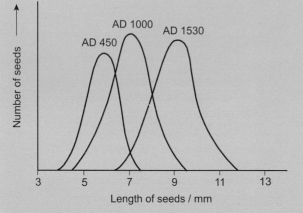

Figure Q4

i. Within each store the maize seeds showed a range of different lengths. Explain **one** cause of this variation.

ii. Use your knowledge of genetics and selection to explain the changes in the mean length of the seeds between AD 450 and AD 1530.

b. The Galapagos Islands are an isolated group about 900 km from South America.

Thirteen species of small birds called finches live on the islands. All species are thought to have evolved from a single species, which reached the islands from South America. This species feeds only on seeds, but the finches on the islands include species which specialise in feeding on buds, nectar and insects, as well as on different sizes of seed.

Explain how evolutionary change could have resulted in this diversity of finch species on the Galapagos Islands.

AQA June 2004 Unit 4 Question 4b–c

6. The Amazonian forest today contains a very high diversity of bird species.

    ❯ Over the last 2 000 000 years, long periods of dry climate caused this forest to separate into a number of smaller forests.

    ❯ Different plant communities developed in each of these smaller forests.

    ❯ Each time the climate became wetter again, the smaller forests grew in size and merged to re-form the Amazonian forest.

    a. Use the information provided to explain how a very high diversity of bird species has developed in the Amazonian forest.

    b. Speciation is far less frequent in the re-formed Amazonian forest. Suggest **one** reason for this.

    AQA June 2013 Unit 4 Question 6

7. Changes in ecosystems can lead to speciation. A high concentration of copper in soil is toxic to most plants. In some areas where the soil is polluted with copper, populations of grasses are found to be growing. These populations of grass belong to a species also found growing on unpolluted soils. It has been suggested that a new species of grass may evolve on soil that has been polluted with copper. Explain how this new species might evolve.

    AQA January 2013 Unit 4 Question 8c

8. Explain how the use of pesticides can result in resistant strains of insect pests.

    AQA June 2012 Unit 4 Question 8c

12 THE CONTROL OF GENE EXPRESSION

PRIOR KNOWLEDGE

You have already looked at the structure of DNA, and at the way it replicates and codes for the manufacture of a protein. You have also seen that the organisation of the body consists of specialised cells that aggregate together to form tissues such as epithelia, nerve and muscle. In turn, the tissues combine to form organs and then organ systems. New cells arise by the process of mitosis.

LEARNING OBJECTIVES

In this chapter we look at the process of mutation and its consequences. We look at the way in which stem cells can give rise to a whole new individual, or differentiate into some of the tissues of the individual. We consider the pros and cons of using stem cells in medicine. We also look at the control of gene expression: how genes are activated and how this can lead to cell differentiation. Finally we look at cancer, which occurs when cell division goes out of control.

(Specification 3.8.1, 3.8.2.1, 3.8.2.2, 3.8.2.3)

The macula is the area of the retina around the fovea that allows us to see in detail. Age-related macular degeneration is a common cause of sight deterioration in older people. Trials have taken place that aim to use stem cells to restore sight.

Several factors make the eye particularly suitable for treatment with stem cells. Despite being a very delicate and seemingly complex organ, they eye is composed of only a few different cell types: the retina contains pigmented epithelium (RPE) cells, light-sensitive cells (rods and cones) and bipolar cells (neurones). It is an easy organ to access, and only a very small number of stem cells are needed for treatment. The eye has 'immune-privileged' status, meaning that stem cells are less likely to be rejected. In addition, there are many sophisticated techniques for measuring the quality of vision, so the progress of treatment is easy to follow.

Recent trials involving the use of stem cells to treat macular degeneration have focused on RPE cells because they are vital for the maintenance of healthy rods and cones, they do not require synaptic reconnection, but they play a key role in many degenerative conditions. Clinical trials are evaluating the transplantation of RPE cells that have been differentiated *in vitro* from embryonic stem cells, for the treatment of three macular degenerative conditions; myopic macular degeneration, Stargardt disease, and age-related macular degeneration. As in most stem cell trials, scientists have reported limited success but are very optimistic for the future.

Stem cell therapy is very simple in theory and very difficult in practice. It offers incredible potential to treat a variety of diseases but the differentiation of stem cells is a complex process and therefore difficult to control reliably.

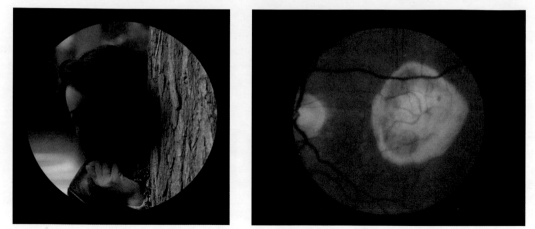

Figure 1 *The image that people with macular degeneration see (left) and a scan of the retina showing deterioration of the central area (the large yellow area – right).*

A reminder of some basics

In the *Year 1 Student Book* you learned the structure and function of DNA.

- DNA molecules consist of two **polynucleotide** strands that are held together by hydrogen bonding between specific base pairs.

- The sequence of bases in the polynucleotide strands enables the DNA to store information.

- The sequence of bases in the **sense strand** of the DNA molecule codes for mRNA, which is then translated into the correct sequence of amino acids that make up individual polypeptides. Each triplet of bases on the mRNA is known as a **codon**, and the order of the codons determines the order of amino acids.

- Since there are 64 possible triplets and only 20 amino acids to code for, the DNA code is said to be **degenerate** (in other words, most amino acids have more than one codon). However, the reverse is not true, there are *no* codons that specify more than one amino acid.

- **Exons** are the functional part of the DNA molecule – the base sequences of DNA that are transcribed into pre-mRNA to make the codons.

- **Introns** are regions of non-coding base sequences of DNA within the gene that need to be spliced out before the protein is made.

12.1 MUTATIONS

A quick recap from last year

A mutation is a change in an organism's genetic material. **Gene mutations** involve a change in the base sequence of a particular gene, while **chromosome** **mutations** involve changes to whole blocks of genes. The causes and consequences of chromosome mutations are beyond the specification, but you do need to know about **non disjunction**: the fault in meiosis that results in changed chromosome number, as seen in Down's syndrome (see Year 1 Student Book).

Gene mutations

Gene mutations occur when DNA is damaged and not repaired, or is copied incorrectly due to errors in DNA replication. As a result of a mutation, the sequence of bases in the DNA is changed.

There are several different types of gene mutation. You may remember the first three from the *Year 1 Student Book*:

Addition: one or more extra nucleotides are inserted, so all the other bases in one direction are pushed along. This is called a **frame shift**.

Deletion: one or more nucleotides are removed, so all the other nucleotides in one direction are effectively moved back. This also results in a frame shift.

Substitution: a nucleotide is replaced by a nucleotide with a different base. This changes just one codon and so does not result in a frame shift.

Inversion: where a sequence of nucleotides is inserted backwards. The inversion can affect as few as two nucleotides or a whole gene, or part of a gene, or even a whole chromosome. Inversions occur when there are two breaks in a stretch of DNA and the repair mechanism rotates the section of DNA between the two breaks by 180 degrees before putting it back in. So, for this section of DNA the sense and non-sense strands have effectively been swapped over. The result is usually a non-functional protein.

Duplication: where a sequence of nucleotides, or a whole gene, or part of a gene, or even a whole chromosome, is added more than once. This is an important source of variation, because the repeated genes can mutate, while the original continues to make the required protein, or vice versa. In duplication, a gene can be copied and inserted somewhere else so there are two copies at different loci. In this case, one of the genes is free to mutate without it harming the organism, as long as the other functions as normal. In this way, new genes can arise, and this is thought to be an important mechanism in mutation.

Translocation: where a base sequence is removed and inserted at a different place either on the same or a different chromosome, so that part of a gene becomes attached to another gene. The new genes will normally make non-functional proteins, but if this happens to proto-oncogenes, tumours may result.

Some mutations involve several nucleotides and so a large amount of the gene is changed. The effect of the mutation will depend on how much the code is disrupted. A single nucleotide substitution will only affect one codon, whereas an addition or deletion may affect all the codons beyond the error. It is also feasible that there could be multiple mutations within a gene, each of which impacts on more than one nucleotide or codon.

QUESTIONS

1. These sentences use three-letter words to represent codons. Identify the types of mutation that have caused the change in each.

   Original sentence – THE OLD MEN SAW THE LAD

   a. THE OLD HEN SAW THE LAD
   b. THE LDM ENS AWT HEL AD
   c. THE OLD SAW THE LAD MEN
   d. THE OLD MEN WAS THE LAD
   e. THE OLD OLD MEN SAW THE LAD
   f. THE COL DME NSA WTH ELA D

The consequences of mutation

When the base sequence of a gene changes, there are three possible consequences. One of these is that the protein is unaffected. There are three possible reasons why the protein might be unaffected:

1. The change in the base sequence may be in an intron, and so is not involved in making the protein.

2. The changed triplet may still code for the same amino acid. That's a result of having a **degenerate code**, in which up to six different codons can translate into the same amino acid.

3. The amino acid sequence of the protein is changed but the protein still functions. For example, the altered gene could code for an enzyme that still works because the active site is unaffected.

Generally, these three reasons will only apply to substitution mutations. In contrast, frame shifts that are caused by additions and deletions are likely to change many codons, which will, in turn, change many, or even most, of the amino acids in the polypepetide. This will usually result in a non-functional protein (the second of the three possible consequences of mutation). If the frame shift occurs at or near the end of the sequence, then only one or a few amino acids will be affected.

The third possibility is that the mutation will produce an allele that makes a different protein, one that gives the individual a selective advantage. This is covered in Chapter 11.

Figure 2 *An albino thrush*

The albino thrush in Figure 2 has a gene mutation that means that it cannot make black pigment. It probably has a poor chance of survival because it is more visible to predators. Sometimes the absence of the correct protein may be harmless, or at least not too serious a problem. This is especially true in diploid organisms, such as humans. For these organisms, it is possible that even if the mutated allele doesn't produce a functional protein, the other, normal allele may produce enough functional protein: for example, in individuals who are heterozygous for haemophilia, or for cystic fibrosis. Occasionally mutations can increase survival chances; such mutant alleles provide the genetic variation that permits natural selection and evolution.

Gene mutations occur naturally at random. As we get older, increasing numbers of cells will contain gene mutations. Mutations in body cells (somatic cells) cannot be passed on to offspring. Mutations that occur during development may cause abnormal growth of the parts that are formed from the cell with the mutation. An example of this can be seen in the photograph in Figure 3, which shows part of a horse chestnut tree that has a patch of leaves without chlorophyll.

Mutations that occur in the gametes are called germ line mutations. If the gamete is an egg or sperm that is involved in a successful fertilisation, then the mutation will be present in every cell in the resulting organism.

QUESTIONS

2. What is the difference between a somatic cell mutation and a germ line mutation?

Figure 3 *A horse chestnut tree showing a patch of leaves that cannot make chlorophyll.*

What causes mutations?

Mutations are random, spontaneous events that can occur when copying DNA or by damage from ionising radiation at any stage of the cell cycle. The more often that DNA is copied, the more chances there are for mistakes to be made. However, the rate of mutation is increased by **mutagenic agents**, which include various chemicals and certain types of radiation.

Mutagens may cause DNA molecules to break, or change the atomic arrangement in a small section of DNA. Breaks in a DNA molecule in a cell can be mended by an enzyme, DNA ligase, which joins the broken ends, but in this process it is possible for a nucleotide to be deleted or for some other defect to occur. High-energy radiation, including X-rays, gamma rays and ultraviolet light, are mutagens, as are high-energy radioactive and ionised particles. X-rays and gamma rays can penetrate deep into the body and may cause mutations in any tissue.

Damage by mutagens is especially serious in tissues in which cell division is rapid, such as in the bone marrow, where blood cells are made. The effect is cumulative, so many small doses have the same effect as one large dose. Radioactive substances such as uranium and plutonium release particles with particularly high-energy radiation, so they can have an even greater mutagenic effect. Atomic particles do not penetrate tissues in the same way as radiation, but absorbing radioactive substances into the body, for example, in food or by breathing them in, is very dangerous, because they continue to decay and emit particles while in the body. Many chemicals, especially organic compounds such as those that occur in tobacco tar, cause mutations. All new drugs and pesticides must be tested to see if they are likely to be mutagenic.

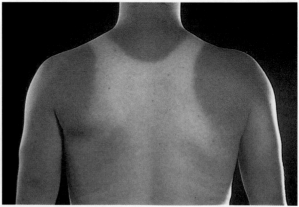

Figure 4 *This person is probably experiencing the discomfort of sunburn. It is a burn, which will heal quickly, but repeated exposure to strong ultraviolet light causes an increase in the mutation rate in skin cells. Skin cancer is then much more likely to develop. It can be a major problem for pale-skinned people living in countries that are near to the equator.*

Mutation rates

A study of the Y chromosome, published in 2009, estimated that every time human DNA is passed on to the next generation, it accumulates 100–200 new mutations. The Y chromosome is useful for this sort of study because it only contains about 200 genes and is passed on – unchanged by crossover – over the generations from father to son.

However, humans are large and complex organisms, and have long generation times. Much work on mutation rate has consequently been carried out using bacteria.

How quickly can bacteria mutate?

In 1997 the complete genome of the bacterium *E. coli* was sequenced. Its circular chromosome contains 4.6×10^6 base pairs (the actual strain sequenced had 4,639,675 base pairs, to be exact). The genome just consists of genes, as bacterial DNA does not include non-coding sequences. Before a bacterium divides, its genome must be replicated. Bacteria can divide every 30 minutes in culture, so that's a lot of DNA replication going on.

When DNA is copied, using the enzyme DNA polymerase, it is possible that one or more incorrect nucleotides are added. This is the commonest cause of mutation. It has been estimated that DNA polymerase III inserts an incorrect nucleotide once in every one hundred million times. This is an error rate of one per 100,000,000, or one per 10^8. However, mutations are not this common because there is a proofreading mechanism, in the form of an enzyme that repairs most of the damage.

This DNA proofreading mechanism fixes 99% of the damage, so only 1% of errors escape and therefore become mutations. The error rate of repair is 10^{-2}, so the overall error rate during DNA replication is 10^{-10} nucleotides per replication ($10^{-8} \times 10^{-2}$).

The overall mutation rate of one in 10^{10} is lower than the size of the *E. coli* genome (4.6×10^6). So, on average, there won't be any mistakes made when one particular cell divides. The DNA will usually be replicated error-free.

However, if one error occurs for every 10 billion nucleotides (10^{-10}) that are added this means that, on average, there will be one mutation every 2200 replications (10 billion divided by 4.6 million). This may not seem to be very common. However, when the numbers of bacteria present in the gut are taken into account, they will be very common. Bacteria divide exponentially (2, 4, 8, 16, and so on). Starting with just one bacterium, it takes only eleven generations to get 2048 cells ($2^{11} = 2048$). At that point you have 2048 dividing bacteria, and with a population that size, there is likely to be at least one mutation every generation.

Calculation: the frequency of bacterial mutations

It has been estimated that for every cell in the human body, we also have 10 bacteria. Most of these are in the gut. It must be remembered that the volume of a bacterium is many times smaller than the volume of an animal cell.

Let's say that, at any one time, the human gut contains one trillion bacteria – that is, 1 000 000 000 000 or 10^{12}.

If there is one mutation for every 2048 bacteria, that would be 1 000 000 000 000 2048 = 488 281 250 mutations per generation. That's nearly half a billion, and that's assuming that the bacteria multiply just once per day. The bacterial reproduction rate varies, dependent upon many factors, but can be as frequent as every half an hour.

With billions of mutations taking place in the gut bacteria of each individual on a daily basis, it is no surprise that populations of bacteria can respond to changing environmental pressures – such as the use of antibiotics – and evolve very quickly.

QUESTIONS

3. Mutations can occur in mRNA molecules as well as in DNA. Explain why a mutation in an mRNA molecule is not likely to have serious consequences.

> A gene mutation occurs when there is a change in the gene's DNA base sequence. Bases may be added, deleted or substituted. The sequence of nucleotides may also be inverted or duplicated.

> A mutation produces a change in a DNA triplet or triplets, which affects the nucleotide sequence of the mRNA codon or codons, and is likely to change the amino acid sequence that is coded for.

> New alleles arise from mutations in existing alleles.

> Mutations in reproductive cells can be passed on to successive generations, but mutations in body cells will only affect the tissues in which they occur.

> Mutations occur naturally, spontaneously and at random, but the frequency at which mutations occur can be increased by mutagens such as ionising radiation and some organic chemicals.

12.2 STEM CELLS

Figure 5 shows a human embryo at the 16-cell stage. You looked like that about nine months before you were born. At the 16-cell stage, each cell in the embryo is capable of making a whole new individual. If the embryo is pulled in half, two new individuals will develop. If 15 cells were destroyed, the remaining one would adapt and get on with the job of making a whole new person. These are the ultimate stem cells.

A multicellular organism, such as a human, grows and develops by two basic processes: cell division (mitosis) and differentiation. Through differentiation cells become specialised into defined cell types and tissues, for example, epithelia, nerve and muscle. Controlling the process of differentiation is critical in development. Cells need to know where they are in the embryo, when to divide, when to stop dividing and what to differentiate into. This control involves switching genes on and off at the right time. For many scientists, this control system is the central mystery of modern biology.

All body cells contain two full sets of genes and so theoretically have the ability to become any of the 200

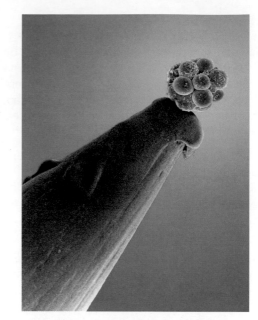

Figure 5 A 16-cell human embryo on the head of a pin

or so different cell types that make up the human body. However, to respond in the right way, cells need to know where they are in space and time, and some of this knowledge is received in the form of chemical signals from other cells. It's a massively complex system that scientists are only just starting to understand, but if we could gain control over cell differentiation the potential benefits would be enormous. We could potentially treat or even cure a wide variety of diseases and trauma, including macular degeneration (see the chapter opener), spinal cord injuries, strokes, burns, heart disease, type 1 diabetes, osteoarthritis, Parkinson's disease, Alzheimer's disease and rheumatoid arthritis.

Different types of stem cells

Stem cells demonstrate two key characteristics:

> **Potency** – the ability to differentiate into specialised cells

> **Self-renewal** – the ability to replicate indefinitely.

Stem cells can be classed according to their potency – the range of cell types that they can produce. There is a sliding scale from the most potent to the least.

Totipotent cells – These cells can mature into any type of body cell (Figure 7) or cell type that is associated with embryo support and development. As a consequence, they are capable of giving rise to a whole organism. The zygote (a fertilised egg) is a totipotent cell, and so are the cells in the early embryo for up to five days after fertilisation (three or four cellular divisions).

Pluripotent cells – After about five days, the totipotent cells in the embryo begin to differentiate, or specialise, and form a hollow ball of cells called a **blastocyst** (Figure 6). The blastocyst has an outer layer of cells that eventually form the placenta, and a cluster of cells inside the hollow sphere called the **inner cell mass**. The cells of the inner cell mass are pluripotent, meaning that they each have the potential to create every type of body cell, but not into cells of the placenta or umbilical cord. Pluripotent cells are not capable of making a whole organism.

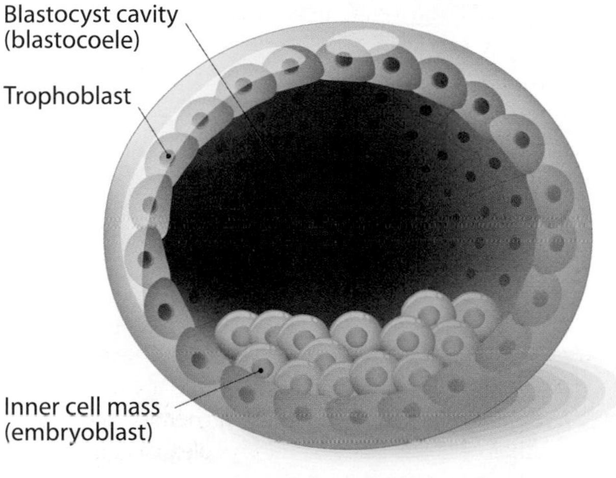

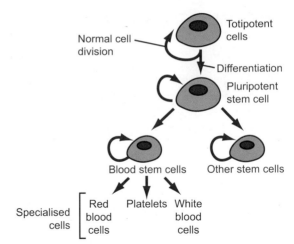

Figure 7 The stem cells in bone marrow have already differentiated. These multipotent stem cells give rise to all types of blood cell.

Induced pluripotent stem cells (iPSCs)

Induced pluripotent stem cells (iPSCs) are adult specialised cells that have been 'reprogrammed' so that they behave like embryonic stem cells.

Figure 8 shows the main sources of stem cells for research. Multipotent cells are found in both the developing foetus and in fully developed human beings. There are certain limitations to the use of multipotent cells, however. Scientists have not identified multipotent cells for every type of mature body cell. Unlike pluripotent cells, multipotent cells are often present in minute quantities and their numbers also usually decrease further with age.

Multipotent cells from a specific patient may take time to mature in culture before they produce adequate numbers for treatment. A potential problem with adult stem cells is that they often contain DNA damage due to ageing, toxins, and random DNA mutation during replication. Care is taken that only healthy stem cells are used for treatment. Research on the early stages of cell specialisation may not be possible with multipotent cells because they are further along the specialisation pathway. This means it is important to study both pluripotent and multipotent stem cells if we are to fully understand cell specialisation and potentially develop new treatments or even cures for diseases.

Figure 6 An embryo at about 5 days is called a blastocyst. Cells from the inner cell mass are pluripotent and therefore have great potential. However, some people feel that an embryo is a human life from the moment of conception, and therefore its destruction is unethical. Others argue that these embryos are the unwanted by-products of IVF treatment, which have been willingly donated by the parents. The use of the embryos involves no suffering and they are cells that would otherwise simply be destroyed.

Multipotent cells – Pluripotent cells soon undergo further specialisation into multipotent cells, which are usually referred to as **adult stem cells**. These cells can give rise to a limited number of other, specific types of cells. For example, haematopoietic cells (blood cells) in the bone marrow are multipotent and give rise to the various types of blood cells, including red cells, white cells and platelets.

Unipotent cells – These cells demonstrate the least potency, and can differentiate into just one cell type. Generally, they provide replacement cells in particular parts of the body, such as the gut lining or liver. However, they still have great therapeutic potential. New skin for burns victims, for example, can be generated from unipotent skin cells, and new heart muscle cells (cardiomyocytes) can be generated from unipotent cardiac progenitor cells (CPCs).

Induced pluripotent stem cells

The differentiation of stem cells in the body is usually a one-way process. The type of specialised cell produced is determined by the gene or genes that are turned on in that particular stem cell. For example, if the genes that control liver formation are activated, the stem cell becomes a liver cell. But, if the genes that control muscle formation are turned

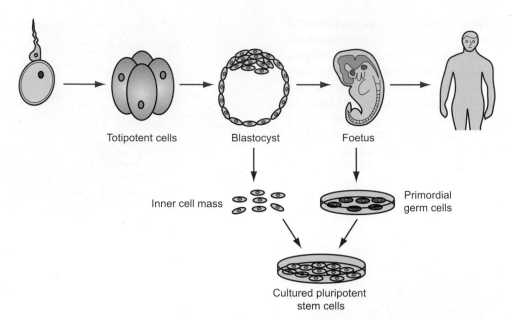

Figure 8 *Obtaining stem cells for research*

on, that same totipotent cell would become a muscle cell. In the process of becoming specialised, stem cells express (or translate) only the relevant parts of their DNA.

Taking stem cell differentiation into a muscle cell as an example, then under normal conditions, once the genes that control muscle formation have been activated, that cell loses the ability to become anything other than a muscle cell – it could never become a liver cell or a brain cell. In other words, the cell can never regain potency – or so it was thought.

However, in 2006, Japanese scientist Shinya Yamanaka (Figure 9) made a ground-breaking discovery: he found a new way to turn specialised adult cells into stem cells. He found that the re-programming required just four specific protein transcription factors: Sox2, Oct4, Klf4 and c-Myc (you don't need to remember their names). These laboratory-grown stem cells are pluripotent – they can make *any* type of cell in the body – and are called induced pluripotent stem cells, or iPS cells. Only embryonic stem cells are naturally pluripotent. Yamanaka's discovery means that, theoretically, any dividing cell of the body can be turned into a pluripotent stem cell.

These iPS cells have two big advantages over embryonic stem cells. Firstly, they don't require the destruction of an embryo, which is an ethical dilemma for some. Secondly, iPS cells can be made from the patient's own cells, so are not likely to be rejected by their immune system.

Figure 9 *Dr Shinya Yamanaka, pictured in 2013. Dr Yamanaka won the Nobel Prize in Physiology or Medicine in 2012 for his discovery of how to create iPS cells.*

Cloning whole organisms

One of the most dramatic demonstrations of the power of stem cells occurred in 1997 when scientists at the Roslin Institute in Edinburgh succeeded in cloning a sheep – the world-famous Dolly – from an adult cell.

In a process called **somatic cell nuclear transfer**, Dolly was cloned from a single udder cell from a six-year old sheep. The nucleus from this somatic (body) cell was placed into a zygote from which the original nucleus had been removed. The genetic material in the udder cell nucleus was able to code for the development of a whole mammal. This showed that the chemical environment in the zygote was able to re-program the nucleus to produce a whole individual.

At first it was thought that Dolly might be genetically damaged and would already be an 'old' ewe when she was born. It is still not certain whether Dolly's DNA had more than average disruption as a result of mutation, but in 1998 she gave birth to a perfectly normal lamb. Dolly died in 2003, following an infection with a virus that causes lung tumours. It is often speculated that she died due to premature ageing but there is no evidence for this.

Using stem cells to treat human disorders

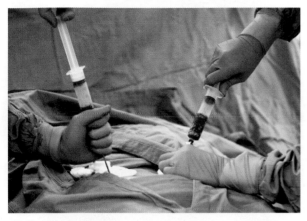

Figure 10 *Preparing to collect human stem cells by removing samples of bone marrow.*

So what is the current state of stem cell therapy?

For 20 years or more, stem cells have been used to grow new skin to treat burns victims. Skin is taken from undamaged areas of the patient's body, where epidermal stem cells produce keratinocytes (skin cells) in sheets (Figure 11). This technique has its limitations: the cells produced simply form a barrier but the stem cells do not give rise to the more complex skin structures such as receptors or hair follicles. Another limitation is the time taken to produce large areas of skin. Research is currently underway using stem cells to overcome these problems.

The use of bone marrow transplants is also a well-established and successful procedure. The basic idea is that bone marrow contains stem cells that give rise to all the different types of blood cell. These cells can be damaged by the high intensity radiotherapy or chemotherapy often used in the treatment of certain cancers, such as leukaemia. Before treatment starts, samples of bone marrow are taken out and frozen (Figure 10). Once the treatment is finished, the bone marrow is put back, where it continues with its normal role.

Figure 11 *Skin that has been produced from stem cells*

Other uses of stem cells are more experimental, and involve treating stem cells so that they will differentiate into one or more specific cell types that will reliably function in the body. As well as technical issues, there are a variety of other problems including reliability, cost, ethics and legal issues.

Overall, as far as new stem cell therapies are concerned, most scientists encourage an approach of cautious optimism: don't expect miracle cures in the very near future. It is often said that stem cell therapy holds great promise in the treatment of diabetes, but scientists have yet to overcome the basic problem of persuading stem cells to differentiate into pancreatic beta cells, and so there are no trials for type 1 diabetes currently underway. That said, trials are underway that show a lot of potential in the treatment of various conditions including some types of blindness, heart disease, Parkinson's disease and nerve damage.

Currently, progress is slow because the cell specialisation process is very complex and cannot yet be reliably controlled. Even if we can control stem cells in a test tube, that that does not mean that they will act the same way in the experimental animal or the patient. The fact that stem cells can replicate indefinitely means that they could also, in theory, give rise to tumours.

On the plus side, stem cell research has many benefits beyond their use in therapy. In our journey to understand how cells differentiate, we will learn a lot about the control systems that affect a cell in the different stages of the cycle, and such knowledge will give us an insight into embryonic development and the underlying causes of cancer. Stem cells can be very beneficial without ever putting them into a patient. They can, for example, be used in drug testing, or in cancer research. Research suggest that many tumours – for example brain or breast – have their own 'cancer stem cells' and so an understanding of the processes that give rise to these cells, and how to selectively destroy them, could lead to major breakthroughs.

KEY IDEAS

> Stem cells have two vital properties: the ability to differentiate into specialised cells (potency), and the ability to divide again and again (renewal).

> Totipotent cells can mature into any type of body cell and so are capable of giving rise to a whole organism.

> Pluripotent stem cells from the inner cell mass of the embryo can differentiate into any of the cell types in the body, but cannot make the placenta or give rise to a whole organism.

> Multipotent stem cells can differentiate into a few closely related cell types.

> Induced pluripotent stem (iPS) cells can be made by adding specific growth factors to already differentiated adult cells.

> During development, stem cells translate only part of their DNA, resulting in cell specialisation.

> Stem cells are used to treat some human disorders, but research into, and the use of, stem cells raises moral and ethical issues.

12.3 REGULATION OF GENE EXPRESSION

We have already seen that cells specialise by the selective activation of genes, but what are the mechanisms that control the process?

Firstly, as a quick reminder, its worth noting that in order for the gene to be expressed, the following steps have to occur:

> The gene is transcribed to make mRNA.

> The introns are spliced out of the pre-mRNA (in eukaryotes).

> The code on the mRNA is translated into a protein.

> The protein may be modified to make it active, often in the Golgi body.

How is a gene activated?

Our current best estimate is that the human genome consists of about 21 000 different genes. A typical human cell normally expresses 3% to 5% of its genes at any given time. By switching genes off when they are not needed, cells can prevent resources from being wasted. Cancer can result when genes do not turn off properly – there will be more about that later in the chapter.

Gene expression in eukaryotes is controlled by a variety of mechanisms that range from those that prevent transcription to those that act after the protein has been produced. The various mechanisms can be placed into four categories, illustrated in Figure 12:

> **Transcriptional** – these mechanisms prevent or promote transcription, and thereby turn off or turn on the synthesis of RNA.

> **Post-transcriptional** – these mechanisms control or regulate mRNA after it has been produced.

> **Translational** – these mechanisms prevent translation; they often involve protein factors that are needed for translation.

> **Post-translational** – these mechanisms act after the protein has been produced.

Let's look at the first of those: transcriptional. A gene will not be transcribed unless all of the required transcription factors are in place. Generally, most of the necessary factors are already present in the cell, and it just needs the addition of a particular molecule from outside the cell to 'complete the set'. Often, this molecule is a hormone.

Hundreds of different transcription factors have been discovered. A transcription factor is a protein that has DNA-binding domains that give it the ability to bind to a specific base sequence of DNA in the promoter regions. Remember that proteins have specific tertiary and quaternary structures, so a transcription factor will have a complementary shape to a specific exposed promoter (region) base sequence, or to other transcription factors that have already attached to the DNA.

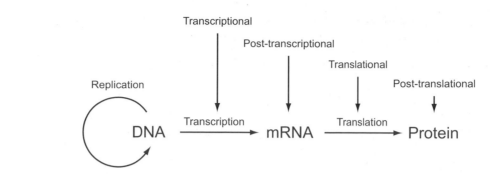

Figure 12 *Regulation of gene expression*

Transcription begins when all of the transcription factors are assembled together. Often, one of the vital factors is attached to the DNA in a position that is quite a distance away from the actual gene. In this case, the DNA must loop round in order to add the required factor to the TIC. This is shown in Figure 13. Once the last piece of the jigsaw is in place, and the TIC is complete, the RNA polymerase enzyme can race along the gene, transcribing as it goes. Details of transcription are in the Year 1 Student Book.

When transcription factors were first discovered, it was thought that they all stimulated transcription. Subsequent research has shown that factors that inhibit transcription are just as important in the grand scheme of gene regulation. Inhibitory transcription factors can act by either binding to and neutralising a particular stimulatory transcription factor, or by binding to the TIC and preventing it from becoming complete and active.

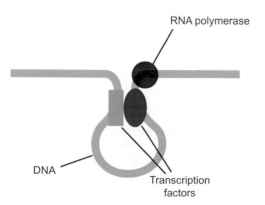

Figure 13 *In order for a gene to be transcribed, all of the transcription factors must be assemble. If a transcription factor is attached to the DNA upstream or downstream of a gene, the DNA must loop round. Note: these details are beyond the specification.*

Hormones as transcription factors

In Chapter 8 we saw that there are two basic mechanisms of hormone action. Water-soluble hormones such as insulin do not enter the cell. Instead, they bind to sites on specific receptor proteins, where their binding sets in motion a cascade of reactions, involving the second messenger, cyclic AMP, which alters the enzyme activity in the cell. In contrast, many steroid hormones, being lipid-soluble, can pass straight into the cytoplasm, where they combine with a receptor molecule to form a complex that passes into the nucleus, where it acts as a transcription factor. The addition of the transcription factor will directly initiate the transcription of a particular gene or genes. For example, oestrogen is the name given to a group of similar hormones that have a vital role in the control of reproduction in females. The oestrogen molecule passes into the nucleus of target cells where it combines with a receptor called **ERα** (Oestrogen Receptor alpha). This forms an active complex that acts as a transcription factor for many different genes. The complex binds to the promoter regions of over 100 different genes, allowing RNA polymerase to bind and therefore beginning transcription.

RNA interference

RNA interference (RNAi) is a system that stops the expression of a particular gene by chopping up the mRNA before it can be used to make a protein. Over the last few years the number of papers published on RNAi has escalated because our ability to harness this mechanism has great potential for the prevention of disease.

There are several different classes of molecules that can bring about RNA interference, including siRNA and miRNAs. Here's how siRNA works:

When foreign RNA (for example, viral RNA) gets into a cell, an enzyme called **dicer** cleaves (splits) the long double-stranded RNA (**dsRNA**) molecules into short double-stranded RNA molecules that are about 21 nucleotides long. These molecules are called **short interfering RNA** (**siRNA**). These siRNAs then split into single-stranded RNAs (**ssRNAs**): the passenger strand and the guide strand. The passenger strand is not needed and is quickly broken down, but the guide strand becomes incorporated into an **RNA-induced silencing complex**, known as **RISC**.

RISC can be thought of as an RNA-destroying machine, but it does so selectively because of the guide strand attached. The guide strand allows RISC to seek out and bind only to those mRNA molecules that have complementary sequences, which stops it being transcribed. The part of RISC that causes RNA cleavage is a protein called **Argonaute.**

Another class of RNAi molecules is the micro RNAs (miRNAs). These are small, naturally occurring RNA molecules that are coded for in the genomes of plants and animals, but that are not, themselves, involved in coding for proteins. miRNAs are similar to siRNAs in that they also inhibit gene expression after transcription, and do so by using Dicer and RISC. The key functional difference between siRNA and miRNA is that whereas siRNAs are very specific, miRNAs are more unselective and can inhibit many different mRNAs. Currently, in research, siRNAs are proving to be very useful tools for studying expression of particular genes. In addition, some siRNAs and miRNAs are being used in clinical trials against various diseases.

RNAi is proving to be a very useful tool for silencing harmful genes. Scientists have produced a whole range of RNAi molecules, which are very effective at silencing thousands of different genes. The Nobel Prize in Physiology or Medicine 2006 was awarded jointly to Andrew Z. Fire and Craig C. Mello *"for their discovery of RNA interference – gene silencing by double-stranded RNA".*

> **QUESTIONS**
>
> 4. RNAi must be specific. Why can't RNAi simply target and destroy all mRNAs made by the cell?

How RNAi works in more detail

During the 1990s, two scientists, named Guo and Kemphus, conducted investigations into the function of the *par-1* gene in a nematode worm (*C. elegans*). They studied the effect of blocking production of the par-1 protein using antisense – a technique in which a small synthesised piece of RNA, which is complementary to a specific sequence in the par-1 mRNA, attaches to and stops the mRNA from being translated into the protein (Figure 14).

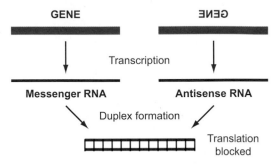

Figure 14 *The use of antisense RNA to block translation of mRNA into protein*

> **QUESTIONS**
> **Stretch and challenge**
>
> 5. a. What is meant by 'antisense'?
>   b. Explain how the small piece of synthesised RNA prevented translation.

The scientists injected an antisense RNA into the worm, and the result was what they expected: all the embryos died. But Guo and Kemphus were puzzled because injecting the sense strand (the same sequence as the par-1 mRNA) – as a standard, negative control for the experiment – also resulted in the death of the embryos.

> **QUESTIONS**
> **Stretch and challenge**
>
> 6. What is meant by 'standard negative control'?

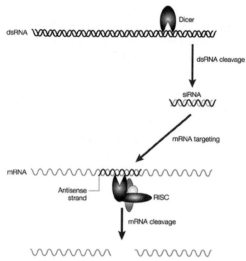

Source: McManus and Sharp. Nature Rev Genet 2002; 3: 737–47. Reproduced with permission from Macmillan Magazines Ltd.

Figure 15 Dicer and the RISC

Two other scientists, Fire and Mello, set up an experiment that was to become significant in the field of RNAi research. In order to see if there would be an additive effect, they injected sense and antisense RNAs into a nematode worm. They found that this double-stranded RNA mixture was a great deal more potent than the sum of its parts. The target gene was silenced ten times more efficiently than it was using either strand alone – an effect that became known as RNA interference.

In molecular biology, the ease with which genes can be silenced using RNAi has resulted in a minor revolution. A group at the University of Cambridge has created a library of more than 16 000 dsRNAs. Further studies on the worms has led to an understanding of the function of 1722 genes, most of which were previously unknown. Using this technique, a group at Cold Spring Harbor, New York, is attempting to determine the function of every gene in the human genome.

ASSIGNMENT 1: OVERCOMING PROBLEMS WITH RNAI AND GENE THERAPY

It is interesting to compare RNAi to gene therapy. In gene therapy, the basic idea is to insert working copies of genes into cells so that they can be expressed and therefore make the missing protein. Conditions such as type 1 diabetes and cystic fibrosis can potentially be treated in this way. In contrast, in RNAi, small pieces of RNA are inserted into cells so that harmful proteins are not expressed. Diseases that can potentially be treated by RNAi include viral infections such as HIV and hepatitis, genetic diseases such as Huntington's disease, and some types of cancer. RNAi has great potential in research because it helps us to find out what particular genes do. In a technique known as knockdown, siRNA can be made to silence the gene of interest, and then the effect of not having the gene can be observed.

For both types of therapy, a big practical problem that needs to be overcome is delivery of the nucleic acids to the target cells. Many things can go wrong: the RNA/DNA may not reach the target cells, it may be broken down by enzymes in the blood plasma and tissue fluid, it may reach cells other than the target cell and have harmful effects, there may be an immune reaction against the vector, or the vector itself might cause problems.

Many different methods of siRNA delivery have been trialled, but they can broadly be divided into two categories, viral and non-viral. There have been many problems associated with viral methods, and so scientists are turning to non-viral methods to get the siRNA into the target cells. A particularly promising non-viral method of delivery is the use of liposomes, which are spheres of phospholipid that surround the siRNA.

Another method for getting siRNA into target cells uses nanoparticles. These are manufactured particles that have the following components:

- a coating made from polyethylene glycol
- the siRNA
- specific antibodies on the outer surface
- a cell-penetrating peptide.

Questions

A1. Explain how siRNA can prevent a protein from being expressed.

A2. What is the difference between *in vivo* and *in vitro*?

A3. What is a vector?

A4. siRNA is a relatively large, polar molecule. Explain why siRNA molecules cannot pass across cell membranes.

A5. Describe the basic structure of a virus.

A6. Explain why viruses have potential utility as vectors of DNA and RNA.

A7. Suggest how viruses might cause problems as vectors of siRNA.

A8. Explain why liposomes are a particularly effective method of getting siRNA into cells.

A9. Suggest the function of each of the nanoparticle components listed above.

A10. Outline the similarities and differences between liposomes and viruses.

KEY IDEAS

> A gene can only be transcribed when it has a complete set of transcription factors.

> When the TIC attaches to the promotor region of a gene, the RNA polymerase enzyme can attach and transcribe the gene.

> Transcription of target genes is stimulated only when specific transcriptional factors move from the cytoplasm into the nucleus.

> Some steroid hormones pass directly into the cytoplasm of the cell where they bind to a specific receptor to form a transcription factor. This directly affects the transcription of a gene or genes in the nucleus.

> Cells in some types of breast cancer have oestrogen receptors in their cell membranes. The binding of oestrogen with these receptors results in transcription switching on genes for cell growth and division. This results in rapid division of the cells forming the tumour.

> Small interfering RNA (siRNA) are short pieces of double-stranded RNA that interfere with the expression of specific genes by degrading mRNA.

12.4 CANCER

Cancer is a disease that results from uncontrolled cell division. The result is usually an abnormal mass of cells called a **tumour** (Figure 16). There are two basic types of tumour:

Benign tumours are not cancerous. They tend to grow slowly and do not spread to other areas of the body as cancerous tumours do. However if a benign tumour is not treated and continues to grow, then its size

will increase and it will push into/against surrounding tissues. Generally, mitosis takes place in the centre and so benign tumours tend to have clearly defined boundaries; it's easy to tell where the tumour stops and the normal tissues begin.

Malignant tumours are cancerous. These tumours tend to grow by mitosis of cells at the edges of the tumour. Some cells may break off and set up secondary tumours elsewhere in the body. This process is called **metastasis**.

Cancer is not one disease. There are more than 200 different types of cancer, which are named and classified according to the tissue or organ in which they occur, and also with respect to how they grow and the cells that they contain. Examples include basal cell carcinoma, malignant melanoma and mesothelioma.

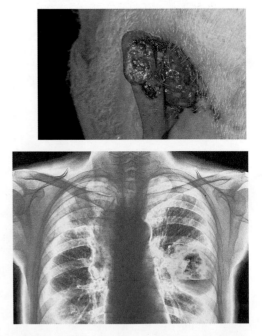

Figure 16 *A skin tumour behind the ear of an elderly man (top) and a coloured chest X-ray showing a cancerous tumour in the left lung.*

One type of cancer, leukaemia, does not result in the development of a tumour. Leukaemia is a cancer of bone marrow that results in over-production of non-functional white blood cells. Blood cells are not joined to each other, so a tumour does not result. However, the problem is that the immune system does not work effectively.

The genetic basis of cancer

Mitosis is controlled by two major groups of genes, **proto-oncogenes** and **tumour suppressor genes**.

Normally, proto-oncogenes code for proteins whose function is to stimulate cell division, inhibit cell differentiation, and halt cell death. All of these processes are important for normal human development and for the maintenance of tissues and organs. If an abnormal cell develops, a self-destruct mechanism is activated. This pre-programmed cell death is called **apoptosis**.

When proto-oncogenes mutate, they become **oncogenes**. The problem is that these mutated genes exhibit increased production of the control proteins, leading to increased cell division, decreased cell differentiation, and inhibition of cell death. These are the three defining features of cancer cells.

A major focus of chemotherapy research aims to develop drugs that target the proteins made by oncogenes.

Tumour suppressor genes act as a failsafe mechanism in cells. For much of the time the activity of tumour suppressor genes inhibits the proto-oncogenes. The proteins made by tumour suppressor genes generally inhibit cell growth and division, and stimulate apoptosis if any abnormal activity is detected. A mutation of the relevant tumour suppressor gene can also allow a proto-oncogene to keep cell division going, leading to the development of a tumour.

A particularly important tumour suppressor gene is called p53, which is located on the short arm of chromosome 17. The p53 gene codes for a protein that plays a key role in preventing cells that have damaged DNA from replicating. It has been described as 'the guardian of the genome' because analysis of tumours reveals that almost 50% contain a mutated p53 gene.

QUESTIONS

7. From the information in this section suggest why mutations to proto-oncogenes are normally dominant, but mutations to tumour suppressor genes are usually recessive.

8. The p53 gene is often mutated in cells taken from colon cancer tumours. Draw a flow diagram to show how mutation of the p53 gene could cause colon cancer to develop.

9. In a metabolic pathway a series of reactions takes place. Each reaction is catalysed by a different enzyme, as shown:

Substance W $\xrightarrow{\text{Enzyme A}}$ Substance X $\xrightarrow{\text{Enzyme B}}$

Substance Y $\xrightarrow{\text{Enzyme C}}$ Substance Z

A mutation of the gene that codes for an enzyme may result in the protein produced having a different tertiary structure so that it cannot function. Suppose that the gene for Enzyme B mutates, and no Enzyme B is produced.

   a. Explain why production of Substance Z stops.

   b. Explain why Substance X accumulates.

   c. Explain what would happen if Substance Y were then supplied.

Epigenetics

Epigenetics is a relatively new area of study that is growing in importance. It concerns the way in which environmental factors – dietary factors, age, environment, and lifestyle disease for example – can affect gene expression.

We have already seen that when cells divide by mitosis, the genome is copied entirely and exactly. Cells then specialise by expressing part of that genome – the epigenome. Environmental changes can cause the transcription of certain genes to be increased or inhibited. So there is no change in the sequence of DNA bases (that is, there are no mutations), but the potential for genes to be expressed does change. Vitally, epigenetic changes are heritable – they can be passed on to the next generation.

There are two main ways in which transcription can be inhibited:

> increased methylation of the DNA

> decreased acetylation of histones.

It can also be inhibited by non coding RNA.

Methylation is simply the addition of a methyl (CH_3) group. In eukaryote DNA, methylation is the addition of the CH_3 group to the base cytosine, forming 5-methylcytosine. The process is carried out by DNA methyltransferase (DNMT) enzymes.

Over recent years it has been discovered that methylation is an important method of epigenetic regulation: that is, increased methylation inhibits transcription and, conversely, decreased methylation increases transcription. It is thought that when a particular promoter region is methylated, the transcription factors cannot bind and so the gene cannot be transcribed.

Histones are the 'organising proteins' around which the incredibly long DNA molecules are wound. Histones and DNA together make chromatin. DNA that is wound around a histone cannot be transcribed, so controlling the degree of attraction between DNA and histones can control transcription.

Acetylation is one of several different histone modifications that can control transcription. Specifically, acetylation is the addition of an acetyl group ($COCH_3$) to the amino acid lysine on the histone. The acetyl group neutralises the positive charge on the lysine residues, reducing the attraction between the DNA and the histone. As a result, the DNA tends to detach from the histone, thus allowing transcription. Conversely, therefore, decreased acetylation of histones will decrease transcription, because the DNA will be more tightly bound to the histones.

A lot of money has been set aside for epigenetic research because it is thought that it has a major role to play in the development of many diseases including cancer, heart disease and various mental illnesses.

Methylation is particularly significant to cancer researchers because inappropriate methylation of tumour suppressor genes switches them off, leading to uncontrolled cell growth.

Interestingly, twin studies can reveal a lot about epigenetics. Identical twins, who have identical genomes at birth, have been found to have very different epigenetic markers, such as methylation and acetylation, later in life. This is thought to be part of the reason that identical twins become more distinguishable as they get older.

Epigenetic changes can be inherited

Since Darwin's time, one of the central pillars of natural selection has been that changes that are acquired during an organism's lifetime cannot passed to its offspring. Until now, there has been a very clear distinction; variation due to genotype can be inherited, and variation due to the environment cannot. Epigenetics blurs this distinction. However, in order to be inherited, any epigenetic changes that occur in an organism's cells must also be made in the germ cells – the eggs and sperm. Is there any evidence that this happens? The simple answer is yes, although the exact mechanisms are unclear and beyond the scope of this book.

Oestrogen and breast cancer

Oestrogen is a general name for a group of closely-related steroid hormones that are central to the development and functioning of females. Oestrogen stimulates cell division in breast and uterine tissue at certain stages of life.

During each menstrual cycle, oestrogen stimulates cells in the breast to divide. Oestrogen also stimulates the cells of the uterus to divide. Hormones from the pituitary gland, notably FSH, stimulate the ovaries to secrete oestrogen. Like all hormones, oestrogen travels in the blood to all cells of the body, but it only affects the cells that have oestrogen receptors in their cytoplasm.

Oestrogen has a shape that allows it to bind to the oestrogen receptor. This results in the formation of an active complex that enters the nucleus and binds to specific regulatory sites on the cell's DNA, which then initiates a series of events that bring about transcription of oestrogen-responsive genes. These genes instruct the cell to make proteins that signal the cell to carry out important activities. Some of the products of these genes are signalling proteins that can cause cells to divide.

Analysis has shown that cells in some types of breast cancer have oestrogen receptors. The binding of oestrogen with these receptors switches on the transcription of genes for cell growth and division. This results in rapid division of the cells, forming the tumour.

PRACTICE QUESTIONS

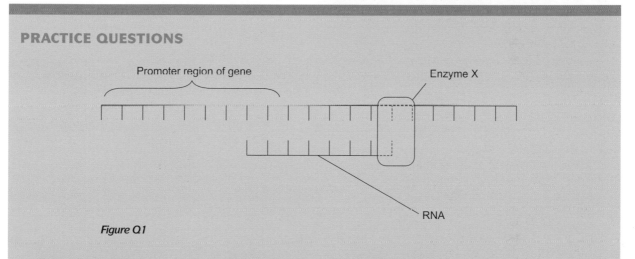

Figure Q1

1. Figure Q1 (above) shows part of a gene that is being transcribed.

   a. Name enzyme X.

   b. i. Oestrogen is a hormone that affects transcription. It forms a complex with a receptor in the cytoplasm of target cells. Explain how an activated oestrogen receptor affects the target cell.

      ii. Oestrogen only affects target cells. Explain why oestrogen does not affect other cells in the body.

   c. Some breast tumours are stimulated by oestrogen to grow. Tamoxifen is used to treat these breast tumours. In the liver, tamoxifen is converted into an active substance called endoxifen.

Figure Q2 shows a molecule of oestrogen and a molecule of endoxifen.

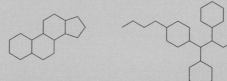

Oestrogen   Endoxifen

Figure Q2

Use Figure Q2 to suggest how endoxifen reduces the growth rate of these breast tumours.

AQA June 2010 Unit 5 Question 5

2. SCID is a severe inherited disease. People who are affected have no immunity. Doctors carried out a trial using gene therapy to treat children with SCID. The doctors who carried out the trial obtained stem cells from each child's umbilical cord.

   a. Give **two** characteristic features of stem cells.

   The doctors mixed the stem cells with viruses. The viruses had been genetically modified to contain alleles of a gene producing full immunity. The doctors then injected this mixture into the child's bone marrow.

   The viruses that the doctors used had RNA as their genetic material. When these viruses infect cells, they pass their RNA and two viral enzymes into the host cells.

   b. One of the viral enzymes makes a DNA copy of the virus RNA. Name this enzyme.

   The other viral enzyme is called integrase. Integrase inserts the DNA copy anywhere in the DNA of the host cell. It may even insert the DNA copy in one of the host cell's genes.

   c. i. The insertion of the DNA copy in one of the host cell's genes may cause the cell to make a non-functional protein. Explain how.

      ii. Some of the children in the trial developed cancer. How might the insertion of the DNA have caused cancer?

   d. Five out of the 20 children in the trial developed cancer. Although the cancer was treated successfully, the doctors decided to stop the trial in its early stages. They then reviewed the situation and decided to continue. Do you agree with their decision to continue? Explain your answer.

   AQA June 2010 Unit 5 Question 6

3. Plant physiologists attempted to produce papaya plants using tissue culture. They investigated the effects of different concentrations of two plant growth factors on small pieces of the stem tip from a papaya plant. Their results are shown in Table Q1.

   Callus is a mass of undifferentiated plant cells.

   Plantlets are small plants.

   a. Explain the evidence from table that cells from the stem tip are totipotent.

   b. Calculate the ratio of cytokinin : auxin that you would recommend to grow papaya plants by this method.

   c. i. Papaya plants reproduce sexually by means of seeds. Papaya plants grown from seeds are very variable in their yield. Explain why.

      ii. Explain the advantage of growing papaya plants from tissue culture rather than from seeds.

   AQA June 2011 Unit 5 Question 6

Concentration of auxin / $\mu mol\ dm^{-3}$	Concentration of cytokinin / $\mu mol\ dm^{-3}$		
	5	25	50
0	No effect	No effect	Leaves produced
1	No effect	Leaves produced	Leaves produced
5	No effect	Leaves produced	Leaves and some plantlets produced
10	Callus produced	Leaves and some plantlets produced	Plantlets produced
15	Callus produced	Callus and some leaves produced	Callus and some leaves produced

Table Q1

4. CREB is a transcription factor in the mitochondria of neurones.

   a. What is a *transcription factor*?

   b. CREB leads to the formation of a protein that removes electrons and protons from reduced NAD in the mitochondrion. Huntington's disease (HD) causes the death of neurones. People with HD produce a substance called huntingtin. Some scientists have suggested that binding of huntingtin to CREB may lead to the death of neurones.

      Suggest how binding of huntingtin to CREB may lead to the death of neurones.

   c. CREB is a protein synthesised in the cytoplasm of neurones. Transport of CREB from the cytoplasm into the matrix of a mitochondrion requires two carrier proteins. Use your knowledge of the structure of a mitochondrion to explain why transport of CREB requires **two** carrier proteins.

   AQA June 2014 Unit 5 Question 7

5. Human immunodeficiency virus (HIV) particles have a specific protein on their surface. This protein binds to a receptor on the plasma membrane of a human cell and allows HIV to enter. This HIV protein is found on the surface of human cells after they have become infected with HIV. Scientists made siRNA to inhibit expression of a specific HIV gene inside a human cell.

They attached this siRNA to a carrier molecule. The flow chart in Figure Q3 shows what happens when this carrier molecule reaches a human cell infected with HIV.

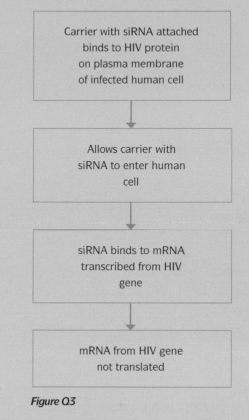

Figure Q3

a. When siRNA binds to mRNA, name the complementary base pairs holding the siRNA and mRNA together. One of the bases is named for you.

_____ with _____

Adenine with _____

b. This siRNA would **only** affect gene expression in cells infected with HIV. Suggest **two** reasons why.

c. The carrier molecule on its own may be able to prevent the infection of cells by HIV. Explain how.

AQA June 2013 Unit 5 Question 6

6. Scientists investigated three genes, C, D and E, involved in controlling cell division. They studied the effect of mutations in these genes on the risk of developing lung cancer.

The scientists analysed genes C, D and E from healthy people and people with lung cancer.

> If a person had a normal allele for a gene, they used the symbol N.

> If a person had two mutant alleles for a gene, they used the symbol M.

They used their data to calculate the risk of developing lung cancer for people with different combinations of N and M alleles of the genes. A risk value of 1.00 indicates no increased risk. Table Q2 shows the scientists' results.

Gene C	Gene D	Gene E	Risk of developing lung cancer
N	N	N	1.00
M	N	N	1.30
N	N	M	1.78
N	M	N	1.45

Table Q2

N = at least one copy of the normal allele is present

M = two copies of the mutant allele are present

a. What do these data suggest about the relative importance of the mutant alleles of genes C, D and E on increasing the risk of developing lung cancer? Explain your answer.

Chemotherapy is the use of a drug to treat cancer. The drug kills dividing cells. The graph in Figure Q4 shows the number of healthy cells and cancer cells in the blood of a patient receiving chemotherapy. The arrows labelled F to I show when the drug was given to the patient.

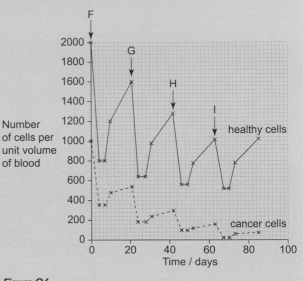

Figure Q4

b. Calculate the rate at which healthy cells were killed between days 42 and 46.

c. Describe similarities and differences in the response of healthy cells and cancer cells to the drug between times F and G.

d. More cancer cells could be destroyed if the drug was given more frequently. Suggest why the drug was **not** given more frequently.

AQA June 2014 Unit 2 Question 8

13 GENE TECHNOLOGIES

We have already looked at the structure and function of DNA, and at the way in which information that is coded in genes is used to make polypeptides and proteins. We have also studied genetics and genetic disease, and the way in which new alleles can arise from mutations. We have looked at the differences between prokaryotic and eukaryotic cells, and at how bacteria feed and reproduce.

LEARNING OBJECTIVES

In this chapter we will read about the progress that has been made in understanding the genomes of various organisms, including humans. We also consider the basics of genetic engineering, in which genes can be transferred from one organism to another. Finally, we consider some of the ways in which genetic engineering techniques can be applied in industry, medicine and agriculture.

(Specification 3.8.3, 3.8.4.1, 3.8.4.2, 3.8.4.3)

Today, the blood glucose concentration of someone with type 1 diabetes can be controlled by giving regular injections of carefully measured amounts of insulin. Until the 1980s, all insulin for injection came from cattle and pigs. Cow insulin differs from human insulin by just one amino acid and although it works perfectly well for a while, an immune reaction against this non-human insulin tends to make it less effective over time. The development of genetic engineering techniques means that we can now use microbes, such as *E. coli* bacteria, to manufacture an exact copy of human insulin.

The gene for human insulin was one of the first to be inserted into bacteria to manufacture drugs for human use. Other substances now made by genetic engineering include human growth hormone and Factor VIII. Growth hormone is used to treat children who do not grow properly because of a pituitary gland disorder. It is also used to treat some adult conditions. Factor VIII is a blood-clotting factor that is used to treat haemophilia, and is extracted from human plasma or made from cultured mammalian cells; sometimes it is not possible to use prokaryote cells to make proteins from eukaryotic cells – more about that later in this chapter.

Genes can also be inserted into crop plants to improve their qualities. For example, specific genes have been added to tomato plants to slow down the ripening process so that the fruit will stay fresh for longer. Genes have been transferred to soya bean and maize crops in the USA to make them more resistant to insect pests. Other suggestions for the future genetic manipulation of plants include adding genes to enable them to make plastics.

However, there is concern about the possible consequences of genetic engineering, especially in crop plants. Might genetically modified foods be a danger to health? Might genes transferred to crops or microbes spread to other organisms and create environmental havoc? Is it possible that widespread use of pest- and herbicide-resistant crops could devastate wildlife? Some of the arguments made by opponents of genetic engineering may appear emotive and unscientific at times, but caution is possibly wise. Indeed, many of the researchers in the field urge a careful assessment of the use of genetic engineering technology.

13.1 STUDYING GENOMES

A genome is defined as 'the entirety of the genetic sequences in an organism'. In short, it's all of the DNA. The human genome consists of 23 chromosomes, about 21000 genes (we are still not certain how many – more about that later) and three billion (3×10^9) base pairs. In humans, the entire genome is present twice in each cell.

Viral genomes were the first to be sequenced, due to their small size. In 1977, the first virus sequenced was the bacteriophage φX174, which has a genome of just 5368 bps (base pairs). It took until 1995 to sequence the complete genome of an organism, the bacterium *Haemophilus influenzae*, whose circular chromosome contains 1830137 base pairs. Since that time, the money invested in developing new sequencing methods increased dramatically. The first eukaryote to be sequenced was baker's yeast (*Saccharomyces cerevisiae*), whose genome is around 12.5 million base pairs.

Sequencing the genome of relatively simple organisms, such as bacteria and *Plasmodium* (the parasite that causes malaria), can reveal very useful information about the **proteome** – the proteins that the organism can make. Knowledge of the proteome of simpler organisms is beneficial in a number of ways. For example, it can help us to understand how equivalent proteins work in humans. It can also tell us about the ways in which these organisms cause disease, and therefore how we can develop drugs to treat infection or produce vaccines. For example, analysing the *Plasmodium* genome could help identify the genes coding for proteins that have antigenic properties and which could be used as the starting points for a vaccine against malaria.

In 2001, and following a massive international collaboration, it was announced that the entire human genome had been sequenced. It had taken about 11 years. However, progress in science is often limited by the technology available and nowhere is this more true than in genomics. The human genome was sequenced using very laborious techniques, known as first-generation sequencing. Then came next-generation sequencing, quickly followed by third-generation sequencing. There are now machines that can sequence an entire human genome in a few hours, and we are constantly refining technologies that allow the machines to work faster. As well as improved speed, genome sequencing is getting cheaper – the sequencing cost per base is becoming dramatically lower.

Figure 1 shows the exponential speed of progress in genome sequencing.

One of the most impressive new sequencing techniques has been developed by Pacific Biosciences, and is called Single-Molecule Sequencing in Real Time (SMRT; Figure 2). This system involves a

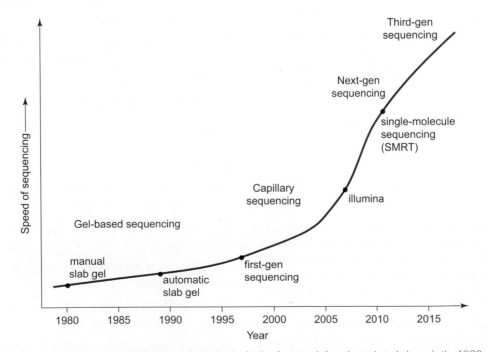

Figure 1 A graph showing how the speed of DNA sequencing technologies has increased since the early techniques in the 1980s. You do not need to know the details of the early techniques.

single-stranded molecule of DNA which attaches to a DNA polymerase enzyme. The DNA is sequenced as the DNA polymerase adds complementary nucleotides that are fluorescently labelled, with a different colour for each base. As each labelled base is added, the fluorescent colour of the base is recorded before the fluorescent label is cut off. The next base in the DNA chain can then be added and recorded. Thousands of DNA polymerase enzymes can do this simultaneously in the same machine, with the result that an entire genome can be sequenced in a morning. It is thought that when this technology is fully developed, it will be possible, and commonplace, to sequence an individual's entire genome in a matter of minutes.

Figure 2 *A Single-Molecule Sequencing in Real Time (SMRT) instrument, developed by Pacific Biosciences. Details of this sequencing technique are beyond the specification.*

QUESTIONS

1. Consider the statement: 'the entire genome is present twice in every body cell'.

   a. Can you think of any examples of animal cells for which this statement may not be true?

   b. To what extent is the statement true for the body cells of:

      i. females

      ii. males?

Where next for our study of the genome?

Once a genome has been sequenced, and we know the order of all the bases, we should be able to work out the sequences of the proteins – the proteome. The problem is that we still cannot tell exactly which bits of eukaryote DNA are involved in coding for proteins, and which are non-coding. One mystery is that the body seems to be capable of making more than 100 000 different proteins, but as far as we can tell we only have about 21 000 genes. One explanation seems to be that the exact structure of a gene is not fixed (see Figure 3).

One gene

| Exon 1 | Intron 1 | Exon 2 | Intron 2 | Exon 3 |

Figure 3 *A gene has traditionally been seen as one sequence of bases that codes for one polypeptide or protein. However, by using different combinations of introns and exons, this gene could be made to make many different proteins.*

So how many genes do humans have?

We don't yet know how many genes there are in the human genome – this is the subject of much ongoing research. It has been estimated that our 21 000 genes only account for about 1.5% of the genome. The rest of the genome has a variety of functions, and includes genes that make RNA molecules, regulatory genes and introns, and sequences whose functions are not yet clear, or are beyond the scope of this specification. Regulatory genes are involved in controlling the expression of other genes, or groups of genes. They do so either by making proteins, or by making RNA molecules.

13.2 MANIPULATING GENES

This section is about what is generally referred to as genetic engineering. The genetic code is **universal** – the same codons code for the same amino acids – and proteins are made in much the same way in all organisms. This means that we can put a piece of DNA from one organism into another and be sure that it will still code for the same polypeptides and proteins.

Some important definitions:

› **Recombinant DNA** is DNA from two different sources (usually different organisms) that has been joined together.

› **Transgenic organisms** are organisms that have had DNA from another individual – often from another species – inserted into their genome. Transgenic organisms therefore contain recombinant DNA.

› **In vivo** means 'in life'. If a gene is cloned *in vivo*, it is made inside a living cell.

› **In vitro** means 'in glass'. If a gene is cloned *in vitro*, it is made in a test tube, or in other lab equipment.

Fragments of DNA can be produced by several methods, including:

› cut out a DNA fragment containing a desired gene from a cell's genome (Figure 4)

› make a required gene from a cell's mRNA, using reverse transcriptase

249

> make artificial genes by working backwards from the protein or the mRNA, that is, use a gene machine to produce a specific protein if we know the protein we want and its amino acid sequence.

Using genetic engineering, we can:

> make millions of copies of genes in a very short time

> insert genes into other cells and organism so that they are expressed

> extract the product of the genes

> use a DNA fragment to find genes or specific DNA sequences.

We will look at each process in turn.

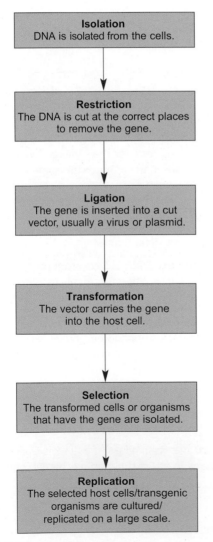

Figure 4 *Transferring a gene.*

Cutting DNA out of the genome

To remove DNA from a cell, the cell membrane needs to be disrupted and the nucleus broken open. The method used depends on the type of cell. In eukaryotes, the cell surface membrane and the nuclear membrane both need to be broken open. In plants, the cell wall must also be disrupted. In prokaryotes, the cell wall and cell membrane needs to be broken, but the absence of a nuclear membrane makes the second stage easier. One common way to disrupt a cell uses a detergent called **sodium dodecyl sulfate** (SDS). This breaks down cell membranes and cell walls. Once the DNA is free, the proteins (histones) that are associated with the DNA are removed using digestive enzymes.

QUESTIONS

2. a. Suggest how the detergent breaks down the cell membranes.

   b. What type of digestive enzyme could be used to remove the proteins in the chromosomes of a human cell?

Once the DNA has been isolated from the rest of the cell, the part of the DNA molecule that contains the required gene has to be cut out and the rest of the DNA discarded. This is important because genetic engineering must be precise; only known genes should be transferred to the donor organism.

The required gene is cut out by using enzymes called **restriction endonuclease** enzymes, which cut DNA molecules at specific positions. Think of them as molecular scissors. Several different restriction enzymes occur naturally in bacteria. Their function is to chop up and destroy the DNA of any viruses that infect the bacterial cell. The name of this group of enzymes comes from the fact that they *restrict* viral growth by cutting *within nucleic acids*. Each enzyme cuts across the double-stranded DNA molecule at a specific nucleotide sequence, known as the **restriction site**. For example, one enzyme, known as EcoRI, cuts the strands only at the sequence shown in Figure 5.

The names of restriction enzymes seem strange when you first come across them, but they are actually quite logical. EcoRI was the first restriction enzyme to be discovered, in the R strain of the bacterium *Escherichia coli*.

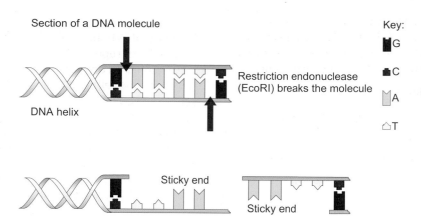

Section of a DNA molecule

Restriction endonuclease (EcoRI) breaks the molecule

DNA helix

Key:
- G
- C
- A
- T

Sticky end

Sticky end

Figure 5 *The action of an endonuclease*

Most restriction enzymes do not cut straight across a DNA molecule – they separate the strands over a stretch of four bases, leaving each part of the broken DNA molecule with a short, single-stranded tail. These tails are called **sticky ends.** The advantage of sticky ends over clean cuts is that you have control over which DNA strands join – a sticky end can only join to a complementary sticky end.

QUESTIONS

3. You will remember from the *Year 1 Student Book* that enzymes are very specific. This is due to the precise configuration of their active site. Use your knowledge of enzymes to explain why EcoRI only cuts DNA at one particular position.

4. a. One of the sticky ends produced by cleavage with EcoRI in Figure 5 has nucleotides with the bases:

   A   T   T   G
   T   A   A   C   T   T   A   A

   Which bases would attach to the sticky end to make a new DNA molecule?

   b. A new DNA molecule can only be made by joining this sticky end with a section of DNA that has the bases on a sticky end. Use your knowledge of DNA structure to explain why.

ASSIGNMENT 1: RESTRICTION ENDONUCLEASES

Table A1 shows the restriction sites of four different restriction endonucleases.

Restriction endonuclease	Restriction site
BamHI	C↓CTAGG G↑GATCC
EcoRII	C↓GGACCG G↑CCTGGC
HindIII	T↓TCGAA A↑AGCTT
PstI	G↓ACGTC C↑TGCAG

Table A1

Questions

A1. Draw diagrams to show the sticky ends produced when each of the restriction endonucleases cuts a DNA molecule.

A2. A section of a DNA molecule has the following sequence of bases:

T C C G G A C C G A C G T C G G T T C G A A T C
A G G C C T G G C T G C A G C C A A G C T T A G

This DNA is treated with a mixture of all four enzymes Table A1. How many DNA fragments will be produced? Draw the fragments produced and name the enzymes involved at each cut.

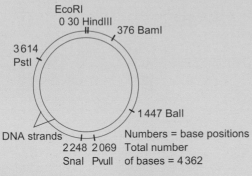

Figure A1

A3. Figure A1 shows a bacterial plasmid with 4362 nucleotide bases in each strand. The cutting sites of seven restriction endonucleases are shown in one strand. The numbers indicate the position of the base; the cutting site of EcoRI is counted as 0.

a. A genetic engineer incubates the intact plasmid with two enzymes, BamHI and PstI. How many bases would be in the smaller section of DNA that is cut out?

b. If the intact plasmid is incubated with all seven enzymes, how many fragments of DNA would be produced? How long would each fragment be?

c. One gene in the plasmid extends from base 1876 to base 2134. Which enzymes should be used to remove this gene with as few extra bases as possible?

A4. Look at the base sequences on both strands of the recognition sequences in Table A1. Most recognition sequences are described as palindromic. Explain what this means.

Conversion of mRNA to complementary DNA

A problem with cutting eukaryote genes out of their genomes is that they still contain introns. Prokaryote DNA does not contain introns, and therefore bacteria do not have the mechanisms for splicing them out. If a gene is inserted into bacteria, and transcribed and translated without splicing out the introns, the protein will be very different and almost certainly will not function. For this reason, it is much better to make artificial genes by working backwards from the mature mRNA or the protein.

To make an artificial gene from mature mRNA, we need to find cells that are actively expressing that gene. Human growth hormone, for example, is synthesised in the anterior lobe of the pituitary gland. The cytoplasm of these cells contains mRNA for growth hormone. This mRNA can be extracted and used to make a complementary strand of DNA (cDNA) using the enzyme **reverse transcriptase** (Figure 6). The single-stranded cDNA can be used to make double-stranded DNA using DNA polymerase. The DNA produced in this way is intron-free, because it is are from mature mRNA which has had its introns spliced out.

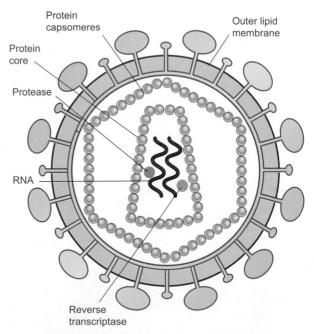

Figure 6 *Retroviruses, such as HIV shown here, contain RNA rather than DNA. In order to reproduce inside a host cell, they make DNA from their RNA, which is transcription in reverse. The virus does this using the enzyme reverse transcriptase. This enzyme is a very useful tool because it can make DNA from samples of RNA.*

Gene machines

The development of automated technologies for synthesising DNA has made it possible to use **'gene machines'** to create artificial DNA including artificial genes from a predetermined polynucleotide sequence (as shown in Figure 7 for making a probe of cDNA). In practice, there is no such thing as a gene machine – it is a general term for all the different technologies that manufacture artificial genes. As an alternative to using mRNA, genes can be synthesised by working backwards from the primary sequence of protein. If you know the amino acid sequence of the protein, today's DNA synthesisers will make the gene that will code for that protein.

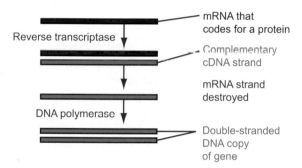

Figure 7 *Producing cDNA*

QUESTIONS

5. Explain how the sequence of bases in DNA can be worked out from the order of bases in the corresponding mRNA.

6. How many bases are in the section of single-stranded DNA that corresponds to the 51 amino acids in the active human insulin molecule?

Making multiple copies of the gene

In the early days of DNA research, sequencing a nucleotide fragment or analysing a sample of DNA was a slow process. It was technically difficult and expensive to obtain a small fragment of DNA in large enough quantities to make analysis possible. It could take months to sequence a short section of DNA, and it was impossible to extract sufficient DNA from spots of blood at the scene of a crime, for example. The whole field of DNA analysis has been revolutionised by the development of PCR (polymerase chain reaction): a technique that can make a billion copies of a strand of DNA in a few hours. In 1993, the American scientist Kary Mullis received the Nobel Prize in Chemistry for his pioneering work in PCR, a process that he began developing a decade earlier.

The polymerase chain reaction (PCR)

PCR is gene cloning *in vitro* (in a test tube). Copies make more copies so the process proceeds at an exponential rate. PCR can amplify tiny amounts of DNA by a factor of over a million within an hour. It has many different uses, including:

> Forensic analysis. Small samples of DNA might be obtained from cells in spots of blood or from a single hair left behind at the scene of a crime. This DNA can be amplified (copied) using PCR to generate enough DNA for **genetic fingerprinting** to be carried out.

> Detection of disease. Using PCR means that only a few cells from an embryo or a foetus are needed for the presence of particular alleles to be detected.

> Tissue typing prior to transplants.

> Analysis of tissue from extinct animals, such as the mammoth or the Tasmanian wolf, to establish their closest relatives.

> Paternity testing.

> Identification of human remains following a fire, or in cases of advanced decay, for example.

> Analysis of ancient human bodies in which some soft tissue has been preserved; these studies are helping us to understand the migrations of early human populations.

The process of PCR needs just four components:

1. The original DNA to be amplified.

2. Nucleotides.

3. DNA polymerase. The enzyme TAQ polymerase is commonly used. It comes from the bacterium *Thermus aquaticus*, which lives in hot volcanic springs. The enzyme is thermostable and is not denatured by high temperatures.

4. Primers. These are short, single-stranded pieces of DNA that bind to the original DNA and signal to the enzyme where to start copying.

PCR amplifies DNA in a series of cycles. Each cycle takes about two minutes and consists of three stages (Figure 8):

1. **Denaturation**. The reaction mixture is heated to 94–98 °C for 20–30 seconds so that the hydrogen bonds between complementary base pairs break and the two strands of double helix DNA separate (or 'melt') – so the DNA is single-stranded.

2. **Annealing**. The temperature is reduced to 50–65 °C for 20–40 seconds so that the primers anneal (stick) to the single-stranded DNA.

3. **Extending**. The temperature is raised again to around 72 °C (which is within the optimum temperature range for TAQ polymerase). The TAQ polymerase moves along the DNA strand, adding complementary nucleotides by forming phosphodiester bonds.

So, at the end of the first cycle there will be two double-stranded copies for every original, then after the next cycle there will be four copies, then after the next cycle eight copies, and so on. The whole process is automated and takes place in a PCR **thermal cycling machine**. These are common in labs all over the world.

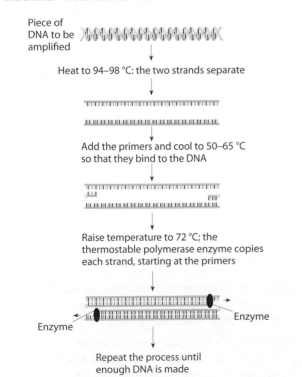

Piece of DNA to be amplified

Heat to 94–98 °C: the two strands separate

Add the primers and cool to 50–65 °C so that they bind to the DNA

Raise temperature to 72 °C; the thermostable polymerase enzyme copies each strand, starting at the primers

Enzyme   Enzyme

Repeat the process until enough DNA is made

Figure 8 A single cycle of the polymerase chain reaction

QUESTIONS

7. Look at Figure 8. How many different types of DNA nucleotide must be added to the mixture in the final stage? Why?

8. Suggest why using DNA polymerase from bacteria living in hot springs is essential.

9. How many cycles of the process would be needed to produce one million copies of a DNA molecule, starting from just one DNA molecule?

Getting the gene into the host cell

So now we have lots of copies of our target gene. It is important to appreciate that if the gene is to be expressed, it also needs to have promoter and terminator regions. However, if the gene has been constructed using mRNA or protein sequencing methods, then it will only contain coded information for the primary structure of the protein. So, in order for it to be expressed correctly in the host, both promoter and terminator sequences need to be added.

The next step is to get the genes into the host cells (bacterial cells, for example), and then incorporated into the host cell DNA so that they will be expressed. This requires a vector – a piece of DNA that can take the gene into the host cell. Bacterial plasmids are commonly used as vectors. Plasmids are small, circular molecules of double stranded DNA that occur naturally in bacteria in addition to the prokaryotic cell's larger molecule of chromosomal DNA, and contain non-essential genes such as antibiotic resistance. Plasmids are very useful in genetic engineering because these loops of DNA can replicate independently from the bacterial chromosome.

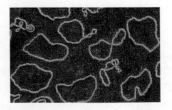

Figure 9 Transmission electron micrograph showing pBR322 plasmids from Escherichia coli

The plasmid is first cut open using a restriction enzyme that will produce a complementary sticky end. This creates a broken loop of DNA with sticky ends that are complementary to those of the donor gene. The donor gene can then be inserted into the plasmid loop using the enzyme DNA **ligase**, which catalyses the ligation reaction that joins two sections of DNA (Figure 10).

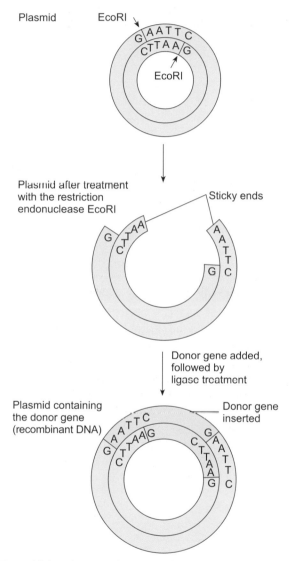

Figure 10 *Inserting a gene into a plasmid.*

In practice, the DNA from the donor organism and the plasmids from the bacterial recipient are incubated, in separate tubes, with the same restriction endonuclease for 2–3 hours to create identical sticky ends. The tubes are then heated to denature the restriction endonuclease. The contents of the tubes are mixed and DNA ligase is added. The sticky ends of the donor DNA join with the corresponding sticky ends of the plasmids. Hydrogen bonds form between

complementary bases and the DNA ligase joins the sugar–phosphate backbone. The new DNA is an example of **recombinant DNA**.

When the vector (e.g. a plasmid) is introduced into the bacteria, the transformed cells are selected and cloned or amplified. Every time the bacteria divide in the culture medium, they copy the new DNA as well. This is *in vivo* amplification. The genes can also be cloned by PCR; *in vitro*.

The process of getting the new DNA incorporated into the genomes of living cells is called **transformation**. There are many different methods of transformation, and techniques are changing all the time.

Cells are often transformed with two sets of genes, where one is a **marker gene**. When plasmids are mixed with bacteria, for every bacterium that takes up a plasmid, tens of thousands do not. So how do you tell which bacteria have accepted the new gene? A marker gene is an extra gene inserted into the plasmid along with the gene that is to be cloned.

A common example of a genetic marker is a gene for antibiotic resistance. The bacteria are grown on a medium that contains the antibiotic. Only those bacteria that took up the plasmid with the new gene and the gene for antibiotic resistance will survive and grow. Another example of a genetic marker is a gene which makes an enzyme that makes a coloured product. The bacteria are then grown with the required substrate in the growth medium, and any transgenic colonies will show up and so are easily seen and collected.

QUESTIONS

10. Explain why it is important to denature the restriction endonuclease before mixing the contents of tubes containing donor DNA and bacterial plasmids.

Gene therapy

So far we have looked at transferring genes into bacteria, but we can also transport genes into the cells of eukaryotes, including humans.

Gene therapy is one area of research that aims to treat genetic disease by giving patients healthy copies of defective alleles. However, achieving this is easier said than done. It's not too difficult to find and make lots of copies of the healthy allele – the techniques involved are outlined in this chapter – but the problem lies in getting the genes to the exact cells that need them, and making sure that they are expressed.

One example of a disease that might feasibly be treated using gene therapy is **cystic fibrosis**. (This example is a good way to contextualise the theory, although you will not be expected to memorise this.) Cystic fibrosis is caused by the effects of mutations in a gene that codes for a protein called the cystic fibrosis transmembrane conductance regulator (CFTR). This complex molecule is one of the essential channel proteins in cell membranes, and it consists of 1480 amino acids. The function of the CFTR channel protein is to transport chloride ions through the cell membrane.

Most people have two normal copies of the CFTR gene, but in some people either one or both copies of the gene are mutated. Individuals with one mutated allele will still be healthy, but are carriers and risk passing on their mutated allele to their offspring. People with two mutated alleles have cystic fibrosis. Gene therapy for cystic fibrosis involves inserting functional CFTR genes into the epithelial cells of the lungs, to replace the defective alleles. Two methods are being tested:

❭ putting CFTR genes into liposomes – tiny spheres of lipid that can easily be absorbed through cell surface membranes

❭ putting CFTR genes into harmless viruses that transfer genes into cells. The structure and life cycle of viruses was covered in the *Year 1 Student Book*. Getting nucleic acids into cells is what viruses do.

Liposomes are spheres made from either one or two layers of phospholipids, so they are similar to vesicles – the small organelles that transport substances around inside cells. Liposomes are able to fuse with phospholipid membranes and so can carry their contents into the cell. CFTR genes are made by one of the techniques outlined in this chapter ('gene machines'), cloned by PCR and inserted into plasmids. The plasmids are then inserted into liposomes.

A major problem with gene therapy is getting the genes to the cells that need them. With cystic fibrosis, the task is relatively easy because the genes are

needed in the cells lining the lungs, and so they can simply be inhaled. Aerosol sprays containing liposomes are used in much the same way as asthmatics use an inhaler. In the lungs, the liposomes fuse with the surface membrane of the epithelial cells, and the plasmids are transported across the membrane into the cells. This is easier said than done. In practice, the liposomes often don't reach the finer bronchioles deeper in the lungs. Furthermore, even when the genes do get to the cells, there is no guarantee that they will be expressed to make the missing protein.

Gene therapy trials to treat cystic fibrosis in humans have taken place. So far, liposomes have shown more promise than viruses. One trial in 2015 showed a 3.7% improvement in lung function compared with the placebo, which is modest but promising.

How do we find the genes we want?

How do you find a specific gene in an entire genome? One way is to make a **gene probe**, which is a single-stranded, fluorescently labelled piece of DNA whose base sequence is complementary to part of the gene that we want to find. This can also be used to detect the presence of a specific allele, for example in screening patients for heritable conditions. When a gene probe is mixed with single-stranded DNA from the genome, the DNA probe hybridises (joins) with the complementary strand of the section of DNA, showing its position. When we have found our gene, we can cut it out (Figure 11)

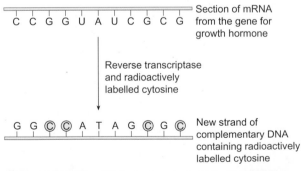

Figure 11 *Producing DNA from a sample of mRNA using the enzyme reverse transcriptase. From the primary structure of the required protein, you can determine the mRNA sequence used in translation and use this to make a complementary strand of DNA. Adding a radioactive tag or fluorescent dye makes the synthesised DNA easy to find and confirms it contains a specific sequence (see section 13.3).*

ASSIGNMENT 2: GENETIC ENGINEERED TOMATOES

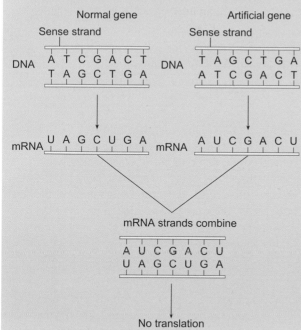

Figure A1 *Blocking the production of pectinase*

Figure A2 *Ripe tomatoes, ready for eating*

Fruit sold in supermarkets is often picked well before it is ripe and transported long distances. It is then ripened artificially just before being sold (Figure A2). It doesn't have the same taste as freshly ripened fruit but it can be displayed for longer as it does not become soft too quickly.

As tomatoes ripen they produce **pectinase** (also called polygalacturonase), an enzyme that breaks down the pectin that normally holds the cell walls together. As the cells separate, the fruit goes soft and squishy and rots. Genetically modified tomatoes have been given an additional artificial gene. The bases on the sense strand of the DNA of this artificial gene are exactly complementary to those on the sense strand of the gene that codes for pectinase (Figure A1). When the two genes are

transcribed, they make complementary strands of mRNA, which are attracted to each other and bind together to form a double strand. This prevents mRNA transcribed from the cell's pectinase gene from joining onto the ribosomes and being translated to make pectinase.

Other aspects of the ripening process are not affected, so the flavour of a ripe genetically modified tomato still develops, but the tomato doesn't go soft because it does not produce pectinase. This means that growers can leave the tomatoes to ripen naturally on the plant; they can be sure that the fruit will remain in good condition for several days longer than traditional tomato varieties, allowing plenty of time for transport to the shops and a few days of display on the shelves.

Questions

A1 Explain why the two mRNA strands transcribed from the two genes bind together to form a double strand of mRNA.

A2 Explain how the artificial gene stops the tomatoes from going soft.

KEY IDEAS

› In genetic engineering genes from one organism can be inserted into another. Genes that code for useful substances, such as hormones, enzymes and antibiotics, can be transferred into microorganisms or cultured eukaryotic cells, which then produce large quantities of these substances. Genes can also be transferred into larger organisms such as plants and animals.

› There are three ways of obtaining a particular gene. One way is to cut the gene out from the DNA of the donor organism using a restriction endonuclease enzyme. Alternatively it is possible to make an artificial gene by working backwards from the mRNA. A third approach is to make an artificial gene by working backwards from the primary structure (amino acid sequence) of the required protein. Automated DNA synthesizers, generally called 'gene machines', are now commonly used in laboratories to construct desired sequences of DNA.

> Restriction enzymes are widely used for cutting DNA. Each restriction enzyme cuts at a specific recognition site. Some make clean cuts, but most create uneven cuts called sticky ends.

> The selected genes need to be transferred into the host cells. Bacterial plasmids are often used as vectors to transfer the selected genes – such as those for useful proteins that we want to produce in large quantities – into bacterial cells.

> Restriction enzymes are used to cut the vector (e.g. plasmid) into which the gene is inserted, so that the sticky ends are complementary. This leaves complementary sticky ends to which the selected gene can be attached by another enzyme, DNA ligase.

> If a transferred gene is to be transcribed when it is incorporated into the host cell's DNA, then it needs to have a promotor and a terminator sequence added to the start and finish of the gene sequence to start and stop transcription.

> Millions of copies of the gene can be made by the polymerase chain reaction (PCR). PCR is gene cloning *in vitro* (in a test tube). It is a cyclical process that consists of three stages: denaturing (separating the two strands), annealing (adding primers) and extending (using enzymes to copy the individual strands).

13.3 USING DNA FOR INVESTIGATION

DNA profiling

Few advances in science in recent years have made as many headlines as DNA profiling, popularly known as genetic fingerprinting, a technique developed by Professor Alec Jeffreys at Leicester University in 1984.

The basic idea behind DNA profiling is that between the genes are long segments of DNA, the function of much of which we still don't really understand, so it's not correct to call it 'junk DNA'. Recent research suggests that some of this DNA may have an important function in gene expression. What we do know is that mutations and recombinations can accumulate in these regions. Specifically, non-coding regions contain many **variable number tandem repeats (VNTRs)**, which are specific base sequences repeated a certain number of times. The greater the number of repeats, the greater the gap between restriction sites. So, when the DNA sample is broken into pieces ('digested') by restriction enzymes, a mixture of differently sized fragments will be produced that is unique to each individual.

The probability of two individuals having the same VNTRs is very low, although closely related people will share some sequences. More recently, DNA profiling has focused on **short tandem repeats (STRs)** because they are less likely to degrade over time and therefore they give more reliable results with older DNA samples.

If there is not enough DNA for analysis, the DNA is first extracted from the sample and PCR can be used to amplify very tiny starting amounts. If fluorescent nucleotides are used in PCR, the resulting fragments are easy to show up after electrophoresis.

When the DNA is cut into fragments, the same restriction enzyme must be used for each DNA sample, so that it is certain that any differences in DNA fragments are due to differences in base sequences, rather than different enzymes cutting at different places.

The DNA fragments are then separated by electrophoresis (Figure 12). The mixture of DNA fragments is placed in a trough at one end of a long piece of agar gel that is placed in a container with a dilute solution of ionic salts. Electrodes are placed in the solution at either end and a voltage is applied. The phosphate groups in the fragments of DNA give them a negative charge, so they are attracted through the gel towards the positive electrode. The smaller fragments move more rapidly through the gel matrix than the larger ones, so the different-sized fragments are separated in much the same way as they are in chromatography.

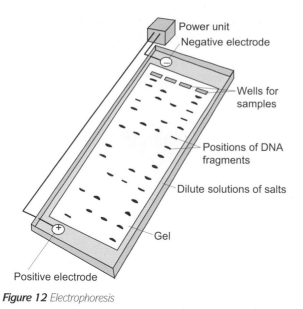

Power unit
Negative electrode
Wells for samples
Positions of DNA fragments
Dilute solutions of salts
Gel
Positive electrode

Figure 12 *Electrophoresis*

complementary to the base sequence of the specified stretch of DNA. This is an important use of DNA probes, as they can identify whether individuals are carrying an allele for an inherited condition, for example.

DNA profiling is also used in animal and plant breeding. For example, individuals in captive breeding or pedigree breeding programmes can be profiled and the specific alleles required to produce a desired phenotype marked. This guides selection of individuals for breeding. In this way genetic fingerprinting helps to monitor and maximise genetic diversity of endangered species, and minimizes inbreeding. In plant breeding the technique of identifying and selecting individuals with a genetic marker for a trait such as disease resistance is more efficient than traditional selective breeding in cases where the trait may be difficult to measure.

QUESTIONS

11. Explain why a restriction enzyme cuts a DNA molecule at specific positions.

12. PCR is used to amplify a section of DNA. When this amplified DNA is treated using a restriction enzyme, 18 DNA fragments of different lengths are always detected by electrophoresis, no matter how many samples of the same DNA are treated with this restriction enzyme. Explain why the samples have a fixed number of DNA fragments.

13. Phosphate groups give the DNA a negative charge. Explain why DNA fragments contain phosphate groups.

KEY IDEAS

> Different people have different non-coding DNA. Specifically, they have different numbers and lengths of VNTRs – variable number tandem repeats.

> DNA profiling is based on highlighting the differences in VNTR or STR length. Samples of an individual's DNA are digested with specific restriction endonucleases that cut DNA wherever a specific short sequence (the recognition site) occurs. This produces a mixture of differently sized fragments.

> DNA fragments can be separated by gel electrophoresis. A voltage is applied to the gel and the negatively charged DNA fragments move towards the positive electrode. Smaller fragments move faster through the gel than larger ones.

> The bands of DNA can be seen if radioactive nucleotides are used in the PCR.

> The digested DNA is separated by gel electrophoresis and various techniques can be used to show up the different fragments. The resulting banding pattern can then be analysed.

As shown in Figure 13, a DNA probe labelled with radioactivity or with a fluorescent dye is then used to reveal the positions of the bands on the sheet containing the DNA sequence of interest. A general probe can be used to make all the bands show up. This allows us to see the familiar barcode pattern of DNA bands, which can be compared side by side with the DNA pattern of another sample. Alternatively, a highly specific probe can be used to show up a particular sequence of DNA. This probe is designed as a piece of single-stranded DNA that is

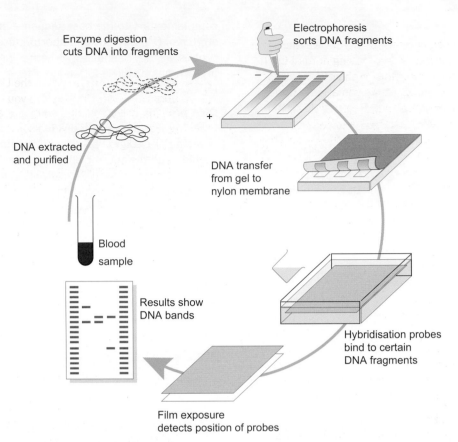

Enzyme digestion
cuts DNA into fragments

Electrophoresis
sorts DNA fragments

DNA extracted
and purified

DNA transfer
from gel to
nylon membrane

Blood
sample

Results show
DNA bands

Hybridisation probes
bind to certain
DNA fragments

Film exposure
detects position of probes

Figure 13 *Analysing DNA samples*

13.4 MEDICAL DIAGNOSIS

We have already seen that labelled DNA probes can be used to find specific alleles or base sequences. The probes are made from cDNA and will hybridise with (bind to) the target sequence and indicate its presence. This technique has great potential for the early detection of genetic disease.

Generally, the process of **screening** refers to the process of testing all of the individuals in a certain cohort, whether they show symptoms of the disease or not. Currently, women of particular age groups in the UK are offered screening for cervical cancer and breast cancer. The development of more sophisticated gene probes and genome analysis means that in the future we will feasibly be able to screen routinely for other genetic conditions, even before birth - for example screening of IVF embryos before implantation to identify heritable conditions. However, given the seriousness of some diagnoses, it is likely that screening will be linked with genetic counselling so that the individual is helped to deal with the possible consequences. For example, people identified to have

a genetic predisposition to conditions such as breast cancer may consider lifestyle changes, more frequent screening or preemptive surgery.

One of the most far-reaching implications of the human genome project, and of the development of sensitive probes for certain genetic diseases, is the possibility of rapid and accurate genetic analysis of an individual's genotype. As a consequence, medicine and other treatments can be tailor-made to an individual's genetic make-up. Personalised medicine can, for example, allow a doctor to select a particular monoclonal antibody for a cancer patient where screening has identified that they have certain alleles that promote cancer. Although this approach is relatively new, it has the potential to make treatment a lot more reliable.

QUESTIONS

14. What is the difference between hybrid DNA and recombinant DNA?

Cystic fibrosis: a case study of genetic testing

Genetic testing can be used to find out whether, for example, a person's cells are carrying normal CFTR genes or whether one or both of their CFTR alleles have mutations. Genetic testing can also be useful for prospective parents if they are possible carriers of a mutant CFTR allele and are planning on having a baby; if the test reveals that both the prospective father and the prospective mother are carriers of one mutant CFTR allele, then there is a one-in-four chance that they will have a child that has cystic fibrosis. If the couple decides to go ahead with a pregnancy, the foetus can be genetically tested. Foetal cells are obtained by amniocentesis or by chorionic villus sampling, which are two antenatal screening methods that are performed routinely. Amniocentesis is performed between weeks 15 and 22 of pregnancy. A small amount of the fluid that surrounds the foetus is removed. This contains cells that have come from the foetus. Chorionic villus sampling is done at an earlier stage of the pregnancy, at about weeks 10 to 12. This method involves removing a small piece of placenta, the organ which links the foetus with the mother, and which has the same genetic make-up as the foetus.

Once the parents know the results of their prenatal test, and if it is positive for cystic fibrosis, then they can receive counselling to help them to decide whether or not to go ahead with the pregnancy. This is never an easy decision, but prenatal genetic testing does provide the family with some choice about their future and the future of their child.

QUESTIONS

15. About 1 in 2000 babies in the UK is born with cystic fibrosis. Do you think genetic screening of foetuses could be used to eliminate cystic fibrosis? Explain your answer.

16. In theory, genetic screening of a foetus could be used for each of the following:

    - to detect Tay–Sachs disease, a genetic disease for which there is no treatment, and which causes serious brain damage, paralysis and death in early childhood

    - to detect a genetic condition that results in deafness

    - to detect the presence of a gene that increases the chances of developing breast cancer in later life

    - to choose the hair or eye colour of a child

    - to choose the sex of a child.

    a. In which of these situations, if any, do you think that it is acceptable to screen the genetic makeup of the foetus?

    b. How would you justify where to draw the line?

ASSIGNMENT 3: GENETICALLY MODIFIED FOODS

Rapid developments in genetic engineering mean that, in theory, it is possible to transfer genes from almost any organism to any other. Scientists are investigating a myriad of potentially useful applications of recombinant DNA technology, including ways of increasing crop yields and improving food supplies. However, many people have become suspicious of these developments and are concerned about the possible ways in which the technology could go wrong. Some people think that it is a bad idea to tamper with natural food sources, and they feel that new technology is being imposed without adequate safeguards by companies that just want to make money. Some people are worried that eating genetically modified (GM) foods may be harmful. Others are concerned about the impact of GM crops on the environment.

The arguments for and against

Consider the following summaries of some of the arguments to statements about GM technology, which are put forward by advocates and opponents of GM foods.

"Foods made from GM crops may be a danger to health."

Anti-GM

It is unnatural to swap genes from one species into another. The food that we eat contains foreign

(continued)

genes, perhaps from bacteria or even humans, and we don't know what we are eating. The new combinations of genes may have unknown effects, such as making poisonous or carcinogenic substances. Also, when a foreign gene is inserted into a crop plant, other genes are normally added too. These might stimulate different genes in the crop to make harmful products. GM crops that are modified to produce substances intended to protect them, for example, from insect pests, may have dangerous long-term effects.

Pro-GM

Genes are not harmful to eat. We eat large amounts of nucleic acids in our food. These are all digested, so we could not somehow incorporate foreign genes from food into our body. All crop plants have been genetically altered by selective breeding, so no food plants today are naturally occurring wild plants. Genetic modification speeds up what has been a slow and expensive process of cross-breeding. Genetic modification is precise; only a small number of genes are transferred. Cross-breeding mixes large numbers of genes with unpredictable effects. Food products are extensively tested for safety before being sold, which includes checking for the presence of possibly harmful products.

"Genes might be transferred from GM plants to others, perhaps creating 'superweeds'."

Anti-GM

Genes can be passed from one organism to another, and from one species to another. Bacteria regularly exchange genetic material, including plasmids. Genes in a crop that protect it from the effect of weedkillers may be passed to other plants, including weeds, and these might also become resistant to weedkillers. Pollen from GM crops may be distributed over long distances by wind or insects, and natural cross-pollination may pass on the transferred genes to non-GM crops, or possibly produce harmful hybrids. Organic farmers are particularly concerned about cross-contamination.

Pro-GM

This is no different from the interbreeding that occurs anyway. Weeds containing genes that confer resistance to a particular herbicide would have no competitive advantage except in environments where the herbicide is being applied. Other weedkillers could still be used, so the weed could not become some sort of uncontrollable monster. Cross-contamination of crops can be avoided by separating organic and GM crops across adequate distances.

"Widespread planting of GM crops will seriously affect wildlife in the environment."

Anti-GM

Pesticides produced by genes in crops to protect them will kill not only crop pests but also other useful insects. This will remove pollinating insects such as bees and therefore affect pollination of fruit trees as well as wild flower populations. The loss of wild plants and insect food for other species such as birds will also cut down the diversity of wildlife in the countryside.

Pro-GM

The use of resistant crops will reduce the amount of pesticide that farmers need to spray on their crops. Only insects that actually feed on a particular crop will be affected and there will be less environmental damage to neighbouring habitats. Reduced diversity of wildlife is an unavoidable consequence of modern intensive farming practices in which large areas are planted with the same crop, and the use of GM crops would make no difference.

"GM crop seeds are more expensive. This would affect the livelihood of poorer farmers, especially in developing countries."

Anti-GM

The use of advanced biotechnology in agriculture will make smaller farms less economical and thus favour large-scale agro-business and the companies that develop and patent particular GM crop varieties. The use of 'terminator genes' that prevent germination of the seeds from a crop will hit poorer farmers particularly hard, because traditionally they keep a proportion of their seeds to plant the following season. Restrictive practices by large GM companies, such as making crops resistant to a particular weedkiller that only one company sells, may lead to inflated prices for the weedkiller and excessive profits for the company.

Pro-GM

The development of GM crops with improved quality, greater yields and reduced wastage due to pests will be of benefit to all and will increase food supplies for an ever-increasing population. The technology allows the development of crops that flourish in harsh environments, such as saline or very arid soils. These will be of great benefit to poorer countries where population expansion is forcing the use of more marginal land. Competition between companies will maintain costs at realistically low levels.

Questions

A1. Use information from the summaries and from additional research of your own to prepare a presentation either in favour of or against the use of GM foods.

PRACTICE QUESTIONS

1. Plasmids can be used as vectors to insert lengths of foreign DNA into bacteria. Figure Q1 shows how this is achieved.

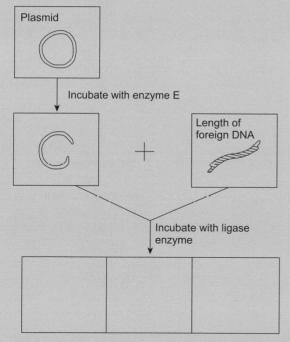

Figure Q1

a. Name enzyme E.

b. Cut plasmids and lengths of foreign DNA can join. What features of their ends allow them to join?

c. Draw **three** different structures that could be formed by incubating cut plasmids and lengths of foreign DNA with ligase. Use the spaces as provided on your copied diagram.

AQA June 2006 Unit 2 Question 4

2. Read this passage:

DNA tests were used to confirm the identity of deposed Iraqi leader Saddam Hussein, after his capture in December 2003. DNA tests were carried out to prove the suspect was not one of the many alleged 'lookalikes' of the former leader. Firstly, the DNA was extracted from the mouth of the captured man using a swab. Great care was taken to check that the swab did not become contaminated with any other DNA. DNA extracted from the swab was then subjected to a standard technique called the polymerase chain reaction (PCR), which takes a couple of hours. Lastly, the sample was 'typed' to give the genetic fingerprint. This was produced within 24 hours of Saddam Hussein's capture. Tests for use in criminal cases often take much longer because samples are very small or contaminated. It appears that Hussein's genetic fingerprint was already stored for comparison. This was obtained from personal items such as his toothbrush. DNA from the toothbrush would

(continued)

have been subjected to PCR before a DNA fingerprint could have been obtained.

Source: adapted from Shaoni Bhattacharya, New Scientist, 15 December 2003

Use information from the passage and your own knowledge to answer the questions.

a. Describe how the technique of genetic fingerprinting is carried out and explain how it can be used to identify a person, such as Saddam Hussein.

b. Explain how DNA could be present on a toothbrush.

c. i. Explain why the polymerase chain reaction was used on the sample of DNA from the toothbrush.

   ii. Explain **one** way in which the polymerase chain reaction differs from DNA replication in a cell.

d. Tests for use in criminal cases often take much longer because samples are very small or contaminated. Explain why it takes longer to obtain a genetic fingerprint if the sample is:

   i. very small

   ii. contaminated.

AQA June 2005 Unit 2 Question 8

3. Figure Q2 shows how the gene for human growth hormone (hGH) can be transferred into a bacterium.

a. Name enzyme 1 and enzyme 2.

b. After mixing with the plasmid, the bacteria are first grown in Petri dishes of agar containing ampicillin. What is the reason for this?

c. Figure Q3 shows how colonies of bacteria can be transferred from a Petri dish of agar containing ampicillin to identical positions on a Petri dish of agar containing tetracycline.

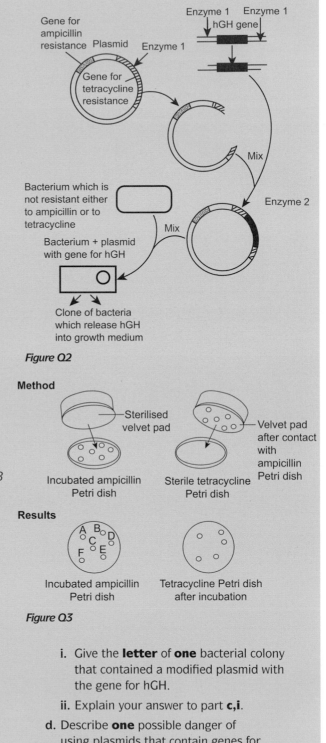

Figure Q2

Method

Incubated ampicillin Petri dish — Sterilised velvet pad

Sterile tetracycline Petri dish — Velvet pad after contact with ampicillin Petri dish

Results

Incubated ampicillin Petri dish (A, B, C, D, E, F)

Tetracycline Petri dish after incubation

Figure Q3

   i. Give the **letter** of **one** bacterial colony that contained a modified plasmid with the gene for hGH.

   ii. Explain your answer to part **c,i**.

d. Describe **one** possible danger of using plasmids that contain genes for antibiotic resistance.

AQA June 2003 Unit 2 Question 7

4. **a.** Plasmids are often used as vectors in genetic engineering.

   i. What is the role of a vector?

   ii. Describe the role of restriction endonucleases in the formation of plasmids that contain donor DNA.

   iii. Describe the role of DNA ligase in the production of plasmids containing donor DNA.

   b. There are many different restriction endonucleases. Each type cuts the DNA of a plasmid at a specific base sequence called a restriction site. Figure Q4 shows the position of four restriction sites, J, K, L and M, for four different enzymes on a single plasmid. The distances between these sites is measured in kilobases of DNA.

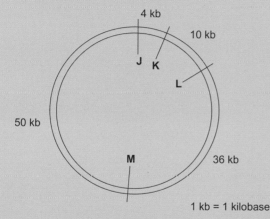

1 kb = 1 kilobase

Figure Q4

   The plasmid was cut using only two restriction endonucleases. The resulting fragments were separated by gel electrophoresis. The positions of the fragments are shown in Figure Q5.

   i. Which of the restriction sites were cut?

   ii. Explain your answer.

   AQA June 2006 Unit 2 Question 6

5. A husband and wife wanted to know whether they were carriers of the mutated form of a gene. This mutation is a deletion that causes a serious inherited genetic disorder in people who are homozygous.

   A geneticist took samples of DNA from the husband and the wife. He used a DNA probe to look for the deletion mutation.

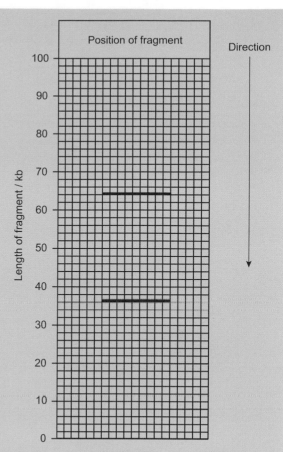

Figure Q6

   The DNA probe was specific to a particular base sequence in an exon in the gene. Exons are the coding sequences in a gene. The geneticist compared the couple's DNA with that of a person known not to carry this mutation.

   Figure Q6 shows the geneticist's results.

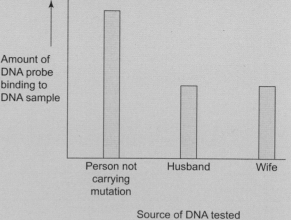

Figure Q6

(continued)

a. The geneticist told the couple they were both carriers of the mutated gene. Explain how he reached this conclusion.

b. The DNA probe the geneticist used was for an exon in the DNA, **not** an intron. Explain why.

AQA June 2013 Unit 5 Question 8

6. Haemophilia is a genetic condition in which blood fails to clot. Factor IX is a protein used to treat haemophilia. Sheep can be genetically engineered to produce Factor IX in the milk produced by their mammary glands. Figure Q7 shows the stages involved in this process.

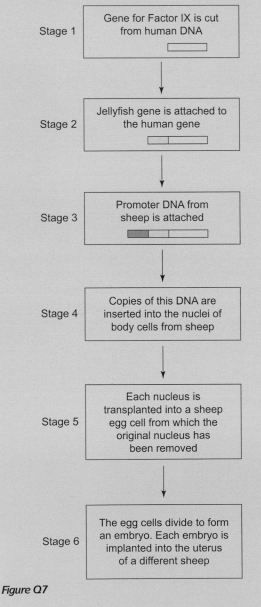

Figure Q7

a. Name the type of enzyme that is used to cut the gene for Factor IX from human DNA (Stage 1).

b. i. The jellyfish gene attached to the human Factor IX gene (Stage 2) codes for a protein that glows green under fluorescent light. Explain the purpose of attaching this gene.

ii. The promoter DNA from sheep (Stage 3) causes transcription of genes coding for proteins found in sheep milk. Suggest the advantage of using this promoter DNA.

c. Many attempts to produce transgenic animals have failed. Very few live births result from the many embryos that are implanted.

i. Suggest **one** reason why very few live births result from the many embryos that are implanted.

ii. It is important that scientists still report the results from failed attempts to produce transgenic animals. Explain why.

AQA June 2012 Unit 5 Question 5

7. Scientists used restriction mapping to investigate some aspects of the base sequence of an unknown piece of DNA. This piece of DNA was 3000 base pairs (bp) long. The scientists took plasmids that had one restriction site for the enzyme KpnI and one restriction site for the enzyme BamHI. They inserted copies of the unknown piece of DNA into the plasmids. This produced recombinant plasmids.

Figure Q8 shows a recombinant plasmid.

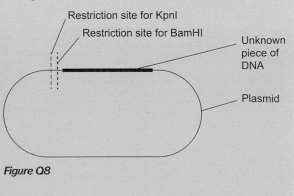

Figure Q8

a. When the scientists digested one of the recombinant plasmids with KpnI, they obtained two fragments. One fragment was measured as 1000 bp. The other fragment was described as "very large".

   i. What does this show about the base sequence of the unknown piece of DNA?

   ii. One of the fragments that the scientists obtained was described as "very large". What is represented by this very large fragment?

b. When the scientists digested another of the recombinant plasmids with BamHI, they obtained three fragments. How many BamHI restriction sites are there in the unknown piece of DNA?

c. i. Scientists can separate fragments of DNA using electrophoresis. Suggest how they can use electrophoresis to estimate the number of base pairs in the separated fragments.

   ii. Scientists need to take precautions when they carry out restriction mapping. They need to make sure that the enzyme they have used has completely digested the DNA. One check they may carry out is to add the sizes of the fragments together. How could scientists use this information to show that the DNA has **not** been completely digested? Explain your answer.

AQA June 2011 Unit 5 Question 5

ANSWERS TO IN-TEXT QUESTIONS

1 PHOTOSYNTHESIS

1. **a.** Most heat is generated in the muscles and liver.

   b. Active transport takes place in most cells, it is particularly important in neurones (nerve cells), muscles, kidney cells and the cells lining the small intestine.

   c. Protein synthesis, DNA replication.

2. One glucose molecule contains more energy than one ATP molecule, so a lot of energy would be wasted if the process that requires the energy doesn't need all the energy in the glucose. Also, glucose molecules are more difficult to break down in order to release the energy – this can be done for ATP much more quickly and easily.

3. **a.** Photophosphorylation.

   b. Photoionisation.

   c. Photolysis.

4. The oxygen that is released as a waste product in photosynthesis comes from water, not from carbon dioxide.

5. NADP is oxidised, and glycerate 3-phosphate is reduced.

6. Both are used in the light-dependent reaction. The NADP accepts protons and electrons to become reduced NADP once more. The ADP and Pi are used to make ATP, in photophosphorylation.

7. Energy from light is transferred to ATP and reduced NADP. This energy is then transferred to glycerate 3-phosphate, resulting in the formation of triose phosphate, which contains this energy in the form of chemical energy.

8. A chloroplast contains chlorophyll for absorption of sunlight. The chlorophyll is arranged on the thylakoid membranes, which have a large surface area so that they can hold a large quantity of pigment molecules and also absorb large amounts of sunlight. These membranes also hold the molecules making up the electron transfer chain, and ATP synthase, allowing photophosphorylation to occur.

   The stroma contains all the enzymes required for the light-independent reactions.

   The envelope (two membranes) surrounding the chloroplast keeps the reactions taking place inside it separate from those taking place in the cytoplasm outside.

2 RESPIRATION

1. Both have an outer envelope, made up of two membranes. Both have a background material that contains enzymes – the stroma in a chloroplast and matrix in the mitochondrion. Both have folded membranes in which the components of the electron transfer chain are embedded – the cristae in a mitochondrion and the thylakoids in a chloroplast. Both have their own DNA.

2. ATP is made in glycolysis, the Krebs cycle and the electron transfer chain.

3. NADH (reduced coenzyme) is made in glycolysis, the link reaction and the Krebs cycle.

3 ENERGY AND ECOSYSTEMS

1. Decomposers feed on all the organisms in the chain, so there would be an arrow from each organism to the decomposers.

2. For example:
   a. Oak tree → caterpillar → titmouse → weasel
   b. Other trees and shrubs → decomposers → earthworms → predatory beetles → shrews
   c. Herbs → decomposers → soil insects → predatory beetles → moles → tawny owls

3. Titmice, parasites, spiders, voles, mice, earthworms, soil insects and mites.

4. a. Mammals are homeothermic, and produce a great deal of heat energy to keep their body temperatures constant, even when the environmental temperature is high. This is all lost from the food chain.

   b. Plant cells are much less digestible than animal cells, because they are surrounded by a cellulose cell wall. Few animals are able to digest cellulose. There is therefore more wastage of energy from eating plant-based foods than from eating animal-based ones. The faeces of herbivores contain undigested cellulose, which contains energy that they have not been able to access.

   c. The invertebrate carnivore transfers the greatest percentage of energy to the next trophic level. It loses less heat than either of the mammals, because it does not generate heat to keep its body temperature up. It loses less energy in its faeces than the invertebrate herbivore, because it does not have to digest cellulose. In general, more energy is lost from mammals than insects because they are endothermic (warm blooded). More energy is lost from herbivores than is lost from carnivores because more indigestible energy-containing materials are lost in faeces.

5. a. Abiotic factors are: intensity of sunlight, duration of light, amount of water, temperature, concentration of carbon dioxide, availability of inorganic ions. The other factors are biotic.

   b. Tropical forest: a high density of trees and other tropical plants, warm temperatures throughout the year extending the growing season, no shortage of soil nutrients or water, all contribute to the high productivity.

Intensive agriculture: a high density planting of crops during the growing season, application of nitrogenous fertilisers and possibly irrigation, all contribute to the high productivity.

   c. Extreme desert and desert scrub: lack of water (and, therefore, lack of plants) and lack of soil nutrients reduce productivity.

6. a. Checking the accuracy of a measuring instrument by using known values/standards.
   b. Burn pure foods with known energy values.

7. Different animals have different digestive systems with different enzymes, and so can digest more/less of a particular food type. Different animals may also differ in the way that they absorb food. The number of villi/microvilli may vary, and so might the number and type of transport proteins in the gut membranes.

8. Energy has to be provided in order to ignite the food (a 'spark'). Some energy will go to heating up the different metal components of the calorimeter, and may be lost to the surroundings. Overall, the value we obtain will be less than the actual energy content of the food.

4 NUTRIENT CYCLES

1. Poorly drained soil becomes waterlogged, and anaerobic denitrifying bacteria can thrive. These reduce the nitrate content of the soil, and hence its fertility. Good drainage will increase the air content of the soil.

2. Nitrogen-fixing bacteria in the root nodules of clover, peas or beans increase the quantity of nitrogen compounds in the soil. These compounds become available for subsequent crops.

3. In the electron transfer system, electrons are transferred from one acceptor to another and then to atmospheric oxygen, producing water. In the absence of oxygen gas, denitrifying bacteria pass the electrons to oxygen in the nitrite or nitrate ions. Energy released in this transfer can be used to synthesise ATP. The oxygen is then available to form water, and nitrogen gas is released.

4. $100-120$ kg ha^{-1}. This concentration results in maximum grain yield. Any less will result in reduced grain yield. Any more will also result in less grain yield and extra expense.

5. a. Phosphorus. It cannot be nitrogen, as even if we give the plants more nitrogen the yield does not increase (orange curve). However, if they are given more phosphorus the yield does increase (green curve).

b. Nitrogen will be the limiting factor – if we give it more nitrogen, it will produce a higher yield (green curve).

6. a. Advantages: natural fertilisers may be cheaper, as they may be waste products from other processes, or from animals on the farm. Natural fertilisers such as manure generally contain plant material (such as straw) that can break down in the soil to form humus. This in turn encourages soil organisms such as earthworms, and increases the ability of the soil to hold water, as well as increasing aeration and drainage. Natural fertilisers often contain components that break down slowly over time, releasing nutrients gradually, rather than all at once.

b. Disadvantages: natural fertilisers do not contain known amounts of nutrients, so the farmer does not know exactly how much to apply to avoid wastage and leaching. Natural fertilisers can be smelly, bulky and difficult to handle. If not stored properly, natural fertilisers can cause pollution (for example, rain falling onto heaps of manure, washing out nutrients that can pollute nearby water courses).

7 a. i. During spring and summer, plants and other producers such as algae grow and use nitrates from the water for protein synthesis.

ii. The nitrate concentration rises again as these organisms die and decay slowly during autumn and winter.

iii. The steep rise in ammonium concentration occurs soon after the vegetation dies back in early autumn. Ammonium ions are the first products of saprotrophic breakdown.

iv. The ammonium ions are slowly converted by nitrifying bacteria to nitrates as part of the nitrogen cycle. This process occurs relatively slowly in the lower water temperatures of late autumn and winter.

b. It is unlikely that there is serious pollution. The nitrate concentration falls almost to zero during the summer, suggesting that there is not a large excess of organic material reaching the lake. Ammonium ion concentration stays at a fairly low level during spring and summer, again suggesting that there are not large amounts of organic matter being broken down.

5 SURVIVAL AND RESPONSE

1. a. If the flatworms used a taxis, they would use light receptors to compare the light intensity on each side, and move to the darker side. If they emerged in the light area they would immediately turn back.

b. If the flatworms used a kinesis, they would move in straight lines until they found themselves in a dark enough environment. They would then turn in tight circles and/or slow down their rate of movement. (This is what flatworms actually do.)

2. Positive phototropism will bring the stems out of the shade so that their leaves will receive more light for photosynthesis.

3. a. The roots will grow downwards into the soil, helping to stabilise the plant and to provide more opportunities for obtaining water and mineral ions.

b. Together with phototropism, this will help the stem to grow upwards into conditions of maximum light intensity.

4. Facilitated diffusion.

5. A stimulus results in the generator potential after a very short time interval. The generator potential has a shorter duration than the stimulus.

6. When in the brightly lit area, much of the rhodopsin in the rods has been bleached (broken down); time is needed to resynthesise it before the rods can become sensitive to light again. The low light intensity does not stimulate the cones, so although their pigment is resynthesised much more quickly, they are not of use in dim light.

7. Snow reflects almost all the light so the light intensity will be very high. The pigment in the cones is broken down faster than it is resynthesised. So the cones become inoperative and the person becomes temporarily blind since the rods also don't work in bright light.

8. a. Only the cones distinguish colours; the cones only work in bright light.

b. Several rods synapse with one bipolar cell, so sufficient transmitter substance is produced to depolarise the bipolar cell. A cone cell would not produce enough transmitter substance to depolarise its bipolar cell.

c. Each cone synapses with a single bipolar cell, so the information from it is discrete rather than being mixed with information from other cells as is the case with rod cells.

d. In bright light we can see colours right to the edge of our field of vision, not just at the centre, so there must be cones in all parts of the retina.

9. a. C, where there is the highest density of cones.

b. A and D because these have the highest density of rods.

c. We would not see the image because there are neither rods nor cones at B. B is the optic disc – the region where the optic nerve leaves the eye.

10. A greater rate of delivery of oxygen (and glucose) to the muscles and a greater rate of removal of carbon dioxide/lactate from the muscles.

11. a. Rate of heartbeat would reduce.

b. A lower rate of heartbeat would result in a fall in blood pressure.

c. They speed up heart rate.

d. They slow down the heart rate.

6 NERVES AND SYNAPSES

1. Electrical insulation.

2. a. A neurone is an individual nerve cell; a nerve is a bundle of neurones/axons.

b. i. Sensory neurone – information will not pass from the receptor in the leg to the brain.

ii. Motor neurone – information will not pass from the brain to the leg.

3. Sodium, potassium and chloride.

4. Because of the impermeability of the myelin sheath, the neural electrode would have to be positioned between the sheath and the cell membrane of the axon. This would be almost impossible to arrange.

5. Facilitated diffusion occurs down concentration gradients. The Na^+/K^+ ATPase pumps produce a high concentration of Na^+ ions on the outside of the membrane and a high concentration of K^+ ions on the inside.

6. The Na^+/K^+ ATPase pumps require ATP from respiration to operate. DNP inhibits respiration so there will be no ATP to operate the pumps. Without the pumps, the ions will only move through the channel proteins, and then only until concentrations

on each side of the membrane are equal. At this time there will be no net difference in the number of ions on each side of the membrane, so there will be no resting potential.

7. a. D

b. C

c. A

d. B.

8. 110 mV (change from −70 mV to +40 mV).

9. 0.5 milliseconds.

10. The internal temperature of invertebrates is largely dependent on the external temperature, and is usually lower than that of mammals. An increase in temperature will increase both the rate of diffusion (molecules/ions bounce around faster) and the rate of the enzyme reactions involved in active transport.

11. Receptors for the transmitter molecules are found only on the postsynaptic membrane.

12. The inhibition of acetylcholinesterase means that the neurotransmitter acetylcholine would not be broken down and removed from the synaptic cleft. The postsynaptic membrane would continue to depolarise and impulses would continually be transmitted along the postsynaptic neurone.

13. The sino-atrial node (SAN).

14. The beta-blocker molecules have a shape that will fit into the receptor molecules in the postsynaptic cells of the SAN. When noradrenaline is released by the nerve fibres, the molecules will not be able to bind with postsynaptic receptors and so will have no effect on the SAN.

15. a. Because it has a complementary shape, caffeine binds to adenosine receptors at synapses and excites nerve cells.

b. Too much caffeine stimulation might cause the brain to reduce the number of adenosine receptors. A person then might feel lethargic without caffeine and have the urge to drink more.

7 MUSCLE POWER

1. Skeletal muscles tissue is not composed of individual cells with membranes. The fibre has many nuclei rather than one. The cell membranes have broken down, allowing giant protein structures (myofibrils) to form.

2. **a.** This is the region where both actin and myosin filaments are found.

   b. **i.** Myosin filaments only.

   ii. Actin filaments only.

3. **a.** No; actin and myosin filaments neither contract nor expand.

   b. The actin filaments slide in between the myosin filaments so there is more overlap leading to a wider A band and a narrower area where there are just actin filaments.

4. **a.** Flow chart should follow this order.

   Nerve impulse arrives at neuromuscular junction → acetylcholine released into synaptic cleft → action potential produced in sarcolemma → action potential transmitted down tubules into centre of myofibril → calcium ions released from sarcoplasmic reticulum → calcium ions bind to tropomyosin switch proteins → binding sites on actin filaments exposed → myosin processes bind to exposed sites on actin filaments → energy from ATP used to move actin filaments.

   b. To provide the abundant ATP required for muscle contraction; each swing of a cross bridge needs the energy from one molecule of ATP.

5. For example, shot, discuss, javelin, weight lifting, high jump, long jump, triple jump.

6. **a.** The liver.

   b. Mainly under the skin.

   c. **i.** Energy can be obtained from it very quickly.

   ii. It is used up very quickly – there is not enough to sustain a long activity.

   d. Lactic acid.

   e. It dissociates into hydrogen ions and lactate ions. If hydrogen ions accumulate in the muscles they affect the tertiary structure of actin and myosin molecules, altering their shape and making contraction less efficient.

   f. Slow-twitch fibres obtain most of their energy from aerobic respiration. Mitochondria are the site of aerobic reactions in respiration.

8 HOMEOSTASIS

1. It will require energy since it is the opposite process to glycolysis, which releases energy.

2. **a.** Glycogenesis is making glycogen from glucose.

   b. Glycogenolysis is splitting glycogen to make glucose.

   c. Gluconeogenesis is making new glucose from non-carbohydrate sources such as glycerol or amino acids.

3. **a.** Production of digestive enzymes, for example, peptidases, amylase and lipase.

   b. A polysaccharide.

   c. The highly branched molecule gives it a compact shape.

   d. Hydrolysis.

   e. Condensation.

   f. The difference in concentration of the substance outside and inside the cell and the number of carrier protein molecules for that substance.

   g. Glucose molecules pass through cell membranes by facilitated diffusion that involves carrier proteins. The more carrier proteins, the more 'passages' there are for glucose through the membranes.

4. Only the target cells for a particular hormone will have the receptors that will recognise and bind with that hormone.

5. **a.** Sugary foods do not need to be digested, or they are digested rapidly by intracellular enzymes in the villi. This leads to sharp increases in blood glucose concentration. Starchy foods take longer to digest because starch molecules have longer chains. Absorption of the sugars produced by starch digestion takes place over a longer period and does not lead to sudden rises in blood sugar.

   b. **i.** Excessive thirst: the glucose in the blood lowers the water potential, which stimulates the thirst centres.

   ii. Weight loss: when cells are starved of glucose, they use up their lipid reserves.

   iii. Fatigue: lack of energy due to lack of glucose, which is the body's main fuel.

   iv. Breath smelling fruity (due to ketones a by-product of lipid metabolism): same explanation as ii.

   v. Excessive urination: a result of taking in large volumes of fluid in response to excessive thirst.

6. The left ventricle of the heart.

7. Excessive urination, because water cannot be absorbed by the kidneys; excessive thirst.

9 GENES AND INHERITANCE

1. Black is dominant, because the dominant allele is the one whose phenotype is seen in a heterozygote.

2. **a.** Codominance, as the heterozygote has a phenotype between that of the two homozygotes.
   b. H^N could be the normal allele, and H^S the sickle cell allele.
   c. $H^N H^N$ normal; $H^N H^S$ sickle cell trait; $H^S H^S$ sickle cell anaemia.

3. Genotype of parents $I^A I^A$ × $I^B I^o$

   Gametes I^A and I^A I^B and I^o

   Genotype of offspring $I^A I^B$ $I^A I^o$ $I^A I^B$ $I^A I^o$

   Phenotypes of offspring   blood group AB, blood group A, blood group AB, blood group A

   We would therefore expect 50% of the children to have blood group A, and 50% to have blood group AB.

4. Phenotype of mother is blood group A, so possible genotypes of the woman are $I^A I^A$ or $I^A I^o$.

   The child has the phenotype blood group O and so must have the genotype $I^o I^o$, since the allele for blood group O is recessive and the child must have two copies of the allele.

   The mother must have the genotype $I^A I^o$ in order to pass an I^o allele to the child.

   For the father with blood group AB:

   Phenotype of parents   mother A   father AB

   Genotype of parents $I^A I^o$ × $I^A I^B$

   Gametes I^A and I^o I^A and I^B

   Genotype of offspring $I^A I^A$ $I^o I^A$ $I^A I^B$ $I^o I^B$

   Phenotypes of offspring   blood group A, blood group A, blood group AB, blood group B

   No child has the possibility of having the phenotype blood group O, so this man definitely could not be the father of the child.

   For the father with blood group A, possible genotypes are $I^A I^A$ or $I^A I^o$.

   Phenotype of parents   mother A   father A

   Genotype of parents $I^A I^o$ × $I^A I^o$

   Gametes I^A and I^o I^A and I^o

   Genotype of offspring $I^A I^A$ $I^o I^A$ $I^A I^o$ $I^o I^o$

   Phenotypes of offspring   blood group A, blood group A, blood group A, blood group O

   Hence it is possible for the man with blood group A to be the father, if he has the genotype $I^A I^o$.

5. **a.** 25% of children − 0% of girls, 50% of boys.
   b. A mother with genotype $X^C X^c$ or $X^c X^c$ and a father who is $X^c Y$ could produce a red/green colour-blind girl.
   c. A boy receives his X chromosome from his mother, not his father.

6. **a.** $X^h Y$.
   b. Mother $X^H X^h$ and father $X^h Y$.

7. **a.** All (100%) black, short fur.
   b. Even numbers (1 : 1) black, short fur and brown, short fur.
   c. Even numbers (1 : 1 : 1 : 1) of all four combinations. (black/long, black/short, brown/long, brown/short).

8. **a.** All genotypes that are ee. (That's eeBB, eeBb, eebb.)
   b. EEbb, Eebb.
   c. EEBB, EEBb, EeBB, EeBb.

9. **a.** The sperm. All eggs carry one X chromosome, but the sperm can have either X (which will produce a girl) or Y (which will produce a boy).
   b. The sperm could be sorted into those carrying an X chromosome and those carrying a Y chromosome. If only the X sperm are used, then all the zygotes would be XX and become cows rather than bulls.
   c. Answers will vary dependent upon personal response.

10 POPULATIONS

1. 0.43, because they must add up to 1.

2. **a.** Using the Hardy–Weinberg equation;
   $p^2 + 2pq + q^2 = 1$

A child with cystic fibrosis is homozygous for the recessive allele, so has the genotype ff. We know that one in 3300 children has cystic fibrosis. So immediately we know that:

$$q^2 = \frac{1}{3300} = 0.0003$$

Now we can work out q, the frequency of the f allele in the population.

$$q = \sqrt{0.0003} = 0.017$$

We can go on to work out the frequency of the F allele, p. We know that $p + q = 1$, so:

$$p + 0.017 = 1$$

$$p = 1 - 0.017$$

so, $p = 0.983$

b. The proportion of heterozygous people in the population

$$= 2pq$$

$$= 2 \times 0.983 \times 0.017 = 0.0334$$

So now we know that, out of every 1000 people in the population of Britain, around 33 people are carriers for cystic fibrosis.

c. PKU

$$q^2 = \frac{1}{15000} = 0.000067$$

so, $q = 0.0082$

so, $p = 1 - 0.0082 = 0.9918$

Proportion of carriers

$$= 2pq = 2 \times 0.0082 \times 0.9918 = 0.0163$$

This means that about 1.6 in every 100 people are carriers of the PKU allele.

3. a. Population.

b. Habitat.

c. Ecosystem.

d. Abiotic factor.

e. Community.

f. Biotic factor.

4. a. 0.0625 m²

b. 1.25 m²

c. 0.57%

5. a. $\frac{25}{30} \times 100 = 83\%$

b. 25%

c. Leguminous plants such as clover have nitrogen-fixing bacteria in their root nodules. These bacteria use gaseous nitrogen to produce organic nitrogen compounds, including amino acids and proteins. When clover plants or their roots and nodules die, they are decayed by saprophytic bacteria. Then, nitrifying bacteria make nitrates from the ammonium ions produced. The improved supply of nitrate ions enables the grass to grow more vigorously.

6. It is much quicker and easier to make decisions using the ACFOR scale. However, this gives less precise data than if you used percentage cover.

7. Oarweed: 0 to 25 cm.

Toothed wrack: 30 cm to 75 cm.

Knotted wrack: 90 cm to 150 cm.

Bladder wrack: 75 cm to 85 cm.

Spiral wrack: 150 cm to 180 cm.

Channelled wrack: 200 cm to 245 cm.

8. a. 20 cm.

b. Tor grass, rock rose, ribwort plantain.

c. Some species, such as daisies, have short stems and spreading leaves. They grow well where the grass is short because they get plenty of light, and their leaves are not easily damaged by trampling. To the side of the path, grasses can grow tall and overshadow them.

9. Total number in population = $(54 \times 63) \div 18 = 189$.

10. a. The high concentration of hydrogen ions affects the ionisation of the side chains and other groups of amino acids in the protein; they will hang on to their hydrogen atoms rather than lose them. This can affect the hydrogen bonds that normally form between different parts of the protein molecule, and therefore change its overall shape and behaviour. Enzyme molecules may no longer be able to bind with their substrate.

Heavy metal ions act as non-competitive inhibitors of enzymes. They bind with the enzyme molecule, usually at a site other than its active site. This causes the shape of the whole enzyme molecule to change, so that its active site can no longer bind with the substrate.

b. i. The oxygen concentration will reduce. Gases such as oxygen are less soluble in warm water than in cold water. Animals may not be able to obtain sufficient oxygen for respiration.

ii. Seaweeds photosynthesise, and therefore produce oxygen. Oxygen concentration would rise during daylight hours, since photosynthesis is much faster than respiration. At night, however, there would be a reduction in concentration due to the respiration of the seaweeds.

iii. When the pool is exposed, water can evaporate and increase the salinity. Heavy rainfall can dilute the seawater in the pool and decrease the salinity. Changes in salt concentration can cause osmotic effects in organisms, with high salt concentrations causing water loss from cells. Low concentrations may cause water to enter cells, and animals' cells may burst.

11. a. Water availability, temperature.

b. Temperature, wind speed, depth of soil.

c. Water current, mineral ion availability.

d. Lack of stable attachment surface, wave action, salinity.

e. Acidity of soil, mineral ion availability, high water content of soil resulting in reduced oxygen content.

12. a.

Generation	Number of bacteria
1	20
2	40
3	80
4	160
5	320
6	640
7	1280
8	2560
9	5120
10	10 240

b. The graph shows an increasingly steep curve. This pattern of population growth is called exponential.

c. A log scale goes up in increments based on factors of the number on which the logarithm is based, so for log 10 (the most common logarithm), the increase would be 10^2, 10^3, 10^4, etc. It allows a large range of numbers to be shown on one scale without losing the smaller numbers.

d. The pattern is similar in that there is slow growth at first, followed by a steep increase. The increase is rather irregular, probably because the cells do not all grow and divide at exactly the same rate. The increase in population size levels off after about 15 days.

e. Light and mineral ion availability.

f. A colorimeter could be used to measure turbidity.

g. (1) Some light could be absorbed by substances other than cells.

(2) Dead cells also contribute to turbidity, but are not part of the viable population.

13. a. There was high mortality among the young rabbits.

b. The population of this colony would decline, and the colony might well die out, because the total number of rabbits at the end of the season (39) was much lower than the number at the start (70).

c. A rabbit colony can produce a large number of young very quickly and so the population could recover rapidly if the population of predators dropped. If the colony were completely wiped out, then the predators might die or move away. Immigration from other colonies could then take place. Also, natural selection might occur, whereby the young that are better at avoiding predators would survive, perhaps by being more cautious or having more acute senses. These more successful rabbits could pass on their characteristics to their offspring.

14. a. The grass was no longer mowed.

b. Competition with larger/taller plants, especially for light.

15. Low water content, high wind speed, instability of sand, high salt content.

16. A network of underground stems provides anchorage in the shifting sand. A thick outer cuticle protects from wind-blown sand and reduces water loss. The leaves can roll up, enclosing the stomata and therefore reducing transpiration. Hairs on the leaf surface, and the positioning of the stomata at the base of deep grooves, traps humid air close to the leaf surface and further reduces transpiration.

17. Mainly by wind-blown seeds. These tend to settle in the sheltered areas on the land side of the ridges. Animals or humans may transport some grass seeds.

11 NATURAL SELECTION AND SPECIATION

1. If biological fitness means reproductive success, 'survival of the fittest' translates to 'survival of the best reproducers', which makes no sense.

2. It is possible that there was not much variation in beak size in this species. If none of the birds had alleles for small beaks, then however strongly selection acted against those with large beaks, there would be no birds with smaller beaks to survive and breed.

3. Very small babies are at a disadvantage for a variety of reasons. They tend to lose heat quickly (having a large surface area to volume ratio) and may have lung problems. They often have weaker immune systems. Large babies cause problems in childbirth.

4. a. They have different *specific* names (but same genus).

   b. They are still evolving apart. They have not had enough time to become genetically isolated.

   c. They have different behaviour patterns, different social structures (wolves are pack animals, coyotes are solitary), different calls/barks, different pheromones.

5. Their genetic problems are caused by faulty (usually recessive) alleles. Closely related individuals often share the same alleles and so when they breed, there is a good chance that the faulty alleles will be paired up and the deleterious genotype expressed.

12 THE CONTROL OF GENE EXPRESSION

1. a. Substitution.

   b. Deletion.

   c. Translocation.

   d. Inversion.

   e. Duplication.

   f. Addition.

2. Somatic cell mutations accumulate in the body but are not passed on to the offspring.

   Germ line mutations occur in gametes and are passed on to the offspring, where the mutation will be present in each cell.

3. Many copies of mRNA are made, and a mutation in one is unlikely to affect more than a few protein molecules. Many other mRNAs will be made that do make the correct protein.

4. If all mRNA molecules were destroyed, the cell wouldn't be able to make its own proteins and carry out its normal functions.

5. a. Single-stranded RNA that is complementary to mRNA.

   b. It paired with the mRNA, preventing access to tRNA molecules.

6. A control is a repeat investigation that contains all the necessary factors/conditions except the independent variable.

7. Mutations in proto-oncogenes are usually dominant because it only takes one of the pair of genes to mutate to make the proteins that stimulate cell division and increase the risk of a tumour developing.

   Mutations of tumour suppressor genes are usually recessive because both genes in a pair need to mutate. The proteins made by the normal tumour suppressor genes inhibit cell division and so if only one gene mutates, the other one would still produce the 'safety' proteins.

8. Both p53 genes mutate → tumour suppressor gene fails to make the right protein → cell division not inhibited → uncontrolled cell division.

9. a. Substance Y is not made, so no Substance Z can be formed from Y.

   b. Enzyme A can still catalyse the production of Substance X from Substance W, but Substance X is then not converted into Substance Y.

   c. Substance Y would be converted to Substance Z, because Enzyme B is bypassed.

13 GENE TECHNOLOGIES

1. a. Red blood cells, because they have no nucleus.

   b. i. Females have two X chromosomes and so have 23 pairs of homologous chromosomes. Their cells have the entire genome twice.

      ii. Males have one X chromosome and one Y. They do not have two copies of all the X-linked genes and so do not have the entire genome twice over.

2. a. Cell membranes are composed of phospholipids. Detergents disrupt lipids.

   b. Endopeptidase, or exopeptidase, or a combination.

3. Active site on enzyme; only a nucleotide sequence with the right shape will fit into this active site; therefore, the enzyme can only cut the DNA at this position.

4. **a.** A A T T

  b. Only complementary bases will join together to produce a molecule with the sugar-phosphate backbones the right distance apart so that the molecule can twist into a regular double helix.

5. The bases in the mRNA correspond to specific bases in the DNA strand. For example if the mRNA sequences reads, UACG, the DNA sequence will read ATGC.

6. 51 amino acids, each with a 3 base code gives $51 \times 3 = 153$

7. Four, with each of the complementary bases, A, C, G and T.

8. The bacteria have enzymes that are stable at much higher temperatures than most enzymes. They are not denatured at $70\,^{\circ}C$.

9. 20

10. To destroy the enzyme; otherwise it would cut the recombinant DNA at the junctions made by the ligase.

11. The active site of the enzyme has a complementary shape to that particular sequence of bases.

12. Each copy of the DNA molecule will be identical. Each will be cut at the same positions, making fragments of the same length.

13. The DNA backbone consists of a phosphate–sugar chain, so every nucleotide contains a phosphate group.

14. Hybrid DNA results when <u>each strand</u> of a DNA molecule comes from a different species.

  Recombinant DNA results when one double stranded piece of DNA is joined to another one from a different source, usually a different individual or species.

15. Eliminating cystic fibrosis completely by genetic screening is unlikely for a number of reasons. Some couples will choose not to undergo genetic screening, or will be unaware that it is an option. Such couples may have a child with CF. If a couple is screened, and both are found to be carriers for the condition, then it is not certain that they will opt for termination. They may decide not to end the pregnancy. This decision may be taken for personal, cultural or religious reasons.

16. **a.** It could be deemed acceptable to screen for genes causing Tay--Sachs disease, deafness and breast cancer.

  b. Tay--Sachs disease, deafness and late-onset breast cancer will affect the quality of life of the unborn baby and a case could be made for screening in each case. A child with Tay--Sachs will have a very short life, and a very poor quality of life. Parents may decide to terminate such a pregnancy. A child who is deaf can live a full and happy life, but parents who know their child will be deaf could plan effectively in advance for the child's care. A child carrying a breast cancer gene will be no different to the general population until later life, but if forewarned the grown adult may wish to may consider lifestyle changes, screening or preemptive surgery.

  It is not acceptable to screen for hair or eye colour, or sex. To choose to keep terminate a pregnancy based on aesthetic features, such as hair or eye colour is morally wrong, and turns a child into a commodity. The same applies to sex.

GLOSSARY

Abiotic factors Non-living chemical and physical parts of the environment that affect living organisms and the functioning of ecosystems.

Abundance scale Set of letters or numbers used to represent the relative proportions of different species in a quadrat or other area being studied.

Acetate A salt or ester of ethanoic acid.

Acetyl coenzyme A The acetyl ester of coenzyme A, involved as an acetylating agent in many biochemical processes.

Acetylcholine Chemical that acts as transmitter substance in many synapses.

Acetylcholinesterase Substance formed from a two-carbon fragment of pyruvic acid and coenzyme A; the two-carbon compound that enters the Krebs cycle.

Actin One of the two proteins that bring about contraction of muscle fibres.

Acuity Ability to use the eyes to make out detail; clarity of vision.

Adaptation The alteration or adjustment in structure or habits, often occurring through natural selection, by which a species or individual becomes better able to function in its environment.

Addition One of the three basic types of gene mutation; an extra nucleotide is inserted, so an extra base is added to the sequence.

Adenylate cyclase An enzyme that catalyses the formation of cyclic AMP from ATP.

Adrenal gland Gland that secretes hormones to control important body functions such as heart rate and blood pressure; there are two — one just above each kidney.

Adrenaline Hormone produced by the adrenal glands; often known as the 'fight or flight' hormone.

Adult stem cells Undifferentiated cell in a tissue; multiplies by cell division to replace dead or injured cells in that tissue.

Aerobic training Exercise taken to improve the efficiency of the body's cardiovascular system in absorbing and transporting oxygen.

Allele Alternate form of a gene.

Allopatric Occurring in separate non-overlapping geographical areas.

All-or-nothing principle Principle which states that the size of the action potential produced by a nerve cell is independent of the size of the stimulus, once the required threshold has been reached.

Ammonification Process in which decomposers break down nitrogenous compounds into ammonia or ammonium ions.

Amyloplast Colourless organelle in plants, similar in structure to a chloroplast; stores starch.

Anaerobic Respiration without oxygen; forms lactic acid in animals, and ethanol + carbon dioxide in plants and microorganisms.

Annealing Process by which complementary sequences of single-stranded DNA or RNA pair by hydrogen bonds to form a double-stranded polynucleotide.

Antagonistic Working against each other; for example, the actions of the sympathetic and parasympathetic fibres when SAN reduces heart rate; can also refer to 'antagonistic' pairs of muscles (such as biceps and triceps) in the upper arm.

Anti-diuretic hormone (adh) A relatively small (peptide) molecule that is released by the pituitary gland at the base of the brain after being made nearby (in the hypothalamus); has an antidiuretic action that prevents the production of dilute urine.

Aortic body One of several small clusters of chemoreceptors, baroreceptors and supporting cells located along the aortic arch.

Apoptosis A natural process of self-destruction in certain cells, such as epithelial cells and erythrocytes, that are genetically programmed to have a limited life span or are damaged.

Aquaporins Channel proteins for water molecules in a cell membrane.

Argonaute Protein that plays a central role in RNA silencing processes, as essential catalytic component of the RNA-induced silencing complex (RISC), which is responsible for the gene silencing phenomenon known as RNA interference (RNAi).

Artificial fertiliser Manufactured fertiliser such as ammonium sulfate.

Ascending limb One of the structures in the nephron of the kidney; drains urine into the distal convoluted tubule.

Auxin Plant hormone that affects processes such as growth and development.

Adenosine Triphosphate (ATP) 'Energy currency' of most cells; consists of adenine, ribose and three phosphate groups.

ATP hydrolase The enzyme that catalyses the release of energy in an ATP molecule.

ATP synthase An enzyme that joins the ADP and phosphate to resynthesise ATP.

Atrioventricular node (AVN) Group of slow-conducting fibres between the atria and ventricles of the heart.

Autosome Any chromosome that is not a sex-determining chromosome.

Axon Long 'thread' that carries impulses from the cell body to the target cells.

Baroreceptors Sensors located in the blood vessels of all vertebrate animals that sense the blood pressure and relay the information to the brain, so that a proper blood pressure can be maintained.

Basement membrane A thin, fibrous, extracellular matrix of tissue that separates the epithelium, mesothelium and endothelium from underlying connective tissue.

Belt transect Line along which quadrats are placed to sample species distribution and abundance.

Benign A condition, tumour or growth that is not cancerous.

Biomass Mass of living material in an ecosystem.

Biotic factor Factor that affects a living organism and is caused by other living organisms, for example, competition for food or predation.

Bipolar cell Cell in the retina of the eye; connects a rod cell and cone cell with a ganglion cell.

Blastocyst Embryonic stage, before implantation, when the embryo consists of a hollow ball of cells.

Bleaching Making whiter or lighter in colour, by exposure to sunlight or a chemical agent; remove the colour from.

Bowman's capsule A cup-like sac at the beginning of the tubular component of a nephron in the mammalian kidney that performs the first step in the filtration of blood to form urine.

Bundle of His The bundle of cardiac muscle fibres that passes from the atrioventricular node to the interventricular septum and then the ventricles.

Calcium ions Initiate the muscle contraction process by moving tropomyosin and causing ATP to hydrolyse.

Calorie The 'small' calorie is the energy required to raise 1 g of water by 1 °C. The 'large' calorie, the food calorie or the kilocalorie (kcal), is 1000 times larger than the small calorie.

Calorimetry The study of measuring heat changes from chemical reactions or physical changes.

Calvin cycle Series of reactions that take place in the stroma of a chloroplast, in which carbon dioxide is fixed and sugars are produced; the light-independent stages of photosynthesis.

Carbon dioxide a colourless, odourless gas (CO_2) produced by burning carbon and organic compounds and by respiration; naturally present in air (about 0.03%) and absorbed by plants in photosynthesis.

Cardiac muscle Muscle that makes up the wall of the heart; produces heartbeat.

Cardioacceleratory centre The part of the brain that sends impulses to speed up heartbeat.

Cardioinhibitory centre The part of the brain that sends impulses to slow down heartbeat.

Cardiovascular centre The part of the brain responsible for the regulation of the rate at which the heart beats.

Carnivores Animals that eat other animals.

Carotid body A small cluster of chemoreceptors and supporting cells located near the fork (bifurcation) of the carotid artery (which runs along both sides of the throat).

Carotid sinus A dilatation of the proximal portion of the internal carotid or distal portion of the common carotid artery, containing in its wall pressoreceptors that are stimulated by changes in blood pressure.

Carrying capacity Maximum number in a population that can be sustainably supported in a particular place.

Cell body The portion of a nerve cell that contains the nucleus but does not incorporate the dendrites or axon.

Central nervous system CNS; brain and spinal cord.

Chance The extent to which an event is likely to occur.

Chemiosmosis The movement of protons through a membrane, down their electrochemical gradient.

Chemoreceptor Receptor that is sensitive to different kinds of molecules.

Chemosynthesis The synthesis of organic compounds by bacteria or other living organisms using energy derived from reactions involving inorganic chemicals, typically in the absence of sunlight.

Chiasmata Breaking and crosswise rejoining of homologous chromatids during meiosis.

Chi-squared Statistical test to check if a null hypothesis is true.

Chlorophyll Green pigment that absorbs energy from sunlight; found in chloroplasts.

Chloroplast Organelle found in some plant cells; contains chlorophyll, and where photosynthesis takes place.

Choice chamber A device that offers animals or groups of animals two or more contrasting environments and allows them to move freely into the one they prefer.

Cholinergic synapse Junction between two nerve cells where acetylcholine is the transmitter substance.

Chromosome mutations Mutations that occur in whole chromosomes or large sections of them.

Chromosomes Thread-like structures in the nucleus of a cell, which carry genetic information.

Climax community Final, relatively unchanging species that occurs in an ecosystem at the end of succession.

Codon Basic unit of the genetic code; consists of three nucleotides.

Coenzyme A A coenzyme derived from pantothenic acid, important in respiration and other biochemical reactions.

Coenzymes A non-protein compound that is necessary for the functioning of an enzyme.

Coleoptile Protective sheath around the shoot emerging from a grass seed.

Collecting duct Part of the renal tubule in a kidney in which water absorption takes place under the control of ADH, producing urine of variable concentration depending on overall water levels in the body.

Community All the organisms, of all the different species, living in the same place at the same time.

Competition Interaction between two or more organisms that require the same resource which is in short supply.

Cones Cells in the retina of the eye; responsible for colour vision.

Consumers Organisms that eat other organisms.

Convergence Coordinated movement of the two eyes so that the image of a single point is formed on corresponding retinal areas.

Coordinator Brain and spinal cord receives impulses and forwards them to the appropriate organs.

Cortex The outer layer of an internal organ or body structure, such as the kidney or adrenal gland.

Crista (plural: cristae) Each of the partial partitions in a mitochondrion formed by folding of the inner membrane.

Cystic fibrosis Genetic disease that results in excess mucus in the lungs and pancreatic duct.

Dark adaptation Changes in the iris and retina of the eye that allow better vision in dim light.

Deamination The removal of an amino group from an amino acid or other compound.

Decomposers Organisms that break down the remains or waste products of other organisms.

Degenerate Describing a triplet that codes for the same amino acid as other triplets.

Degenerate code DNA base sequence that codes for the same amino acid as a different DNA base sequence.

Degrees of freedom A measure of how many values can vary in a statistical calculation; equal to $N - 1$, where N is the number of values in a data set.

Deletion One of the three basic gene mutations; loss of part of a chromosome or part of a DNA base sequence.

Denaturation A process in which a protein or nucleic acid is altered from its native state, due to exposure to certain chemical or physical factors (e.g. heat, acid, solvents, etc.), causing the protein to become biologically inactive.

Dendrite Highly branched, slender process from a nerve cell.

Denitrifying bacterium Bacterium that gets its energy by converting nitrates to nitrogen gas.

Depolarisation Events at a nerve cell membrane resulting in an influx of positively charged ions, making the inside of the cell less negative.

Descending limb The portion of the renal tubule constituting the first part of the loop of Henlé.

Diabetes mellitus The commonest form of diabetes, caused by a deficiency of the pancreatic hormone insulin, which results in a failure to metabolise sugars and starch.

Dicer Enzyme used to chop mRNA strands into shorter lengths.

Differential reproductive success The difference between individuals in a given generation and how many offspring they are able to produce; the 'fittest' produce more offspring while those not suited to the environment produce fewer or even none.

Diploid Containing two sets of chromosomes.

Directional selection Type of natural selection in which organisms with characteristics away from the median value are selected for, so that the range of this characteristic changes over many generations.

Disease Impairment of a bodily function.

Disruptive selection Changes in population genetics in which extreme values for a trait are favoured over intermediate values.

Distal (or second) convoluted tubule (DCT) A portion of kidney nephron between the loop of Henlé and the collecting duct system.

Duplication A particular kind of mutation involving the production of one or more copies of any piece of DNA, including a gene or even an entire chromosome.

Ecological factors Environmental features that affect living organisms.

Ecological niche Role of an organism in an ecosystem; what it needs to survive, and the ways in which it affects other organisms.

Ecosystem All the living organisms and non-living features in an area that interact with one another.

Edaphic factors An abiotic factor relating to the physical or chemical composition of the soil found in a particular area.

Effector An organ or cell that carries out a response to a nerve impulse.

Electrochemical gradient A gradient of electrochemical potential, usually for an ion that can move across a membrane; consists of two parts, the electrical potential and a difference in the chemical concentration across a membrane.

Electron carrier Molecule situated in the inner membrane of a mitochondrion and the thylakoid membranes in a chloroplast; passes electrons from one molecule to the next and generates ATP.

Electron transfer chain Chain of electron carrier molecules in the inner membrane of a mitochondrion or the thylakoid membranes in a chloroplast.

Endothelium A layer of cells that forms the lining of organs and other parts of the body.

Energy continuum The interaction of the three energy systems to provide energy to resynthesise ATP.

Energy transducers Convert the energy of a stimulus into a frequency of impulses, or action potentials.

Envelope The two membranes that surround a chloroplast.

Environmental resistance Factors in an environment, such as predators, competition, climate and food availability, that keep its various populations from reaching their maximum growth potential.

Epigenetics An area of study that concerns the way in which environmental factors can affect gene expression.

Ethanol A colourless, water-soluble alcohol; produced along with carbon dioxide by anaerobic respiration in plants.

Eutrophication Addition of nutrients to a body of water; often results in the growth and then death of algae and the growth of large populations of aerobic bacteria, decreasing the oxygen concentration in the water.

Excitable tissues Tissues that are capable of being activated by and reacting to stimuli.

Excitatory A synapse that increases the activity of the next cell.

Exons The sections of a gene that code for amino-acid sequences in a protein.

Exponential Involving one or more numbers or quantities raised to an exponent.

Extending The third step in the polymerase chain reaction (PCR).

Extracellular digestion A process in which saprobionts feed by secreting enzymes through the cell membrane onto the food.

Faeces Waste matter remaining after food has been digested, discharged from the bowels.

Fast skeletal muscle fibres Muscle fibres that can produce ATP very quickly via glycolysis.

Fatigued Synapses become fatigued when they are repeatedly stimulated at a high rate making the impulse unable to cross the synapse.

Fenestrations Pores in endothelial cells that allow a faster rate of diffusion between capillaries and tissues.

Filtrate Fluid that results from filtration.

Food chain Series of organisms along which energy is transferred in the form of food.

Fovea Area of the retina with the most acute vision; consists almost entirely of cones.

Frame quadrat Area delineated by a square that is made of, for example, wood or wire, in which sampling of a community is carried out.

Frame shift A genetic mutation caused by insertions or deletions of a number of nucleotides in a DNA sequence.

Frequency A measure of how common a particular allele is in a population.

Gated channel proteins A transport protein that opens a 'gate', allowing a molecule to pass through the membrane.

Gene Part of a DNA molecule that codes for a polypeptide.

Gene machines A general term for all the different technologies that manufacture artificial genes.

Gene mutations Changes in the nucleotide base sequence of genes.

Gene pool All the different genes, and alleles of those genes, present in a population.

Gene probe Marker used to find the position of a gene in a DNA sequence.

Generator potential The charge built up when sodium ions flood into a receptor cell.

Genetic diagram Conventional way of showing a cross in genetics.

Genetic drift The change in the frequency of an allele in a population due to chance.

Genetic fingerprinting Technique for analysing and comparing DNA samples with different origins.

Glomerulus A cluster of nerve endings, spores or small blood vessels, especially a cluster of capillaries around the end of a kidney tubule.

Gluconeogenesis The process by which glucose is generated from certain non-carbohydrate carbon substrates.

Glycerate 3-phosphate (GP) Three-carbon compound, formed in the Calvin cycle.

Glycogenesis Production of glycogen from glucose.

Glycogenolysis Breakdown of glycogen into glucose.

Glycolysis Conversion of glucose to pyruvate during respiration.

Gross primary production (GPP) Rate at which a plant produces organic materials through photosynthesis.

Habitat Place where an organism lives.

Haploid Cells that contain only one set of chromosomes.

Hardy–Weinberg equation Equation that allows the calculation of the frequency of two different alleles in a population, if the proportion of homozygotes or heterozygotes is known.

Hardy–Weinberg principle States that allele and genotype frequencies in a population will remain constant from generation to generation in the absence of other evolutionary influences.

Herbivores Organisms that eat plants.

Heterozygous Possessing two different alleles of a gene.

Homeostasis Keeping a constant internal environment.

Homozygous Possessing two identical alleles of a gene.

Hyperglycaemia High blood sugar level.

Hypertonic A solution where the concentration of solutes is greater outside the cell than inside it.

Hypoglycaemia Low blood sugar level.

Hypothesis A proposition made as a basis for reasoning, without any assumption of its truth.

In vitro 'In glass.' A gene made in a test tube, or in other lab equipment.

In vivo 'In life.' A gene cloned inside a living cell.

Indicator species Species of an organism that requires particular conditions in which to live, which can therefore be used to indicate whether pollution has occurred in an area.

Indoleacetic acid (IAA) Plant hormone; its main function is to control plant growth.

Ingested Taken (food, drink or another substance) into the body by swallowing or absorbing it.

Inhibitory A synapse that decreases the activity of the next cell.

Inner cell mass Cluster of pluripotent cells inside the hollow sphere of a blastocyst.

Insulin Hormone produced by the pancreas that lowers the blood sugar level.

Intensive rearing Rearing animals using high inputs such as artificial feeds.

Interrupted belt transect Belt transect in which quadrats are placed at intervals along the transect.

Interspecific competition Competition between organisms of different species.

Intraspecific competition Competition between organisms of the same species.

Introns Non-functional parts of genes.

Inversion Reversal of the sequence of nucleotide bases on part of a chromosome.

Iodopsin Light-sensitive pigment found in cone cells.

Islets of Langerhans Regions of the pancreas that produce the hormones glucagon and insulin.

Joule (J) SI unit of work or energy; the energy required to raise 1 g (1 cm^3) of water by 0.24 °C.

Kinesis Change in direction as a response to a directional stimulus.

Krebs cycle Series of reactions that takes place in the matrix of a mitochondrion, in which NADP is generated and carbon dioxide given off.

Lactate The conjugate base of lactic acid.

Lag phase Initial period of slow growth in a population.

Lamellae Thin layers of bone or tissue.

Leaching Washing out of soil.

Ligase Enzyme used to join together two pieces of DNA.

Light-dependent reaction Stage of photosynthesis in which light energy is used to make reduced NADP and ATP, and to split water.

Light-independent reaction Stage of photosynthesis in which reduced NADP and ATP from the light-dependent reaction are used to convert carbon dioxide to sugars; the Calvin cycle.

Limiting factor Environmental factor that prevents a process (such as photosynthesis or population growth) from taking place any faster.

Line transect Line along which living organisms are sampled to find out what lives there and the abundance of each species.

Link reaction Conversion of pyruvate to acetylcoenzyme A in respiration.

Linked Genes that are inherited together with the other gene(s)

as they are located on the same chromosome.

Log phase Period of rapid growth in a population.

Loop of Henlé The part of a kidney tubule which forms a long loop in the medulla of the kidney, from which water and salts are resorbed into the blood.

Malignant Cancerous.

Marker gene Type of gene, for example, an antibiotic-resistance gene, used to determine which bacteria have taken in modified plasmids.

Mark–release–recapture Technique used to estimate the population size of mobile animals.

Mate-selection Situation in which individuals of one particular genotype are more likely to mate with individuals of a similar genotype.

Maze A simple device, often made from cardboard, that allows you to give an animal a range of different stimuli.

Mechanoreceptor A sensory receptor that responds to mechanical pressure or distortion.

Medulla oblongata (Medulla) A cone-shaped neuronal mass in the brain responsible for multiple autonomic (involuntary) functions.

Meiosis Cell division in which the number of chromosomes is halved.

Metastasis The development of secondary tumours at a distance from a primary site of cancer.

Microclimate Particular climatic conditions in a small part of a habitat.

Migration Movement of individuals with different genotypes into or out of a population.

Mitochondria The places in a cell where aerobic respiration takes place.

Motor neurone Nerve cell that carries information from the central nervous system to a muscle or a gland.

Motor unit A motor neuron and its associated muscle fibres.

Multiple alleles Several alleles that affect a characteristic, for example, height.

Multipotent cells Cells that are able to develop into several different types of cells.

Mutagenic agents Chemicals or types of radiation that can induce a mutation.

Mutation A change to the base sequence in DNA or to the number or structure of the chromosomes in cells.

Myelin sheath Insulating sheath around a nerve cell.

Myofibrils Thin filaments in muscles; in bundles, which bring about contraction.

Myosin Thicker of the two types of protein filaments that bring about muscle contraction.

Na$^+$/K$^+$ ATPase pump The enzyme-based mechanism that maintains correct cellular concentrations of sodium and potassium ions by removing excess ions from inside a cell and replacing them with ions from outside the cell.

NADP Nicotinamide adenine dinucleotide phosphate; a hydrogen acceptor (enzyme cofactor) involved in photosynthesis.

Natural fertiliser Substance such as manure; made from living material and contains nutrients which can help plant growth.

Natural selection Differential survival of organisms; having features that best adapt organisms to their environment, making them more likely to survive and reproduce.

Negative gravitropism Growth response away from the direction of the force of gravity.

Negative phototropism Growth response away from the direction of the stimulus of light.

Net Remaining after all deductions.

Net primary production (NPP) Net gain of dry mass stored in a plant after it has used up some material in its own respiration.

Neuromuscular junction Junction between a nerve cell and a muscle.

Neurone Nerve cell.

Neurotransmitters Chemicals that is carry information across the synaptic cleft.

Nitrate Salt of nitric acid composed of ions with the formula NO_3^-.

Nitrate, phosphate and potassium (NPK) The three primary nutrients for healthy plant growth; NPK value of a crop is the ratio of nitrogen : phosphorus : potassium that it requires.

Nitrification Conversion of ammonia to nitrite, and of nitrite to nitrate.

Nitrifying bacteria Bacteria that convert ammonia to nitrite or nitrite to nitrate.

Nitrogen fixation Changing unreactive nitrogen gas, N_2, into a more reactive compound such as ammonia or nitrate, for use by plants.

Nitrogenous Containing nitrogen in chemical combination.

Nodes of Ranvier Small gaps in the myelin sheath surrounding a neuron.

Non-disjunction A chromosome mutation that occurs during cell division in which one cell gets an extra chromosome, leaving another cell with one less than it should have.

Noradrenaline Transmitter substance in some synapses; has the same effect on the body as adrenaline.

Obligate By necessity.

Omnivore An animal that eats a variety of food of both plant and animal origin.

Oncogenes A gene that in certain circumstances can transform a cell into a tumour cell.

Opsin Substance produced by the breakdown of the pigment rhodopsin in the rod cells of the eye.

Osmoreceptor cells Cells in the hypothalamus that monitor the concentration of solutes in the blood.

Osmoregulation The maintenance of constant osmotic pressure in the fluids of an organism by the control of water and salt concentrations.

Oxidation reactions Reactions in which oxygen is gained or electrons are lost.

Oxidative phosphorylation Production of ATP during respiration.

Parasitism Close relationship between two organisms in which one (the host) is harmed and the parasite benefits.

Parasympathetic Relating to the part of the autonomic nervous system which balances the action of the sympathetic nerves.

Parasympathetic neurones Part of the parasympathetic nervous system; the cell bodies lie in the brain and sacral region of the spinal cord.

Pectinase An enzyme that breaks down pectin, a polysaccharide found in plant cell walls; produced by tomatoes as they ripen.

Percentage cover Percentage of ground that is covered by a particular species.

Peripheral nervous system Parts of the nervous system, not in the brain or the spinal cord.

Photoionisation Ionisation produced in a medium by the action of electromagnetic radiation.

Photolysis Splitting of water, using light energy.

Photophosphorylation Production of ATP during photosynthesis.

Photosynthesis The process by which green plants use sunlight to synthesise nutrients from carbon dioxide and water.

Photosystems Groups of chlorophyll and other pigment molecules found in the membranes inside chloroplasts.

Phototropin Photoreceptor protein that mediates phototropism responses in higher plants.

Pioneer species Species that is able to colonise newly disturbed habitats.

Pluripotent cells Types of cell that can differentiate into several different kinds of cells, for example, different types of blood cells.

Podocytes Cells in Bowman's capsule in the kidneys that wrap around capillaries of the glomerulus.

Point quadrat A quadrat that is so tiny that it consists of only one point.

Polymerase chain reaction (PCR) Technique for producing large numbers of copies of a DNA fragment.

Polynucleotide Long chain of nucleotides.

Population All the organisms of a species that live in the same place at the same time and can breed with one another.

Positive phototropism Growth response towards the direction of the stimulus of light.

Post-transcriptional Mechanisms in gene expression that control or regulate mRNA after it has been produced.

Post-translational Mechanisms in gene expression that act after the protein has been produced.

Potency The ability of a cell to differentiate into specialised cells.

Predation Killing and eating of an animal.

Primary consumers Organisms that eat producers.

Primary production Rate at which plants convert carbon dioxide to organic materials.

Probability The extent to which an event is likely to occur, measured by the ratio of the favourable cases to the whole number of cases possible.

Producers Organisms that take energy from the non-living environment to synthesise organic substances from inorganic substances; plants are producers.

Productivity The rate of production of new biomass by an individual, population or community.

Protein kinase A An enzyme system that is activated by cyclic adenosine monophosphate (cAMP) and that catalyses the activity of intracellular proteins.

Protein kinases A kinase enzyme that modifies other proteins by chemically adding phosphate groups to them (phosphorylation).

Proteome The complete set of proteins that are coded for in a cell.

Proto-oncogenes Gene with the potential to become an oncogene, which is responsible for producing cancer.

Proximal (or first) convoluted tubule (PCT) The portion of the duct system of the nephron of the kidney which leads from Bowman's capsule to the loop of Henlé.

Purkinje fibres Any of the specialised cardiac muscle fibres, part of the impulse-conducting network of the heart, that rapidly transmit impulses from the atrioventricular node to the ventricles.

Pyruvate Three-carbon substance, which is the final product of glycolysis.

Quadrat Square-shaped area within which a community is sampled.

Rate The relative speed of progress or change of something variable.

Receptor Cell that is sensitive to a stimulus, for example, light or temperature.

Recombinant DNA DNA fragment, formed by cutting two DNA fragments, thereby joining them together.

Reduced NAD (NADH) NAD that has taken up hydrogen or electrons.

Reduction reactions Chemical reactions in which a substance gains electrons or hydrogen.

Reflex action Involuntary response to a stimulus.

Reflex escape response Automatic response to remove an animal from danger.

Refractory period Time period after an action potential, when a neuron cannot respond to another stimulus.

Relay neurone A nerve cell that acts as the coordinator between sensory neurones and motor neurones and causes nerve impulses in the motor neurone.

Releasing factor Secreted by the hypothalamus to stimulate the posterior (rear) lobe of the pituitary gland.

Renal artery One of the pair of large blood vessels that branch off from the abdominal aorta (the abdominal portion of the major artery leading from the heart) and enter into each kidney.

Renal vein The short thick veins which return blood from the kidneys to the vena cava.

Repolarisation Restoring the resting potential in a nerve cell after depolarisation.

Reproductively isolated Unable to breed with other populations, because of differences in, for example, behaviour or physiology.

Respiration A process in living organisms involving the production of energy, typically with the intake of oxygen and the release of carbon dioxide from the oxidation of complex organic substances.

Respirometer Device used to measure the rate of aerobic or anaerobic respiration.

Restriction endonuclease enzyme Enzyme used to cut DNA molecules.

Restriction site Location on a DNA molecule containing specific sequences of nucleotides, which are recognised by restriction enzymes.

Retinal Concerned with the retina of the eye.

Reverse transcriptase Enzyme involved in copying an mRNA code into a DNA molecule.

Rhodopsin Photosensitive chromoprotein in the retinal rods that is bleached by light, allowing stimulation of retinal sensory endings.

Ribulose bisphosphate (RUBP) The compound that combines with carbon dioxide inside chloroplasts during the Calvin cycle.

RNA-induced silencing complex (RISC) Group of proteins involved in silencing a gene.

Rods Cells in the retina used for vision in dim light.

Rubisco Enzyme that catalyses the reaction between RuBP and carbon dioxide in the Calvin cycle.

Saltatory conduction Rapid conduction of an impulse along a myelinated nerve cell; impulse jumping from one node of Ranvier to the next.

Sampling at random Measuring the abundance of organisms at randomly placed points within an area.

Sampling techniques Methods used to investigate small parts of large areas, in order to obtain estimates of the distribution and abundance of different species.

Saprobiotic digestion digestion of proteins to amino acids by decomposers; digestion involves hydrolysis, catalysed by enzymes

Saprobiotic nutrition Feeding on an organic substrate by secreting enzymes outside the body, and then absorbing the products of digestion.

Sarcoplasmic reticulum The specialised endoplasmic reticulum of cardiac muscle and skeletal striated muscle that functions especially as a storage and release area for calcium.

Schwann cells Cells that surround myelinated nerve cells, insulating them.

Screening Examination or testing of a group of individuals to separate those who are well from those who have an undiagnosed disease or defect or who are at high risk.

Secondary consumers Organisms that feed on primary consumers.

Selection A process in which environmental or genetic influences determine which types of organism thrive better than others, regarded as a factor in evolution.

Selective re-absorption and secretion The absorption of some of the components of the glomerular filtrate back into the blood as the filtrate flows through the nephrons of the kidney.

Self-renewal The ability to replicate indefinitely.

Sense strand DNA strand that codes for a polypeptide.

Sensitivity The strength of a specific stimulus required for the receptor to detect it.

Sensory neurone Neurone that carries an impulse from a receptor to the central nervous system (CNS).

Sensory receptors A sensory nerve ending that responds to a stimulus in the internal or external environment of an organism.

Sessile Remaining in one spot for most of the time, for example, sea anemones.

Sex chromosome A type of chromosome in the genome that is involved in the determination of the sex as well as the development of sexual characteristics in an organism.

Short interfering RNA (SIRNA) Short fragments of RNA used to silence genes.

Short tandem repeat (STR) A microsatellite, consisting of a unit of two to thirteen nucleotides repeated hundreds of times in a row on the DNA strand.

Significant Important or noticeable

Simple reflex An automatic response to a stimulus. It does not involve any thought, but is an involuntary action.

Sinoatrial node (SAN) Natural pacemaker of the heart, situated in the right atrium.

Skeletal muscle Muscle attached to the skeleton, which brings about movement of bones.

Slow skeletal muscle fibres Muscle fibres that contract at about half the speed of fast skeletal muscle fibres.

Smooth muscle Muscle tissue in which the contractile fibrils are not highly ordered, occurring in the gut and other internal organs and not under voluntary control.

Sodium dodecyl sulfate (SDS) Chemical used in electrophoresis.

Somatic cell nuclear transfer A laboratory technique for creating an ovum with a donor nucleus. It can be used in embryonic stem cell research, or in regenerative medicine where it is sometimes referred to as 'therapeutic cloning'.

Species The taxonomic category comprising individuals with common characteristics that distinguish them from other individuals at the same taxonomic level.

Species frequency Percentage of quadrats in which a species is found.

Species richness The number of different species that live in a particular habitat.

Stabilising selection A type of natural selection that causes no change due to a lack of change in the environment and an already adapted population.

Standard deviation A measure of the variability in a population.

Sticky ends Ends of DNA fragments which have been cut with a restriction enzyme, and which can be joined to another similarly cut piece of DNA.

Stimulus Change which can be detected and which may invoke a response.

Stretch-mediated sodium channels Sodium channels whose permeability to sodium changes when they change shape.

Stroma 'Background material' in a chloroplast.

Substitution One of the three basic types of gene mutation; one or more nucleotides in a nucleic acid are replaced by others.

Substrate-level phosphorylation Production of ATP by a reaction directly coupled to one of the steps in the Krebs cycle.

Succession Directional change in the composition of a community over time, caused by one set of species changing the environment in such a way that others are able to live there.

Summation The additive effect of several electrical impulses on a neuromuscular junction.

Sympathetic Of or relating to the part of the autonomic nervous system consisting of nerves that arise from the thoracic and lumbar regions of the spinal cord, and functioning in opposition to the parasympathetic system, as in stimulating heartbeat, dilating the pupil of the eye, etc.

Sympatric Taking place without geographical separation.

Synapses Junctions between two nerve cells.

Synaptic cleft Space between two adjoining neurones.

Systematic sampling Measuring the abundance of organisms at regularly placed points within an area.

Taxis Movement of an animal in response to a directional stimulus.

Tertiary consumers Organisms that eat secondary consumers.

Tetanus The prolonged contraction of a muscle caused by rapidly repeated stimuli.

Thermal cycling machine A laboratory apparatus most commonly used to amplify segments of DNA via the polymerase chain reaction (PCR).

Threshold level Minimum level to bring about a response.

Thylakoids Membranes in chloroplasts, on which the light-dependent reactions of photosynthesis takes place.

Topographical factors The non-living, physical conditions in an ecosystem, such as temperature, light, soil conditions.

Totipotent cells Cells that can mature into any type of body cell or cell type that is associated with embryo support and development, or even a whole organism.

Transcriptional Mechanisms in gene expression that prevent or promote transcription, and thereby turn off or turn on the synthesis of RNA.

Transect Straight line across a habitat along which organisms are sampled.

Transformation Inserting DNA into a cell or a plasmid.

Transgenic organisms Organisms that have genes from another organism.

Translational Mechanisms in gene expression that prevent translation; they often involve protein factors that are needed for translation.

Translocation The process in which organic substances move around a plant by way of phloem tissue.

Triose phosphate (TP) Three-carbon sugar; the first carbohydrate to be made in photosynthesis.

Trophic level Step in a food chain at which an organisms feeds.

Tropomyosin A thin protein that is involved in muscle contraction.

Tumour A swelling of a part of the body, generally without inflammation, caused by an abnormal growth of tissue, whether benign or malignant.

Tumour suppressor genes A protective gene that normally limits the growth of tumours.

Ultrafiltration Filtration under pressure.

Unipotent cells Cells that can differentiate into just one cell type.

Universal Describing the way that the genetic code is almost identical in all living organisms.

Ureter The duct by which urine passes from the kidney to the bladder.

Variable number tandem repeats (VNTRS) A location in a genome where a short nucleotide sequence is organised as a tandem repeat. These can be found on many chromosomes, and often show variations in length between individuals.

Vasa recta A network of blood capillaries surrounding the loop of Henlé.

Wave of depolarisation A reversal of the resting potential that moves rapidly along the axon.

Zygote A diploid cell resulting from the fusion of two haploid gametes; a fertilised ovum.

INDEX

ACKNOWLEDGEMENTS

The Publishers gratefully acknowledge the permissions granted to reproduce copyright material in this book. Every effort has been made to contact the holders of copyright material, but if any have been inadvertently overlooked, the Publisher will be pleased to make the necessary arrangements at the first opportunity.

Practical work in biology

p2 Miles Studio/Shutterstock; p3 top: lmfoto/Shutterstock, middle: sfam_photo/Shutterstock, bottom: Miles Studio/Shutterstock; p4 top: Photographee.eu/Shutterstock, bottom: Ozgur Coskun/Shutterstock

Chapter 1

p5 background: Shutterstock/ Milosz_G; p5: PASCAL GOETGHELUCK/SCIENCE PHOTO LIBRARY; p10: Brian Maudsley/Alamy Stock Photo; p20: Shutterstock/Kingarion; p21: Shutterstock/oticki

Chapter 2

p21 background: PASCAL GOETGHELUCK/SCIENCE PHOTO LIBRARY; p35: STEVE GSCHMEISSNER/SCIENCE PHOTO LIBRARY; p40: Shutterstock/ Michaelpuche

Chapter 3

p45 background: Shutterstock/ Papa Bravo

Chapter 4

p59 background: WENN Ltd/ Alamy Stock Photo; p60 left: Shutterstock/Lisa A; p60 right: Shutterstock/Andreas Zerndl; p62: HUGH SPENCER/SCIENCE PHOTO LIBRARY; p63 top: DR. MERTON BROWN, VISUALS UNLIMITED/ SCIENCE PHOTO LIBRARY; p63 middle: Shutterstock/JL-Pfeifer; p65: Shutterstock/Chrislofotos; p66 top: Shutterstock/Emjay Smith; p66 middle: Shutterstock/Svend77; p67: Shutterstock/courtyardpix

Chapter 5

p75 background: Shutterstock/ a9photo; p77: Shutterstock/

Pommeyrol Vincent; p79: Shutterstock/Marek Velechovsky; p82 left: GRAHAM JORDAN/ SCIENCE PHOTO LIBRARY; Cathy Melloan/Alamy Stock Photo; p82 right bottom: MARTIN SHIELDS/ SCIENCE PHOTO LIBRARY; p86 top: NASA (Johnson Space Center); p88: Shutterstock/Convit; p90: STEVE GSCHMEISSNER/SCIENCE PHOTO LIBRARY

Chapter 6

p101 background: Shutterstock/ vitstudio; p101: ALFRED PASIEKA/ SCIENCE PHOTO LIBRARY; p102: Shutterstock/Bildagentur Zoonar GmbH; p103 left: CNRI/SCIENCE PHOTO LIBRARY; p103 right top: ASTRID & HANNS-FRIEDER MICHLER/SCIENCE PHOTO LIBRARY; p103 right bottom: MANFRED KAGE/SCIENCE PHOTO LIBRARY; p115: Shutterstock/ Kanusommer

Chapter 7

p124 background: Shutterstock/ beerkoff; p126: CNRI/SCIENCE PHOTO LIBRARY

Chapter 8

p139 background: Shutterstock/ Ondrej83; p141: ASTRID & HANNS-FRIEDER MICHLER/ SCIENCE PHOTO LIBRARY; p144: Shutterstock/Ondrej83; p147: MARTYN F. CHILLMAID/ SCIENCE PHOTO LIBRARY; p150: Ozgur Coskun

Chapter 9

p158 background: Shutterstock/ Gio.tto; p159 top: Shutterstock/ Meletios; p159 bottom: POWER AND SYRED/SCIENCE PHOTO LIBRARY; p165: Shutterstock/ Vasiliy Koval; Shutterstock/ mdmmikle; Shutterstock/Eric Isselee; p173: Shutterstock/ c.byatt-norman; p174 right: Getty Images/TOSHIFUMI KITAMURA

Chapter 10

p179 background: Shutterstock/ Erni; p180: Shutterstock/ Bildagentur Zoonar GmbH; p181 top: Shutterstock/Martin Fowler; bottom: Shutterstock/Steve

McWilliam; p183 left: Shutterstock/ Nicolas Primola; p183 right: Shutterstock/MarkMirror; p184: Shutterstock/Birdiegal; p192: Shutterstock/James Wheeler; p193 left: Shutterstock/Critterbiz; right: Shutterstock/MVPhoto; p196: Shutterstock/neil hardwick; p197: Shutterstock/Lebendkulturen. de; p199 top: Shutterstock/Yuriy Kulik; bottom: Shutterstock/Martin Fowler; p200 top: Shutterstock/ Zamytskiy Leonid; bottom: blickwinkel/Alamy; p202 top: Shutterstock/Oliver Foerstner; left bottom: Shutterstock/Ruud Morijn Photographer; right bottom: Shutterstock/Dariusz Majgier; p206 left: Shutterstock/jps; right: Shutterstock/Katarzyna Mazurowska

Chapter 11

p212 background: UrbanZone/ Alamy Stock Photo; p213 top left: Wikimedia Commons/Lee Roger Berger research team; top right: Wikimedia Commons/ Lee Roger Berger research team; bottom: Shutterstock/Everett Historical; p217: Shutterstock/ Designua; p219: Shutterstock/ Robert Eastman; Shutterstock/ Volodymyr Burdiak; Shutterstock/ S.R. Maglione; p220: Wikimedia Commons/Joseph Berger; p222: Shutterstock/Bildagentur Zoonar GmbH; p223: Hans Hillewaert; Jefferson Heard; Stevenj

Chapter 12

p227 background: Shutterstock/ Image Point Fr; p228 left: B. BOISSONNET/BSIP/SCIENCE PHOTO LIBRARY; right: PAUL PARKER/SCIENCE PHOTO LIBRARY; p230 left: Biophoto Associates; p232: DR YORGOS NIKAS/SCIENCE PHOTO LIBRARY; p233 left: Shutterstock/Designua; p235: Corbis/Lester Lefkowitz; right: Corbis/ANSA; p240 bottom: Graham Chapman

Chapter 13

p247 background: Shutterstock/ Matej Kastelic; p254: DR GOPAL MURTI/SCIENCE PHOTO LIBRARY; p257: Shutterstock/Kulniz